HARCOURT

· T R O P H I E S ·

A HARCOURT READING/LANGUAGE ARTS PROGRAM

DISTANT VOYAGES

SENIOR AUTHORS
Isabel L. Beck ◆ Roger C. Farr ◆ Dorothy S. Strickland

AUTHORS
Alma Flor Ada ◆ Marcia Brechtel ◆ Margaret McKeown
Nancy Roser ◆ Hallie Kay Yopp

SENIOR CONSULTANT
Asa G. Hilliard III

CONSULTANTS
F. Isabel Campoy ◆ David A. Monti

Harcourt

Orlando   Boston   Dallas   Chicago   San Diego

Visit *The Learning Site!*

www.harcourtschool.com

ISBN 0-15-322479-7

5 6 7 8 9 10 048 10 09 08 07 06 05 04 03

Dear Reader,

Everyone loves to take part in an adventure—whether it's traveling to an exciting place, playing a new instrument, or joining a team. Also, as you may know from reading a good book or listening to friends, learning about the experiences of others can be a thrill.

Prepare to take a voyage around the world—from high above Earth's atmosphere to the powerful oceans below, from Alaska's snowy wilderness to cities and schools just like yours. You will read stories developed in the minds of imaginative writers and adventures experienced by real people in real places. In **Distant Voyages,** you will meet brave characters, including some American heroes, who either seek a challenge or are faced with one unexpectedly. Maybe you will find that someone else's voyage is like one of your own! Come travel with us in search of excitement, surprise, and adventure.

Sincerely,

The Authors

The Authors

LOOK INSIDE

CONTENTS

Reading
Across
Texts

Reading
**Across
Texts**

5

Team Work

CONTENTS

Reading
Across
Texts

Reading
Across
Texts

Reading
Across
Texts

7

THEME 3

A CHANGING PLANET

CONTENTS

Reading Across Texts

Reading Across Texts

Express Yourself

CONTENTS

Reading Across Texts

Reading Across Texts

School Rules

CONTENTS

AMERICAN ADVENTURE

CONTENTS

Reading
Across
Texts

Using Reading Strategies

A strategy is a plan for doing something well.

You probably already use some strategies as you read. For example, you may **look at the title and illustrations before you begin reading** a story. You may **think about what you want to find out while reading.** Using strategies like these can help you become a better reader.

Look at the list of strategies on page 17. You will learn about and use these strategies as you read the selections in this book. As you read, look back at the list to remind yourself of the **strategies good readers use.**

Strategies Good Readers Use

- Use Decoding/ Phonics

- Make and Confirm Predictions

- Create Mental Images

- Self-Question

- Summarize

- Read Ahead

- Reread to Clarify

- Use Context to Confirm Meaning

- Use Text Structure and Format

- Adjust Reading Rate

Here are some ways to check your own comprehension:

✔ Make a copy of this list on a piece of construction paper shaped like a bookmark.

✔ Have it handy as you read.

✔ After reading, talk with a classmate about which strategies you used and why.

LOOK INSIDE

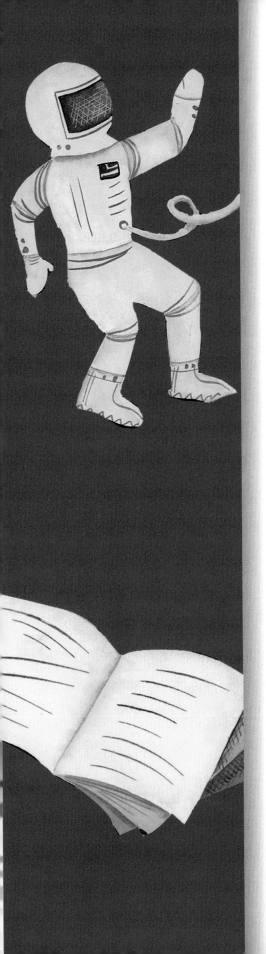

CONTENTS

▲ **The Hot and Cold Summer**

authority

incredible

vow

exhausted

souvenir

commotion

Vocabulary Power

"The Hot and Cold Summer" tells about some friends and how they spend a special summer. Many people keep scrapbooks to help them remember special times in their lives, as you can see and read about below.

Here I am shaking hands with Mr. Dobbs. He is an **authority** on wildlife photography, which means he is an expert on taking pictures and on understanding animals, too. He told us

about adventures he has had with animals. Some of his stories are so **incredible** that it would be hard to believe them if he didn't have pictures as proof! That's one reason why I take my own pictures.

I made a **vow**, a serious promise, to get a picture of a hummingbird hovering in the air. This picture shows that I kept that promise. I don't understand how such a small bird can beat its wings so fast for such a long time without getting very tired. I think I'd be **exhausted**!

After the hummingbird in my picture flew away, this feather was left behind. I kept it as a **souvenir** to remind me of that special day.

These crows are a lot bigger and noisier than hummingbirds. They caused such a burst of noise and confusion that people came outside to find out what all the **commotion** was about!

Vocabulary-Writing CONNECTION

Think of a special event when you or someone else took a photograph to keep as a **souvenir**. Write a caption to describe how you felt at the time.

Genre

Realistic Fiction

Realistic fiction tells about characters and events that are like people and events in real life.

In this selection, look for

- **Characters that have feelings that real people have**

- **Challenges and problems that might happen in real life**

The Hot & Cold Summer

by Johanna Hurwitz
illustrated by Russ Wilson

Rory and Derek's summer plans don't include playing with a surprise visitor — a girl named Bolivia. To avoid meeting her, the boys force themselves to spend time with their classmate Maurice. When the boys are served sprout-and-tofu sandwiches and have to listen to Maurice play his violin, they decide that meeting Bolivia is not such a bad idea after all. Derek and Rory agree to attend a cookout that is planned for Bolivia, but they make a pact not to speak to her. Can the boys keep their pact of silence?

Derek and Rory grinned at one another. The cake, the hamburgers, and the bottle of root beer that was waiting on the table were the least that they should get in compensation for Bolivia. The boys waited, knowing the two girls would emerge from behind the Goldings' hedge at any moment.

Sure enough, the hedge parted and first Mr. and then Mrs. Golding and then a redheaded girl walked into the Dunns' yard. "This is Bolivia!" said Mrs. Golding proudly. She said it in the same way she often introduced a new type of cookie or cake, as if Bolivia was something she had created in her kitchen. Rory took a quick look and then shifted his gaze. He didn't want to appear interested. He noticed, however, that he had been right about one thing. Bolivia was several inches taller than he was.

"Hi, Bolivia. Welcome to Woodside!" said Mr. Dunn. "I'm just putting on the hamburgers. How do you like yours?"

"I like mine well done," said Bolivia.

"Fine," said Mr. Dunn. "So do Rory and Derek." He turned to the boys, who were trying to edge away from the guest of honor. Derek's mother grabbed him. "Bolivia, this is Derek. He and Rory will be your friends this summer."

Neither boy said anything.

"How's Lucette settling in?" asked Mrs. Dunn. Rory realized for the first time that Bolivia's little sister hadn't come to the barbecue.

"She's fine. At first she was very quiet, but just before we left the house she said her first word to me. She knows ten words. It's so exciting," said Mrs. Golding.

Bolivia turned to Rory and Derek. "I couldn't bring Lucette to the barbecue because the smoke might be bad for her," she explained. "Do you want to come to my aunt's house and see her?"

These were the first words Bolivia spoke directly to the boys.

Rory shook his head no. Derek also shook his head.

"Don't be shy," said Mr. Golding. "Go meet Lucette."

Rory shook his head again.

"You fellows are missing something really special," said Mrs. Dunn as she removed the plastic wrap from the salads.

Rory couldn't understand his mother. Why should he get excited over someone else's baby sister? He didn't care that Lucette had said her first word. Edna had known a lot of words by the time she was two. What was so special about Lucette?

Derek leaned toward Rory and whispered, "If we keep our mouths full of food, we can't talk."

Rory grinned. If his mother had told him once, she had told him a thousand times not to talk with food in his mouth.

"Right." He nodded.

The boys picked up paper plates. "Can we start eating?" asked Rory.

"If you're so hungry that you can't wait, go ahead," said Mrs. Dunn. Both boys piled their plates with potato salad and cole slaw.

Bolivia picked up a plate, too.

Edna pulled on Bolivia's skirt. "I made the cole slaw," she said.

"No kidding," said Bolivia.

"I made the potato salad, too," said Edna.

"The burgers are ready," called Mr. Dunn.

The three older children went to get their meat.

"You know," Bolivia said, turning to Rory and Derek, "last summer I was in Israel with my parents. They make hamburgers out of turkey there."

It was hard to imagine turkey hamburgers, although Rory thought they probably would be better than vegetable burgers with sprouts.

"Gobble, gobble," said Derek.

"What?" asked Bolivia.

"Gobble, gobble," he repeated.

Rory kicked Derek. His friend wasn't exactly speaking to Bolivia, but it was close.

Derek got the message. He stuffed his mouth with potato salad.

"Do you like my potato salad?" asked Edna.

"Rory, tell Bolivia about Woodside. This is her first visit here," Mr. Dunn called from his position at the grill.

Rory shoveled in a large forkful of potato salad and turned to his father, pointing to his mouth.

"There's a lot of things to do around here," said Mrs. Curry, since neither of the boys were speaking. "There's the town pool." She turned to Derek. "Which are the days when the public library is showing free movies for kids?" she asked.

Derek took an enormous bite out of his hamburger and shrugged his shoulders.

Rory licked some ketchup off his fingers and went back to refill his plate. Luckily he was very hungry after the lunch at Maurice's house.

"You like my cole slaw?" asked Edna.

"Where else have you traveled with your parents?" asked Mrs. Dunn.

Good, thought Rory. Let the grown-ups keep Bolivia busy talking. She sounded like a geography book, listing all the foreign countries where she'd been: Israel, Egypt, Mexico, France, Spain. . . .

After a little while, Bolivia turned to the boys again. "Would you like to come over tomorrow and play with Lucette?" she asked. "We could teach her some new words. I'll let you feed her if you like."

Girls really have no idea what boys like to do, Rory thought. What boy in his right mind would want to sit around playing nursery school with a little baby? He shook his head no.

"How about you?" asked Bolivia, turning to Derek.

"No," said Derek. Then realizing what he had done, he pushed another forkful of potato salad into his mouth.

Bolivia sat down on the ground next to Edna. She began playing "This little piggy went to market" on the little girl's bare toes. It was probably the eighty thousandth time that someone had played that baby game with Edna, but still she laughed and laughed.

Rory moved away, taking Derek with him.

"Boys, don't rush off," shouted Mrs. Curry. "We're going to cut the cake soon."

Bolivia was not going to scare them off the cake, Rory decided. Especially since it had chocolate frosting. So the boys moved back to the center of activity. Mrs. Golding was busy discussing something with the two mothers. Mr. Golding, the neighborhood authority when it came to cars, was talking to Mr. Dunn and Mr. Curry about motors.

Rory saw Bolivia go through the hedge back to the Goldings' house. Maybe she had to use the bathroom, he thought. But just maybe, she was getting the message that he and Derek didn't want her around.

With Bolivia gone, at least for a few minutes, the boys could stop eating and rest. It was hard work keeping your mouth stuffed with food.

"What should we do tomorrow?" asked Derek.

"Let's go to the pool," said Rory. "Mrs. Golding never signs up for a pool card and so Bolivia won't be allowed in."

"What if it rains?" asked Derek.

Rory looked up at the sky. It was still light and there wasn't a single cloud. "It won't rain," he said. "But if it does, we'll go over to Maurice's again."

"Okay," said Derek. "But if we go, I'm taking ear plugs with me. I've heard enough of that *Carmen*."

Rory stuck his hand into his pocket and pulled out a sprout from the sandwich he had disposed of earlier in the day. "A souvenir of the first afternoon hiding from Bolivia," he said, presenting it to Derek.

"This is just the beginning of July," said Derek. "Do you realize how many more days there are till she goes home?"

"As many days as there were sprouts in that sandwich," said Rory, sighing.

"It's going to be a long, long summer," agreed Derek.

At any other time, the thought of a long, long summer would have filled the boys with delight. But now it stretched endlessly before them.

The morning after the barbecue, Derek and Rory met outside at nine-thirty. The boys wore their trunks under their clothes and each had a towel and a sandwich. Mrs. Dunn called after them, "Ask Bolivia to go with you," but Rory pretended not to hear. He had no intention of knocking on the Goldings' door. Anyway, Bolivia wouldn't have a membership card to the pool yet. And Rory didn't know if she had a bike. He didn't want to go anywhere with that girl and especially not if he had to go on foot. He looked around and was relieved that she was not in sight. He glanced up at the window of Bolivia's room and for a second, he thought he saw one of the curtains move. But then all was still again. It was probably just a little breeze.

"Let's get going," he said to Derek, who had been checking the air in his tires. "We want to make our getaway while the coast is clear."

Suddenly the boys heard a shriek.

"Help, help! Lucette has escaped!"

Derek and Rory looked at each other. What was the big fuss? Had Bolivia's little sister climbed out of her playpen or something?

Bolivia stuck her head out of the upstairs window. "Have you seen Lucette?" she called.

The boys shook their heads. How could little Lucette manage the heavy door? "She's got to be inside the house," said Derek.

"No. I saw her go out the window," Bolivia shouted.

Rory dropped his bike in surprise. How could the baby get out the window?

"Go around the back," demanded Bolivia. "I'll come and look with you. She must be in one of the trees."

Derek and Rory stood stunned. Had Bolivia lost her senses? If the baby had fallen out the window, she would be lying on the ground. It was impossible that she would land in a tree.

Mrs. Golding came running out of the house. "Should we

call the fire department?" she asked
her niece.

"Call an ambulance or the police,"
said Rory. His heart was beating loud.
He knew how he would have felt if
Edna had fallen out the window.

Mr. Golding had gone out the back
door. "I see her. I see her," he called
from the backyard. "She's in the Dunns'
mimosa tree."

Rory ran to the back of his house followed
by Derek, Bolivia, and Mrs. Golding. He couldn't
see any baby in the tree. "Where is she?" he shouted to Mr.
Golding. He wondered if she had fallen out the window and then
climbed the tree. It seemed incredible. He and Derek had been
trying to climb that tree for years.

"It's all my fault." Bolivia was crying. "I opened the door so
she could walk on my arm, and the next thing I knew she was
flying around and around the room."

"She must be scared in a new place," said Mrs. Golding,
putting her arm around her niece. "Don't cry. We'll all help catch
her."

"I'll get a ladder," said Mr. Golding.

Rory watched as the old man leaned his ladder against the side
of the tree.

"Hey, look at that!" shouted Derek.

Rory looked where his friend was pointing. On the very
topmost branch of the mimosa tree was a large green bird with a
blue-and-red head.

"It's a parrot!" he shouted. He had never seen one before
except in the encyclopedia, but there was no mistaking that size
or color.

"Of course it's a parrot," Bolivia shouted at him. "What did
you think Lucette was? An elephant?"

It wasn't only their vow of silence that kept Rory and Derek from admitting they had thought Lucette was a baby.

While they were shouting, the bird flew from the mimosa tree to the maple.

No sooner had the ladder been put in place there than the bird flew over the hedge and into the next yard, landing in a locust tree. Mr. Golding looked red in the face from the exertion of moving the ladder back and forth.

"Let me help," called Mr. Dunn, coming from the house. Twice a week, even during the summer, he took classes in school administration so that he might someday become a principal. Now he forgot his courses as he dropped his attaché case with his papers and books and ran toward Mr. Golding.

"Hello there. Hello there," shrieked Lucette as she flew from tree to tree.

"Hello there, yourself!" Derek called back. He looked at Rory. Rory hadn't told him not to speak to a bird.

Mrs. Dunn came outside, followed by Edna. The little girl began jumping up and down. "I see her!" she shouted. "Catch her! Catch her!"

"Hello there!" Lucette called down to them.

"I'm going to call the fire department," Mr. Golding said. "They have taller ladders, and we have an awful lot of trees around here for Lucette to investigate."

"Hello there!" Edna called up to the bird.

Mrs. Dunn put her arms around Bolivia. "Don't worry. We won't let her get away." She comforted the girl as Lucette flew into the branches of one tree and then another. The swimming pool was forgotten as Rory and Derek chased in and out of the hedges, keeping their eyes on the bird.

"Could we get her down with some food?" asked Derek when he stopped to catch his breath. "What does she like to eat?"

"Fruit," said Bolivia.

Everyone rushed home except the two men with the ladder. Rory brought back some grapes. Derek had an apple. "Hello there!" shouted Edna, waving a banana for Lucette.

They made a pile of all the fruit in the Golding yard. Lucette hovered in the air above it for a moment, but she didn't land.

"What else does she like?" asked Mrs. Dunn. "This isn't working."

Mr. Dunn climbed down the ladder as the bird flew off once again. "None of my courses in running a school have prepared me for a morning like this," he said, wiping the sweat off his forehead.

In the distance they could hear approaching sirens. The fire department was on its way.

Dogleg Lane was filled with onlookers. People driving by got out of their cars to see what was happening. Neighbors came out of doors. Three large fire trucks pulled up in front of the Golding house. The firemen, wearing their helmets and tall boots, leaped off the trucks dragging ladders and long hoses with them.

"My vegetables could use a little water," said Mr. Dunn from where he was stationed.

"There's no fire," shouted Mrs. Golding. "It's a bird in the tree."

"Birds belong in trees," said one of the firemen, not yet understanding that Lucette was a pet bird who belonged in a cage.

"Hello there. Hello there!" Lucette greeted the new arrivals. She seemed to be having a great time.

Rory looked over at Bolivia. She was smiling. She looked like she was having a great time, too. For someone who had been crying a few minutes ago, she didn't seem unhappy now. Either she had wonderful faith in the Woodside Fire Department or she was not really worried about the bird.

"Music!" Bolivia remembered suddenly. "Lucette loves country music."

Derek ran into his house and came out with the little transistor radio he had gotten on his last birthday. He fiddled with the dials, looking for a station that played country music.

"That's good," shouted Bolivia. "Leave it there."

Derek stood holding his radio at full volume and looking up at Lucette.

"Hello there," shouted the bird, swooping lower.

Strains of "Country Roads" came over the radio. The neighbors that had crowded around began to sing and clap their hands in time to the music.

Mrs. Golding began introducing Bolivia to the people that she recognized. Bolivia smiled at everyone. She was really enjoying this commotion very much, Rory decided.

"Can your parrot do any tricks?" asked one of the onlookers.

"She knows ten words, and she can play dead, and she comes flying to my arm when I call her," said Bolivia proudly.

She noticed Rory standing nearby listening and added hastily, "But she won't come now. She's in a new place and she's overexcited by all the people."

The firemen got a call on their radio. There was a real fire somewhere. As quickly as they arrived, they disappeared with their sirens wailing. "We'll come back later if you still need us," one of the men called back as they departed.

Lucette seemed to be getting tired. She wasn't flying so much. She sat in the Currys' maple tree and looked around her.

"Who's my bird?" shouted Bolivia.

"Lucette. Lucette," the bird answered.

"Hey, she knows her name!" shouted Derek.

Rory was as excited by the bird as Derek. But he also had a strong suspicion that the whole morning had been planned by Bolivia. The more he thought about it, the more certain he was that she had opened the cage and the window on purpose. She had probably seen him through her window as he waited for Derek and she had decided to mess up the morning for them.

"I've got her. I've got her," shouted Mr. Dunn in triumph, as he slowly came down the ladder.

"Hello there!" Lucette greeted all the people in the yard. Everyone burst into applause and ran to get a closer look at the bird. The Goldings looked exhausted and relieved that this first emergency was over. Mr. Dunn handed Lucette over to Bolivia, looking very pleased with himself. It wasn't every morning that he climbed into trees to catch a bird.

"I feel like Tarzan," he said to Mrs. Dunn.

Derek just couldn't keep from asking Bolivia questions. "Where did you get her?" he wanted to know. "How many words can she say? Could she learn my name?" He was thrilled that Lucette was this clever bird and not the baby sister he and Rory had expected.

"You naughty girl," Bolivia scolded her pet. "I'm going to put you into your cage right now." She looked at Derek and said, "This has been a tiring morning for her. But tomorrow you can come over and help me clean her cage and feed her. Maybe I can teach her to say your name," she offered.

"Super," said Derek, not remembering until the words were out of his mouth that he had promised Rory he would never, ever speak to Bolivia.

Think and Respond

❶ What happens to Derek and Rory's **vow** not to speak to Bolivia? What do they learn from what happens?

❷ What reasons might Bolivia have to be glad that Lucette got away?

❸ What mistaken idea do the boys have about Lucette before they see her? Why might they have made this mistake?

❹ Do you think Bolivia would be an interesting friend? Why or why not?

❺ What reading strategies did you use to help you understand "The Hot and Cold Summer"? When did you use them?

Meet the Author
Johanna Hurwitz

What influenced you to become a writer?

Books have been a part of my life as long as I can remember. My father owned a secondhand book store. Even though he eventually gave up the store, he never gave up the books. Every room of our house was filled with books. No wonder everyone in our family loved to read! I especially liked to read series books. That might be the reason why I've continued to write about the characters in *The Hot and Cold Summer*.

Where do you get ideas for your books?

My own children, who are now grown up, sparked many of my ideas when they reported on activities at school and with their friends. Other ideas come from students I meet on visits to schools and libraries. Anything can happen in my books because everything in them comes from real life.

Where do the characters from *The Hot and Cold Summer* come from?

I really met someone who had a daughter named Bolivia. As soon as I heard that name, I knew it was perfect and I would have to "borrow" it for a book. Derek and Rory are based on my own son and his friends, boys I see in my neighborhood. Boys that age do not want to talk to girls or fuss over babies, and they will do anything to avoid it.

Making Connections

Compare Texts

1 What happens in this story that connects it to the theme Look Inside?

2 How is the picture on pages 32–33 different from the other illustrations in this story? Why do you think the artist drew it this way?

3 Think of another story you know in which a character's pet is important to the plot. Compare it with "The Hot and Cold Summer," and tell why the pet is important in each story.

4 How is this selection similar to or different from other realistic fiction stories you have read? Give examples.

5 What do you think the rest of the summer will be like for Rory, Derek, and Bolivia?

Write Text for a Flyer

Imagine that Lucette has flown away. Create a flyer to post around the neighborhood to help Bolivia find Lucette. Include information on how to identify Lucette and how to return her to Bolivia. Use a graphic organizer like the one shown here to list the information you want to include.

Writing CONNECTION

How to recognize Lucette:

How to return Lucette:

Other helpful information:

Create a Menu

In "The Hot and Cold Summer," Bolivia says that Lucette likes to eat fruit. Research the topic of what parrots eat. You might find information in a print, CD-ROM, or online encyclopedia. Organize your information in a chart. Then use your chart to create a menu for parrots.

What Parrots Eat		
Type of Food	Where Found	Other Details

Draw a Bird's-Eye View

The illustration on pages 32-33 is called a bird's-eye view because it shows the scene from above. Photographers sometimes fly in planes or go to the top of tall buildings to capture a bird's-eye view of a landscape or city. Find books on photography that include photographs of this type. Then imagine how the streets, buildings, and other landmarks around your school would look from above. Draw your own bird's-eye view.

Prefixes, Suffixes, and Roots

Focus Skill

Look closely at the underlined words in these sentences.

- Rory and Derek did not want to make the surprise <u>visitor</u> a part of their summer plans.

- Bolivia did not make a good <u>impression</u> on Rory and Derek at the barbecue.

- At first, the boys thought it was <u>impossible</u> that Lucette would land in a tree.

- "Go around the back," <u>demanded</u> Bolivia.

In each underlined word, a word part has been added to a root word or a root to form a new word.

- A word part added to the beginning of a word is a **prefix**.

- A word part added to the end of a word is a **suffix**.

- A **root** is a word part, often taken from Greek or Latin, that usually cannot stand alone. It must be attached to other word parts to make a word.

- A **root word** can stand alone.

Prefix	Root	New Word
de-	*man*, meaning "hand"	demanded—"handed down," as an order

Suffix	Root Word	New Word
-or	visit	visitor—"person who visits"

Visit *The Learning Site!* www.harcourtschool.com

See *Skills* and *Activities*

Test Prep
Prefixes, Suffixes, and Roots

▶ **Read the passage. Then answer the questions.**

> It seemed <u>unimaginable</u> that Tori and her new neighbor, Marie, would become friends. Tori thought they had nothing in common. Then Marie introduced Tori to Tranquil, Marie's pet parrot. Tranquil was quite <u>vocal</u>. He could say twelve words, and he could even tell a joke. Tori realized that she and Marie both enjoyed playing with Tranquil. Maybe they had other things in common, too. Perhaps they would become friends after all.

1. **If the prefix *un-* means "not," then what does <u>unimaginable</u> mean?**

   A not able to be imagined

   B full of imagination

   C without imagination

   D able to imagine

Tip

Use the meaning of the prefix to figure out the meaning of the word.

2. **If the Latin root *voc* means "voice," then what does <u>vocal</u> mean?**

   F full of humor

   G able to use one's hands

   H likely to use one's voice

   J not friendly

Tip

Use the meaning of the root to figure out the meaning of the word.

Vocabulary Power

exaggerate

quiver

compose

sternly

tread

moss

The characters in "Sees Behind Trees" live close to nature. In our modern world, it isn't always easy to stay in touch with nature. Natural history museums can help us do just that, as this diary entry shows.

Thursday, October 6

Yesterday our class visited the natural history museum in Hamilton. I would not **exaggerate** and call it a large museum, because it is not. It's very small, but it's very interesting. The museum has items made by Native Americans and by other early settlers in our area.

When we went outside to learn about plants and animals, some of us began acting silly. Ms. Ortiz told us

This special case, called a **quiver**, is used to hold or carry arrows.

to **compose** ourselves, and we settled down right away. That way she didn't have to speak to us **sternly**, in a harsh or strict way.

We learned a lot at the museum. For example, we learned how to identify an animal's **tread**, or how it walked, by the prints it left in the soft ground. I drew these pictures to help me remember some of the other things I learned.

The patch of **moss** on this rock is made up of many tiny plants. Moss has no flowers. It grows on trees as well as on rocks.

Vocabulary-Writing CONNECTION

Choose something in nature. Write three sentences that **exaggerate** what that thing is like. For example: The butterfly had fifty different colors on its wings! It flew eighty miles per hour and made more noise than a train!

Historical Fiction

Historical fiction is a story that is set in the past and portrays people, places, and events that did or could have happened.

In this selection, look for

- **A real time and place in the past**
- **Some made-up events**

Sees Behind Trees

by Michael Dorris
illustrated by Rocco Baviera

"TRY HARDER. TRACK IT with your eye before you shoot."

My mother's anxious voice snapped in my ear as loudly as the string of my bow.

"Track what?" I asked for the third time this morning. Before me all I could see was the familiar blur of green and brown that meant I was outside in the forest on a sunny day. Then, by squinting, I could sense something coming toward me, smell the familiar pemmican scent of berries mixed with dried meat, recognize the tread of moccasins I had heard a thousand times before. Gradually one blurry image began to stand out from all the others and an instant later it turned into my approaching mother. When she was close enough for me to touch, I could tell from her face and from the tenseness of her body that she was worried.

"This," she said, shaking the clump of moss that she held in one hand. In the other were the four arrows I had already shot, which she dropped at my feet. "When I throw the moss in the air, imagine its flight and then aim where you think it will be by the time your arrow meets it. It's not so hard, and every boy must learn how to do it before he can become a man."

A rumbling noise came from my stomach and my mother smiled her I've-got-an-idea smile. "Think of the moss as your breakfast," she suggested. "Imagine it is a corn cake, hot from the ashes, soooo delicious."

I could almost taste it on my tongue, feel its crunch as I bit down, smell the sweet fullness it would bring. "Couldn't I eat first, just this once?" I pleaded. "I'm sure I could find the moss in the sky if I weren't so hungry."

For a moment I thought my mother would give in, and I leaned toward her, blinking as though a steaming golden corn cake would appear in her hand to replace the straggly plant. But all that changed was my mother's expression.

"Walnut." My name in her mouth was tired, pounded into flour. "You know the rule: you must find the target before breakfast can find you."

I nodded. If that was the rule, I wouldn't eat for a long time. We had faced this matter of what I couldn't see many times before — when my mother would point to something I couldn't locate or throw a ball I couldn't catch —

but it had never before been such serious business. Now we couldn't just act as though nothing was wrong. Now we had to solve the problem. We had struggled with it every morning since, three days ago, my mother had decided it was time to teach me, her oldest child, how to use a bow and arrow. I had never once succeeded and I knew that sooner or later she would give up, make some excuse, and feed me. But it would not be soon.

"Maybe if you made your eyes smaller?" My mother encouraged me by bringing her cheeks so close to her forehead that she looked like a dried onion, and I made the mistake of laughing.

"Today . . . ," my mother said in the same voice she had used when I was younger and she told me not to play with sharp knives. She picked up an arrow from the ground and sternly held it out for me to take. She walked back toward the place where she threw the moss into the air. "Today, we will *not* surrender." Before I could object she had disappeared again into that mist of color and noise that surrounded me like the roof and walls of a very small house.

"Now!"

I quickly pointed my arrow high above the place where her voice came from, and released it.

"Better," she called. "The sunlight must have confused you. Try again."

There were many *other* things I could do, I told myself when finally, with not a single victory, we came home. I could make a whistle from a stiff reed using only the sharp edge of a clamshell. I could sing a song after hearing it just one time. I could find wild strawberries, even clusters of violets, by closing my eyes and following the directions of my nose. I could hear my father's footsteps before anyone else. "He's back," I would inform my brothers and sisters, giving them a little longer to stop playing and compose themselves. So why couldn't I shoot?

"Is there some trick to it?" I asked my mother's brother, Brings the Deer, one evening as we were sitting in front of our house, watching fireflies as they flickered before our faces. He was the best archer in our whole family, so he should know.

"Practice is the only trick," my uncle said, sounding more like my father than himself. Usually, since he was younger than my mother and didn't yet have any children of his own, he was less serious.

"It's been days and days, and I'm no better."

"Maybe . . ." Brings the Deer's tone was gentler, more understanding. "Maybe your bowstring is not tight enough?" He reached over to where it rested by my leg and tested it. "No, it seems all right. Maybe you're closing your eyes at the last moment before you shoot? *I* did that myself when I first started."

I shook my head.

"Maybe . . . How many fingers am I holding up?"

I tipped my head. The dusky light was dim, but I could still see my own hands, balled into fists. "Fingers?"

"How many?"

I couldn't tell how many arms he was holding up, much less fingers. "Three?" I guessed.

"How many now?"

"Two?"

"Now?"

"Five?"

There was a silence. "Walnut, I was holding up no fingers at all."

"I knew that," I said, though it wasn't true. "I was making a joke."

But Brings the Deer didn't laugh.

The next morning when my mother woke me for shooting practice, we went to a new part of the forest. That was only the first odd thing.

"Put down your bow and sit on this rock," my mother said, patting a large flat stone at the base of a pine tree. Then, from her sack she brought out a tightly woven sash, placed it over my eyes, and tied it with a length of grapevine.

"What are you doing?" I wanted to know.

"Shhh," she said. "Describe this place to me."

"But I've never been here before and I can't see."

"Shhh," she said again. "Look with your ears."

At first, there was nothing to hear—just . . . forest. But the longer we didn't talk, the more separate parts announced themselves: the hush of a brook just behind me and, farther beyond that, the rush of a river. The buzz of a beehive on a tree not far over to my right. The beat of a hummingbird's wings as it dove in and out of a cluster of . . . what was that smell? . . . *roses* near where my mother— who, I could tell, had just oiled her hair this morning—sat.

"Don't move," I said as I heard her prepare to shift her weight. "It's only a hummingbird."

"*What's* only a . . . ? Oh," she whispered. "How beautiful. What else do you see, Walnut?"

So I told her—there were so many things that it took the whole morning to list them all. And the amazing fact was, I completely forgot to be hungry for breakfast. From that day on, instead of shooting arrows we went each dawn to a new spot and stayed until I had surprised my mother at least four times by what I could see but she could not.

At the end of the summer there was always a great feast— and that was when boys my age had to prove by their accurate shooting that they were ready to be grown up.

"I'm not going," I told Brings the Deer. We were lying on our backs on the bank of the pond at the south end of the village, waiting for fish to swim into our net. "You said I had to practice and I have not practiced. Instead I played games with my mother."

"So she's told me," he said. All around us was the noise of people working. Some were gathering hollow green and yellow gourds in huge piles that made a popping sound when they knocked together. Others were stacking firewood—I could hear them stumbling up with their arms full, dropping the load with a rolling crash, and then the even tap-tap-tap of setting the logs straight. Even Brings the Deer was replacing the old bluebird feathers on his fancy headband with new ones. From off to one side I picked up the rich hickory smell of stewing venison.

"My father will be ashamed." My best friend Frog was, I knew, even now out somewhere practicing his aim. I didn't know why he was nervous—he told me that he had been able to shoot moss out of the air on his very first try.

"Have you asked him?"

"Who, Frog?" Had even Brings the Deer heard of Frog's talent?

"Your father. Have you talked to him about this?"

"No, but . . . he's coming now."

Brings the Deer stood up and looked all around. "Where?"

"On the other side of the pond," I told him, just as my father called our names.

"Walnut? Brings the Deer? Where are you?"

"I see him now," said my uncle. "Over here," he yelled.

While we waited for my father—he walked like a beaver, his feet flat and wide apart—to make his way over to us, Brings the Deer sat next to me and shook his head. "It's amazing," he laughed, and admired the design of the new feathers. "My sister did not exaggerate."

Before I could say anything, my father burst from the rest of the colors around us and sat down on my stomach.

"Ah," he sighed, and stretched his arms. "A dry, comfortable seat at last."

"I can't breathe!" I tried to shove him off me, but he was too heavy.

"How very strange," my father said to Brings the Deer. "I thought I heard my son speak from inside my own body."

"Yes," Brings the Deer replied. "It's what a bird must feel when she sits on her nest after the chicks hatch."

"I am sinking into the mud," I muttered, and poked my father beneath his ribs with my finger.

Why was he being so playful, as if I were still a very little boy?

"What's this? What's this?" he cried, cocking his head and jumping up. "Walnut, what are you doing down there? Come home quickly. The contests are going to start early."

"Father . . . ," I began. How I hated to embarrass him.

"No time for talking. This year there is going to be an extra trial, *much* harder."

"Harder than hitting a target?" I might as well stay in the mud instead of cleaning up.

Boys my age were already waiting in the clearing where ball games were played. Each one had his bow and quiver of arrows. As we passed my friend Frog close enough for me to glance directly into his face I realized that though he was nervous and excited, he wasn't half as unhappy as I felt.

The flat afternoon sun made the colors of the earth and rocks as bright as if they were wet. There was no wind to stir the branches of the trees and give me an excuse for missing my shots. The sky was the pale, shiny blue of a trout's scale.

Brings the Deer gave my arm a squeeze and then went over to join the crowd of adults and small children watching in the shade nearby. I was sure my mother must be among them. I wondered what she was thinking. When people learned she hadn't taught me how to shoot, they might criticize her. Ay-yah-yah.

The weroance, our most important person, the expert on hunting, stood nearby. She raised her hands for quiet, and when everyone was still, she spoke in the slow, booming voice she saved for the most solemn moments. It seemed to come from deep within her body, to be blown through a horn of shell, to rattle like the skin of a hand drum.

"Sometimes," she said, "the people need someone to do the impossible. As necessary as hunting is, as necessary as growing and harvesting plants, sometimes we need even more than those tasks can provide. We need someone with the ability to see what can't be seen. And we won't have the regular contest until someone passes this new one."

There was a silence, then all the boys around me began to whisper to one another.

"What does she mean?" worried one.

"How can they expect us to do that?" another demanded. "Isn't it enough that our mothers have taught us how to shoot moss from the sky?"

"So," the weroance went on steady as the beat of a large bird's wings, "the first test will be for . . ."

I missed what she said because something fell at my feet. I looked down—it was the sash and a length of grapevine. My mother must have tossed it.

"See behind *trees*?" Frog repeated the weroance's words, and the boy next to me looked toward the forest uncertainly.

But I knew what to do. I tied the sash around my eyes and remained very still. The wind made fingers through the trees and I used them to feel my way in each direction. My mind flew the way a hawk must fly, skimming over all that was ordinary, alert for a dart of something out of place. I paid no attention to the rustle of leaves or the rain of a waterfall. Those expected sounds—those sounds I knew from all my morning games with my mother—I put to one side, and waited.

What was that? A dead branch snapped. A rock, slightly closer, tumbled down a hill. A breath was drawn in.

"Who will begin?" The weroance interrupted my ears. "You," she said.

And Frog tried, without much hope, "I see a raccoon. He is asleep in the bough of a tree."

"You," she said. Another voice, Sleeps Late, no more confident, answered. "I see a . . . spiderweb, strung on the brambles of a mulberry bush."

"Now you," she said, but this time there was no reply. "You. Walnut."

I thought so hard that my head felt tight between my ears. I was afraid to make a mistake in front of so many people, but then I pretended it was my mother asking me to listen, curious and interested as she had been every morning.

"A man is coming from the south," I said. "He is light on his feet but has a limp. He is not young, for he must breathe hard to climb. He is . . ." I stopped talking, shut my eyes even behind my blindfold, and concentrated. There was no mistaking it. "He is laughing! It is Gray Fire!"

I heard people turning to look behind me, whispering among themselves. I could almost *feel* them looking to see if I was right. That part of the forest was dense, the paths overgrown and winding.

"There!" Brings the Deer's voice was loud above the rest. "It is, it *is* Gray Fire!" The weroance's brother! He had been given his name because he was so quiet he could pass through the village like smoke.

Strong hands untied the vine that bound the sash around my eyes. My father's hands. They lingered for just an instant on my hair. I'm sure no one else but me noticed.

"This part of the contest is over," the weroance announced. "Each boy except the one who passed must now prove himself with a bow in order to earn the right to his grown-up name."

"And what of the boy who passed?" my mother called out from where she stood. "What about my Walnut?"

"When a boy passes the test he is no longer a boy," the weroance answered. "He no longer wears a boy's name."

Everyone stopped what they were doing to hear what she would say next. I turned the sash in my hand, the sash my mother had woven. It was soft to the touch, as if it had been made from silky moss.

"Sees Behind Trees," the weroance pronounced, "is now a young man."

Think and Respond

1. Why does Walnut's mother speak sternly to him when she tries to teach him to shoot? Why and how does her attitude change?

2. How does the author show you the way Walnut sees?

3. What important lesson does the weroance teach when she gives Walnut his new name?

4. Do you think you might judge people differently after reading this story? Explain.

5. How did you use reading strategies to help you understand this story?

About the Author
Michael Dorris

Michael Dorris was a member of the Modoc Indian tribe on his father's side of the family. He said, "I lived on a reservation part of the time when I was a child, so I knew my Indian relatives. That part of my background was front and center." He also read a lot when he was young. He said, "The thing I like about reading is that it puts you in charge. You can stop and start, you can reread something, and you can imagine what the characters and places look like. When you read, you're a participant in the story. When you're watching television, you're not."

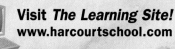

Visit *The Learning Site!*
www.harcourtschool.com

Sounds of Nature

Three Poems

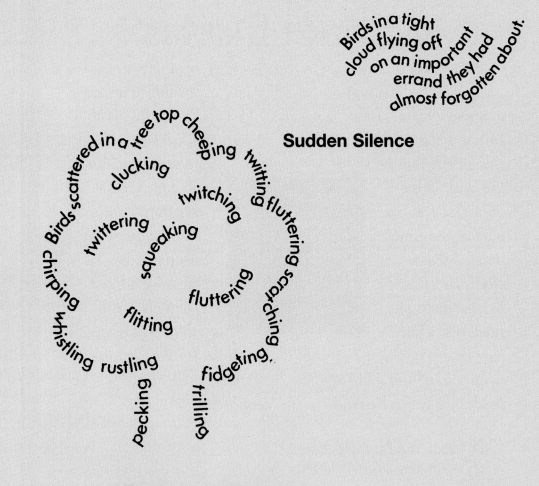

Birds in a tight
cloud flying off
on an important
errand they had
almost forgotten about.

Sudden Silence

Birds scattered in a tree top cheeping twitting fluttering scratching
clucking
twitching
twittering
squeaking
fluttering
chirping
flitting
whistling rustling
fidgeting
pecking
trilling

SHAPE POEM

When Birds Remember

by Robert Froman
lettering by Ray Barber

64

LIMERICK

So by chance it may be you've not heard
Of a small sort of queer silent bird.
      Not a song, trill, or note
      Ever comes from his throat.
If it does, I take back every word.
              —David McCord
          illustrated by Laura Greer

HAIKU

Above the chorus, listen! A single cricket shakes a golden bell.
—Kyoshi
    illustrated by Molly Bang

65

Making Connections

Compare Texts

1 Why is this story included in a theme that focuses on learning our inner strengths?

2 How does the author show a change in Walnut's mother's feelings?

3 How is the subject of the three "Sounds of Nature" poems like that of "Sees Behind Trees"?

4 What cultural information makes "Sees Behind Trees" a work of historical fiction?

5 Do you think Sees Behind Trees will make valuable contributions to his community as an adult? Why or why not?

Write Sentences

Suppose that Walnut heard the three poems, "When Birds Remember," "Haiku," and "Limerick." Write one or more sentences expressing Walnut's thoughts and point of view about each poem. Use a chart like this one to organize your thoughts.

Writing CONNECTION

Poem	Walnut's Thoughts
"When Birds Remember"	
"Haiku"	
"Limerick"	

Construct a Model

Native American peoples constructed different types of homes depending on their needs and the materials that were available. Find information about Native American dwellings. Choose one type of dwelling, and construct a model of it. Fill in a chart like this one and display the chart with your model.

Type of Dwelling	People Who Built It	Geographical Location	Materials Used

Make a Chart

To teach Walnut to shoot, his mother throws a clump of moss into the air. Later, he hears the people gathering green and yellow gourds. Research mosses and gourds, using a print, CD-ROM, or online encyclopedia. Make a two-column chart to compare the characteristics of mosses and gourds.

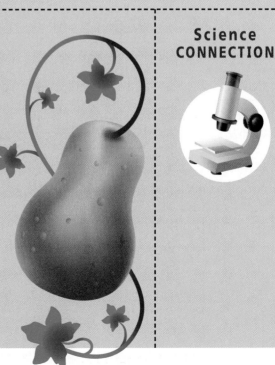

Narrative Elements

Focus Skill

The narrative elements of a story include the plot, the setting, and the characters. The **plot** is a sequence of related events in a story. At the center of the plot is a **conflict**, or **problem**, that the main character must resolve. In the development of plot,

- the **rising action** is a series of events that shows how the main character tries to solve the problem.

- the **turning point** determines how the problem will be resolved.

- the **falling action** leads to the **resolution** of the problem and the final outcome of the story.

This plot diagram shows the development of the plot in "Sees Behind Trees."

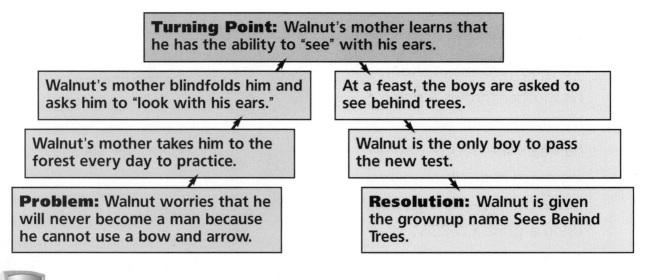

Turning Point: Walnut's mother learns that he has the ability to "see" with his ears.

Walnut's mother blindfolds him and asks him to "look with his ears."

At a feast, the boys are asked to see behind trees.

Walnut's mother takes him to the forest every day to practice.

Walnut is the only boy to pass the new test.

Problem: Walnut worries that he will never become a man because he cannot use a bow and arrow.

Resolution: Walnut is given the grownup name Sees Behind Trees.

Visit *The Learning Site!*
www.harcourtschool.com

See *Skills* and *Activities*

68

Test Prep
Narrative Elements

▶ **Read the passage. Then answer the questions.**

"They should have named me Goes in Circles," Little Moon mumbled to himself. Today, Hears the Wind had led Little Moon deep into the woods. Little Moon was supposed to find his way home before sundown, or he would experience the shame of having someone come to find him.

Little Moon had been preparing for this test for months. Each day, his older brother had taken him into the woods to show him how to use the sun and its shadows as a compass and how to mark a trail. Little Moon had paid close attention, but Little Moon had no natural sense of direction.

1. **Which sentence best describes the plot?**

   A Little Moon must learn how to mark a trail.

   B Little Moon must find Hears the Wind before others find him.

   C Little Moon must find his way out of the forest before sundown.

   D Little Moon must show that he can use the sun as a compass.

Tip

Sum up the series of related events that tell the story.

2. **What is Little Moon's problem?**

   F He lacks a sense of direction.

   G He is walking the wrong way.

   H There is no sun to guide him.

   J He forgot to mark the trail.

Tip

Look for details that tell what is preventing the main character from achieving his goal.

▲ Yang the Third
and Her Impossible
Family

grimaced

audition

sonata

accompaniment

accompanist

simultaneously

Vocabulary Power

Music plays an important role in the lives of the characters in the next selection. Some people play musical instruments for their own enjoyment. Others, like the fiddle player in the following interview, play music for a living.

Fiddle Player's Roots

BY ANNA MCGEE

Ken Cross, the fiddle player for the country band Frog Hoppers, wasn't always a country fiddle player. He told this reporter in a recent interview how he got his start in music.

REPORTER: How old were you when you began playing the fiddle?

KEN CROSS: I was eight when I learned to play the violin. I always wanted to play country music, but my mother had other ideas. She **grimaced**, just got this look of pain on her face, any time I called that violin a "fiddle."

REPORTER: When did you make the change from classical music to country?

KEN CROSS: When I was in the sixth grade, my mother arranged an **audition** for a special music program. For this tryout, I had to play a **sonata**, a musical composition that has several different sections. The sonata was written for violin with piano **accompaniment**. That meant I had to get a piano player to play with me. My **accompanist**, the guy who played the piano part, turned out to be a fan of country music, too. We'd start out practicing the sonata and just sort of look at each other and **simultaneously**, at the same moment, change over to playing a country song.

REPORTER: How did your audition go? Did you get into the special music program?

KEN CROSS: No, I didn't make it, but everything turned out all right. I love what I'm doing, and today my mother is the Frog Hoppers' biggest fan.

Vocabulary–Writing CONNECTION

Have you ever dreamed of becoming a star? Imagine you've just been given the **audition** of your dreams. Write a short paragraph describing what happened and how you felt about it.

Lensey Namioka
Yang the Third and Her Impossible Family

The companion to
Yang the
Youngest
and
His Terrible
Ear

by Kees de Kiefte

Genre

Realistic Fiction

Realistic fiction tells about characters and events that are like people and events in real life.

In this selection, look for

- **A main character who faces a problem or challenge**

- **First-person point of view**

Though they now live in Seattle, Washington, Yingmei's family still follows many Chinese customs, such as referring to the children by their birth order: Eldest Brother, Second Sister, Third Sister, and Fourth Brother. Yingmei (Third Sister) wants to become an American more than anything else. To accomplish this —

- She changes her name to Mary.
- She keeps a list of American words and phrases.
- She accepts a kitten from Holly Hanson, the most popular girl at school, even though it is forbidden.

Yingmei tries very hard, but she can't control everything that happens. In particular, she can't prevent her family members from saying and doing things that embarrass her in front of her new friends.

Yang the Third and Her Impossible Family

by Lensey Namioka
illustrated by Kees de Kiefte

I tried to squeeze my left leg behind my cello case in the backseat. It was a week after Kim's birthday party, and we were on the way to a rehearsal of the All-City Orchestra. The best players from the Seattle elementary schools had been selected to form a citywide orchestra, which rehearsed once a week.

Holly and I had been chosen from our school; so had Kim. The rehearsals were held in an auditorium across town from our neighborhood, so Mrs. Hanson and Mrs. O'Meara took turns driving the three of us to the rehearsals.

It was nice of Mrs. Hanson and Mrs. O'Meara to include me. My cello was only half-size, but it still took up a lot of room, and I had a struggle fitting it in the car.

"What time is your tryout on Wednesday, Holly?" asked Mrs. Hanson, who was driving that week. "I have to make sure I can get time off to take you over."

Holly was silent for a moment. "I might have to call it off. The accompanist is sick, and I'm not sure she'll be able to play."

Mrs. Hanson turned her head sharply to look at Holly. The car swerved, and she got it back into the lane before she spoke again. "But that's awful! You've been practicing the piece for ages! And it's too late for you to prepare some unaccompanied piece! Why didn't you tell me earlier?"

"It's not the end of the world, Mom," muttered Holly.

"Can't your music teacher find another accompanist?" asked Mrs. Hanson. "There must be other pianists around!"

"It's a hard piece, that Brahms. We won't be able to get anybody ready by Wednesday."

I could see the tendons on Mrs. Hanson's neck. It occurred to me that *she* was the one who was really bothered, not Holly.

A brilliant idea suddenly hit me. "Mrs. Hanson, my mother can play the accompaniment for Holly's tryout."

We had arrived at the auditorium. Mrs. Hanson stopped the car and slowly turned to look at me. "Are you sure? She can't stop if she makes a mistake, you know. It would ruin Holly's piece."

Mother might do a lot of embarrassing things, but if there was one thing I felt confident about, it was her musical ability. "My mother has played a lot of chamber music with other people, so she never loses the beat even if she makes a mistake."

"Thank you for the offer, Mary," Mrs. Hanson said. But she still looked doubtful.

It might be mean of me, but I hoped Holly's accompanist would stay sick. This was a chance for Mother to get on Mrs. Hanson's good side for a change. Holly would be grateful to me for saving her audition.

Halfway through the rehearsal we had a break. Holly came to the cello section and made her way to my stand. "Can I talk to you for a minute, Mary?"

I could tell that she was unhappy about something. "Sure, Holly," I said. "What's wrong?"

She absently ran her finger across the horsehair of her viola bow, and some of the resin flew up in a fine powder. "It's about your mother accompanying me for the tryout," she said finally. "I don't really care about getting in to the Junior Chamber Orchestra, you know. My mom wants me to join, because it's such a select group and they have a summer camp on Orcas Island."

A summer camp where people just made music! It sounded like heaven. Playing in the All-City Orchestra was fun, but being in the Junior Chamber Orchestra would be a real privilege. I tried not to feel envious. "I'd give anything to join something like that! Is it very expensive?"

Holly nodded. "It costs a bundle, but my dad will pay for it. In fact he's one of the main supporters of the orchestra. But frankly, I'd rather have the money for something else — like raising purebred dogs."

She grimaced as she looked around the rehearsal hall. I didn't know what to say. Were we really that different? Did she really think purebred dogs are more important than music?

On the way home, Mrs. Hanson seemed more friendly. "Your mother is a professional pianist, isn't she? Maybe I *will* ask her to play for Holly's tryout if the regular accompanist can't make it, Mary."

I looked at Holly and saw that she was gently shaking her head. If I asked Mother to play the accompaniment, Holly might get mad and wouldn't let me be her friend anymore. After I had worked so hard to get this far with her!

Then I thought of Mother. I thought of how many social blunders she had been making. If she got to play in Holly's tryout, the Hansons would find out what a good pianist she was and respect her a lot more.

It was hard to decide. So I just mumbled something.

"Fine!" Mrs. Hanson said cheerfully. "I'll give your mother a call tomorrow."

It was nice that Fourth Brother cared about my feelings...

76

As Mrs. Hanson dropped me at our house, I ran into Mr. and Mrs. Sylvester. "We saw that kitten again, Mary," said Mr. Sylvester. "It seems to hang around a lot. I wonder if it's a stray. Maybe we can take it home."

"I don't want a cat, Benny," said Mrs. Sylvester. "Cats are stuck-up animals, and they care only about themselves. I want another dog. I want a beagle like Jenny!"

Her voice quavered a little, and I knew she still missed their dog.

"Now, now, Denny," said Mr. Sylvester. "We'll find a beagle just like Benny one of these days."

When I went in the house, Fourth Brother was making himself a peanut butter and jelly sandwich in the kitchen.

"I thought you didn't like peanut butter," I said.

"I knew you were embarrassed because I was always eating bean sprouts for lunch," he said. "So I thought I'd try to get used to peanut butter."

It was nice that Fourth Brother cared about my feelings. He took a big bite of the sandwich. "Anyway, I couldn't find anything else to eat," he mumbled.

I remembered why I wanted to talk to him. "Did you hear what the Sylvesters said? They saw Rita again!"

Fourth Brother licked the peanut butter from the roof of his mouth and swallowed. Then he said, "It's okay as long as she comes when I play the dinner signal."

"But if Mrs. Sylvester gets another dog, it might tear Rita to pieces!"

"We'll have to talk her out of it," said Fourth Brother.

That was easy enough to say. But what could we do if the Sylvesters finally found a beagle to replace Jenny?

Mother's face turned pink. I could tell she was pleased.

I had too many things to worry about. Rita kept escaping from the basement. Having Mother accompany Holly might ruin my friendship with her. And my family kept disgracing themselves in public.

Once I saw a juggling act in China. A girl balanced three plates simultaneously by spinning them at the ends of three chopsticks. I felt like that juggler. At any minute, one of the plates might fall and smash into bits.

Mrs. Hanson called Tuesday night when we were having dinner. I answered the phone. "Mary," she said, "do you still think your mother could play the accompaniment tomorrow for Holly's audition?"

I felt torn. If I said yes, I risked losing Holly's friendship. But if she didn't want to be in the orchestra, why couldn't she just play badly at the audition? Maybe she was too proud. She didn't want her mother to see that she wasn't good enough or that she wasn't trying hard.

From where I stood in the hallway, I could see into the dining room. Mother was bringing in a stir-fried dish, and after setting it down, she wiped her forehead.

"I know it's very short notice," Mrs. Hanson was saying. "Hello? Are you still there, Mary?"

I cleared my throat. "Yes, Mrs. Hanson. I'm sure my mother would be able to do it. Can you bring the music over tonight?"

Mrs. Hanson breathed a sigh of relief. "Thank you, Mary. I'll be over as soon as I can."

"Well, we're still having supper . . . ," I told her.

"Of course, of course!" she said quickly. "I'll come at eight, shall I?"

It was strange to hear Mrs. Hanson sounding so anxious to please. I told her that eight o'clock was fine, then walked slowly back to the dining room table.

The family looked at me curiously. "What was that about?" asked Father.

"Mother," I said in a rush, "Mrs. Hanson needs a pianist to play the accompaniment for Holly's tryout. It's a Brahms viola sonata. She's bringing over the music tonight at eight. Can you do it?"

Mother's face turned pink. I could tell she was pleased. "Why, yes, I think I can. Is that the one transposed from a violin sonata?"

I didn't know, but Father and Eldest Brother did. For the rest of the meal, we discussed the piece and whether Mother could play it at such short notice.

Mother wasn't the only one who looked happy. Father said it was about time people learned how good Mother was, while Eldest Brother and Second Sister both beamed and nodded agreement.

Fourth Brother was the only one who didn't look completely happy. "I hope Mrs. Hanson doesn't mention Rita," he said to me as the two of us cleared the table.

I had forgotten about Rita! Mrs. Hanson was under the impression that we had already told my family about her. I had to prevent Mrs. Hanson from saying something.

Mrs. Hanson and Holly arrived promptly at eight. Mrs. Hanson looked around at our living room. I had given up trying to neaten the room, and there were music stands all over. My cello leaned against the sofa, and next to it was an open case containing Elder Brother's violin. Heaps of sheet music were piled on the stands, on the sofa, and on the floor. To walk across the room, you had to negotiate carefully between piles.

"Goodness, you have a lot of music!" Mrs. Hanson exclaimed. "If you had the kitten in here . . ."

I knew what she was going to say next, and I had to head her off. Before I could do anything, there was a clatter behind me. Fourth Brother had acted first: He had knocked over a couple of music stands.

As I helped him set the stands up again, he whispered to me, "You'll have to think of something else to distract her."

"As I was saying—," Mrs. Hanson began again.

"Mother," I interrupted desperately, "we haven't tuned the piano for some time. Do you think that will bother Holly?"

Mother walked over to the piano and played a blurringly fast chromatic scale across the keyboard. "It should do well enough." She turned to Mrs. Hanson. "Have you got the music?"

At last that took Mrs. Hanson's mind from Rita—for the time being. She fetched the music and handed it to Mother.

Mother looked at the score. "My husband thought it might be this sonata. I've accompanied him on it—in a different key, of course." She sat down at the piano and looked at Holly. "Shall we try it?"

Holly looked uncomfortable—the first time I had ever seen her really uncomfortable. Slowly, she took out her viola and tuned it. "I'm getting stage fright," she muttered, looking around at the circle of eyes.

"Then it would be good practice for the real audition," said Mrs. Hanson with a nervous laugh.

We moved aside piles of instruments and music and found seats. Holly and Mother began.

After a few bars, I began to worry—but not about Mother. There was nothing wrong with her piano playing. She had played the piece before, after all.

The problem was Holly. She had obviously been well taught. Her bowing was correct, her fingering neat, and her pitch true. She seemed to be following the score carefully, obeying all the dynamics signs. But there was something lifeless about her playing— and that was fatal.

My family and I looked around at one another, and I saw the same conclusion in everybody's eyes. Even Fourth Brother, who can't tell "Old MacDonald Had a Farm" from "Mary Had a Little Lamb," seemed to know from the expression on Holly's face that her heart wasn't in the music.

At the end we all clapped politely, but nobody was fooled. "I told you I had stage fright," Holly said in a low voice.

Mrs. Hanson swallowed. "You'll get over it by tomorrow, darling," she said, and the forced smile on her face was painful to see. She turned to Mother. "Thank you very much, Mrs. Yang. You played beautifully."

"Oh, no, I was simply awful!" said Mother. She knew she had done well, but for a Chinese it would be very rude to agree.

"You're a marvelous pianist, really!" insisted Mrs. Hanson.

Mother again disagreed. "I'm very poor. You must not flatter me."

"No, no!" said Mrs. Hanson. "I'm not trying to flatter you."

Holly looked impatient. "Mom, we'd better go."

"Of course, darling," Mrs. Hanson said quickly. She turned to Mother. "Holly has to get a good night's rest. We don't want her to go to the audition all tired and sleepy, do we?"

"Yes!" said Mother, smiling broadly.

Mrs. Hanson blinked. "I mean, we wouldn't want Holly to fail the audition!"

"Yes, yes!" said Mother.

The rest of the Yangs agreed. "Yes," we all said earnestly.

Mrs. Hanson and Holly stared at us. I could tell that something was wrong, but I didn't know what it was. Finally Mrs. Hanson turned abruptly and walked to the front door. "Good night!" she said curtly. Opening the door, she walked out, followed by Holly.

I went after them, determined to find out what the matter was.

"Uh — did my mother say something funny again just now?" I asked when I had caught up with the Hansons.

Mrs. Hanson stopped. "Well, it just sounded awfully strange, what all of you said. I could hardly believe my ears!"

I didn't know what she was talking about. "What did we say? What sounded strange?"

"It sounded like you wanted me to fail the audition!" said Holly.

It was my turn not to believe my ears. "We said no such thing!"

"I said we wouldn't want Holly to fail the audition," Mrs. Hanson said slowly, very slowly. "Then your family said yes — every single one of you!"

"Of course we said yes!" I cried indignantly. "We agreed with you completely! We certainly don't want Holly to fail the audition!"

The three of us stood frozen and looked at one another. To a passerby, we must have looked like three store dummies.

Suddenly Mrs. Hanson began to laugh. "Yes! We have no bananas!" she sang in a high, cracked voice.

She had gone completely mad! Maybe the anxiety over Holly's audition had driven her out of her mind. I looked at Holly. But she was laughing as well. "It's an old song my grandma used to sing," she told me.

Mrs. Hanson turned to me, still laughing. "You all said yes because you agreed with me, just like in the song 'Yes! We Have No Bananas.'"

I still didn't understand. "Was that wrong?"

Holly tried to explain. "In English, you'd say, 'No, we wouldn't want Holly to fail the audition.'"

I had thought that learning English was just a matter of memorizing a lot of new words and phrases. It is much more complicated than that. Even knowing when to say yes or no is tricky!

I turned slowly away and started for home. I'd have a lot to write in my notebook tonight. Behind my back, I heard Mrs. Hanson and Holly giggling and softly singing, "Yes! We have no bananas today!"

Suddenly I felt I had to say something. I turned again and caught up with the Hansons. "Mrs. Hanson," I said, "we're new in this country, and we can't do everything right immediately. I hope you'll try to be patient."

Without waiting for her to reply, I turned to Holly. "When you picked up your viola for the first time, you probably played a few sour notes. I bet your teacher didn't break down laughing."

By now both Mrs. Hanson and Holly had sobered. "You're quite right, Mary," Mrs. Hanson said quietly. "We should have been more understanding."

I turned slowly away and started for home. I'd have a lot to write in my notebook tonight.

She looked at Holly. "You should apologize, too."

Holly murmured something. Her face didn't show much expression, so I couldn't tell how she felt.

As I walked home, I thought about how unfair I had been to my family all these months. I thought they had been impossible, because they didn't make more of an effort to learn American ways.

But I am actually one of them: In spite of my list of new words and my careful study of American ways, I still make mistakes, just like the rest of the family.

I had blamed Mother more than the rest, because she had made the most embarrassing mistakes. I should have remembered that she had to spend all her time cooking and feeding us. She didn't have time to meet a lot of Americans and learn the customs of this country.

I had been ashamed of Mother. Now I was more ashamed of myself.

Think and Respond

❶ Why does Mary have mixed feelings about asking her mother to be Holly's **accompanist** at the **audition**?

❷ Why does the author describe Mrs. Hanson's smile as "forced" and "painful to see" after Holly has finished playing?

❸ Why do you think the author included the description of the juggling act that Mary saw in China?

❹ Do you think Mary is right to tell Mrs. Hanson and Holly how their laughter makes her feel? Why or why not?

❺ How did you use reading strategies to help you understand this story?

Meet the Author
Lensey Namioka

Was your family musical like the Yangs?

I'd say so. My father has composed music, and my sister is a professor of musicology, so they had very good "ears." But not me! Once, my sister hid my violin exercise book. She confessed years later that she just couldn't take listening to me practice anymore! Still, my family was supportive of other things I did.

What were some of the other things you did?

Actually, I liked playing the piano. It was really only the violin that I disliked. I hated tuning it up! I preferred reading. I was a real bookworm. After I found the public library, it became my home away from home.

What else in the story comes from your own life?

I was born in Beijing, China, and came here with my family when I was nine years old. I didn't know English when I came here, and I had to learn it at school.

Was it hard to learn English?

It wasn't as bad as it sounds. Kids learn fast, and I had good friends.

**Visit *The Learning Site!*
www.harcourtschool.com**

85

Making Connections

Compare Texts

 1 What might Mary write about in her notebook tonight that relates to the theme Look Inside?

2 Why are some sentences of this story in large red type?

3 Mary's interest is music. Think of another character you have read about who has an interest in a particular area. How is this character similar to and different from Mary?

4 Do you think the events in this story would be better presented in the form of journal entries? Explain.

5 What could you do to find out more about classical music?

Write an Advice Column

Imagine that you write an advice column for your school newspaper. A character from this story has written to you, asking for advice about a situation in the story. Write the question and your reply. Explain what the character may learn from the experience. Use a chart like this one.

**Writing
CONNECTION**

Character	
Character's problem	
Advice	

Create a Time Line

In "Yang the Third and Her Impossible Family," Mary's friend Holly plays a sonata by Brahms, a famous composer. Do research to find out when Brahms lived, important events in his life, and dates of his best-known musical compositions. You might use an encyclopedia, music textbooks, or other nonfiction books about music. Then construct a time line to show the information you found.

Social Studies CONNECTION

Draw a Diagram

Mary's family members play many instruments. Choose an instrument that interests you, and use an encyclopedia or other resource to find information about it. Then draw a diagram of the instrument and label the parts.

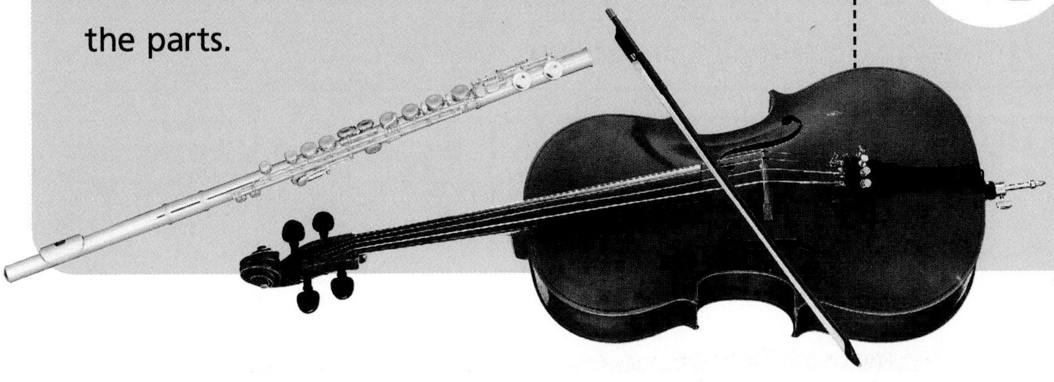

Music CONNECTION

▲ **Yang the Third and Her Impossible Family**

Prefixes, Suffixes, and Roots

Look at these words from "Yang the Third and Her Impossible Family."

disagreed   doubtful   signal

The prefix *dis-* has been added to the root word *agreed*. The suffix *-ful* has been added to the root word *doubt*. You know that adding word parts called **prefixes** and **suffixes** to **root words** changes the meanings.

The word *signal* is made by combining the Latin root *sign*, which means "mark," with the suffix *-al*. Remember that a **root** is a word part, often taken from Greek or Latin, that must be attached to another word part or parts to make a word.

Look at the chart below. Study the word parts and their meanings. Think about other words you have come across in your reading that contain these word parts.

Prefix	Meaning	Selection Examples
dis- *mis-*	"not" or "opposite of" "wrongly" or "bad"	disagreed mistake

Suffix	Meaning	Selection Examples
-ful *-less*	"filled with" or "able" "without" or "lacking"	doubtful lifeless

Latin Root	Meaning	Selection Examples
sign *port*	"mark" "carry"	signal import

Visit *The Learning Site!*
 www.harcourtschool.com

See *Skills* and *Activities*

88

Test Prep

Prefixes, Suffixes, and Roots

▶ **Read the passage. Then answer the questions.**

> Lydia stared in <u>amazement</u> at Marty. He had played the violin and the oboe with great skill. What a <u>multitalented</u> musician he was! As they waited for the judges' decision, Lydia folded up her portable music stand. She had played her best and could only hope that she would be selected for the orchestra.

1. **If the suffix *-ment* means "state of," then what does <u>amazement</u> mean?**

   A lack of confusion

   B relief

   C a state of great surprise

   D a jealous feeling

   Tip
   Use the meaning of the suffix to figure out the meaning of the word.

2. **If the prefix *multi-* means "many" or "much," then what does <u>multitalented</u> mean?**

   F not as talented as everyone else

   G fearful about trying new things

   H very good at just one thing

   J talented in many ways

   Tip
   Use the meaning of the prefix to figure out the meaning of the word.

▲ Dear Mrs. Parks

Vocabulary Power

Young people often write to famous adults like Rosa Parks to ask for advice. Has anyone ever given you good advice that helped you solve a problem? Sometimes it pays to seek advice from someone who is older and wiser than you are.

Partnership Program

Are you a younger person?

Do you feel you need help to reach your **potential**, to be the best that you can be? Do you need someone to **inspire** you, to help you feel excited about working toward your goals? Do you need a place to express your thoughts and dreams without fear of being laughed at or **ridiculed**?

Then you need to know about the Partnership Program!

Are you an older person?

Do you feel you have the ability to **counsel** others, to give them advice and support?

Do you think you could be a **mentor**, a wise and caring adviser, to a growing youngster?

Do you think you can show others the proud, calm behavior that we call **dignity**?

Then you need to know about the Partnership Program!

Learn more about the Partnership Program.

Friday, November 14

8 P.M.

Kinley Road School

For more information, send your **correspondence** by mail or e-mail to Mrs. Gates, principal of Kinley Road School.

Vocabulary–Writing CONNECTION

Imagine that your best friend has been **ridiculed** by a school bully. Write a brief note to your friend. What would you **counsel** him or her to do?

Genre

Letters

Letters are written communication addressed to a person or an organization.

In this selection, look for

- **Questions or comments written to a person**

- **Responses that express personal beliefs**

Rosa Parks has been called the mother of the modern-day civil rights movement. In 1955 she showed courage when she insisted on her rights on a city bus in Montgomery, Alabama. Over the years, she has received many letters from students seeking advice on different issues. This selection is a collection of some of those letters and the letters Rosa Parks wrote back to the students.

DEAR MRS. PARKS

A DIALOGUE WITH TODAY'S YOUTH

ROSA PARKS

WITH GREGORY J. REED

ILLUSTRATED BY LORI MCELRATH-ESLICK

Dear Mrs. Parks,
In school and when I am around certain people, I want to ask questions, but I am having trouble doing this. What would you do, Mrs. Parks?

Jimmy
Cleveland, Ohio

You can never learn very much if you do not ask questions. Many times questions are more important than answers. A person should never be afraid to admit he or she does not know an answer. Once you do this, then you are on the path of learning. The right question and a steady mind to listen help us to grow and build confidence and character. Asking questions will help you to make better choices in life.

I am 83 years of age, and I am still learning. I am fascinated by the computer age, and I am still learning how to use some of the new technology. I just started taking water aerobics and swimming lessons last year. I ask a lot of questions during my swimming lessons. Take a deep breath! You can drown yourself with problems if you do not ask questions.

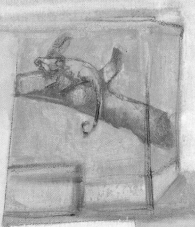

Dear Mrs. Parks,
I heard you were having your 83rd birthday celebration. I told my dad you must know everything now. My dad disagrees with me, but I don't believe him.

Richard
London, England

Your dad is right. No one knows everything. There is so much to learn and live for. There is a world of experiences awaiting us if we take the time to take part in them. Learning helps us grow and become the best person we can be. Age does not determine what we know. There are many young geniuses in life. I am still learning about life.

Today there are many changes. When I was young, cars went about 25 miles per hour. Now there are cars that can go 200 miles per hour. (I do not know why some people want to drive that fast!) Man has gone to the moon. I now keep up with much of my correspondence "on-line" on the Internet. People refer to this as "cyberspace." All this is new to me, but I am still learning.

Listen to your dad. We often act as though we know everything when we know too little. Your dad knows quite a bit. Keep an open mind. I hope your mind stays open after reading this.

Dear Mrs. Parks,
I like going to school. But I'm worrying about getting straight A's. My peers make fun of me when I get an A. I am trying to fit in.

Shata
Detroit, Michigan

I am happy to know you enjoy school. School is one of the most important developments of life that a student can experience if it is not taken for granted. Each person in life has certain gifts or talents to give back to life. I know today it is difficult at times to express your gifts because you are afraid of being ridiculed. You are not alone in your feelings. There are many other students in other cities who tell me they feel the same way. To all of you, I have one message: Work hard, do not be discouraged, and in everything you do, try to do your best. Those who make fun of you for achieving your highest potential have turned their values around backward. We are all leaders of something in life. You are a leader. Start leading, and the others will soon follow.

Dear Mrs. Parks,
I am 12 years old, and my favorite subject is math. I want to work with computers when I grow up. Did you like school when you were young?

Anthony
Las Vegas, Nevada

Because of my health, my early years were spent at home. I was a very sickly child, and my mother, who was a schoolteacher, did not think that I was strong enough to attend school. It made me very sad when it was time for me to go to school and my mother kept me at home. But that did not stop me from learning!

My grandmother was my main teacher during those times. I watched my grandmother care for others, and as a teenager, I was able to care for my grandmother based on the things I had seen her do.

I learned the importance of personal dignity. I learned the importance of treating other people with respect. My Grandma Rose taught me the history of our family and our community.

By the time I was strong enough to start school, I was ready. I knew the subjects I wanted to study— math, science, and literature. I have always loved learning, and I loved being in school!

Dear Mrs. Parks,
My teacher told us that you just celebrated your 83rd
birthday. My great-grandmother is 85 years old. She
talks about the old days all the time. Sometimes I
wonder what the old days have to do with me.

Adrienne
Vienna, Virginia

When your great-grandmother talks to you about those days, you must listen, listen, listen. When she talks to you that way, she is trying to keep history alive. She seeks to inspire you by sharing stories of the past, of good times and bad times. There is no better way for us to learn from the mistakes of the past than through stories handed down from people who have lived through those times.

You will learn from listening to your great-grandmother that human nature—the way people act—does not change. The lessons that she learned when she was a child and teenager will still apply to your life today. My grandmother often spoke to me of the times when she was a little girl. As I look back, I can see that I was being informed about my ancestors and those people who paved the way for the freedoms we now have. From this I learned of their courage, faith, and sacrifices.

Listen to your great-grandmother and her stories from her past. She is preparing you to take your place in the world of tomorrow. Treasure her stories, and remember them so that you can share them with future generations.

Dear Mrs. Parks,
I am 13 years old. Did you ever think that you would live to be 83 years old? What changes have you seen in the last 50 years?

Michael
Gary, Indiana

Eighty-three years—and I do not feel old! I am grateful for every day.

I have been blessed with a wonderful life. I have met people from all walks of life who come from every ethnic group. I have been touched by all of humanity.

I am grateful to God for this long life. I am thankful that He has used me to fulfill some of His plans.

I am proud to be an American. America is a wonderful country. In just over 200 years, since the signing of the Declaration of Independence, we have come a long way. Slavery has been abolished. Child labor laws have been established as the law of the land. Women have the right to vote and have taken their places in politics, the arts, sciences, and business. I am proud to see that history and herstory are coming together as one as we move ahead.

Our country is the model for every other developing country in the world for achieving justice and equality for its citizens. Our Constitution has lasted longer than any other constitution in modern history.

We cannot take these blessings for granted. We must share these gifts from God. Whether we are 13 or 83, we must show the world that we are able to correct our mistakes—including homelessness, poor race relations, and violence—and move forward to a better society. I know that we can. This nation has always overcome the obstacles it has faced.

Dear Mrs. Parks,
How can I make a difference in the world today?

Larry
St. Paul, Minnesota

By asking that question, you are making a difference. You are thinking about your place in the world and what you can do for other people.

Anyone who wants to make a difference in the world can do it. There are many ways to serve. Sometimes it can be your career choice, such as being a teacher, lawyer, minister, engineer, health care worker, or medical researcher. All of these jobs, and others, give you a chance to have a direct impact on people's lives. Other times, you can serve your community by taking part in activities during the evenings or throughout the weekend at your church or with a community group.

I always encourage those who ask how they can make a difference to consider working with young people. They have so many needs and concerns as they prepare themselves for their place in the next century. You might be the one to counsel them when they are troubled or to be a mentor to those who need someone to guide them.

All of us have talents that we can share with others. I am grateful to those who care about humanity and want to make a difference.

Think and Respond

1 Why do you think Mrs. Parks took time from her busy life to carry on **correspondence** with young people?

2 Why do you think this selection is presented in the form of letters rather than in the form of an article or a biography?

3 What kind of person is Mrs. Parks? How can you tell what she is like?

4 Which student letter and response did you find the most interesting?

5 How did you use reading strategies to help you understand this selection?

AESOP'S

FABLES

RETOLD BY ANN McGOVERN

About Aesop

Aesop was a slave who lived in Greece about 3,000 years ago. He became famous for the clever animal fables through which he showed the wise and foolish behavior of men.

Not much is really known about the life of Aesop. It is said that his wisdom so delighted one of his masters that the slave was given his freedom. It is said, too, that he became an honored guest at the courts of kings.

Aesop's fables have become a part of our daily language—a way of expressing ourselves. Haven't you heard people talk about "sour grapes" or "not counting chickens until they are hatched"?

Aesop never wrote down his stories. He told them to people, who in turn told them to others. Not until 200 years after his death did the first collection of his fables appear. Since then they have been translated into almost every language in the world. Today there are many, many versions of the tales that Aesop told in the hills of Greece so long ago.

The Crow and the Pitcher

A Crow, who was almost dying of thirst, came upon a pitcher which had once been filled with water. But to his dismay the Crow found that the water was so low he could not reach it. He tried with all his might to knock the pitcher over, but it was too heavy.

Then he saw a pile of pebbles nearby. He took one pebble in his beak and dropped it into the pitcher. The water rose a tiny bit. Then he took another pebble and dropped that in. The water rose a tiny bit more. One by one he dropped in all the pebbles. When he had dropped in a hundred pebbles, the water at last rose to the top. As the Crow drank deeply of the cool water, he said to himself, *"Where force fails, patience will often succeed."*

The Travelers and the Bear

Two men were traveling together when a Bear suddenly came out of the forest and stood in their path, growling. One of the men quickly climbed the nearest tree and concealed himself in the branches. The other man, seeing that there was no time to hide, fell flat on the ground. He pretended to be dead, for he had heard it said that a Bear will not touch a dead man.

The Bear came near, sniffed the man's head and body, and then lumbered away, back into the forest.

When the Bear was out of sight, the man in the tree slid down and said to his friend, "I saw the Bear whispering to you. What did he have to say?"

The other man replied, "The Bear told me never to travel with a friend who deserts me at the first sign of danger." He looked his companion straight in the eye. "The Bear said that, *in time of trouble, one learns who his true friends are.*"

Think and Respond

How are the two fables you read similar?

108

Making Connections

Compare Texts

1 What do the letters to Mrs. Parks and her replies have to do with the theme of discovering your strengths and abilities?

2 Why are the letters to Mrs. Parks set in different type from her replies?

3 How are Aesop's fables like Mrs. Parks's replies? How are they different?

4 How is the Rosa Parks selection different from a biography or autobiography of her?

5 Do you think the lives of the letter writers might change because of the advice from Mrs. Parks? Explain.

Write an Anecdote

Rosa Parks reminds us that it is important to listen to stories about the past. Think about a story you have heard or might hear from an older family member or friend. Write down the story. Use a graphic organizer like this one to gather your thoughts.

Who told you this story?
Why did this person tell the story?
When did the story take place?
What are the important details of the story?

Writing CONNECTION

110

Create a Certificate

Social Studies CONNECTION

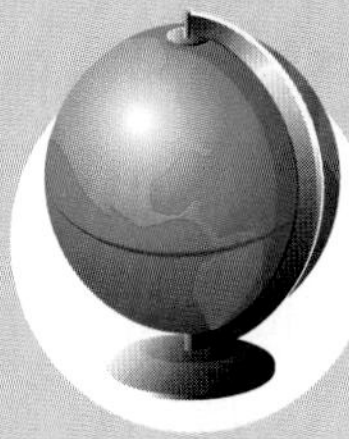

Rosa Parks says she is proud of the achievements of American women. Choose another woman who made a significant contribution to our country in earlier times. Research this woman. Create a certificate that might have been presented to her to thank her for her achievements.

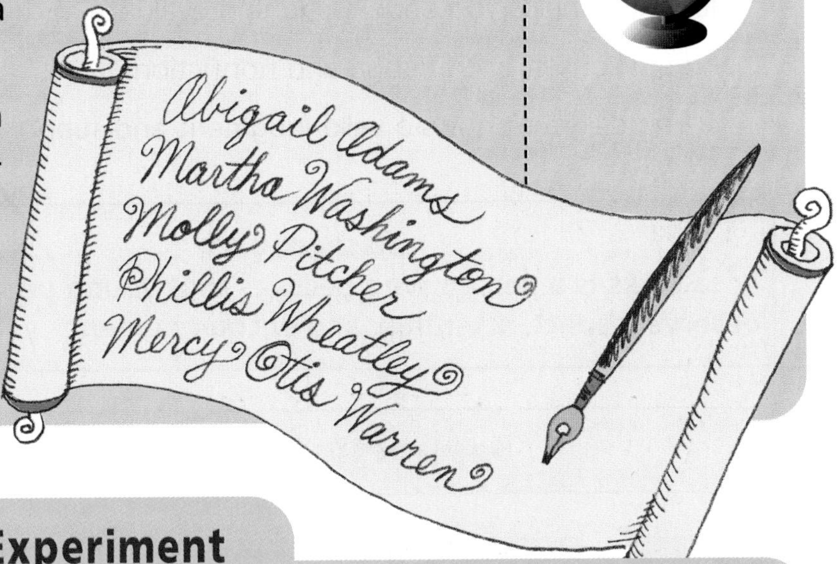
Abigail Adams
Martha Washington
Molly Pitcher
Phillis Wheatley
Mercy Otis Warren

Design an Experiment

Science CONNECTION

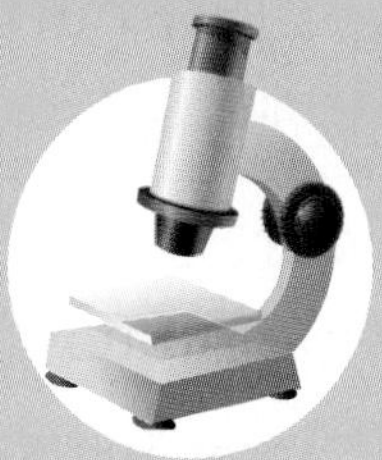

Mrs. Parks writes that she is learning to swim. You know that moving through water feels different from moving through air. Design an experiment to show that an object moves differently in water from the way it moves in air. Give a presentation of your experiment to classmates and explain what it shows.

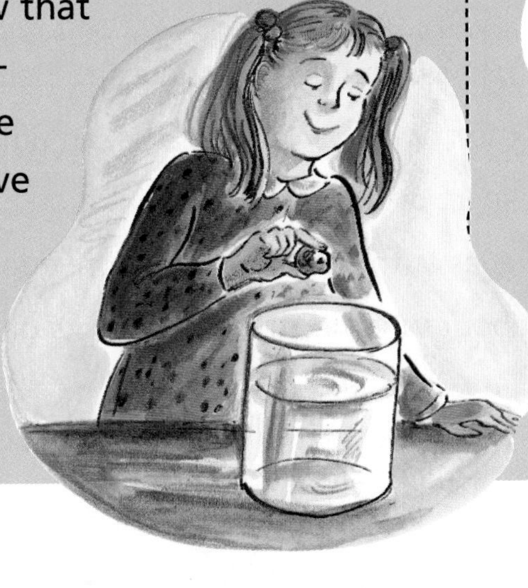

Make Judgments

Focus Skill

Making judgments means making decisions. A valid judgment is one you make based on evidence from the text. Making valid judgments helps you understand and evaluate authors' viewpoints and opinions in both fiction and nonfiction.

This diagram shows a valid judgment and supporting evidence.

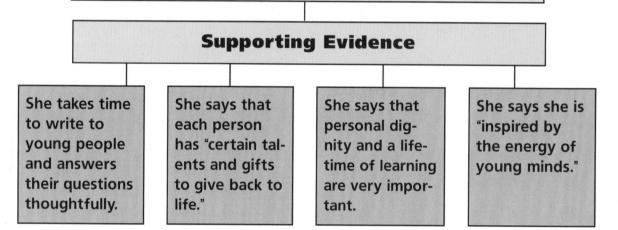

Judgment
Rosa Parks is a person who believes that young people deserve respect, attention, and encouragement.

Supporting Evidence

| She takes time to write to young people and answers their questions thoughtfully. | She says that each person has "certain talents and gifts to give back to life." | She says that personal dignity and a lifetime of learning are very important. | She says she is "inspired by the energy of young minds." |

Authors use a variety of techniques to persuade readers to agree with their opinions. For example, an author might quote a respected expert or appeal to your emotions. As you read, notice what techniques authors are using to influence you. Then make judgments about whether their arguments or conclusions are valid.

Test Prep

Make Judgments

▶ **Read the paragraph. Then answer the questions.**

> The peer counseling program in our school really seems to be working. Since the program began last year, the number of referrals for discipline has been cut almost in half. Our principal, Mrs. Barrett, says, "I think the program is making a real difference in the way our students relate to each other and settle their problems."

1. **Which of these is a valid judgment you can make about the peer counseling program?**

   A It has helped students improve their grades.

   B It has helped students relate better to each other.

   C It is too early to tell whether the program is helpful.

   D It has not been successful.

Tip

Look for evidence that supports your choice. A true statement is not a valid judgment unless it is supported by the text.

2. **What information supports your judgment about the peer counseling program?**

Tip

Go back to the passage to identify the statements that support the judgment you chose in question 1.

▲ Elena

ravine

plunged

condolences

revolution

determination

mocking

Vocabulary Power

In the selection titled "Elena," you will read about a mother who shows great courage. Other ordinary people have also done great things in difficult times.

Our first award for courage goes to Gary Manning. Gary was hiking with friends when he heard cries for help. He ran to see what was wrong and found the Crane family standing at the edge of a **ravine**, a narrow passageway surrounded by steep rocky sides. "Our dog, Pepper, ran on ahead of us and **plunged** into the ravine. He fell down into this deep pit in the earth!" Mr. Crane told Gary.

With his friends' help, Gary used a rope to slide to the bottom of the ravine. There he found Pepper injured but alive. Then Gary's friends pulled Gary and Pepper to safety. Instead of receiving **condolences**, or expressions of sympathy or comfort, on the loss of their pet, the Cranes are here today with Pepper to see Gary Manning receive this award for bravery.

This next award goes to Luz Hernandez, who showed great courage during the recent **revolution** in her country. The government was taken over by citizens who wanted to have elections to choose their own ruler. There was a great deal of anger on both sides, and it was a dangerous time.

When the adults in her village began arguing, this young girl spoke up with great **determination**, or strength of purpose. She told the adults to stop **mocking** and insulting each other. "If the people of your generation cannot speak and listen with respect and understanding for each other, what will become of my generation?" she asked.

The adults listened to Luz Hernandez and worked calmly toward a peaceful solution. We honor her today for her courage in speaking up and for the wisdom of her suggestion.

Vocabulary-Writing CONNECTION

Think about a time when you or someone you know acted with a great deal of **determination**. What did you do? Write about it for five minutes.

Genre

Historical Fiction

Historical fiction is a story that is set in the past and portrays people, places, and events that did or could have happened.

In this selection, look for

- **A real time and place in the past**

- **Actual historical figures**

Elena

by Diane Stanley

illustrated by

Michael

Steirnagle

In the year 1910, when I was about five years old, my father had to go to Guadalajara on business. He went there once or twice a year. It was nothing unusual. As he mounted his horse, my mother went out to say good-bye. "Be careful," she told him. She was worried about who he might meet on the road. We had heard talk of a revolution. There were said to be rough soldiers and armed *campesinos* about. They were dangerous men. But Father just squeezed her hand and smiled. "I will be careful," he said.

Father was joined by several villagers who were making the trip with him. They waved to us and headed off across the rugged countryside, for there were no proper roads. It was just at the end of the rainy season and the path was wet. About an hour after they left, the ground under Father's horse suddenly gave way, creating a landslide. Down they plunged into the ravine below.

The villagers raced back for help, and many men hurried off with ropes to haul my father up to safety.

They brought him to our house and laid him on the bed. The doctor came and dressed my father's wounds. As he was leaving, we asked the doctor, "Will he live?" He shrugged his shoulders. "Who can tell?" he said. "Perhaps Pablo knows. It is a gift some Indians have."

My mother stood and watched the doctor walk away from our house. "He is right," she thought to herself. "Pablo knows." So she went into the darkened room and knelt down beside the bed. She took his big hand and gently stroked it.

"Husband," she whispered, "how is it? Do you think you will recover?"

For a long time he did not look at her and he did not answer. At last he turned his head and spoke. "No," he said. He said there would be war and that she and the children must leave their home.

"You will always be in my heart," he said. He never spoke again.

Three days later, at the very hour he had spoken, my father died.

Mother went crazy with grief. She ran weeping into the patio, and with a big stick began to swing wildly, knocking down her beautiful flowers. Then she opened all the cages and let the birds free.

After that, my mother grew quiet. Though she went on caring for us just as before, that *chispa*, the bright spark that was always a part of her, went out. Papá's absence filled our house with emptiness. I could not really understand what had happened, because I was so young. It seemed to me that Papá had just gone to where I couldn't see him—perhaps he was in the next room. I kept expecting him to walk in our door one day and make everything good again. But he never came, of course, and in time I understood that he never would.

I remember that it was warm and beautiful at that time, the skies a brilliant cloudless blue, day after day. It was as if nature were mocking us.

One day I was playing upstairs with my brother Luis. I heard the loud clop-clop of horses on the stone pavement outside—not one, but many horses. So I ran to the window to see. Looking down, I saw our street transformed into a river of sombreros. The revolution had reached our little village—it was the army of Pancho Villa riding by!

With a gasp, Mother pulled me away from the window, for Pancho Villa was a notorious man. It was true that he was fighting to help free Mexico from the dictator Porfirio Díaz and that he wanted to give back to the *campesinos* the land that had been stolen from them. He was, in fact, on his way to becoming a genuine folk hero, the Robin Hood of Mexico. But it was also well known that he had once been a bandit and that his men were just as bad as the government soldiers. Neither army respected the law. Wherever they went, they stole from the people, killed anyone who challenged them, and left burned villages in their wake. What would happen to us?

Mother knelt down and gathered us in her arms. She understood in a flash that everything that had happened to her before had been for a reason. The books she had read, the hard numbers she had conquered, the battle she had won over her marriage—all this had made her strong. Now she had no father and no husband to help her. She had, instead, great courage and determination. Had there not always been wars? And in every country and every age, brave men and

women had faced terrible dangers. She could do it, too—God had put it into her heart. We saw this understanding pass across her face like a ripple of light. "Children," she said urgently, "we must find Esteban."

She knew that soldiers often took older boys and forced them into the army. My brother was sixteen.

None of us had seen him for hours. We searched the house for him, but he wasn't there. A book lay open on his bed. He had put it down and gone off somewhere. Maybe he was out in the streets among all those men. Maybe they had already taken him. At last María found him—up on the roof watching the soldiers. Boys are so foolish sometimes!

We made a hiding place for him in a kitchen cabinet, behind the big clay pots. Then Mother had another thought—the horses. They were sure to steal the horses. But maybe if they found the stable empty, they would think the horses had already been seized. They would certainly not think to look for them in the kitchen, so she brought the horses in there, too.

Before my mother could hide anything else, there was a loud knock on the door. We could hear deep voices laughing and talking outside. Mother hesitated a moment, wondering what to do. Then she sent us into the back room. We did as we were told but opened the door a crack so we could see what happened. Mother took a deep breath and opened the door.

There stood four or five soldiers, rough men who smelled of sweat and horses. The man in front was stout and wore a huge drooping mustache. *Bandoleras* crossed his chest. We had seen his face before, on a government poster. It was Pancho Villa himself!

"Señora," he said, "is this the house of Pablo, the famous maker of sombreros?" It was the last thing she expected to hear.

"It is," she said, "I am his widow."

"Then please accept my sincere condolences," said the leader of the rebel army, bowing slightly. He paused for a moment and then added almost shyly, "And the hats? The fine hats? Are there no more left?"

My mother actually smiled. "Excuse me a minute," she said. She went to a cupboard in her bedroom and returned with one of Father's beautiful silver-trimmed sombreros. "This is the last one," my mother said.

Pancho Villa was delighted. He put it on right away and actually paid her for it. Not only that, he posted a guard outside our house. As long as Villa's army was there, we were not harmed.

"Pablo was surely watching over us this day," my mother told us later. "But it may not always be so. Before your father died, he told me there would be soldiers. He told me we must leave our home. I wonder how I could have forgotten it."

"You were sad, *Mamacita*," María said.

When the *Villistas* had gone, Mother went to the plaza and opened the shop to the people of the village. She emptied the store of everything, taking down great bolts of manta and giving them to people who had nothing. We took only our money, some clothes, and food for the journey. We were leaving behind our aunts and uncles, our little house, the furniture, the pictures, the pots and pans and dishes. We said good-bye to the friends of a lifetime.

Everyone urged us not to go. "It is not proper for a woman to travel unprotected like that," they said. "It is not safe."

"The world is changing around us," Mother answered. "We must change, too."

We left the village early in the morning. When we reached the train station, we found that it was packed with frantic, pushing people. It seemed as though everyone in Mexico was trying to get on that train. Mother and María managed to make it inside. Then before Esteban got on, he handed Luis and me in through the window, along with the basket of food.

We were lucky to have benches to sit on. Most of the people were in boxcars or crowded in the aisles.

For five days the train chugged north. Through the open windows came soot, dust, and flies. I had worn a beautiful lacy white dress for the trip. Soon it was damp with sweat and covered with dirt.

We headed for California because we had a cousin, Trinidad, who lived there. We didn't have his address, though. In fact, we didn't even know what town he lived in. So we went to San Francisco, which was famous. We made our way to the *barrio*, where many people from Mexico lived. We asked everyone we met there, "Do you know our cousin Trinidad?" No one did. And besides, we didn't like it

there. It was damp and cold. In Los Angeles, no one had heard of Trinidad, either. We were happier there, because the weather was warmer. But the city was too big, not like our lovely little village in Mexico. We heard about a place called Santa Ana. There were lemon and orange and walnut groves there and good schools for the children. So that is where we went and that is where we stayed. We never did find Trinidad.

By then, we had spent most of our money. So Esteban got a job picking fruit. Sometimes he was gone for weeks, living in the camps near the farms. When he came home he was sore and tired. He didn't laugh and play with me the way he had before.

Mother ran a boardinghouse, which was hard work. She did the cleaning, made the beds, mopped the floors, and scrubbed the bathtub. She washed and ironed the boarders' clothes. After all that, she went into the kitchen and cooked mountains of rice and beans and *tortillas* and *enchiladas* for them to eat. We all sat down to dinner together at a long pine table. Sometimes the boarders were very nice and became our friends. Some even came from the same part of Mexico as our family had. It made me feel like I wasn't so far from home.

María and I did what we could. We hung the laundry out on the clothesline, and we brought it back in if it rained. We helped wash the dishes and changed all the sheets once a week. And we looked after little Luis.

But Mother said that our real job was to get an education. School and homework always came first. When we were done with that, she said, we could help. I felt bad sometimes, sitting in a chair with a book on my lap while Mother was never still, always bustling about at her chores. She did it with a good spirit, though. If I said to her, "You work too hard, *Mamacita*," she would just shake her head and smile.

"And what is so bad about work?" she would say. "Work is how I take care of my family. Work is how I keep busy. Work is how I am useful. It is not so bad."

At school we learned to speak English and heard all about George Washington crossing the Delaware and Thomas Jefferson writing the Declaration of Independence. We wrote essays on the American Revolution and the American Civil War, and one day it dawned on me that Americans had suffered in terrible wars just as we had. And not long after that, I realized that Americans weren't "they" anymore. After all, we wore American clothes, read American books, knew American songs, and ate American candy. We had all become *real* Americans—all of us, that is, but Mamá.

She never quite knew what she was. Part of her was still back in Mexico and part of her was with us in California. Sometimes in the evening, after the dishes were done, we all went out on the porch to sit and enjoy the cool night air. At those times, Mother liked to talk about the old days. She told us about growing up in her father's great house in the beautiful mountains of Mexico. She talked of her gentle sisters who sang so beautifully to the guitar. She remembered her own little house full of flowers and birds. But she especially loved to talk about Father—how they fell in love first and got to know each other later, how he was such an artist, making beautiful sombreros, and how he knew things it was impossible to know, yet he knew them just the same. I had been so small when Father died, I could scarcely remember him. Those stories gave him back to me.

In all those years she talked only of happy times. It was much later that we learned what had happened in our little village. Only when we were grown—strong and full of hope—did we find out that it was gone, burned to the ground by the soldiers. And when we heard about the people who had died, people we had known, then we understood what our mother had done. With her courage and daring, she had saved us all.

Think and Respond

1 How does the mother in this story show courage and **determination**?

2 How does the narrator of this selection feel about her mother? How can you tell?

3 What does the narrator's mother mean when she says, "The world is changing around us. We must change, too"?

4 Do you think the mother was right not to tell her children what happened to their village? Why or why not?

5 What reading strategies did you use to help you understand "Elena"? When did you use them?

Diane Stanley

Diane Stanley developed her talent for drawing during her senior year at Trinity University in San Antonio, Texas. She earned a degree in medical illustration, and worked as a medical illustrator while raising her children.

"When I became a mother and started visiting the library to check out books for my children," Stanley says, "I realized that what I really wanted to do was make books for children. It was the perfect combination of my love of words, art, and book design." Since 1977 Diane Stanley has published many books, including a series of ten picture-book biographies. Her books have been recognized with many national awards, including The Orbis Pictus Award for Outstanding Nonfiction for Children and the ALA Notable Book award.

Diane Stanley says, "Today, my life is all about the books: writing them, illustrating them, reading them, and sharing them with children."

Michael Steirnagle

Michael Steirnagle was born in El Paso, Texas. He studied art at the University of Texas and at the Art Center College of Design in Pasadena, California. As an artist, Michael Steirnagle is fascinated by light and the way it "plays" across a moving figure. He tries to use light to add more meaning to his subjects. When he illustrates historical fiction like "Elena," Steirnagle carefully researches the time and the place of the story's setting. The facts he gathers help him choose how to portray the characters and what details to paint in the backgrounds. Talking about his paintings, he says, "I like to tell stories. I like to let viewers participate in my paintings by drawing their own conclusions about what is taking place." Michael Steirnagle has illustrated the books *Billy Lazroe and the King of the Sea: A Northwest Legend* by Eric A. Kimmel and *All by Herself: Fourteen Girls Who Made a Difference* by Ann Whitford Paul.

Visit *The Learning Site!*
www.harcourtschool.com

131

Making Connections

Compare Texts

1 What does the narrator of "Elena" discover about herself?

2 How does the narrator's description of her mother change between the time after her father's death and the day Pancho Villa comes to their house?

3 Name another historical fiction selection that you have read besides "Elena." Which story did you like better, and why?

4 Think of a courageous person in history that you have read about in a textbook or nonfiction selection. How is reading about a historical figure different from reading about a fictional character like the mother in "Elena"?

5 After reading this story, what questions do you have about Pancho Villa and the Mexican War for Independence?

Write a Diary Entry

"**E**lena" is told from the daughter's point of view. Imagine that you are another character in the story. Write a diary entry about an event in the story from this character's point of view. Use a graphic organizer like this one to plan your diary entry.

Writing CONNECTION

Character	
Event or events to tell about	
Details to include from this character's point of view	

Make a Graph

Over the years, immigrants from many different lands have come to the United States. Use an encyclopedia or other reference source to find the total immigration from 1880 to the present. Choose three countries and note the approximate percent of immigrants from each of them. Make a circle graph to show this information. Use the category *other* for all the rest of the immigrants.

**Social Studies/Math
CONNECTION**

Create a Fact Sheet

The hat that Pancho Villa buys from the mother in "Elena" is trimmed with silver. Find silver on the periodic table of the elements. Then make a fact sheet that gives the atomic symbol, atomic number, atomic weight, hardness, melting point, boiling point, and other scientific information about silver and its properties.

**Science
CONNECTION**

133

Narrative Elements  Focus Skill

Every story has a setting, characters, a plot, and a theme. The author develops the plot by telling what the characters say and do during a series of events. The events might take place in more than one setting. The theme is the meaning of a story. To identify the theme, ask yourself what message the author is hoping to send to readers.

Look at the diagram below. The characters and the changing settings will help you understand the theme, or message, of "Elena."

Characters	Setting
Elena Mother Father Pancho Villa	**When does the story take place?** 1910, the start of the Mexican Revolution **Where does it take place?** (1) Mexico (2) California

Theme
What is the message of the story? People find the courage—in the face of danger—to save the lives of those they love.

Think about how Elena's story might have been different if she had lived in a different time or had settled in a state other than California. How would a change in setting affect the theme?

Test Prep

Narrative Elements

▶ **Read the passage. Then answer the questions.**

> It was one of those sticky, sweltering southern days in the summer of 1877. I was thirteen years old, and Mama and I had gone into town to pick up groceries. That's where Mama first saw the poster, nailed to the front of the general store. Unlike some formerly enslaved people, Mama could read.
>
> Mama's face lit up as she read the poster out loud. Her voice was strong. "Eva," she said, "we are going west to Kansas. This poster says I can claim my own stretch of land to farm. Imagine that!" She was quiet for a moment. Then she said, "The journey will be difficult. The winters can be cold and long. The hot summer wind blows something fierce. The work will be hard, but I'm strong, and the reward is a new life. Imagine that!"

1. This story is set —

   A in Kansas on a farm

   B in the South during the time of slavery

   C in the South after the end of slavery

   D on the trail west

Tip

Look for dates, place names, and other clues about when and where the story takes place.

2. What is the theme of this passage? How do the setting and the characters' words and actions help you identify the theme? Support your answer with references from the story.

Tip

Pay attention to what the narrator reveals about her mother. Think about what Mama says and how she says it.

135

Team
Work

CONTENTS

▲ We'll Never
Forget You,
Roberto Clemente

error

lineup

dedicated

artificial

ace

control tower

Vocabulary Power

The next selection tells about a very special baseball player named Roberto Clemente. He is remembered not only for his baseball skills but also for helping and caring about others. Read on to learn about some other people worth remembering.

This statue honors Mr. Calvin Woods, a Little League coach for over thirty years. Former players of all ages remember Mr. Woods as a man who taught them about baseball and about life. He never took a player out of the game for making an **error**, such as a wild throw. Instead, he would keep players in the **lineup** and encourage them to do their best so they could improve their skills.

The Nature Society planted this tree to honor Mrs. Phyllis Redmond. She has **dedicated** her time to saving trees, setting aside countless hours for that purpose. Members of the Nature Society agreed that a living tree was a more appropriate symbol than something **artificial**, or made by humans.

Paul Markham was a pilot who flew in World War II. He was considered an **ace**, or expert, at flying fighter planes. The people of his home town put up this statue at the airport to remember his skill and bravery. The statue is located near the **control tower**, the building from which takeoffs and landings are directed.

Vocabulary–Writing CONNECTION

Think of someone you know about who has **dedicated** time to helping others. Write a few sentences about this person and what he or she does to help people.

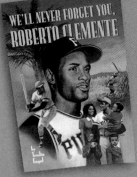

Genre

Biography

A biography is the story of a person's life written by another person.

In this selection, look for

● **Information about why the person is important**

● **Information showing how the person made a difference**

Roberto Clemente loved baseball. When his parents couldn't afford to buy him a ball and a bat, Roberto used a skinny broomstick to hit empty tomato cans. He could not be struck out.

Roberto was born in 1934 on the tropical island of Puerto Rico. He first played for a youth league team. Then he moved up to the Puerto Rican Winter League. Because of his exceptional talent, Roberto was chosen to play for a minor league team in Montreal, Canada. He was soon recruited by a major league team, the Pittsburgh Pirates.

Roberto was a spectacular success. He shared that success with his family, friends, and the community. His generosity became as well-known as his sports ability.

WE'LL NEVER FORGET YOU,
ROBERTO CLEMENTE

by Trudie Engel
illustrated by Gil Adams

By 1972, only ten players in the history of baseball had gotten 3,000 hits.

Roberto badly wanted to be number 11. When the season began, he needed only 118 hits to reach the magic number. Roberto had gotten more than 118 hits every year he had played in the major leagues.

He won't have any trouble, said his family and friends. He'll make it.

With 3,000 hits, Roberto was sure to be the first Latin American ballplayer to be voted into baseball's Hall of Fame.

But during much of the season, Roberto was either hurt or sick. He had the flu, a stomach virus, trouble with his heels. He lost ten pounds and had to wear a uniform that belonged to a thinner teammate.

By the middle of August, Roberto had missed almost half of the Pirates' games. People stopped talking about 3,000 hits. There just weren't enough games left in the season, they thought. And nobody knew if he would be well enough to play again the next year.

With only 26 games left, Roberto still needed 25 hits to get to 3,000.

And then in September, he started to hit. Was there a chance he might get his 3,000th hit after all?

On September 28 in Philadelphia, Roberto faced Steve Carlton, the great Phillies pitcher. He hit a single to right field. It was hit number 2,999.

Right away, Roberto was taken out of the lineup. Everyone wanted him to get the 3,000th hit in Pittsburgh in front of the hometown fans.

The next night in Pittsburgh it was cold and rainy. Even so, 24,000 fans turned out to cheer Roberto on.

The Pirates were playing the New York Mets. Tom Seaver was pitching. If Seaver could win this game, it would be another twenty-game season for the Mets' ace pitcher.

The crowd cheered loudly as Roberto walked up to the plate in the first inning.

One of Seaver's fastballs whizzed over the plate. Roberto swung hard but did not get much wood on the ball. It bounced over Seaver's glove. The second baseman ran in to grab it. The ball bounced off his glove. Roberto pulled up at first base.

Was the play a hit or an error? If the scorekeeper said it was an error, Roberto would not get his 3,000th hit.

It was so noisy in the stadium that only a few people heard the words, "Error, second baseman," over the loudspeaker.

All eyes turned toward the scoreboard. For what seemed like a long time, there was nothing. Then the big H for hit went up.

The crowd cheered and clapped. The people were sure that Roberto had gotten hit number 3,000.

Suddenly, everyone became quiet. The H disappeared. An E for error went up on the scoreboard.

The scoreboard crew had not heard the call. They made a big mistake when they put up the H.

Boos sounded in the stadium. The Pirate fans felt cheated. So did Roberto. He was up three more times that night but could not get another hit.

"I'll be out there swinging again tomorrow," Roberto said after the game.

The next day, Jon Matlack pitched for the Mets. That was bad news for Roberto. He had not hit one of Matlack's pitches all season.

In the first inning, Roberto struck out.

He came up to bat again in the fourth inning.

All-Star first baseman Willie Stargell was Roberto's best friend on the team.

He handed Roberto a bat.

"Go get it!" Stargell said.

And Roberto did! He sent a hard line drive bouncing off the left-field wall for a double. The cheering that filled the stadium lasted for a full minute. On second base, Roberto tipped his helmet to the fans.

Willie Mays left the Mets' dugout and came over to shake Roberto's hand.

On that day, September 30, 1972, there were just three men playing baseball who had 3,000 hits. They were Willie Mays, Hank Aaron, and now, Roberto Clemente.

Roberto is now one of 11 players in major league history to get 3000 or more hits

On December 23, 1972, the earth shook in Nicaragua.

Nicaragua is a small, poor country in Central America, not far from the island of Puerto Rico. Two days before Christmas in 1972, a terrible thing happened there.

NICARAGUA

A giant earthquake hit the biggest city in Nicaragua.
Over 6,000 people were killed. Another 20,000 were hurt. Thousands more were left homeless. People needed food, water, and medicines.

Roberto had been in Nicaragua a month before the earthquake.

While he was there, Roberto heard about a fourteen-year-old boy who had a terrible thing happen to him. He had lost both his legs in an accident. The boy's parents had died. He needed artificial legs but had no money to pay for them.

A team in the Puerto Rican Winter League had raised part of the money the boy needed. Roberto himself gave the rest. He went to see the boy and told him he would be able to walk again. Roberto then returned to Pittsburgh.

When the earthquake hit Nicaragua, Roberto thought of his young friend. Had he lived through it? Was he all right? He had to find out.

Roberto also thought about the thousands of other people who had lost their homes and everything in them.

Caring about others who had less than he did was nothing new for Roberto. He had followed his father's teachings. He helped out other members of his family when they were in need. After his brother had died, he supported his nieces and nephews.

Roberto was kind to many people. One day during a game, the Pirates' announcer brought a deaf boy to meet Roberto. Roberto talked to the boy, using his hands and smiling. Later, Roberto took one of his bats into the stands where the deaf boy was sitting. He gave him the bat.

On the side of the bat he wrote, "You don't have to be able to hear to play baseball and enjoy the game. Best wishes, Roberto Clemente."

So no one was surprised when Roberto started helping people in Nicaragua after the earthquake.

He went from door to door in his neighborhood in San Juan asking for money. He spoke on radio and television asking the people of Puerto Rico to give money, food, clothes, and medicines.

He helped collect the supplies that came in. And he found ships and a plane to take the food and clothing to Nicaragua.

All during the Christmas holidays in 1972, Roberto helped pack the supplies into boxes.

Two planeloads of goods had already been flown to Nicaragua. Another would go on New Year's Eve, the last day of the year 1972.

New Year's Eve is an important holiday in Puerto Rico. People come together from all over the island for family celebrations.

But Roberto decided to leave his family and fly to Nicaragua.

"I must see that the people who need the supplies really get them," he said.

And what had happened to his young friend who had lost his legs? This was his chance to find out.

The plane going to Nicaragua was a twenty-year-old propeller plane. Three weeks before, it had been in an accident. The brakes had not worked and the plane crashed into a wall. The propeller tips were badly bent.

Now, the brakes were fixed and the plane had new propellers. The plane was said to be ready to fly again.

It was supposed to take off at 4:00 P.M. in the afternoon.

149

But at 9:00 A.M. in the morning, the owner of the plane was still trying to find a crew to fly it to Nicaragua.

At last a pilot was found. There was a flight engineer, but he did not know much about that kind of plane.

They could not get a copilot. The owner of the plane no longer had a license to fly, but he decided to be the copilot anyway.

At 3:30 Vera, his wife, took Roberto to the airport.

The plane was not ready.

Teenage helpers were loading the plane. It was already full, but they kept putting more and more boxes in. Everyone wanted to get the last of the supplies to Nicaragua.

"Is it safe?" Vera asked.

"Look, the plane is fine," the owner said. "It will be ready soon. If it were in bad shape I wouldn't go myself." And he climbed into the cockpit.

At 5:00 P.M. Roberto got onboard. Vera waved good-bye.

It wasn't until after 9:00 P.M. that the plane rolled down the runway toward the ocean for takeoff. The San Juan Airport is just a mile from the beach.

The plane was only in the air for a few seconds before there was a loud bang. Flames shot out from one of the engines.

The people in the control tower heard the pilot say, "I'm coming back around."

Then there were two more explosions. The plane went off the radar screen in the control tower.

A man who lived in a house near the ocean heard a plane roaring overhead. He looked out the window and saw it flying so low, it almost hit the palm trees by the shore. Then he saw the plane fall into the ocean.

The man left the window to tell his son to call the police. When he came back, the plane had completely disappeared, sinking into the ocean.

It was after midnight when the phone rang at the Clementes' with the news about the plane crash. Vera rushed to the beach.

Bright orange flares lit up the night sky. Police cars parked on the beach and shone their headlights into the ocean. Coast Guard ships were in the water. Search crews looked for bodies and parts of the plane.

Nothing was found.

The next day the search went on. In the morning, the beach was full of people. Some were standing in the water. Some were holding small radios to their ears.

The search went on for weeks. Crowds were there every day. Every afternoon, Vera Clemente came and stood in the sand and watched.

Then one day she stopped coming.

The Coast Guard picked up parts of the plane. Later, Roberto's briefcase washed up on shore.

But Roberto's body was never found.

It was hard to believe Roberto was gone. "I expected him to swim to shore someplace," one of his Pirate teammates said.

Q: How did the plane just blow up out of the blue?

ere is a billboard that
everyo lit up brightly at
night.

Aft _amigo._" Good-bye,
friend.

Ma erto. That he was the
best b est hero Puerto Rico
ever h

Ro player voted into the
Baseb

But there was something else about Roberto that was even more
important. "He was a good man," said Willie Stargell.

On opening day of 1973, the Pirates scoreboard read, "Thank
you, Roberto. We will never forget THE GREAT ONE."

The city of Pittsburgh and the Pittsburgh Pirates kept their
promise. They did not forget Roberto.

In July 1994, more than twenty years after the plane crash in
which he lost his life, a statue of Roberto Clemente was dedicated at
the Pirates' stadium in Pittsburgh.

The statue was paid for by the people of Pittsburgh and shows
Roberto dropping his bat after hitting the ball. It must
have been a good hit. He is just starting to
run, as his eyes are fixed on the
ball, far in the distance.

The statue tells us
that Roberto lives on in
our hearts and minds.
But he lives on in

ADIÓS,
AMIGO

more than our memories. Roberto lives, too, in all the children that he helped.

Before he died, Roberto had plans to build a "sports city" in Puerto Rico where the poor children of the island would have a chance to learn to play different kinds of sports.

After Roberto died, Sports City was built by his family. Over the years, thousands of children have gone there.

One baseball player who got his start at Sports City is Ruben Sierra, an outfielder for the Oakland Athletics. Sierra not only made it to the major leagues, but he also played in the 1994 All-Star game.

Sierra was a poor boy from a poor village in Puerto Rico. He says he would still be there today if it hadn't been for Roberto's Sports City.

When Sierra came up to bat during the All-Star game, millions of people were watching. They saw that he wore the number 21 on his uniform.

That was Roberto's number.

Sierra says, "He was the greatest. That's why I wear his number, in honor of him."

Think and Respond

1 Why was a statue **dedicated** to Roberto Clemente?

2 Why do four sentences, including the first sentence in the selection, begin with large, fancy letters?

3 Why do you think the author used so much detail to tell about the game in which Roberto did not get a hit?

4 What do you admire most about Roberto Clemente? Explain your answer.

5 What reading strategies helped you to better understand this biography about Roberto Clemente?

 Visit *The Learning Site!* www.harcourtschool.com

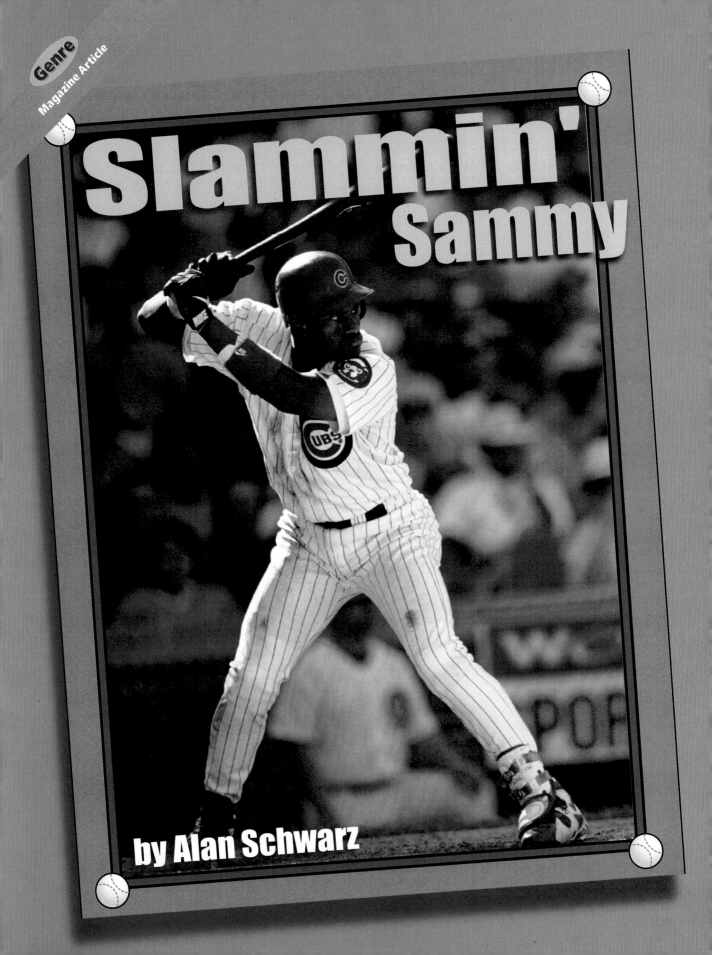

Slammin' Sammy

by Alan Schwarz

SAMMY SOSA OF THE CHICAGO Cubs is baseball's sunshine superman. He slams home runs with awesome power. His smile is as bright as the sun.

"Sammy isn't just a great hitter," says Mark Grace, the Cub first baseman. "He always plays with a smile. He's fun to be around."

FAN FAVORITE

Sammy often takes a playful hop as he starts his home-run trot. He blows kisses to the fans at Wrigley Field. The fans chant *Sam-my! Sam-my!* when he's at bat and when he runs out to rightfield at the start of the game.

"I enjoy everything that I do," says Sammy. "I'm happy."

THE HOME-RUN RACE

The Great Home-Run Race of 1998 was one of baseball's most exciting events. Sammy and Mark McGwire of the St. Louis Cardinals pounded away at Roger Maris's record of 61 homers all season long.

The pressure from fans and the media was intense. Mark got cranky at times, but Sammy kept smiling.

"I never feel pressure," says Sammy. "Pressure was when I was a kid and didn't have any food on the table."

Sammy made the race fun. He also shifted all the attention to Mark—with a big grin!

"Mark is going to break the record," he constantly told reporters. "He's the man."

Mark hit his record-breaking 62nd homer on September 8, against the Cubs. Sammy ran in from rightfield and hugged Mark.

Mark finished the season with a record 70 homers. Sammy hit the second-highest number of homers in baseball history, 66.

Sammy tosses his fans a souvenir ball in Wrigley Field.

In many ways, Sammy had a more impressive season than Mark did. Sammy hit .308 and led the majors with 158 RBIs. The Cubs made the playoffs for the first time since 1989. Sammy was named the National League MVP.*

POOR BOY

Sammy grew up in San Pedro de Macoris, Dominican Republic. His family was poor. His dad died when Sammy was 7. Sammy, his mom, and his four brothers and two sisters lived in a two-room apartment. He shined shoes, washed cars, and sold oranges to earn money for his family.

Sammy couldn't afford real baseball equipment as a kid. He used a milk carton for a glove and balled-up socks for a baseball. He didn't play organized baseball until he was 14 years old.

---

* Most Valuable Player

Two years later, Sammy borrowed a uniform and a pair of old spikes to try out for a scout from the Texas Rangers. The scout liked the 16-year-old's power. He gave Sammy a $3,500 bonus to sign a pro contract. It was more money than Sammy's family had ever seen!

Sammy gave the money to his mom. Well, not *all* the money. He used some to buy his first bicycle!

TO MAMA WITH LOVE

Sammy's skills were raw when he began his pro career in 1986. He was traded twice before he blossomed into a star with the Cubs in 1993. He hit 33 homers and drove in 93 runs that season.

Each time Sammy hits a homer, he sends a special message to his mom.

SAMMY SOSA
YOU
DA
MAN!

Babe

Sammy and Mark McGwire (left) during the 1998 season.

She watches the Cubs on TV in the Dominican Republic. Sammy kisses two fingers, touches his heart, and blows a kiss.

"It's my way of saying I love her," says Sammy. "My life is pretty much a miracle." No *wonder* he's so happy!

•••► **The number 21** is special to Sammy. It's his jersey number. He wears it in honor of Hall of Fame outfielder Roberto Clemente, who also wore number 21. Roberto died in a 1972 plane crash while delivering supplies to earthquake victims in Nicaragua.

•••► **Baseball gave** Sammy its 1998 Roberto Clemente Man of the Year Award for his charity work. Sammy raised money to help victims of Hurricane Georges in the Dominican Republic. He also delivered food to them.

•••► **Sammy smacked** a 500-foot home run that landed in the middle of a party on the roof of a building across the street from Wrigley Field!

•••► **The "30-30 Club"** is for players who hit 30 or more homers and steal 30 or more bases in one season. Sammy was the first player from the Dominican Republic to join the club. He had 33 homers and 36 steals in 1993, and 36 homers and 34 steals in 1995.

THINK AND RESPOND

What were the highlights of Sammy Sosa's 1998 baseball season?

Making Connections

Compare Texts

1 Do you think Roberto Clemente achieved all he did on his own, or did he need the help of others? Explain.

2 How does the tone of the writing vary in the different sections of the selection?

3 After reading "Slammin' Sammy," what similarities do you see between Roberto Clemente and Sammy Sosa?

4 Think of another biography you have read. How do the author of that biography and the author of this selection show their feelings about their subjects?

5 Where would you find information about sports records?

Write a Statement of Opinion

Many people believe that team sports help young people learn to get along and work together. Do you agree? Write a statement of your opinion, and explain why you think as you do. Give examples to support your opinion. Use a graphic organizer to plan your statement.

Writing CONNECTION

My Opinion

My Reasons

Examples

Make a Map

The map on pages 146 and 147 shows two geographic locations. Make a map that shows all of the places referred to in this selection. Begin by listing the names of all the cities, states, islands, and countries that the author mentions. Draw your map carefully. Use stick-on labels or add a map key to explain what each place has to do with Roberto Clemente.

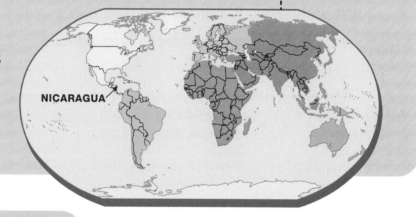

NICARAGUA

Create a Game

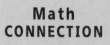

With 26 games left in the season, Roberto Clemente still needed 25 hits to reach 3,000 in his career. A player is usually up at bat at least three times per game, so Clemente had about 78 more chances to get those hits. Look in the sports section of a newspaper or in a world almanac for other baseball facts. Make up math problems, and create a board game or card game that is played by solving the problems.

The Pirates played 5 games and lost 2. The Mets played 12 games and lost 4. Which team has the better record?

Draw Conclusions (Focus Skill)

Authors don't always tell you everything about the characters, situations, or events in a story. They expect you to use what you know and your own personal experiences to **draw conclusions** as you read. Think about your experiences and what you know about a topic, a situation, or a similar text. Use that knowledge and the information the author provides to draw conclusions that will help you understand the story.

What you know	+	Information from the story	=	Conclusion
I know that planes are designed to carry up to a certain weight.	+	Teenage helpers kept putting more and more boxes on the plane.	=	The weight of the extra boxes made the plane too heavy to fly.
I know that airplanes require an experienced crew.	+	The copilot of the plane did not have a license to fly, and the flight engineer didn't know much about the plane.	=	The plane Roberto Clemente flew on had an inexperienced crew.

A **generalization** is an expanded conclusion. To make a generalization ask yourself how you might apply an idea beyond the text.

160

Test Prep
Draw Conclusions

▶ **Read the paragraph. Then answer the questions.**

> In 1943 America was involved in World War II, and a large number of professional baseball players were in the military. President Roosevelt was on the verge of suspending major-league baseball for that year when a group of businesspeople, headed by P. K. Wrigley, the owner of the Chicago Cubs, offered a solution. The businesspeople created the first professional baseball league for women. The goal was to keep baseball alive and Americans entertained until the war was over.

1. **Which is the best conclusion for the information in the paragraph?**

   A Minor-league baseball became popular during the war.

   B Americans opposed the women's baseball league.

   C The women's baseball league helped keep baseball alive during World War II.

   D Women refused to play on teams with ten players.

Tip

To draw a conclusion, combine what you know with facts and details from the passage.

2. **How can you expand on the conclusion you chose for Question 1? What generalization can you make based on that conclusion?**

Tip

To make a generalization, figure out how a conclusion might apply in a broader sense.

161

Vocabulary Power

▲ Folk Tales
from Asia

plodded

entrusted

assured

bountiful

diligence

destiny

Folk Tales were passed down orally from person to person over a long period of time before they were ever written down. Families also may pass stories down over the generations to keep important memories and information alive.

How I wanted to linger, or stay on, this morning to listen to more of Uncle William's stories! Mama said we had to go to school, though, so I **plodded** along, walking with heavy steps. I was too deep in thought to run and jump as I usually do.

Uncle William told us that our great-grandfather **entrusted** him with, or put in his care, the job of telling our family stories. "He gave me a big task," Uncle William said, "but I **assured** him that I would carry it out, and I've tried to keep that promise."

I love these wonderful stories of the old folks and the old days. I laughed hard at the one about the big bee that hovered over our great-aunt Ruthie as she weeded the vegetable patch. That bee just stayed right there in one place, buzzing and buzzing. Finally Ruthie got so angry that she stood up and yelled. She said that if the bee left her alone, she would name her next child Bee. That's how Grandmother's cousin Bee got her name!

I felt sad when I heard how my relatives long ago lost a **bountiful**, or very large, crop of corn. It was all destroyed in a terrible windstorm. I feel proud, though, when I listen to the stories that tell of their **diligence**, their willingness to work steadily and carefully toward their goals.

I wonder whether someday it will be my **destiny**, or fate, to pass along the stories as Uncle William does. Maybe I'll be the one to write them down so they can never be forgotten!

Vocabulary–Writing CONNECTION

Imagine a task with which you may be **entrusted**. Write a brief description of the task and tell how you would carry it out.

Folk Tales

**A folk tale is a story
written to entertain.**

In this selection, look for

- Stories that have a quick
resolution

- Information about different cultures

Folk

Tales from Asia

illustrated by Suling Wang

Why do people all around the world, in every culture, tell folk tales? It could be because folk tales describe what all people have in common:

- We all live under the same sun and moon.
- We all wonder how to lead a good life.
- We all, sometimes, have to put up with other people's faults.

The following three folk tales come to the United States from three Asian countries—Vietnam, Thailand, and China—but their messages are universal.

How the Moon Became Ivory

from *Sky Legends of Vietnam*

by Lynette Dyer Vuong

Long ago, when the world was young, Jade Emperor entrusted to his eldest and brightest daughter the task of overseeing the earth.

"Each day," he told the sun, "you will ride your golden palanquin across the sky. You will watch over humankind. You will turn your face toward them to give them light and warmth so that they can till their fields and grow their crops."

Two groups of four bearers each took turns carrying the sun's palanquin. The winter bearers, black-haired young men, strong and muscular, sprinted through the sky, quickly reaching the western horizon to finish their journey. The summer bearers, gray-bearded and tired, left the eastern portals early and plodded their way across the heavens, arriving late in the west.

The long days gave the people time to care for their crops and assured them a bountiful harvest. But the nights were dark, and no light brightened the travelers' way. So Jade Emperor called his second daughter, the moon, and gave her the task of watching over the earth at night.

The moon rushed back to her palace. She scrubbed and polished her face till it shone as brightly as her sister's. She opened her jewel chests and chose the brightest gems to wear.

She trimmed every lamp in her palace until all the windows blazed with light.

Down on earth, the farmers trudged toward their huts, their hoes slung over their shoulders. They gazed up at the sky in wonder. Only moments ago the sun had brushed the western horizon, and now again light beamed around them. They turned around and hurried back to their fields.

At last, exhausted, the people laid their hoes aside. They could work no longer. They plodded home and sank onto their sleeping mats. All night they tossed and turned on their pillows, trying to escape the moonlight that shone in through the windows. Finally they gave up; they lay and fanned themselves, longing for the cool breezes that used to refresh them at night.

Day by day the people grew more weary. No longer did they greet the dawn with shouts of joy. Each morning they dragged themselves to their fields later than the day before. Even the rooster forgot to crow, and the birds neglected to sing. Bewildered, the sun looked down on the sad scene as she rode through the sky, wondering what had happened. But she found no clues.

When she finished her journey, she hovered just above the horizon and peeked over the clouds. She would stay and keep watch until she found out what was the matter.

All at once the sky grew bright again. The moon stepped out of her palace and turned her face toward the earth. Behind her, every window gleamed.

The sun sank behind the clouds and hurried off to tell her parents.

"Humans are not like us," she said. "They need a time to rest." She glared at her younger sister. "How could you be so proud and selfish?"

The moon hung her head in shame. "But what am I to do? My face is as bright as yours."

"Then you must cover your face!"

"Calm yourselves, daughters." Tay Vuong Mau, Queen Mother of the West, rose from the throne beside her husband. "I will take care of it."

She returned a few minutes later with a pot of ashes.

"Come here, daughter," she called to the moon. She reached into the pot and scooped out a handful of ashes, which she smeared over the moon's face. "Now your face will shine with a soft, ivory light. The people will love you, even more than they love your sister. Take these ashes home with you and spread them over your windows as well."

Jade Emperor smiled in approval. "Your sister, the sun, shows the seasons. Now you will show the time of the month so that people will know when to plant their crops. I am sending the heavenly bear to be your watchman. It will take him twenty-eight earth-days to patrol your palace. On the fourteenth day of each month, when he passes the back of your palace, humans will see the full moon. When he goes to the right or to the left, your face will become a crescent. And on the last day of each month, when he walks in front of your palace, he will hide your face from the earth. Watch him so that he does not retrace his steps, or linger in front of the palace, and cause an eclipse."

As the moon bowed to her father, she glimpsed her face in the gold of his throne. She wiped away a tear as she turned to leave the room. Never again would she show her face to humans.

She stepped out into the night. She would take one last look at the world and then rush home and hide in her palace forever.

Suddenly shouts filled the air. The people were singing and cheering, their faces turned toward the sky.

They were cheering her! Queen Mother of the West had been right. The people did love her new face.

The moon's ivory light softened to a satin glow. But the fire in her heart burned even brighter as she hurried home to smear the ashes on her windows.

WHO ~Is~ Best?

from *Thai Tales: Folktales of Thailand*

retold by Supaporn Vathanaprida

A long time ago, there were three men who were close friends. The first was named Boon (Merit), the second was named Man (Diligence) and the third was named Panya (Wisdom). Once, during a time of famine, the three men decided to leave for another town to look for jobs. At last, they found a rich farmer who would hire them to clear land for more rice fields. The rich farmer had only one condition. They must finish the task in seven days.

Every morning, a servant brought the three men food for the day. Every evening, the rich farmer came to see how much they had accomplished. The rich farmer was pleased to see that the three men worked very hard. They would be able to accomplish this task within the seven days.

On the last day, the three finished their work early, but nobody brought them their food. They waited and waited, still the servant did not come. While they waited they began to boast among themselves about their names. "My name is the best," said Mr. Boon. "If you lack *boon* (merit) you will not become rich and prosperous even if you are diligent and clever."

Mr. Man interrupted, "No, *my* name is best. Even if you have *boon*, if you do not have *man* (diligence) you will starve to death."

But Mr. Panya disagreed. "No. Even if you have *boon* and *man* you cannot prosper unless you have *panya* (wisdom)."

Suddenly, the three were attacked by hunger. Panya got up and walked around looking for something to eat. He soon noticed a trail of ants. Each ant was carrying a single grain of rice. Right away, he realized that the rich man had sent the food, but that the servant had been instructed to hide it from them. He told his friend Man, "The servant did bring the food. It is hidden. Look for it."

Mr. Man got up and looked around. He searched diligently until he discovered the packet of food, wrapped in its banana leaf covering, hidden in the forest. He brought back the food and shared it with his friend Panya, saying, "If Boon is truly blessed by his previous good deeds and merits, he will have somebody bring him food. He will not need this."

After Panya and Man were full, there was still a bit of food left. So Panya and Man tossed it to Boon.

Boon accepted the food gratefully and ate hungrily. But as he finished the food, Boon discovered several pieces of gold in the bottom of the packet! The rich farmer had hidden their promised reward under the food.

Boon was delighted. He showed the money to his friends, who promptly asked for their shares.

Panya said, "If it had not been for my wisdom, we would not have known the food was hidden."

Man said, "If it had not been for my diligence, we would not have found the hidden food."

Boon said, "You two still lack *boon*. Good deeds bring good in return. As you lack merit, you threw your gold away with the food scraps. You cannot say that this gold belongs to you. What is thrown away is no longer yours."

While the three quarreled, the rich farmer arrived. The three asked the rich farmer to be the judge. After hearing their story, the rich man took the six gold pieces and divided them equally among the three. He explained, "Each of you is equally important. No one alone is sufficient. All three are needed. In order to succeed and prosper, a man must have all three of your qualities: merit, diligence, and wisdom."

Virtue Goes to Town

a Chinese folk tale from *The Rainbow People*

by Laurence Yep

After Virtue had buried his parents, he went to see the wise woman. "They say you can read a face like a page in a book. Tell me what my destiny is."

But the wise woman just kept sipping her tea. "What would you have? A quiet, happy life as a farmer? Or a life of sorrow and glory?"

"I hate being bored," Virtue said.

The wise woman studied his face a long time. She patted his shoulder sadly. "Then go into town."

When Virtue arrived there, he saw a long line of men. "I heard that town folk did the oddest things. Are you all practicing to be a fence?" he asked.

A townsman leaning against a wall looked at Virtue and then looked away again. But Virtue's voice was loud, and he was such a pest that the townsman finally said, "They're hiring workers, Turnip."

"The name's Virtue. And they can sign me up too. I left the farm to see the world and get rich." He got in line behind the townsman.

However, it was a hot, summer day and Virtue quickly became impatient. As he wiped at the sweat on his forehead, he shouted, "Hey, can't you go any faster?"

The foreman sat at his table in the shade. He ignored Virtue and went on just as slowly as ever.

"Hey, we're not getting any younger," Virtue yelled.

Still the foreman ignored him.

"Maybe he's deaf." Virtue started forward.

The townsman stuck out his arm. "Hey, Turnip, wait your turn."

"I told you. My name's Virtue. So why don't I just take you right with me, friend?" Virtue tucked his arm into the townsman's. The others were too afraid to say anything else, but everyone watched as he stomped up to the foreman.

"I can outplow a water buffalo and can harvest more than twenty folk," Virtue said.

The foreman took an instant dislike to Virtue. "You may be strong; but you're not that strong. No one likes a braggart."

"It's not bragging if you really can do it," Virtue said.

The foreman grunted. "I'm the boss here. I say how we do things. Get back there."

"Come on, friend." With a sigh, Virtue carried the townsman back to the end of the line.

It took most of the day before Virtue finally reached the table. Virtue made a muscle for the foreman. "No job's too hard for me."

The foreman put down his brush and folded his hands over his big belly. "I have all of my work crew already. All I need is a cook. Can you do that?"

Virtue frowned. He thought a cook's job was beneath him, but times were hard and jobs were scarce. "Can I cook?" Virtue said. "I could cook a whale and fricassee a dragon."

The foreman twiddled his thumbs. He would have liked to turn Virtue away, but he needed a cook. "You only have to cook rice, dried fish and vegetables. I guess even you couldn't ruin that."

"Whatever I do, I always do well," Virtue promised. "I would make a better worker. But if you want me as a cook, then I'll be the best cook I can be."

The workers had to get up at sunrise, but Virtue had to get up even earlier to boil the water for their tea. Even so, he always had the tea poured and the cold rice served in bowls before the first man was up. He tried to have a friendly, cheerful word for each of the other workers. "Smile, friend," he would say to one. "We're keeping farm hours now—not town hours."

And to another, he would say, "We're all in this together, neighbor."

And to a third, he would grin. "Teamwork. That's how we do it on the farm."

But all the other men were from town. They never thanked him. In fact, they never spoke to him. Behind his

back, they laughed and called him the loud-mouthed turnip.

Still, Virtue did not give up easily. "These townsfolk will come around once they get to know me."

At noon, he served them supper. Then, picking up a huge cauldron in each hand, he went down to the river. Each of the cauldrons could have held a half dozen men, but Virtue dipped them into the water and lifted them out as easily as if they were cups.

After making several trips, he would set the cauldrons of water on big fires. By sunset, they would be bubbling. When the work crew came back, they would wash before they sat down to eat their dinner.

But one noon, the other workers were delayed. Virtue got hungrier and hungrier as he smelled the food. Finally, he ate his bowlful of rice. Still, there was no sign of anyone. Virtue was so bored that the only thing he could think of doing was to eat another bowlful of rice and wait.

When no one had shown up yet, he began to feel sorry for himself. "I do my job, but no one appreciates me. So maybe I'll just have another bowlful. That'll show them."

When he had finished his third bowl, he looked at the cauldron simmering on the big fire. "This rice is going to get burned. I shouldn't let it go to waste." Bored and lonely, Virtue began to eat right from the cauldron. Before he knew it, he had finished the whole cauldron of rice.

Tired and dirty, the work crew finally came back to camp. They were angry when they found the empty cauldron. "Where's our food, Turnip?" they demanded angrily. But no one went too close to Virtue.

Virtue gave an embarrassed cough. "My name's Virtue."

They glared at him. "You're nothing but a big sack of wind. How do you expect us to work on empty bellies?"

Virtue brightened. "Since I ate all your lunch, let me do all your work. It's only fair."

The foreman got ready to fire Virtue. "One person couldn't meet our goals by himself."

"We take turns back on the farm. I'll do their work and they can do mine," Virtue said.

"You'll kill yourself," one of the work crew objected.

The foreman thought for a moment and then smirked. "Let him."

So Virtue left the others back in camp and marched off to work with the foreman. The foreman set a hard pace, but Virtue did not complain. By the end of the day, he had done all the work and more—much to the surprise of the foreman.

When Virtue came back, he shook his head when he saw the one pot of hot water. "You're supposed to have hot water for me. That wouldn't wash a cat's tail." And then he saw the pot of rice they had cooked for him. "I've done the work of twenty men. I've got

the hunger of twenty men. That wouldn't even feed a mouse."

"We don't have enough firewood," one of the work crew said.

"Then I'll take care of it myself this time." Picking up an ax in either hand, he marched up to the nearest tree. In no time, he had chopped it into firewood. Then, taking the huge cauldrons, he went down to the river and

filled them.

One cauldron he used for his rice. The other he used for his bath.

When he finally sat on the ground, he wolfed down the whole cauldron of rice. The others just watched in amazement. Virtue laughed. "I work hard, I eat hard, friends."

All this time, the foreman had been thinking. "You're not just bragging. You really can do the work of a whole crew." The foreman still didn't like Virtue, but it was more important to get the job finished. "Tomorrow you can do the work again."

But Virtue had learned a few things since he had left the farm. He winked at the rest of the crew. "We're all a team." He turned back to the foreman. "You're not going to fire them, are you?"

The foreman had been planning to do that very thing. Then he could pocket all the extra wages. But there was something in Virtue's look that made the foreman think again.

"No, they can be the cooks," the foreman said grudgingly.

One of the work crew grinned at Virtue. "No one will ever mistake you for a modest man, but your heart's in the right place." Then he bowed his head to Virtue. And one by one, the others did too.

And that was why there was only one worker but twenty cooks.

And even though Virtue went on to become a mighty warrior and general, he never lost his talent for making friends . . . and enemies.

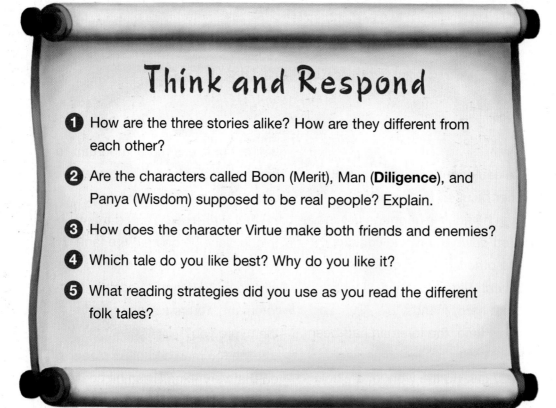

Think and Respond

1 How are the three stories alike? How are they different from each other?

2 Are the characters called Boon (Merit), Man (**Diligence**), and Panya (Wisdom) supposed to be real people? Explain.

3 How does the character Virtue make both friends and enemies?

4 Which tale do you like best? Why do you like it?

5 What reading strategies did you use as you read the different folk tales?

Meet the Illustrator
Suling Wang

Suling Wang grew up in Newport Beach, California. She graduated from Stanford University planning to pursue a career in mechanical engineering. Before long, however, she went back to school, to the Academy of Art College. There she earned another degree, this time in illustration. She now works as an artist in San Francisco, California.

Suling gets the inspiration for her drawings from the stories she is illustrating. She reads the text closely and focuses on capturing the story's mood with her artwork. She says, "I like this kind of work very much. I'm really glad I changed careers."

Visit *The Learning Site!*
www.harcourtschool.com

Making Connections

Compare Texts

1 What does each of the three folk tales show about working together?

2 How are the styles of the three folk tales alike? How are they different?

3 Think of a tall tale that you have read. In what ways are "Virtue Goes to Town" and the tall tale alike?

4 Think of another folk tale that tells how something in nature came to be, as "How the Moon Became Ivory" does. Compare these two folk tales.

5 How could you learn more about folk tales from other lands?

Write a Classified Ad

Writing CONNECTION

Suppose a character from one of the folk tales is looking for a job and puts an advertisement in the classified section of a newspaper. How would the character describe the job he or she is looking for and his or her qualifications? Organize your ideas in a chart like this one, and then write the ad.

Character's Name	Job the Character Wants	Qualifications	Other Information

Construct a Model

Science CONNECTION

"**H**ow the Moon Became Ivory" gives a creative explanation for how the sun and moon appear to move and how the moon looks from Earth. Do research to discover the scientific explanations. You might use an encyclopedia or a science text book. Then make a model that shows how the sun, moon, and Earth are related and how they move.

SUN

Moon

EARTH

Make a Poster

Social Studies CONNECTION

The three folk tales in this selection are from three different countries in Asia. Choose one of those countries to learn more about. Do research to discover interesting facts about the culture of that country. You might find information in a library's reference section or on the Internet. Make a poster to share the information with your classmates.

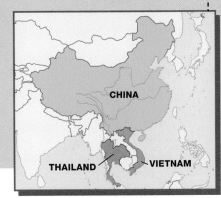

CHINA

THAILAND — VIETNAM

▲ **Folk Tales from Asia**

Summarize and Paraphrase

Focus Skill

When you **summarize**, you tell only the main ideas or important events of a selection, using a combination of the author's words and your own words.

The list below mentions some important events from "How the Moon Became Ivory." Notice that unimportant details are omitted, ideas are not repeated, and the events are listed in order.

- Jade Emperor asks his daughter the sun to oversee the earth during the day.

- He asks his daughter the moon to watch over the earth at night.

- The moon polishes her face till it shines.

- The moon is so bright that people work late and can't sleep at night.

- The Queen smears ashes on the moon's face so that she will shine with a soft, ivory light.

- The moon is sad, until she realizes that the people love her new, ivory face.

When you **paraphrase**, however, you use your own words to restate information or to tell a story. The meaning of the original text stays the same.

Visit *The Learning Site!*
www.harcourtschool.com

See Skills and Activities

Test Prep
Summarize and Paraphrase

▶ **Read the passage. Then answer the questions.**

> The sun and the wind once got into an argument over who was stronger. "Ah," said the sun, "I have an idea. We will have a contest to see who can make that traveler down below take off his coat. You go first."
>
> The wind blew hard. The traveler shivered. The wind blew harder and harder, and the man wrapped his coat tighter around him.
>
> "Let me try," the sun said. The sun climbed high in the sky and shone down on the traveler. Soon the traveler got so hot that he took off his coat and stopped by a brook for a cool drink. So, in the end, the sun proved that he was stronger.

1. **Which of these would *not* belong in a summary of the passage?**

   A The sun and the wind argued.

   B The sun and the wind both tried to make the traveler take off his coat.

   C The wind blew hard but the man wrapped the coat tighter around him.

   D The traveler stopped by a brook for a cool drink.

Tip

A good summary contains only main ideas or important events.

2. **Combine the first two sentences for a paraphrase.**

Tip

Write one sentence that means the same as the first two sentences but uses different words.

183

Vocabulary Power

In the next selection, "Iditarod Dream," a boy named Dusty takes part in a very special and difficult race. Read this newspaper article about another unusual race.

pace

headquarters

positions

handlers

tangle

SNAP THE SNAIL WINS BIG RACE

The **pace** was slower than the rate of speed in most races, but a win is still a win. The Carter County Snail Race took place yesterday at the **headquarters** of the Carter County Snail Racing Club. The opera- tions of the club are all di- rected from the headquar- ters, located in a small room at Sam's Bait Shop.

The mood was tense as the snails and their owners took their **positions**, or places, for the start of the race. As one of the

Winner of the Carter County Snail Race

handlers remarked, "It isn't easy to control a snail. They don't pay attention to what their handlers say."

Shortly after the start of the race, some of the snails got into a **tangle**. By the time the handlers got them straightened out, the race was over. Snap, owned by Terry Kane, was declared the winner. Once again, as in the fable of the tortoise and the hare, a slow and steady pace brought success.

Vocabulary–Writing CONNECTION

Write a two line poem cheering your horse to victory in a race. For example:

Set your **pace** and win the race.
Don't delay. Today's your day!

IDITAROD DREAM

Dusty and His Sled Dogs Compete in Alaska's Jr. Iditarod

TED WOOD

Genre

Nonfiction

Nonfiction tells about people, things, events, or places that are real.

In this selection, look for

- Events in time-order
- Ordinary people who face extraordinary challenges

In 1925, the people of Nome, Alaska, desperately needed help. In response, people from Anchorage set out with sled-dog teams on the Iditarod Trail to deliver life-saving medicine. Today, in honor of those brave teams, two races take place along the trail: the famous Iditarod Trail Sled-Dog Race and, for young competitors, the Jr. Iditarod. This selection describes the experiences of Dusty Whittemore as he competes in the Jr. Iditarod.

IDITAROD DREAM

BY TED WOOD

The day is clear and cold. Mount McKinley, the highest peak in North America, stands like a giant before the truck. The trip south to race headquarters in Wasilla takes four hours.

Dusty's thoughts return to last year's Jr. Iditarod, his first. He remembers the thirty-below-zero temperatures and how his glasses were so coated with ice he couldn't see the trail. And how on the return — when perhaps he'd been headed for victory — he got lost, wandering for four hours before he found the right trail. He finished fourth. But this year his glasses are gone, replaced with contact lenses, and his dog team is the best he's ever had. He can only hope the huskies take him down the right trail.

That evening they reach Iditarod headquarters, where all the racers are gathered for the pre-race meeting. He sees familiar faces from last year — Andy Willis, the favorite to win this year, and Noah Burmeister, who came all the way from Nome. One at a time the fifteen racers pick numbers from a hat to set their starting positions in tomorrow's race. (There is no number 1 position competing in the race; instead the slot is reserved to honor a dedicated supporter of that year's Jr. Iditarod race.) The racers start two minutes apart. Dusty picks number 6, a good position and the same he had last year. Andy will start fourteenth and Noah ninth. Dusty leaves with his father for his final night's sleep before the race.

The next morning Dusty and his dad arrive two hours before the race. It's zero degrees, which is perfect for the dogs. Any warmer, and they would overheat. The race begins on frozen Lake Lucille and runs seventy-nine miles north through forests, over windswept swamps, and up the ice-covered Yentna River to a cabin called Yentna Station, the halfway point.

Last year the race started ten miles farther up the trail. Dusty is worried about starting here. The lake ice is barely covered with snow and is so hard that if he loses control at the start, he could get dragged across the lake. His safety hook, used to stop and hold the sled, won't be able to grab the ice. Dusty checks the brakes on his sled and begins to pack the required supplies. Every racer must carry two pounds of food per dog in case of emergency, and must finish with the same amount. (The four pounds each dog will eat for dinner has been flown to Yentna Station the day before.)

Ten minutes before his start, Dusty, his father, and three friends working as handlers hook the dogs up to the sled. Each dog looks

189

small but is tremendously powerful. Dusty has to walk each dog from the truck, lifting its front legs off the snow. With all four legs down, a sled dog would pull Dusty off his feet. Even hooked up, the dogs are so excited by the other teams it takes every hand to hold them in place.

Dusty's team moves to the starting line, straining against the handlers. His mother rides the sled with him, stepping on the brakes to help control the sled. She's nervous, remembering how Dusty got lost last time. But she's also very proud, and she kisses him good-bye before hopping off the sled.

The dogs are pulling so hard now that five people can barely hold them back. Then the announcer yells, "Go!"

The handlers step away and Dusty flies from the start.

They cross the lake safely, following the red plastic cones marking the route. But as they enter the woods Dusty is on edge. He's never done this part of the trail, and it's crowded with obstacles. Snowmobiles roar along the same trail, and within ten miles he has to cross four roads. Sometimes the roads are so slick the dogs fall, or they get confused by the cars and spectators. Dusty knows he just needs to survive this part until he hits the main Iditarod trail.

At the first road, the team roars over the pavement and around a sharp turn coming off the road. But they're going too fast, and the sled skids sideways, crashing into a tree. Dusty stops dead and can't believe he didn't break the sled. *I'm out of control,* he says to himself. *I'd better slow the team down.*

Back on the trail, he uses his track brake to slow the dogs. He gets them into a strong, steady pace and is able to pass two racers only five miles from the start. He crosses the next road and quickly overtakes another racer. Right before the final road crossing, ten miles out, Dusty passes the last racer. He knows he's in the lead now, that his team is running well, but he can't think about that. He just wants to get through this part and onto the main Iditarod trail, which he knows from last year's race.

Finally, eleven miles out, Dusty hits the familiar trail leading into the thick Alaskan forest. The team is running perfectly now, strong and fast, as they head into the hilly section of the race. Dusty is in a rhythm, too. He runs beside the sled up hills to lighten the load for his team. Around tight corners he jumps from left runner to right runner, digging in the edges to steer the sled through the curves.

The trail is only a few feet wide in the woods, and coming around a blind corner the dogs run smack into two snowmobiles stopped in the path. Unable to pass, the dogs spin and run in circles, tangling their lines before Dusty can get to them. It takes him five minutes to straighten them out and get under way. As he goes around the next curve and down a hill, he spots another snowmobile roaring full speed toward him. The machine almost hits Annie and QT in the lead, but it flies off the trail to avoid the collision. The two lead dogs stop dead, but the others can't. They pile into each other, making a huge tangle of dogs and line.

Dusty can't believe it. Two tangles in less than five minutes. He frantically unknots his team, sure that another racer will catch up to him because of the delays. A tangle is a musher's second-worst nightmare. The dogs can injure their feet in the lines, or strangle when they wrap around each other.

Finally under way, Dusty and the dogs are on edge and can't settle into a pace. *Please don't see another snowmobile*, he says to himself. Then he spots moose tracks on the trail, and his fears mushroom. Running into a moose is a musher's worst nightmare. Because dogs look like wolves to a moose, a moose may attack a team and can kill several dogs before a musher can frighten it off. There's no going around a moose. If Dusty sees one, all he can do is wait for it to move and hope it doesn't charge.

But the team carries him safely out of the forest and onto a wide, open meadow.

Dusty passes a small wooden sign that says "Nome 1,049 miles" and knows from the year before that he can relax for a while through these barren flats. The flats lead to frozen Flathorn Lake, three and a half hours from the start. Here, on the edge of the lake, Dusty takes his first break. He tosses all the dogs fish snacks, big chunks of frozen salmon that will keep their energy up. He says hi to each as well, checking their feet for injuries. QT and Blacky have splits in the webs between their toes, so Dusty puts booties on their feet to protect them as they run.

He takes only five minutes, still expecting to see another racer coming close behind. Trails cross in every direction at the lake, and it's here that Dusty got lost last year. Today, he chooses the right path and speeds out onto the huge snowy lake. It's like running on an ocean of white; Dusty feels relaxed and at home. Out on the lake he suddenly realizes how big his lead is. He can see five miles behind him and there's not one racer in sight. He can't believe it. *Where are Andy and Noah?* he asks himself.

From the lake Dusty turns on to the Susitna River. It looks like a winding snow highway disappearing into the wilderness. Here, he stops at the one checkpoint in the race, and while an official examines his sled and required cargo, Dusty checks the dogs. He decides to take Annie off the lead. She's been looking back while running and seems nervous. She must not have recovered from the encounter with the snowmobile, Dusty thinks.

Dusty moves young Jazz to lead with QT. But Jazz proves too inexperienced, and three miles from the checkpoint Dusty switches Jazz for Bettie. Now the team is running well again, and they move quickly, silently, up a tributary of the Susitna called the Yentna River. There's no need to yell orders here. They know the way to Yentna Station, but Dusty still calls their names to keep them happy.

Just after five P.M. — seven hours after he started — Dusty arrives at Yentna Station, the halfway point and overnight stop. The station is a little log house that can only be reached by plane, snowmobile, or dog sled. Visitors can stay in the house, but racers can't. By the rules, they have to stay with the dogs.

Dusty feels great. He knows he's had a fast race — but, more important, the dogs look fresh and are still eager to run. He smiles to himself, knowing that his training has paid off.

But there's no time to relax. He has hours of dog chores to do. Each racer gets one bale of straw for bedding; after Dusty ties the sled off to a small tree, he spreads the straw around the dogs. It will protect them from the cold snow as they sleep.

Next, he fires up his stove to melt snow for water. While it heats, he fills a cooler with twenty pounds of hamburger and dry food. He pours the heated water into the cooler, letting the frozen meat soak up the warm liquid. Twenty hungry eyes watch as Dusty finally dishes up the warm meal.

After dinner, Dusty checks the dogs' feet for web cracks, putting on ointment where needed. Then he hears other dogs and looks up. He'd forgotten about the other racers. It's Noah, the second racer to arrive at Yentna — thirty-eight minutes behind Dusty. Andy arrives next, eight minutes after Noah. Over the next four hours the remaining racers straggle in. Everyone is required to stay at Yentna ten hours. Dusty arrived so early that his departure time is three-thirty the next morning. He decides not to sleep and helps the other racers build a big fire in the snow. They all help each other; that's the rule of the wilderness.

Before his three-thirty start, Dusty melts more water for the dogs, feeds everyone, packs his sled, and finally makes sure his headlamp batteries work for the trip back.

It's snowing lightly as he leaves Yentna, and there's no moon. The only light comes from Dusty's headlamp. The dogs are excited to run, but Dusty doesn't like the night. He can't see the trail markers or nearby moose. The dogs are his only eyes, so he chooses Bettie and QT to lead him out. They did the trail once, Dusty figures, so they can do it again.

Once again the dogs are gobbling up the miles. They run the Yentna River and Flathorn Lake in the dark; at first light, Dusty stops at the Nome sign. As he gives the dogs fish snacks, he finally lets himself believe that if nothing bad happens he can expect to win. Dusty and his team move through the hills easily and take all four road crossings smoothly.

Finally, the lake appears, like a welcome mat, and Dusty begins to smile as he heads for the finish. He's running so fast that the spectators and most of the racers' families haven't arrived yet. But he spots his mother and father cheering him on, and when he crosses the finish line his mother showers him with hugs and kisses. His father's proud smile is so big it almost looks frozen with happiness.

TV and radio announcers swarm Dusty. "How does it feel to win, Dusty?" they ask.

"I would have had a big smile even if I'd come in last," he says. "But it feels great to win."

Because he ran so fast, rumors are flying that Dusty has mistreated his dogs, pushing them too hard. But now, looking at them, everyone knows this isn't true. The dogs are still strong, barking, jumping, and eager to run farther. Dusty has treated them just right. He knows they are his trusted partners — and they're champions.

Think and Respond

1 How does the Jr. Iditarod protect the racers and the dog teams?

2 Why do you think the author uses photographs to illustrate this selection?

3 How does Dusty feel when the dogs get in a second **tangle** less than five minutes after the first one?

4 Would you enjoy training for and competing in the Jr. Iditarod? Why or why not?

5 What reading strategies did you use to help you understand "Iditarod Dream"? When did you use them?

Meet the Author

TED WOOD

Ted Wood, also known as Edward John Wood, sometimes writes under the name Jack Barnao. In addition to being the author of science fiction stories, two mystery series, television scripts, a play, and many novels, he is also a photographer. His photos of Dusty and his sled dogs are featured in *Iditarod Dream* as well as in many magazines.

Visit *The Learning Site!*
www.harcourtschool.com

Making Connections

Compare Texts

1 How does "Iditarod Dream" fit into the theme Team Work?

2 In the first two paragraphs on page 192, what does the author tell you about Dusty's emotions? How does this compare with the emotions described on page 196?

3 How is this nonfiction selection similar to a newspaper article about the Jr. Iditarod? How is it different?

4 How is this nonfiction selection like and unlike a realistic fiction story?

5 What other questions do you have about sled-dog racing?

Write a Conversation

Suppose the sled dogs could talk among themselves. Write their imaginary conversation. List the names of some sled dogs from the selection. Then list some comments the dogs might make. Use both lists to help you write the conversation.

Writing CONNECTION

Sled Dog	Comment
QT	My feet hurt.
Blacky	I want booties.
Jazz	I love to run.
Bettie	I love to win.

Draw a Landmark

The Jr. Itidarod takes place in Alaska. The highest peak in North America, Mount McKinley, is in Alaska. Do research to find out how high Mount McKinley is, what national park it is located in, and who has climbed it. Then draw a picture of it, including its surrounding landscape.

**Social Studies
CONNECTION**

Compare Temperature Scales

Dusty obtains water by melting snow on his stove. At what temperature does snow or ice melt to form liquid water? At what temperatures does water freeze and boil? The numbers that represent these temperatures depend on whether you are using a Fahrenheit or Celsius scale. Use an encyclopedia or a science text to find out the temperatures on these different scales. Create a bar graph to compare the two temperature scales.

**Science
CONNECTION**

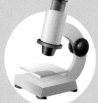

199

▲ Iditarod Dream

Draw Conclusions

Focus Skill

As you read "Iditarod Dream," you may have drawn conclusions or made inferences. To draw conclusions, you combine prior knowledge and facts and details from the text. You can also use this information to make inferences about something that is not stated directly in the text. Look at the chart below.

Prior knowledge	+ Information from the text	= Inference
In a race my mom ran, the people who had good starting positions had an advantage.	Each of the fifteen racers draws a number. The racers start two minutes apart.	The racer who draws number two has a twenty-minute advantage over the racer who draws number twelve.

Prior knowledge	+ Information from the text	= Conclusion
Handling a sled dog team takes skill, strength, and experience.	Dusty raced in the Jr. Iditarod the year before; he untangles the dogs on the trail; he repositions the dogs along the way.	Dusty has the skill, strength, and experience to handle a team of sled dogs.

A generalization is a conclusion that can be expanded or applied beyond the text. Can you make a generalization about Dusty and the next Jr. Iditarod?

Visit *The Learning Site!*
www.harcourtschool.com

See *Skills* and *Activities*

200

Test Prep
Draw Conclusions

▶ **Read the passage. Then answer the questions.**

> Rob Davis and hundreds of other young people across the country share Dusty Whittemore's enthusiasm for sled dog racing. Rob, a sledder from a small town in Massachusetts, had a narrow escape in one 60-mile sled dog race in New Hampshire. His sled skidded on the ice, slammed into a trail sign, and tipped over. His dogs kept running, pulling him along the ice at 20 miles an hour. Fortunately, Rob was able to get the sled, its 50 pounds of gear, and himself back up and running.

1. **What is one inference you can make based on the information in the passage?**

   A   Rob and Dusty are friends.

   B   Rob dreams about the Iditarod.

   C   Some sled dog races are held outside Alaska.

   D   Rob will never race sled dogs again.

   Tip
   Make sure your choice is logical. A logical inference is based on what you know and on information in the text.

2. **Which conclusion can you draw from this passage?**

   F   In spite of hardships, Rob participates in sled dog racing.

   G   Rob will not sign up for the next sled dog race held in New Hampshire.

   H   Rob has had many dreams of winning.

   J   Snowmelts are a constant problem during sled dog races.

   Tip
   Choose a conclusion that combines personal experience or knowledge with details in the text.

▲ Woodsong

resembled
harness
bulk
pointedly
snort
disengage
retired

Vocabulary Power

"Woodsong" tells about a special dog named Storm. Animals can't talk to us, but they do have their own ways of showing how they feel. If we pay attention, we can sometimes figure out what an animal would say if it could talk, just as Marcus Brown "listened" to Peaches.

Marcus Brown

Peaches

I love looking at the old pictures in my grandmother's album. Marcus Brown was my grandmother's grandfather. He had a pony named Peaches. Peaches **resembled**, or looked like, a toy horse that I had, so she seems like an old friend to me.

Marcus Brown used a leather **harness** to hitch Peaches to a cart. Peaches pulled many loads over the years. She took children for rides in the cart. When she got older, she hauled logs, sacks of flour, and bales of hay. Some of the loads had great **bulk**, but Peaches was strong enough to handle even the largest and heaviest ones.

After years of hard work, the day came when Peaches **pointedly**, with great emphasis, showed that she was too old and tired to work any more. When Marcus Brown hitched her to the cart, she stood like a mule and would not budge. All she would do was **snort** loudly, forcing air noisily through her nostrils. Marcus Brown decided to **disengage** the straps of the harness.

"You're right, Peaches," he said. "It's time you were **retired**. No more work for you, old girl." So Peaches lived out the rest of her life in peace and contentment.

Vocabulary-Writing CONNECTION

Some pets **resemble** their owners. What kind of pet would most resemble you? List your reasons.

Personal Narrative

A personal narrative tells a true story about something important to the author.

In this selection, look for:

- First-person point of view

- The use of vivid words and details

Author Gary Paulsen once lived deep in the Minnesota wilderness in the company of forty-one sled dogs. He observed these beautiful animals closely, made connections with many of them, and learned powerful lessons about toughness, trust, and teamwork.

Woodsong

BY GARY PAULSEN

ILLUSTRATED BY LEE CHRISTIANSEN

It is always possible to learn from dogs and in fact the longer I'm with them the more I understand how little I know. But there was one dog who taught me the most. Just one dog.

Storm.

First dog.

He has already been spoken of once here when he taught me about heart and the will to pull. But there was more to him, so much more that he in truth could take a whole book.

Joy, loyalty, toughness, peacefulness—all of these were part of Storm. Lessons about life and, finally, lessons about death came from him.

He had a bear's ears. He was brindle colored and built like a truck, and his ears were rounded when we got him so that they looked like bear cub ears. They gave him a comical look when he was young that somehow hung onto him even when he grew old. He had a sense of humor to match his ears, and when he grew truly old he somehow resembled George Burns.

At peak, he was a mighty dog. He pulled like a machine. Until we retired him and used him only for training puppies, until we let him loose to enjoy his age, he pulled, his back over in the power curve so that nothing could stop the sled.

In his fourth or fifth year as a puller he started doing tricks. First he would play jokes on the dog pulling next to him. On long runs he would become bored and when we least expected it he would reach across the gangline and snort wind into the ear of the dog next to him. I ran him with many different dogs and he did it to all of them—chuckling when the dog jumped and shook his or her head—but I never saw a single dog get mad at him for it. Oh, there was once a dog named Fonzie who nearly took his head off, but Fonzie wasn't really mad at him so much as surprised. Fonzie once nailed me through the wrist for waking him up too suddenly when he was sleeping. I'd reached down and touched him before whispering his name.

Small jokes. Gentle jokes, Storm played. He took to hiding things from me. At first I couldn't understand where things were going. I would put a bootie down while working on a dog and it would disappear. I lost a small ladle I used for watering each dog, a cloth glove liner I took off while working on a dog's feet, a roll of tape, and finally, a hat.

He was so clever.

When I lost the hat it was a hot day and I had taken the hat off while I worked on a dog's harness. The dog was just ahead of Storm and when I kneeled to work on the harness—he'd chewed almost through the side of it while running—I put the hat down on the snow near Storm.

Or thought I had. When I had changed the dog's harness I turned and the hat was gone. I looked around, moved the dogs, looked under them, then shrugged. At first I was sure I'd put the hat down, then, when I couldn't find it, I became less sure and at last I thought perhaps I had left it at home or dropped it somewhere on the run.

Storm sat quietly, looking ahead down the trail, not showing anything at all.

I went back to the sled, reached down to disengage the hook and when I did, the dogs exploded forward. I was not quite on the sled when they took off so I was knocked slightly off balance. I leaned over to the right to regain myself, and when I did I accidentally dragged the hook through the snow.

And pulled up my hat.

It had been buried off to the side of the trail in the snow, buried neatly with the snow smoothed over the top so that it was completely hidden. Had the snowhook not scraped down four or five inches I never would have found it.

I stopped the sled and set the hook once more. While knocking the snow out of the hat and putting it back on my head I studied where it had happened.

Right next to Storm.

He had taken the hat, quickly dug a hole, buried the hat and smoothed the snow over it, then gone back to sitting, staring ahead, looking completely innocent.

When I stopped the sled and picked up the hat he looked back, saw me put the hat on my head, and—I swear—smiled. Then he shook his head once and went back to work, pulling.

Along with the jokes, Storm had scale eyes. He watched as the sled was loaded, carefully calculated the weight of each item, and let his disapproval be known if it went too far.

One winter a friend gave us a parlor stove with nickel trim. It was not an enormous stove, but it had some weight to it and some bulk. This friend lived twelve miles away—twelve miles over two fair hills followed by about eight miles on an old, abandoned railroad grade. We needed the stove badly (our old barrel stove had started to burn through) so I took off with the team to pick it up. I left early in the morning because I wanted to get back that same day. It had snowed four or five inches, so the dogs would have to break trail. By the time we had done the hills and the railroad grade, pushing in new snow all the time, they were ready for a rest. I ran them the last two miles to where the stove was and unhooked their tugs so they could rest while I had coffee.

We stopped for an hour at least, the dogs sleeping quietly. When it was time to go my friend and I carried the stove outside and put it in the sled. The dogs didn't move.

Except for Storm.

He raised his head, opened one eye, did a perfect double take—both eyes opening wide—and sat up. He had been facing the front. Now he turned around to face the sled—so he was facing away from the direction we had to travel when we left—and watched us load the sled.

It took some time as the stove barely fit on the sled and had to be jiggled and shuffled around to get it down between the side rails.

Through it all Storm sat and watched us, his face a study in interest. He did not get up, but sat on his back end and when I was done and ready to go I hooked all the dogs back in harness—which involved hooking the tugs to the rear ties on their harnesses. The dogs knew this meant we were going to head home so they got up and started slamming against the tugs, trying to get the sled to move.

All of them, that is, but Storm.

Storm sat backward, the tug hooked up but hanging down. The other dogs were screaming to run, but Storm sat and stared at the stove.

Not at me, not at the sled, but at the stove itself. Then he raised his lips, bared his teeth, and growled at the stove.

When he was finished growling he snorted twice, stood, turned away from the stove, and started to pull. But each time we stopped at the tops of the hills to let the dogs catch their breath after pulling the sled and stove up the steep incline, Storm turned and growled at the stove.

The enemy.

The weight on the sled.

I do not know how many miles Storm and I ran together. Eight, ten, perhaps twelve thousand miles. He was one of the first dogs and taught me the most and as we worked together he came to know me better than perhaps even my own family. He could look once at my shoulders and tell how I was feeling, tell how far we were to run, how fast we had to run—knew it all.

When I started to run long, moved from running a work team, a trapline team, to training for the Iditarod, Storm took it in stride, changed the pace down to the long trot, matched what was needed, and settled in for the long haul.

He did get bored, however, and one day while we were running a long run he started doing a thing that would stay with him—with us—until the end. We had gone forty or fifty miles on a calm, even day with no bad wind. The temperature was a perfect ten below zero. The sun was bright, everything was moving well, and the dogs had settled into the rhythm that could take them a hundred or a thousand miles.

And Storm got bored.

At a curve in the trail a small branch came out over the path we were running and as Storm passed beneath the limb he jumped up and grabbed it, broke a short piece off—about a foot long—and kept it in his mouth.

All day.

And into the night. He ran, carrying the stick like a toy, and when we stopped to feed or rest he would put the stick down, eat, then pick it up again. He would put the stick down carefully in front of him, or across his paws, and sleep, and when he awakened he would pick up the stick and it soon became a thing between us, the stick.

He would show it to me, making a contact, a connection between us, each time we stopped. I would pet him on top of the head and take the stick from him—he would emit a low, gentle growl when I took the stick. I'd "examine" it closely, nod and seem to approve of it, and hand it back to him.

Each day we ran he would pick a different stick. And each time I would have to approve of it, and after a time, after weeks and months, I realized that he was using the sticks as a way to communicate with me, to tell me that everything was all right, that I was doing the right thing.

Once when I pushed them too hard during a pre-Iditarod race—when I thought it was important to compete and win (a feeling that didn't last long)—I walked up to Storm and as I came close to him he pointedly dropped the stick. I picked it up and held it out but he wouldn't take it. He turned his face away. I put the stick against his lips and tried to make him take it, but he let it fall to the ground. When I realized what he was doing, I stopped and fed and rested the team, sat on the sled and thought about what I was doing wrong. After four hours or so of sitting—watching other teams pass me—I fed them another snack, got ready to go, and was gratified to see Storm pick up the stick. From that time forward I looked for the stick always, knew when I saw it out to the sides of his head that I was doing the right thing. And it was always there.

Through storms and cold weather, on the long runs, the long, long runs where there isn't an end to it, where only the sled and the winter around the sled and the wind are there, Storm had the stick to tell me it was right, all things were right.

Think and Respond

1. How do Storm and the author communicate with each other?

2. How does the author help you create a clear mental picture of Storm? Give examples.

3. Why do you think the author used Storm to train puppies after he **retired** him from pulling?

4. Do you think you would like to have a dog like Storm for a pet? Why or why not?

5. Which reading strategies did you use to help you understand this selection?

MEET THE AUTHOR
Gary Paulsen

Gary Paulsen was not a strong reader as a child. Then one event changed his life forever. He says, "One day as I was walking past the public library in twenty-below temperatures . . . I went in to get warm and, to my absolute astonishment, the librarian asked me if I wanted a library card. . . . When she handed me the card, she handed me the world."

Gary Paulsen is now a successful author of adult westerns, fiction, nonfiction, short stories, plays, and children's literature. He says, "I knew . . . that whether I was successful or not, whether it *worked* or not, I would write until I died. I had absolutely no choice." He has written nearly one hundred books and almost two hundred articles and short stories for adults and young people. He says, "I have become what I hoped for . . . and sometimes prayed for, and never, not in a million years, thought I would become—a successful author."

Visit *The Learning Site!*
www.harcourtschool.com

ICE LANDS

The continent of Antarctica is a land of ice. Almost the entire continent, which includes the South Pole, is blanketed with ice. The ice blanket is several miles deep in parts, covering all but the very tops of the highest mountain peaks. Near the coast, glaciers (slow-moving rivers of ice and snow) crawl down the mountains and flow into the ocean. Sometimes, chunks of the glaciers, some as large as a city, split off, crash into the ocean, and float off to become icebergs.

At the opposite region of the Earth, an ice-covered ocean surrounds the Arctic, or North Pole. The ice cracks, crashes, and swirls on top of ocean currents. The ice cover shrinks in summer and expands in winter, but it never disappears.

North and South, the polar regions of the Earth are unusually beautiful places, frozen with ice.

Rime is frozen water ▶
vapor. This frozen
water vapor, or fog (a
type of cloud), freezes
on tree branches and
other solid objects. The
wind blows the ice
crystals horizontally
(parallel to the hori-
zon). The rime looks
like a white, jagged flag
on a tree branch.

Snowy Snapshots

◀ Every kind of crystal has
its own regular struc-
ture of atoms. Snow
crystals are hexagons
(six-sided figures). The
crystals combine in var-
ious ways to form snow.
The type of snow
formed depends on
temperature, density
(how packed the atoms
are), moisture, and
other factors.

The cracked ice below looks eerily like the ice sheets that cover the Arctic Ocean. Yet it's not on planet Earth. The cracked ice covers Europa, a moon of Jupiter. Europa might have a liquid, watery ocean under its icy shell. Where there is liquid water, there might be life.▼

▲ It was formerly thought that the moon had no water. Recently, scientists discovered ice in the moon's deepest craters. Perhaps comets put it there. Comets' heads are chunks of ice—of which 80 percent is water ice—and rock that sometimes slam into planets and moons. Some of Earth's water may have arrived via comets, but this is simply a guess.

A Glacier on the Move

Glaciers (French for "ice") begin as piles of snow in mountain valleys. As some snow evaporates or melts, freshly fallen snow replaces it.

Snow weighs a lot. Layers of snow press down, forming a compact ice called firn.

Gravity causes the firn to travel down the mountain at a rate of several feet per day.

In places, deep cracks called crevasses form.

As the land becomes flatter, the glacier slows down and buckles, creating bumpy icefalls.

The tip of the glacier advances and, at other times, retreats, depending on the amount of snowfall and the temperature.

▲ Each winter in St. Paul, Minnesota, artists create giant castles. They use a building material that is common in winter–blocks of ice from Minnesota's frozen lakes and rivers. Since 1886, the ice castles of St. Paul have been world-famous. The 1992 structure set a world record of 15 stories–that's approximately 150 feet!

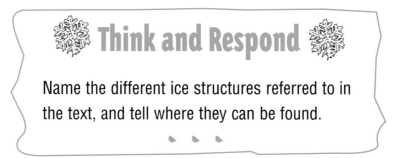

❄ Think and Respond ❄

Name the different ice structures referred to in the text, and tell where they can be found.

▸ ▸ ▸

Making Connections

Compare Texts

1 How does Storm's ability to communicate with the author help the two of them work together?

2 Look at the last three paragraphs on page 211. How is the first of these paragraphs different from the other two? Why do you think the author changes his style?

3 "Woodsong" and "Ice Lands" are both nonfiction. What is the author's purpose for writing each selection?

4 Think of another personal narrative you have read that tells about someone's experiences with an animal. Compare the other narrator's opinion of animal intelligence with Gary Paulsen's.

5 After reading this selection, what would you like to learn about dogs and how to train them?

Write a Brief Narrative

The narrator tells about Storm's sense of humor. Think of a time when someone's sense of humor helped make a job easier for you. Write a narrative about what happened. Organize your thoughts by answering these questions.

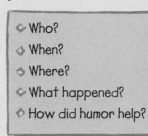

- Who?
- When?
- Where?
- What happened?
- How did humor help?

Writing CONNECTION

Prepare a Presentation

The events in "Woodsong" take place in the state of Minnesota. Research the history and geography of Minnesota. When did it become a state? What are its major rivers? You might use an encyclopedia, an atlas, or the Internet as sources of information. Prepare an oral presentation with graphic aids, such as photographs or maps.

Social Studies CONNECTION

Present a Slide Show

The author says that Storm carried the stick through storms and cold weather. Research the subject of snowstorms to find out what causes them. Prepare a series of drawings to show the stages in the develop-ment of a snowstorm. Present your drawings to classmates.

Science CONNECTION

Summarize and Paraphrase

Focus Skill

To make sure that you recall important points, or to make sure that you understand what you have read, you can **summarize** or **paraphrase** a selection.

- To summarize, briefly tell the most important ideas of the selection, using the author's words and your own words.

Author's words: "Storm had bear's ears. They were rounded when he was young, and that made them look like a bear cub's ears."

Your own words: Storm would play jokes on the dog pulling next to him. He hid things from the author and pretended to be innocent.

Summary of the two: Storm had a comical look and a good sense of humor.

- To paraphrase, use your own words to restate information or to tell a story without changing its meaning.

Author's words: "Storm calculated the weight of the sled load with his eyes. If he thought the sled was too heavy, he let his disapproval be known."

Paraphrase: Storm could tell if there was too much weight piled on the sled. Then he acted in a way that let the author know it.

Visit *The Learning Site!*
www.harcourtschool.com

See *Skills* and *Activities*

222

Test Prep
Summarize and Paraphrase

▶ **Read the passage. Then answer the questions.**

> When Misha came to live with us, she was the cutest golden lab puppy I'd ever seen. I could tell right away why she had been chosen for the service training program. But when Mom asked if I'd like to be in charge of her puppy training, I hesitated.
>
> Even though I felt honored, I knew that if I trained Misha, the two of us would become best friends. Once her training was complete, though, she would leave us to live with the family of a young person who needed her help.
>
> I noticed Misha's tail wagging furiously. She seemed to be smiling at me. I knew that when the time came, it would be very hard to say good-bye. Until then, however, Misha and I would be a team.

1. **Write a summary of the entire passage.**

Tip

Focus on main points. Follow the author's sequence. Leave out unimportant details.

2. **Write a paraphrase of the second paragraph.**

Tip

Use your own words, but be careful not to change the meaning. Replace key words with synonyms.

forlorn
overcome
abalone
pitched
lair
gorged
vainer

Vocabulary Power

The main characters in the next selection live close to nature. People today often have to go on vacation to have that experience.

I was so excited about leaving for our camping trip! We were going to spend two weeks camping and learning about nature. I felt sorry for my little brother, though. He was **forlorn**, very sad about being left behind. He was almost **overcome**, or made weak and helpless, by it all. I made him feel better by promising to bring back something special for him.

I found this **abalone** shell when we were exploring the beach. The abalone is a type of shellfish. The flat shell is lined with shiny mother-of-pearl. It will be a good souvenir to take home

for my little brother. I wonder if it **pitched** in the waves, rising and falling the way boats do, before it washed up on shore.

We came upon a cave while we were hiking in the mountains. We thought it might once have been the **lair** , or den, of some kind of wild animal. I guess the animal **gorged** itself, because there were a lot of bones lying in the dirt. Maybe it stuffed itself with food so it could sleep through the winter. Angie and I fell in a puddle. It's a good thing the other girls didn't fall. They're **vainer** than we are. They're always admiring themselves. I don't think they'd like to be all muddy!

Vocabulary-Writing CONNECTION

Imagine that you live in a modern cave. In a brief paragraph, describe some characteristics of your **lair**.

Newbery Medal
ALA Notable Book

Genre

Historical Fiction

Historical fiction is set in the past and portrays people, places, and events that did or could have happened.

In this selection, look for

- A setting that could be a real place

- Details that show the story took place in the past

Island Blue Do

by Scott O'Dell
illustrated by Rich Nelson

of the

lphins

Karana lives peacefully with her people on an island off California's coast. When her father, the chief, trusts a group of strangers and allows them to hunt on the island, the peace is shattered. The hunters turn their weapons on Karana's people, killing many, including her father, and leaving them with no way to defend themselves.

The new chief decides to lead his people away to a new island — to what he hopes will be a safer home.

We took nothing with us when we thought we would have to flee, so there was much excitement as we packed our baskets. Nanko strode up and down outside the houses, urging us to hurry.

"The wind grows strong," he shouted. "The ship will leave you."

I filled two baskets with the things I wished to take. Three fine needles of whalebone, an awl for making holes, a good stone knife for scraping hides, two cooking pots, and a small box made from a shell with many earrings in it.

Ulape had two boxes of earrings, for she was vainer than I, and when she put them into her baskets, she drew a thin mark with blue clay across her nose and cheekbones. The mark meant that she was unmarried.

"The ship leaves," shouted Nanko.

"If it goes," Ulape shouted back, "it will come again after the storm."

My sister was in love with Nanko, but she laughed at him.

"Other men will come to the island," she said. "They will be far more handsome and brave than those who leave."

"You are all women of such ugliness that they will be afraid and soon go away."

The wind blew in fierce gusts as we left the village, stinging our faces with sand. Ramo hopped along far in front with one of our baskets, but before long he ran back to say that he had forgotten his fishing spear. Nanko was standing on the cliff motioning us to hurry, so I refused to let him go back for it.

The ship was anchored outside the cove and Nanko said that it could not come closer to the shore because of the high waves. They were beating against the rocks with the sound of thunder. The shore as far as I could see was rimmed with foam.

Two boats were pulled up on the beach. Beside them stood four white men and as we came down the trail, one of the men beckoned us to walk faster. He spoke to us in a language which we could not understand.

The men of our tribe, except Nanko and Chief Matasaip, were already on the ship. My brother Ramo was there too, Nanko said. He had run on ahead after I had told him that he could not go back to the village for his spear. Nanko said that he had jumped into the first boat that left the cove.

Matasaip divided the women into two groups. The boats were pushed into the water, and while they bobbed about we scrambled into them as best we could.

The cove was partly sheltered from the wind, but as soon as we went through the passage between the rocks and into the sea, great waves struck us. There was much confusion. Spray flew, the white men shouted at each other. The boat pitched so wildly that in one breath you could see the ship and in the next breath it had gone. Yet we came to it at last and somehow were able to climb onto the deck.

The ship was large, many times the size of our biggest canoes. It had two tall masts and between them stood a young man with blue eyes and a black beard. He was the chieftain of the white men, for he began to shout orders which they quickly obeyed. Sails rose on the tall masts and two of the men began to pull on the rope that held the anchor.

I called to my brother, knowing that he was very curious and therefore would be in the way of the men who were working. The wind drowned my voice and he did not answer. The deck was so crowded that it was hard to move, but I went from one end of it to the other, calling his name. Still there was no answer. No one had seen him.

At last I found Nanko.

I was overcome with fear. "Where is my brother?" I cried.

He repeated what he had told me on the beach, but as he spoke Ulape who stood beside him pointed toward the island. I looked out across the deck and the sea. There, running along the cliff, the fishing spear held over his head, was Ramo.

The sails had filled and the ship was now moving slowly away. Everyone was looking toward the cliff, even the white men. I ran to one of them and pointed, but he shook his head and turned from me. The ship began to move faster. Against my will, I screamed.

Chief Matasaip grasped my arm.

"We cannot wait for Ramo," he said. "If we do, the ship will be driven on the rocks."

"We must!" I shouted. "We must!"

"The ship will come back for him on another day," Matasaip said. "He will be safe. There is food for him to eat and water to drink and places to sleep."

"No," I cried.

Matasaip's face was like stone. He was not listening. I cried out once more, but my voice was lost in the howling wind. People gathered around me, saying again what Matasaip had said, yet I was not comforted by their words.

Ramo had disappeared from the cliff and I knew that he was now running along the trail that led to the beach.

The ship began to circle the kelp bed and I thought surely that it was going to return to the shore. I held my breath, waiting. Then slowly its direction changed. It pointed toward the east. At that moment I walked across the deck and, though many hands tried to hold me back, flung myself into the sea.

A wave passed over my head and I went down and down until I thought I would never behold the day again. The ship was far away when I rose. Only the sails showed through the spray. I was still clutching the basket that held all of my things, but it was very heavy and I realized that I could not swim with it in my arms. Letting it sink, I started off toward the shore.

I could barely see the two rocks that guarded the entrance to Coral Cove, but I was not fearful. Many times I had swum farther than this, although not in a storm.

I kept thinking over and over as I swam how I would punish Ramo when I reached the shore, yet when I felt the sand under my feet and saw him standing at the edge of the waves, holding his fishing spear and looking so forlorn, I forgot all those things I planned to do. Instead I fell to my knees and put my arms around him.

The ship had disappeared.

"When will it come back?" Ramo asked. There were tears in his eyes.

"Soon," I said.

The only thing that made me angry was that my beautiful skirt of yucca fibers, which I had worked on so long and carefully, was ruined.

The wind blew strong as we climbed the trail, covering the mesa with sand that sifted around our legs and shut out the sky. Since it was not possible to find our way back, we took shelter among some rocks. We stayed there until night fell. Then the wind lessened and the moon came out and by its light we reached the village.

As we neared the huts I heard a strange sound like that of running feet. I thought that it was a sound made by the wind, but when we came closer I saw dozens of wild dogs scurrying around through the huts. They ran from us, snarling as they went.

The pack must have slunk into the village soon after we left, for it had gorged itself upon the abalone we had not taken. It had gone everywhere searching out food, and Ramo and I had to look hard to find enough for our supper. While we ate beside a small fire I could hear the dogs on the hill not far away, and through the night their howls came to me on the wind. But when the sun rose and I went out of the hut, the pack trotted off toward its lair which was at the north side of the island, in a large cave.

That day we spent gathering food. The wind blew and the waves crashed against the shore so that we could not go out on the rocks. I gathered gull eggs on the cliff and Ramo speared a string of small fish in one of the tide pools. He brought them home, walking proudly with the string over his back. He felt that in this way he had made up for the trouble he had caused.

With the seeds I had gathered in a ravine, we had a plentiful meal, although I had to cook it on a flat rock. My bowls were at the bottom of the sea.

The wild dogs came again that night. Drawn by the scent of fish, they sat on the hill, barking and growling at each other. I could see the light from the fire shining in their eyes. At dawn they left.

The ocean was calm on this day and we were able to hunt abalone among the rocks. From seaweed we wove a rough basket which we filled before the sun was overhead. On the way home, carrying the abalone between us, Ramo and I stopped on the cliff. The air was clear and we could look far out to sea in the direction the ship had gone.

"Will it come back today?" Ramo asked.

"It may," I answered him, though I did not think so. "More likely it will come after many suns, for the country where it has gone is far off."

235

Ramo looked up at me. His black eyes shone.

"I do not care if the ship never comes," he said.

"Why do you say this?" I asked him.

Ramo thought, making a hole in the earth with the point of his spear.

"Why?" I asked again.

"Because I like it here with you," he said. "It is more fun than when the others were here. Tomorrow I am going to where the canoes are hidden and bring one back to Coral Cove. We will use it to fish in and to go looking around the island."

Think and Respond

1 What problem does Karana face, and how does she solve it?

2 Why do you think the author includes the description of the wild dogs?

3 How do Karana's feelings change when she sees how **forlorn** Ramo looks?

4 If you had been a passenger on the ship, would you have been in favor of waiting for Ramo? Why or why not?

5 Which reading strategies did you use to help you read "Island of the Blue Dolphins?" When did you use them?

About the Author

Scott O'Dell

Scott O'Dell lived in many places when he was growing up. One strange and wonderful place was Rattlesnake Island, across the bay from Los Angeles, California. His family lived there in a house on stilts.

In 1960, when O'Dell began to write *Island of the Blue Dolphins*, he remembered those early years on Rattlesnake Island. He and other boys used logs as canoes and paddled with their hands around the bay, exploring the surrounding islands.

Years later, O'Dell and his wife rented a house on the island. Karana, the main character of the story, is based on a Mexican girl named Carolina, whose father took care of that house.

Fond memories of Rattlesnake Island and of Carolina were part of what inspired O'Dell to write *Island of the Blue Dolphins*. O'Dell hoped that his book would communicate a simple message: "Forgive your enemies and have respect for life — all life."

Visit *The Learning Site!*
www.harcourtschool.com

237

Souvenir

by Eve Merriam
illustrated by Kurt Nagahori

I bring back a shell so I can always hear
the music of the ocean when I hold it to my ear:

then I feel again the grains of sand
trickle sun-warm through my hand

the sea gulls dip and swoop and cry
as they dive for fish then climb the sky

the sailboats race with wings spread wide
as the wind spins them round and they glide ride glide

my lips taste a crust of salty foam
and sandpipers skitter and crabs scuttle home

where I build a castle of Yesterday
that the high tide washes away away

while I keep the shell so I can always hear
the music of the ocean when I hold it to my ear.

Making Connections

Compare Texts

1 Why does this selection belong in the theme Team Work?

2 How does the artist show Karana's emotions in the illustration on pages 230 and 231?

3 How is the description of the beach in the poem "Souvenir" different from the description of the beach in "Island of the Blue Dolphins"?

4 Name another older, well-known story that you have read. What qualities do the two stories have in common?

5 Do you think Karana and Ramo will be rescued from the island? Tell what you think may happen next in this story.

Write a List

Imagine that, like Karana, you must leave your home quickly and can take only as much as will fit in two baskets. List the items you would take, and add a brief note explaining each one. Separate the items into categories such as necessities, treasures, or useful tools.

Writing CONNECTION

Create a Brochure

"Island of the Blue Dolphins" is based on actual events that took place on San Nicolas (or San Nicholas) Island. This island is part of Channel Islands National Park, located off the coast of California. Use print or online sources such as encyclopedias and atlases to learn more about these islands. Then create a travel brochure that gives a brief description and history.

Social Studies CONNECTION

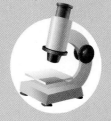

Paint a Mural

Along the Pacific shore of North America, giant kelp beds form kelp forests. Use the Internet, encyclopedias, or nonfiction books to learn more about kelp forests. Use your information to make a mural. Label the levels of the kelp forest, and show the species of sea life that inhabit each level.

Science CONNECTION

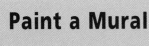

Kelp Forests

Narrative Elements

Focus Skill

You know that being able to recognize narrative elements such as setting, plot, characters, and theme can help you better appreciate and understand a story. This chart shows the narrative elements in "Island of the Blue Dolphins."

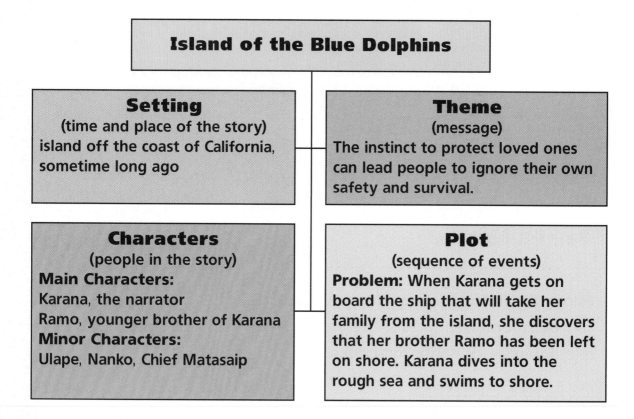

Island of the Blue Dolphins

Setting
(time and place of the story)
island off the coast of California, sometime long ago

Theme
(message)
The instinct to protect loved ones can lead people to ignore their own safety and survival.

Characters
(people in the story)
Main Characters:
Karana, the narrator
Ramo, younger brother of Karana
Minor Characters:
Ulape, Nanko, Chief Matasaip

Plot
(sequence of events)
Problem: When Karana gets on board the ship that will take her family from the island, she discovers that her brother Ramo has been left on shore. Karana dives into the rough sea and swims to shore.

Discuss the narrative elements as you answer these questions:

- Who were the main characters in the story?

- How might the story have been different in a different setting?

- How do Karana's actions affect the plot?

Visit *The Learning Site!*
www.harcourtschool.com

See *Skills* and *Activities*

Test Prep
Narrative Elements

▶ **Read the passage. Then answer the questions.**

The last time Paulo and Carla had seen their parents was on the boat. The four of them had been on deck eating lunch when a loud noise shattered the peace and quiet of the sea. The next thing Paulo knew, he and Carla were in the water, surrounded by thick, dark smoke. Paulo could hear his parents calling to him and Carla, but he couldn't see them. When a life preserver floated by, Paulo grabbed it and told Carla to hang on. Carla had started to cry, but after a while she stopped and wanted to go to sleep. To keep her awake, Paulo made her sing songs with him. Just before dark, the two were washed ashore, still clinging to the life preserver.

1. **Which phrase best identifies the setting?**

   A on a boat

   B in the sea

   C on an island

   D on a boat dock

> **Tip**
>
> A story can have more than one setting. Choose the place where most of the action in this passage takes place.

2. **What is Paulo's main problem?**

   F Paulo must find a way for Carla and himself to survive until they are rescued.

   G Paulo must search the island for his parents.

   H Paulo has to find a way to get back to the boat.

   J Paulo has to build a shelter for Carla and himself as quickly as possible.

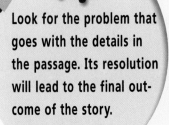

> **Tip**
>
> Look for the problem that goes with the details in the passage. Its resolution will lead to the final outcome of the story.

A CHANGING PLANET

CONTENTS

▲ Everglades

Vocabulary Power

plenitude

pondered

scurried

peninsula

multitude

eons

Our world is filled with a variety of fascinating places. In the selection "Everglades," you will read about one special place and how it has changed over time. These photographs show some other fascinating parts of the world.

From high above, it is easy to see that the world has a **plenitude** of, or more than enough, water. Have you ever **pondered**, or carefully thought about, the importance of water to all forms of life? Sea creatures are not the only ones that depend on it. Land dwellers of all kinds, from the mighty dinosaurs to the tiniest creatures that **scurried** about or ran quickly, have needed water to live.

The land area that looks like a giant boot jutting into the water is the country of Italy. Italy is a **peninsula**, a piece of land nearly surrounded by water and joined to a larger land mass.

There are a great number of islands, a **multitude** of them, in the Caribbean Sea. How will this part of the world look **eons** from now? Will some of the islands have disappeared or changed shape hundreds of thousands of years in the future?

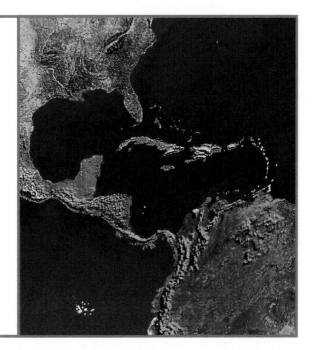

Vocabulary-Writing CONNECTION

If you could travel **eons** into the future, what do you think you would find? Write a paragraph predicting what you might see.

EVER

Genre

Informational Text

Informational text gives information, but the people and events might not be real.

In this selection, look for

- **Elements of fiction and nonfiction**

- **Descriptive language that helps readers picture the setting**

GLADES

BY JEAN CRAIGHEAD GEORGE • PAINTINGS BY WENDELL MINOR

The storyteller poled the children under arching trees into a sunny water glade. He sat down and leaned toward them.

"I am going to tell you a story," he said. "It is not a story about a person or a mythical creature. It is not even a story about an animal."

The children looked at each other and waited.

"It's a story about a river." He swung his arms in a wide circle. "This river, the miraculous Everglades of Florida.

"My story will be different from any you have heard, because this river is like no other river on Earth. There is only one Everglades."

The children leaned forward. He began.

First there was sunshine on a blue-green sea.

It was the Age of the Seashells.

The seashells formed a rock called limestone on the sea bottom. Over the eons the sea lowered, and the rock became land. The long Florida peninsula took shape in warm, sunny waters.

Purple clouds, flashing with lightning, roiled and boomed above the land. Rain gushed from the storm clouds in summer. Sun bathed the land in winter. Moss grew, then ferns, then grass and trees.

The rain eroded holes in the soft limestone and filled them with water. Florida glistened with green land and blue-green lakes.

One was Lake Okeechobee, round, deep, and as clear as window glass.

Lake Okeechobee filled to its brim and spilled over. The spill became a river that seeped one hundred miles down the peninsula from Lake Okeechobee to the Florida Bay. It was fifty miles wide and only six inches deep in most places.

This river did not chortle and splash. It did not crash over falls and race. It was a slow river that gleamed like quicksilver. We know it today as the Everglades.

Into the shallow, warm river came tiny one-celled animals and plants. They lived and died and made gray-green soil on the bottom of the river. Saw grass took root in the soil.

The grass prospered. When the winds blew, the saw grass clattered like a trillion swords. Each sword was edged with cutting spines. Of the larger animals, only the leathery alligator could walk unharmed among the terrible spears of the saw grass.

Around the stems of the grass scurried the young of insects, and tiny crabs and snails. Little fish found these to be excellent eating. Turtles and alligators found the fish to be excellent eating. Every wild thing ate well, and there was still an enormous abundance.

To the abundance came the birds. Clouds of lacy, white egrets made their home in the Everglades.

Every day a blizzard of wood storks dropped into the grass and dined on the snails, crabs, bugs, and fish.

A profusion of pink flamingos hunted in the shallow mudflats.

Hundreds of miles of roseate spoonbills vacuumed the ponds and shallows with their sievelike bills.

A myriad of little songbirds fluttered through the trees that grew on the islands in the river of saw grass.

Quantities of alligators roamed the grass and dug pools for their young. Into their pools came fish and turtles, herons and anhingas, and billions of frogs, snakes, and snails.

A multitude of panthers, raccoons, deer, and otter came to the river. They made their homes on the beautiful islands.

A plenitude of orchids bloomed and turned the island trees into colorful cathedral windows.

A plethora of lizards and anoles clambered over the orchids, and two thousand kinds of plants, including palms, vines, bushes, grasses, and trees.

When all were in place, the Everglades was a living kaleidoscope of color and beauty. It glittered with orchids, grass, trees, birds, panthers, raccoons, snakes, mosquitoes, fish–all things large and small that make the Earth beautiful.

The storyteller paused. The children looked around and pondered. The storyteller went on:

When the Everglades was perfect, people who called themselves Calusas arrived. They lived gracefully on the fish and game and made tools out of seashells.

The Spanish conquistadors arrived, and the Calusa people disappeared.

The conquistadors were afraid of the flesh-ripping grass and roaring animals of the Everglades, and they moved on.

North of Florida, European men pushed the Creek Indians out of the Carolinas. Some of them walked south until they came to the silvery Everglades. They poled deep into the saw grass and settled on the islands. They are the Seminole Indians. A few of them live here today.

The storyteller paused. The children looked around.

"Where are the clouds of egrets?" a child asked.

The hunters shot them by the tens of thousands and sold the feathers to decorate women's hats. Only a few survived the slaughter.

"Where are the quantities of alligators?" another child asked.

The hunters shot them by the acres and sold their gleaming hides to make wallets and shoes. Only a few remain.

"Where did the cathedral windows of orchids go?" a third child asked.

The orchid hunters picked gardens and gardens of them and sold them to put on ladies' dresses. Practically none can be found.

Another child looked around. "And where did the mammals and snails and one-celled plants and animals go?"

They vanished when the engineers dug canals in the Everglades and drained the fresh water into the sea to make land. Farmers tilled the land; businesspeople built towns and roads upon it. Pesticides and fertilizers flowed into the river waters and poisoned the one-celled animals and plants. The snails died, the fish died, the mammals and birds died.

"But this is a sad story," said a fifth child. "Please tell us a happy story."

The storyteller picked up his pole and quietly skimmed the dugout canoe across the water and down a trail in the saw grass. Then he sat down and told the children a new story.

Five children and a storyteller poled into the Everglades.

Eventually the children grew up and ran the Earth.

The clouds of birds returned to an abundance of fish in the water. The flowers tumbled into bloom. Quantities of alligators bellowed through the saw grass again. A multitude of panthers, deer, raccoons, and otters cavorted on the islands.

"That's a much better story," said the children. "Now pole us home quickly so we can grow up."

Think and Respond

➊ How have the Everglades changed over the **eons**?

➋ Why do you think the author created the characters of the storyteller and the children?

➌ What do the children mean when they ask to go home so they can grow up?

➍ Do you agree with the children that the second story is much better than the first one? Explain.

➎ What reading strategies did you use to help you understand "Everglades"? When did you use them?

Meet the Author
Jean Craighead George

Born into a family of nature lovers, Jean Craighead George learned about nature on weekend camping trips in the woods near Washington, D.C. Her first wild pet was a turkey vulture. Since then she has had more than 172 other wild animals as pets. These animals have always been free to come and go. Some of them have even gone into her books as characters.

Jean Craighead George began writing in the third grade, and she hasn't stopped since. She has written more than 100 books, including the 1973 Newbery Award winner *Julie of the Wolves*. She says, "I write for children. Children are still in love with the wonders of nature, and I am, too. I tell them stories about a boy and a falcon, about a girl and an elegant wolf pack, about owls, weasels, foxes, prairie dogs, the alpine tundra, the tropical rain forest. When the telling is done, I hope they will want to protect all the beautiful creatures and places."

Meet the Illustrator
Wendell Minor

Wendell Minor attended the Ringling School of Art and Design in Sarasota, Florida. After graduation, he began creating original art for book publishers in New York City. His illustrations have decorated the covers of 2,000 books, including *Julie's Wolf Pack* by Jean Craighead George.

Wendell Minor draws on his love of the environment to create illustrations for children's books. He hopes to inspire children to go out into nature and see wildlife in its natural state. He wants all children to know about the great beauty that exists in the world.

Visit *The Learning Site!*
www.harcourtschool.com

▲ Everglades

Making Connections

Compare Texts

1. Why does "Everglades" belong in a theme called A Changing Planet?

2. When and how does the tone of the storyteller's story change?

3. How is the illustration on page 264 different from the other illustrations in "Everglades"?

4. In what ways is "Everglades" like a nonfiction selection? In what ways is it like a fiction selection?

5. Where could you learn more about a particular plant, insect, bird, or animal mentioned in "Everglades"?

Write a New Ending

At the end of "Everglades," the children want to go home quickly so they can grow up. What do you think these five children might do when they are adults to help restore the Everglades? Write a new ending to the story, telling the changes the children make when they grow up. Use a graphic like this one to organize your ideas.

Writing CONNECTION

What changes do they make?	How do they make each change?

Make a Diagram

Choose one of the many plants or creatures that you read about in "Everglades." Research the conditions it needs to grow and thrive. Make a diagram or chart that shows how the plant or creature fits into the ecosystem of the Everglades.

Make a Poster

The storyteller in "Everglades" mentions three groups of people who came to the Everglades long ago—the Calusas, the Spanish conquistadors, and the Seminole Indians. Do research to find out more about one of these groups. Use an encyclopedia, a social studies text, other non-fiction books, or the Internet to find out who they were, where they came from, what impact they had, and what happened to them. Create a poster display to share the information you find.

FLORIDA

▲ Everglades

Prefixes, Suffixes, and Roots

You can often figure out or clarify the meaning of unfamiliar words by using what you know about the meaning of prefixes, suffixes, root words, and roots.

Look at the examples below.

Prefix + Root Word	uni (one)	+ form (shape)	=	uniform (constant)
Prefix + Root Word	un (not)	+ harmed (injured)	=	unharmed (not injured)
Root Word + Suffix	miracle (wonder)	+ ous (full of)	=	miraculous (full of wonder)
Root + Root	centi (hundred)	+ ped (foot)	=	centipede (wormlike creature that may have a hundred or more legs)
Root + Root Word	aqua (water)	+ marine (having to do with the sea)	=	aquamarine (blue green, like sea water)

Visit *The Learning Site!*
www.harcourtschool.com

See *Skills* and *Activities*

Test Prep
Prefixes, Suffixes, and Roots

▶ **Read the paragraph. Then answer the questions.**

> A group of children gained great insight as they listened to a <u>chronicle</u> of the Everglades. They were saddened to learn that humans, <u>incautious</u> of their actions, had practically eliminated certain plants and animals that had lived in the Everglades for centuries. The children made a promise to work to preserve the Everglades for future generations.

1. The word *cautious* means "careful." What is the meaning of <u>incautious</u>?

   A careless

   B showing attention

   C taking your time

   D concerned

Tip

Identify the prefix at the beginning of *incautious* and think about its meaning.

2. The root *chron* means "time." What does the word <u>chronicle</u> mean?

   F musical instrument

   G place where wildlife lives

   H history of events over time

   J sad song about nature

Tip

This word contains the Greek root *chron*. Choose the word meaning that is related to the meaning of the root.

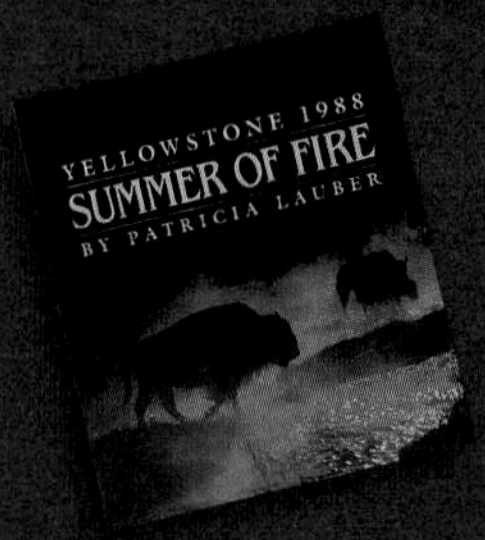

Vocabulary Power

The sound of fire engines racing to a fire makes everyone's heart beat a little faster. This newspaper article tells about a fire that could happen in almost any town or city.

tinder

policy

geyser

veered

canopy

dwindled

embers

Fire Burns
Local Business

A major fire nearly burned a local warehouse to the ground last night. Firefighters believe that the fire at the Potter and Sons warehouse began in an area where old papers were stored. "Dry materials such as paper can act as **tinder** to start a fire," Fire Chief Vern Wilson said. "All it takes is a single spark."

The chief added that it is not a good **policy**, or plan of action, to store old papers in an open area.

The firefighters directed a huge spray at the blaze. It looked like a **geyser**, the fountain of water that shoots up from a natural spring. Then the wind suddenly changed direction.

When it **veered**, it began blowing the water from the hoses right back at the firefighters.

They continued fighting the fire into the night, with the sky now a **canopy** of stars over their heads. Little by little, the fire **dwindled**, steadily becoming smaller. By dawn, the flames had finally died out, and only faintly glowing **embers** remained.

Vocabulary–Writing CONNECTION

Develop a step-by-step fire-drill **policy** for your school or classroom.

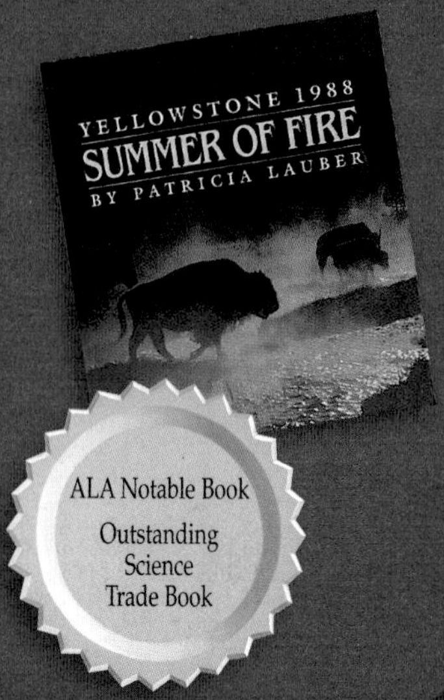

Genre

Nonfiction

Nonfiction tells about people, things, events, or places that are real.

In this selection, look for

- **Events in time-order**

- **Photographs with captions**

- **An interesting historical event**

SUMMER of FIRE

PATRICIA LAUBER

In the summer drought of 1988
lightning strikes started wildfires
across the northern Rockies.

*T*he summer of 1988 was hot and dry in much of the United States. Above plains and prairies, the sun blazed out of an ever blue sky, baking fields and withering crops. Ponds and streams dried up. Rivers shrank. In places the very earth cracked open as underground water supplies dwindled away.

Farther west, forests were tinder dry. Sometimes skies grew dark with storm clouds. Thunder growled and lightning crackled, but little rain fell. Lightning strikes started forest fires that raged across the Rockies and other ranges with the roar of jumbo jets on takeoff. Night skies turned red and yellow where flames soared 300 feet into the air. Smoke, carried on the winds, darkened skies as far away as Spokane and Minneapolis–St. Paul. Airline passengers, flying high above the fires, could smell the smoke. Before the rains and snows of autumn came, 2,600,000 acres had burned in the West and Alaska, an area twice the size of Delaware.

In Yellowstone the fire season started on May 24, when lightning struck a tree in the northeastern part of the park. The fire stayed small. Rain fell later in the day and put it out. That was what usually happened. In Yellowstone, winters are long and cold, summers short and often rainy. Many people thought you couldn't set fire to the forest if you tried.

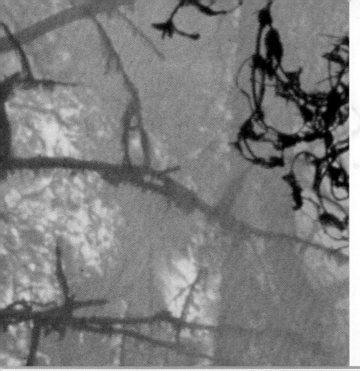

On June 23 lightning started a fire near Shoshone Lake in the southern part of the park. On June 25 another bolt of lightning started a fire in the northwest. These fires did not go out, and no one tried to put them out. Park policy was to let wildfires burn unless they threatened lives or property. Also, there seemed no reason to worry about the fires. Although winters in the 1980s had been dry, with little snow, summers had been unusually wet. The summer of 1988 was expected to be wet too.

But in 1988 the rains of summer did not come. The Shoshone and other fires blazed and spread. By mid-July, 8,600 acres had burned. Park officials decided that all fires should be put out, no matter whether they were wildfires or caused by human carelessness.

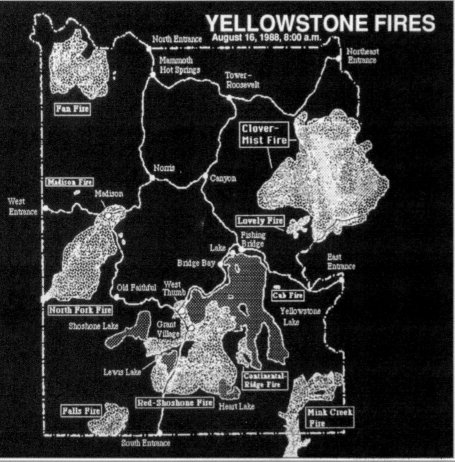

YELLOWSTONE FIRES
August 16, 1988, 8:00 a.m.

North Entrance
Northeast Entrance
Mammoth Hot Springs
Tower-Roosevelt
Fan Fire
Clover-Mist Fire
Norris
Canyon
Madison Fire
Madison
West Entrance
Lovely Fire
Fishing Bridge
Lake
Bridge Bay
East Entrance
Old Faithful
West Thumb
Cub Fire
North Fork Fire
Shoshone Lake
Grant Village
Yellowstone Lake
Lewis Lake
Continental Ridge Fire
Falls Fire
Red-Shoshone Fire
Heart Lake
Mink Creek Fire
South Entrance

Flames raced through the forests when rain failed to come.

Fire fighters arrived by the hundreds to attack fires from the ground. Helicopters and airplanes attacked from above. But new fires started in the park. In 1988 Yellowstone had more than 50 lightning strikes, twice the normal number. Fires in neighboring national forests swept into the park. Old fires burned on. And still the rains did not come.

Cold fronts passed through, bringing winds of hurricane force with gusts of 60 to 80 miles an hour. Winds whipped and spread the fires and fed them oxygen, which fires must have to keep burning. Big fires met, merged, and became even bigger fires. In forests flames galloped through the tops, or crowns, of trees, through the canopy. Snags—dead trees that are still standing—burned like Roman candles. Boulders exploded in the heat. Sheets of flame leaped forward. Gigantic clouds of smoke ringed the horizon, looking like thunderheads, only bigger. There were days when the sun was no brighter than a full moon.

Fire fighters could put out small blazes . . . but they were helpless in the face of the big ones.

Fires jumped rivers, roads, canyons, parking lots. Glowing embers, some the size of a man's fist, shot a mile or more ahead, starting new fires. Flames were roaring through the park at a rate of four or five miles a day. One fire ran 14 miles in only four hours. On August 20, a day known as Black Saturday, more than 150,000 acres burned inside the park and in neighboring forests. The 2,000 fire fighters could no more put out these fires than they could have stopped a hurricane. But what they could do was defend the park communities—the information centers and the buildings where people slept, ate, and shopped.

By September 6 fire fighters were moving in to defend the area around the park's most famous geyser, Old Faithful. The geyser itself could not be harmed by fire, but the buildings around it could. One of them, the Old Faithful Inn, was the world's largest log building. Now one of the eight major fires in the park was bearing down on it.

Called the North Fork fire, it had started in the Targhee National Forest on July 22, when a careless woodcutter threw away a lighted cigarette. Driven by shifting winds, the fire raced into Yellowstone, turned back into Targhee, neared the town of West Yellowstone,

Flames rocketed into the crowns of trees.

then veered back into the park. There it jumped roads and rivers, snarling its way through the crossroads at Madison on August 15. By the afternoon of September 7 it was approaching Old Faithful. Long before they could see the flames, fire fighters heard the fire's deep rumble and saw a churning wall of dark smoke towering skyward.

Planes dropped chemicals to damp down fires. On the ground weary fire fighters were wetting down buildings.

The fire came on, a mass of red flames whipped by winds gusting up to 50 miles an hour. Sparks and embers were everywhere, flying over the inn, parking lots, and geyser, and setting fire to the woods beyond. At the last moment the wind shifted and the fire turned to the northeast, away from Old Faithful.

Saturday, September 10, began as another bad day. One arm of the North Fork fire was threatening park headquarters at Mammoth Hot Springs, and another arm was a quarter of a mile from Tower Junction. The forecast was for winds of up to 60 miles an hour. But the sky was thick with clouds, and the temperature was falling.

By early afternoon, September 10 had turned into a day of hope. Rain was drenching the area around Old Faithful. The next morning snow blew along the streets of West Yellowstone. It sifted through blackened forests and dusted herds of bison and elk. Scattered islands of fire would burn until November blanketed them in snow. But the worst was over.

At long last the summer of fire had ended. During it, eight major fires and many smaller ones had burned in Yellowstone. To people who had watched the fires on television news, it seemed the park must lie in ruins. But this was not so. The geysers, steam vents, and hot springs were unharmed. Park communities had been saved. Nearly two thirds of the park had not even been touched by fire.

Long hours of hard work tired the women and men who fought the fires.

Pockets of flames and embers continued to burn after the worst was over.

It was true that many once-green areas were now black and gray. Yet it was also true that they were not ruined. Instead, they were beginning again, starting over, as they had many times in the past. Fire has always been part of the Yellowstone region. Wildfire has shaped the landscape and renewed it. Yellowstone needs fire, just as it needs sun and rain, and its plants have developed ways of surviving fire.

Finally the snows of November put an end to the fires.

Think and Respond

❶ In what way was the summer of 1988 different from other summers at Yellowstone?

❷ How do the pictures and captions help you better understand the story?

❸ How do the author's descriptions help you understand what happened?

❹ Do you think the park's **policy** on wildfires makes sense? Why or why not?

❺ How did you use reading strategies to help you understand this selection?

MEET THE AUTHOR

PATRICIA LAUBER

How did you gather information to write a book like
Summer of Fire?

When I am thinking about writing a book,
I start by reading everything I can find on the subject.
Then, if possible, I like to go and see the place
for myself. That was why I visited
Yellowstone National Park the summer
after the big fires.

**What did you discover on your visit
to the park?**

The fire wasn't the disaster it seemed
on television. Yellowstone has long, cold
winters and short summers. In these conditions,
decay takes place slowly and dead matter piles up. A
forest fire is nature's housekeeper. It releases nutrients
locked up in dead matter and makes them available again
to plants.

Even though I knew how nature worked, I was surprised
to see how quickly life had returned to the burned areas.
Wildflowers were in bloom. Meadows were green. New trees
and shrubs were sprouting. Scientists were busy studying how
some forms of life helped out others. Yellowstone Park was a
showcase of how nature takes care of itself.

Visit *The Learning Site!*
www.harcourtschool.com

287

The noise of the plane's engines is deafening. So is the wind, which rushes past the open door at 110 miles an hour. Inside, men and women wait, taking deep breaths. Then . . . they jump! After five tense seconds their parachutes open. They float to the ground, and everything is perfectly calm—for now.

Smoke Jum

Wherever fires erupt and vehicles cannot reach—that's where you'll find smoke jumpers. They parachute into remote mountain wilderness throughout the western United States, including Alaska. Their mission: to prevent small wildfires from growing into large ones. Employed by the Forest Service and the Bureau of Land Management, smoke jumpers have been fighting fires since 1940.

Smoke jumpers land close to a forest fire. They work to prevent the fire from spreading. They rely on obstacles such as rivers, creeks, lakes, and logging roads to help contain the fire. Sometimes they dig a fire line—a dirt path several feet wide through the surrounding vegetation. Their goal is to let the fire burn out while keeping it from reaching the treetops. If it does reach the treetops, there is no way to put out the fire from the ground. A plane carrying fire retardant might be called in to help.

Once the fire is out, smoke jumpers watch for smoke and feel chunks of timber. They must make sure that no areas are still hot. They call this part of their job mopping up.

Smoke jumpers spend sleepless nights listening to a forest fire roaring in the distance. They breathe thick smoke, work up a terrible sweat, and get covered by dirt and ash. At the end of a mission, smoke jumpers have aching bodies. They may face a 20-mile hike to get home. Smoke jumpers have a dangerous but vital job—they save millions of acres of forestland every year.

by Janice Koch

Learning to Leap and Land

Jump to It!

Rookie smoke jumpers practice the correct way to land. When they hit the ground, smoke jumpers roll. This distributes the shock of the landing over the entire body.

Stepping Out

A future smoke jumper leaps from a four-story tower. The proper exit technique prevents a smoke jumper from getting tangled in the parachute or hitting the side of the plane.

Wet Landing

In a swimming pool smoke jumpers learn how to free themselves from their parachutes. A gust of wind can carry smoke jumpers over a lake —a dangerous place to land with open parachutes.

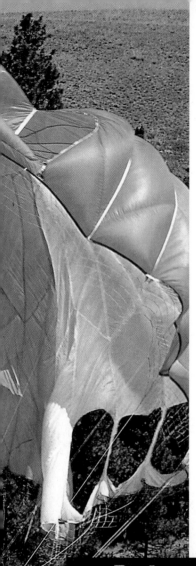

All Geared Up and Ready to Go

Smoke jumper Margarita Phillips is well suited to fight a fire. Smoke jumpers put together and repair their own gear—except for their boots and helmets. The equipment Phillips jumps with weighs 85 pounds.

Jumpsuit
The heavily padded jumpsuit is made of the same material as bulletproof vests worn by police officers. Smoke jumpers wear fire-resistant clothing underneath.

Reserve Chute
If the main parachute does not open, the reserve chute gets pulled into service.

Pack-Out Bag
Tucked away in a jumpsuit, this bag is empty at first. Most fire fighting equipment is dropped to the ground in a separate container. Once a fire is out, a smoke jumper puts the equipment in the bag so it can be carried out.

Crosscut Saw
Dropped to the ground in a cargo box, the saw is used to clear timber and branches from a fire line. Here the saw is bent over the pack-out bag and its teeth are covered.

Main Parachute
Within five seconds of leaving the plane, a smoke jumper's parachute opens. It is carried inside a backpack.

Static Line
A yellow nylon strap connects the main parachute to a cable inside the plane. The strap helps pull open the chute, which then disconnects.

Helmet
A motorcycle helmet has a protective metal face guard.

Leg Pockets
Inside go candy bars, long johns, and the "bird's nest"—looped nylon strap (shown on top of the pack-out bag) that smoke jumpers use to descend if they land in a tree. Also inside are signal streamers for communicating with the pilot from the ground.

Rocky Touchdown
A mountain slope presents a challenge to a smoke jumper. This one landed face down. Knowing how to land on different kinds of terrain —thick forests, steep hills, lakes— is an essential smoke jumper skill.

Think and Respond

How are smoke jumpers and traditional fire fighters alike? How are they different?

▲ Summer of Fire

Making Connections

Compare Texts

1. What do readers learn from "Summer of Fire" about the changes caused by wildfires?

2. Looking at the photographs in this selection, would you think the fires were a good thing or a bad thing for Yellowstone? How does the text influence your opinion?

3. How is the focus of the article "Smoke Jumpers" different from the focus of "Summer of Fire"?

4. Think of another nonfiction selection you have read. Does the author write in a style similar to Patricia Lauber's, or are the styles of the two authors different? Explain your answer.

5. Where could you find more information about Yellowstone National Park?

Write Interview Questions

What challenges do firefighters face in your own community? Work with a group to write five or six questions you would like to ask. Then make arrangements to interview a firefighter in your community. Use a K-W-L chart to organize your thoughts.

Writing CONNECTION

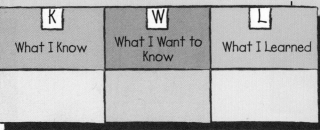

K What I Know	W What I Want to Know	L What I Learned

Make a Model or Diagram

In "Summer of Fire," you learned that Yellowstone's geysers were not harmed by the fires. Do research about geysers to find out where they are found, what they are, and why they erupt. You might find information in a print or online encyclopedia, on science websites for students, or in a science text book. Share the results of your research by constructing a model of a geyser or by drawing a diagram.

Science CONNECTION

Write a Summary Report

Every year forest fires destroy thousands of acres of national forest land. Use a print or online encyclopedia to find information on forest fires. Write a summary report listing the total acres burned in several different areas of the United States for a particular year.

Social Studies CONNECTION

Graphic Aids

Focus Skill

Maps, charts, diagrams, and graphs are examples of **graphic aids** that help you "see" and understand information in a selection.

The map in "Summer of Fire" shows all of Yellowstone National Park. Using the map, you were able to locate the Yellowstone fires mentioned in the text and visually track their movement.

Look at the following graphic, which makes comparisons about the fires of 1988.

Fires in Yellowstone National Park and Surrounding Forests		
Time Period	**Location**	**Acres Burned**
1972-1987 (fifteen years)	Inside Yellowstone	33,000 (Fires allowed to go out on their own)
Summer of 1988 (less than one year)	Inside Yellowstone	800,000

Maps, graphs, and charts can be used to support or clarify the information in a text. They can also be used to supply additional information. Paying careful attention to the key and symbols on a map, the headings on a chart, and the labels on a graph will help you interpret facts and numbers accurately.

Visit *The Learning Site!*
www.harcourtschool.com

See *Skills* and *Activities*

Test Prep

Graphic Aids

▶ **Study the map from a campground pamphlet. Then answer the questions.**

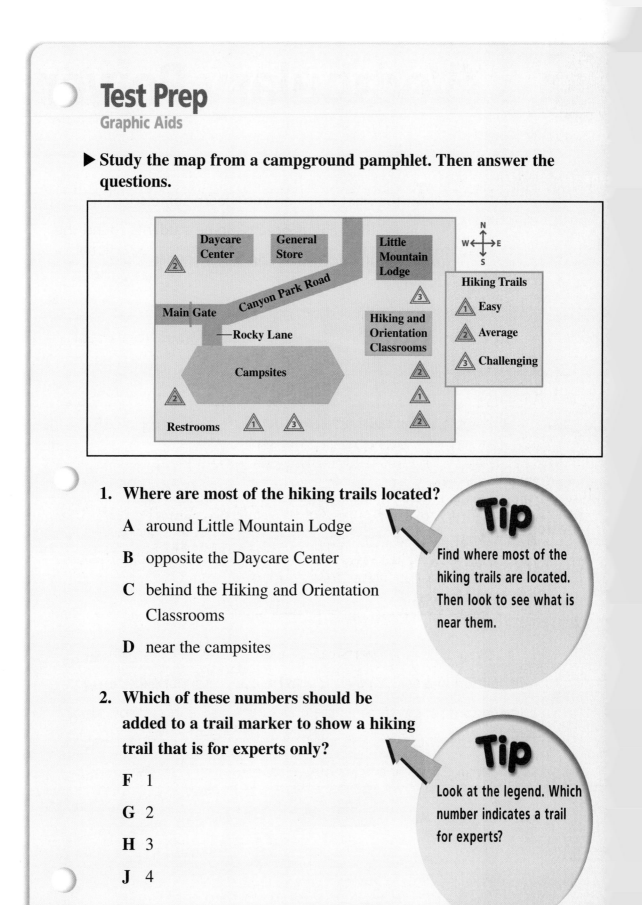

1. **Where are most of the hiking trails located?**

   A around Little Mountain Lodge

   B opposite the Daycare Center

   C behind the Hiking and Orientation Classrooms

   D near the campsites

   Tip

   Find where most of the hiking trails are located. Then look to see what is near them.

2. **Which of these numbers should be added to a trail marker to show a hiking trail that is for experts only?**

   F 1

   G 2

   H 3

   J 4

   Tip

   Look at the legend. Which number indicates a trail for experts?

Vocabulary Power

▲ Oceans

energy

generated

inlet

shallow

bulge

gravitational

In the next selection you'll learn some scientific information about oceans. Some students found the following information on other science topics.

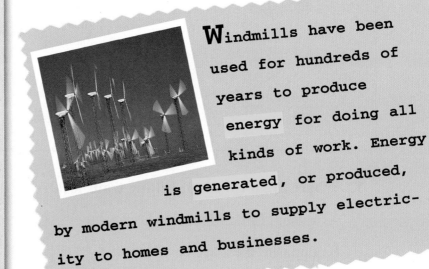

Windmills have been used for hundreds of years to produce **energy** for doing all kinds of work. Energy is **generated**, or produced, by modern windmills to supply electricity to homes and businesses.

This body of water is an **inlet**, a narrow strip of water leading into land. The water is deep enough for small boats, but it is too **shallow** for large ships.

Why are the shapes of the balls different? The ball on the left has a bulge, or part that swells outward. The weight of the girl is forcing some of the air to the sides. Another type of force is gravity. Gravitational force is the force by which any two objects pull toward each other. This force explains why the pull of the moon moves the ocean tides on Earth.

Vocabulary–Writing CONNECTION

Write a list of things that you can do to save **energy**.

297

OCEANS

Genre

Expository Nonfiction

Expository nonfiction presents and explains information or ideas.

In this selection, look for

- Photographs and illustrations with captions

- A text structure that is organized by main ideas and supporting details

E A N S

by Seymour Simon

Earth is different from any other planet or moon in the Solar System: It is the only one with liquid water on its surface. In fact, more than 70 percent of the earth's surface is covered by oceans. Although we speak of the Atlantic and Pacific as separate oceans, the world is really covered by a single body of water in which the continents are islands.

The Tides

If you visit the shore, you'll soon notice the daily rise and fall of the water, which we call tides. Tides are caused by the gravitational pull of the moon and the sun. Even though the moon is much smaller than the sun, the moon is so much closer to the earth that its pull is much stronger. As the earth rotates, the ocean waters nearest the moon are pulled outward in a traveling bulge called high tide. There is also a traveling tidal bulge on the side of the earth opposite the moon. Here, the moon's pull on the waters is less, so there is a second high tide. Because of the double tidal bulges, most places on the coast have two high and two low tides every twenty-four hours and fifty minutes.

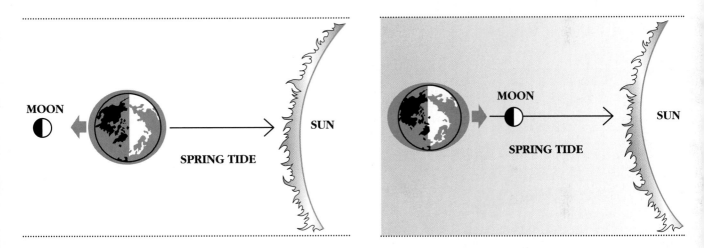

Twice a month, when the sun and the moon are lined up with the earth, their gravitational pulls combine and produce the biggest tides, called spring tides. The sun and moon also pull at right angles to each other twice a month. Then we get the smallest tides, called neap tides.

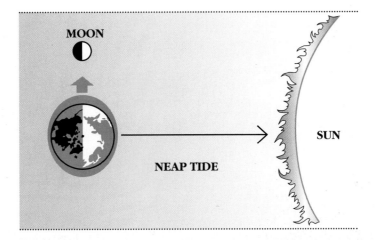

Even in places close together, tides do not always occur at the same time or have the same size. The time and size of the tides depend upon the shape of the shore and the width of the gulfs and bays. Think of an ocean as a kind of large, shallow pan of water sloshing back and forth. The water in the middle of the ocean moves up and down very little. The water at each end of the oceans moves up and down much more. Because of this, islands in the middle of the ocean, such as Hawaii, often have small tides compared to the lands around the edges of an ocean.

If a tide can spread out, such as in the wide Gulf of Mexico, it may rise and fall only a few inches a day. When the tide cannot spread out, the tides are much greater. The photos show an inlet in the narrow Bay of Fundy in Nova Scotia, where high tide may be fifty feet higher than low tide.

Waves

The waves commonly called tidal waves really have no connection with the daily tides. The name scientists use for this kind of wave is tsunami, pronounced SUE-nami, a Japanese word for sea wave. A tsunami is generated by a violent undersea earthquake or volcanic explosion. The shock forms a wave that can move across an ocean at five hundred miles per hour, as fast as a jet plane. In the open ocean, a tsunami is only two or three feet high and hardly noticeable; but when it approaches a shore, a tsunami may build up to a huge size and hit with the force of a runaway train.

These three photos show the arrival of a tsunami on the shores of the island of Oahu, Hawaii. The tsunami was generated by an earthquake 2,500 miles away in the Aleutian Islands, Alaska. This tsunami resulted in over fifty deaths and much property damage.

When the wind blows across the surface of ocean waters, little ripples form. As the wind continues to blow, the ripples grow into waves. The size of a wave depends upon the speed of the wind, how long it blows, and the fetch. The fetch is the distance over which the wave travels. The faster the wind, the longer it blows, and the greater the fetch, the bigger the waves.

In the open ocean, where the wind is blowing and making waves, the waves are all different sizes and shapes and go in different directions. As the waves move away from where they began, some travel faster than others and they form groups of about the same wavelength. The waves are now long and smooth and are called a swell.

Waves moving across the ocean carry the energy of the wind, but the ocean water does not move along with the wave. As the wave passes, the particles of water move up and down and around in a little circle. If you watch a stick floating on water as waves pass by, you'll see that it bobs up and down but stays in just about the same place. Only the energy of the waves moves forward.

The high spot of a wave is called a crest and the low spot is called a trough. The distance between two crests (or two troughs) is called the wavelength. The height of a wave is the distance from crest to trough.

Storm-driven waves in the ocean can build up to great heights. The largest wave on record was 112 feet high, the height of a ten-story building. Oceangoing ships can ride over most waves. Small ships can ride up one side of a wave and down the other. Large ships can usually ride through waves without too much difficulty. During a hurricane or severe storm, however, a huge wave can dump hundreds of tons of water onto a ship in a few seconds, smashing it apart and sending it to the bottom.

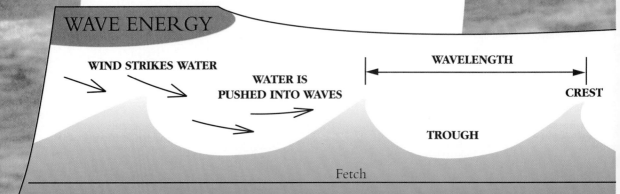

WAVE ENERGY

WIND STRIKES WATER

WATER IS
PUSHED INTO WAVES

WAVELENGTH

CREST

TROUGH

Fetch

CRESTS RUSH FORWARD AS BREAKERS

BASE OF WAVES STRIKES OCEAN FLOOR AND SLOWS DOWN

When an ocean wave reaches the shallow water of shore, it begins to travel more slowly and its shape begins to change. Some people say that "the wave begins to feel the bottom." Waves begin to pile up and grow higher as those in the back come in faster than those in the front are moving.

As the waves slow down, the crest of the wave tries to continue at the same speed, until finally it topples over into the trough of the wave in front and becomes a breaker.

When waves break on the shore, the surf begins. Sometimes surf can break just a few yards from shore. However, if the shore is shallow, surf can form hundreds of yards out to sea. The waves on shallow beaches, such as this one in Hawaii, spill over slowly as they roll up the shore.

Even rocky coastlines are worn away by the power of the surf. The softer kinds of rock are worn away first, leaving rocky spires or platforms of harder rock. These, too, will eventually be worn down by the pounding of the waves. In other places, the incoming surf carries sand particles from one spot to another, slowly building up beaches and dunes. Every moment of every day, the sea is at work reshaping the land.

Think and Respond

1. Why is it important for us to learn about the oceans?

2. How does the author help you understand the scientific facts in this selection?

3. Are tidal waves **generated** in the same way as regular ocean waves? Explain.

4. Would you like to read other selections by this author? Why or why not?

5. What reading strategies did you use to help you understand "Oceans"? When did you use them?

Seymour Simon

I taught science for twenty-three years, and often I couldn't find the right book on a topic I wanted to teach. So I began to write my own books. I try to write the way I talk when I'm teaching and actually talking to students. I want to explain *why* and *how* something happens, not just *what* happens.

If you take a walk and *really* look, listen, and feel the world around you, it can be a strange experience. You begin to observe things you never paid much attention to. You begin to wonder about things that you've seen thousands of times—clouds, trees, rocks, machines. You ask questions: Does that dark cloud mean that it is going to rain? Why do some leaves turn red in the fall, while others turn yellow? What kind of rock has glittery little specks in it? How is an airplane able to fly? These kinds of questions, and the questions my students asked me, prompted me to write science books. My books are full of questions.

**Visit *The Learning Site!*
www.harcourtschool.com**

CLIMATE AND SEASONS

From **Guide to Weather**

A photographic journey through the skies

by Michael Allaby

If you took a journey from the north pole to the equator, you would discover that there are different patterns of weather around the world. At the north pole the Sun is always low in the sky (except in winter, when it never rises) and the weather is very cold and clear. As you travel south the Sun gets higher and the weather warmer. At the equator the Sun is directly overhead at midday and the weather is hot and humid. The warm air absorbs a lot of moisture from the oceans, which means frequent rain. Weather also depends on the time of year. Toward the poles there are warm and cold seasons, while nearer the equator it is warm all year but there may be wet and dry seasons.

▲
Equatorial climates like that in the Amazon rain forest are warm all year round and receive a lot of rain.

▲
Temperate climates like that in Europe have mild weather and hot and cold seasons.

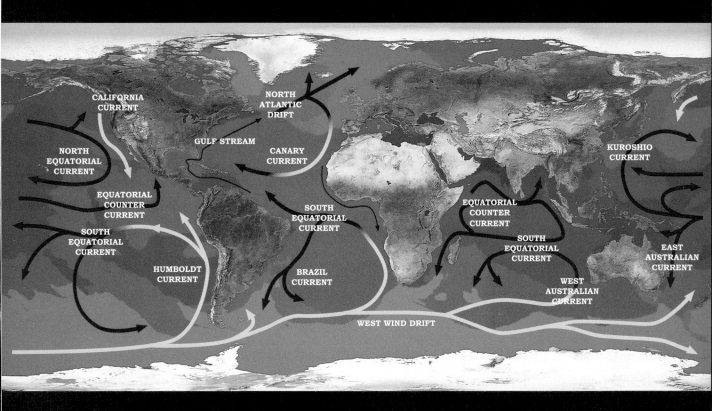

Surface ocean currents are shown here in blue (cold water) and red (warm water). Besides these surface currents, there is a very deep, cold current called the Atlantic conveyor, which takes 1,000 years to circulate from Greenland to Australia and back.

WEATHER AND THE SEA

Oceans have an enormous influence on the weather. Water acts as a heat store, absorbing the Sun's warmth near the equator and carrying it toward the poles in ocean currents, which are driven by the wind. For instance, the Gulf Stream, which carries warm water from the Caribbean to western Europe, makes British winters very mild. The warm, moist air associated with the Gulf Stream increases rainfall, so British summers are often overcast. In each ocean the currents form a giant circle, with cold water generally flowing along the western coasts of continents and warm water along the eastern coasts.

Although the poles have many hours of daylight in summer, the Sun's rays are weak because they fall on land obliquely, like a flashlight held at an angle. As a result, the climate is always cold.

CLIMATE

The pattern of weather that a country experiences through the year is known as its climate. The coldest climates are found at the poles, the driest in deserts, and the wettest near the equator, where tropical rain forests flourish in constantly warm and rainy weather. Europe and North America have a temperate climate, with distinct warm and cold seasons. A country's climate depends not just on how far it is from the equator, but also on how close it is to the sea. Central Asia has a very dry climate because it is very far from the sea.

Deserts occur wherever rainfall is very low. They may be hot, such as the Sahara, or cold, such as the Gobi.

SUNNY SIDE UP

Earth spins on a tilted axis as it orbits the Sun. Because of this, first one pole is turned toward the Sun and then the other, and this is what causes seasons. In June the northern hemisphere gets the most sunlight, bringing summer weather to Europe, Asia, and North America. In December it is summer in the southern hemisphere. The equator always receives plenty of sunlight, so it stays hot and sunny all year round.

Spring

Summer

Autumn

Winter

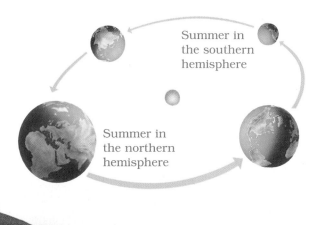

Summer in the southern hemisphere

Summer in the northern hemisphere

Think and Respond

If you took a journey from the North Pole to the equator, what would the weather be like on your trip?

Making Connections

Compare Texts

1. Why is the selection "Oceans" included in a theme about our changing planet?

2. Why does the author include information in three different forms—text, photographs, and diagrams?

3. How are the selections "Oceans" and "Climate and Seasons" alike? How are they different?

4. Compare "Oceans" with another nonfiction selection you have read. Does one selection present its information more clearly than the other, or are the two selections equally effective? Explain why you think as you do.

5. What questions do you still have about the oceans after reading these selections?

Write a Caption

Writing CONNECTION

Imagine that you are setting up a photo exhibit. Choose a dramatic photograph from "Oceans" to include in the exhibit. Write a caption to be exhibited with the photograph. The caption should be a short paragraph that gives viewers information about the photograph. Use a graphic organizer like the one shown here to collect your ideas.

What does the photograph show?	
How does it help viewers understand more about the oceans?	
Why is it included in the exhibit?	

Create Graphic Aids

Begin a research project on tsunamis by setting up a K-W-L chart. Use a variety of research materials, including print and online encyclopedias, to find information. Create one or more graphic aids to explain your findings to classmates.

Science CONNECTION

[K] What I Know	[W] What I Want to Know	[L] What I Learned
caused by earthquake or volcano	Can scientists predict them?	
can move 500 miles per hour	How high can the wave be?	
grow to huge size	What happens when a tsunami is forming?	
can cause great damage	Where do tsunamis occur?	

Study Tide Tables

Did you know that scientists can predict the times and heights of tides all over the world? Using a map, choose several locations on coastlines. Then use the Internet to find tide tables that predict tides for those locations. Study the times and heights at the different locations, and write some generalizations about them.

Social Studies/Math CONNECTION

Tides Around The World

Different places in the world have their own individual patterns of tides.

Text Structure:
Main Idea and Details

Focus Skill

A nonfiction selection such as "Oceans" often involves complicated information. The author may decide to use a pattern of main ideas and details to organize or structure the text.

In "Oceans" the author divided the text into three topics related to the oceans—Tides, Tsunamis, and Waves. Each topic has a main idea. Look in the text to find details which support the main topic.

Topic	Main Idea	Details
Tides	Tides are caused by the gravitational pull of the moon and the sun.	
Tsunamis	A tidal wave has nothing to do with tides.	
Waves	Several things contribute to the size of a wave.	

Sometimes the main idea is directly stated in a topic sentence. When the main idea is not stated directly, you will need to use the important details in the passage to help you figure out the main idea.

Visit *The Learning Site!*
www.harcourtschool.com

See *Skills* and *Activities*

318

Test Prep
Text Structure: Main Idea and Details

▶ **Read the passage. Then answer the questions.**

> Tides, although predictable, have inspired people throughout the ages. Tides occur every day along the shore. Tides come in and go out approximately every twelve hours. Yet, in spite of their predictability, tides have a romantic quality that has inspired the works of writers, artists, and poets.

1. **Which sentence from the passage is the topic sentence?**

   A the first sentence

   B the second sentence

   C the third sentence

   D the fourth sentence

Tip

Figure out the main idea of the passage. Then find the sentence that states the main idea. That sentence is the topic sentence.

2. **How is the text of this passage organized?**

Tip

Think about the passage as a whole and about how the information is organized.

Vocabulary Power

barren

meander

sensors

atoll

reef

lagoon

Have you ever wished you could travel in space? Read what an imaginary space traveler of the future wrote in her diary.

July 26

We passed through the black hole and saw the strange planet. Now we are preparing to land. I see how **barren** this planet looks, as if no plant life could possibly grow here. Yet small streams **meander** along, winding and turning like tiny rivers. The **sensors** on our spaceship, the devices that record and signal information, remain quiet.

August 4

Today we made an amazing discovery. We followed one of the streams and found that it led to a sea. In the sea is an **atoll**, a ring-shaped island. Like atolls on Earth, this one seems to be a coral **reef**, or ridge near the surface of the water. The reef forms a ring that encloses a body of water called a **lagoon**.

If our tests show that the reef is made of coral, it will mean that there is life on this planet after all. We are all hoping that this will be the case.

Vocabulary-Writing CONNECTION

Mars is a **barren** planet. Quickly list all of the things you know about the planet Mars.

BY PATRICIA LAUDER

Genre

Photo Essay

A photo essay presents information through a combination of photographs and related text.

In this selection, look for

- Photographs that are supported by the text

- A text structure that is organized by main idea and supporting details

SEEING
EARTH
FROM
SPACE

BY PATRICIA LAUBER

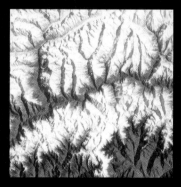

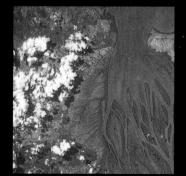

PLANET EARTH ••

On their way to the moon, Apollo 8 astronauts looked back and saw a bright blue globe, partly masked by white clouds and set against the black of space. At that moment they became the first people ever to see Earth as a planet. Their photographs and others show us Earth

as we can never see it for ourselves. They also show us something we know but find hard to believe: We are all flying through space. Our spaceship is the Earth, whirling around the sun at 67,000 miles an hour.

Other new views come from photographs taken by astronauts orbiting a few hundred miles above Earth's surface. These astronauts are too close to see the full face of the Earth. But they see large pieces of it at one time, something we cannot do. Trying to see the Earth from its surface is like looking at a large painting while standing up against it. We see only details. To see the picture, we must back off.

Astronauts in orbit have backed off from Earth. They see the full length of rivers, the folds of mountains, the birth of hurricanes, the straight lines of roads and bridges that mark the cities of the world. Their photographs give us a space tour of our home planet.

Still different pictures of Earth come from satellites carrying sensors, radar, and other instruments. They show us things that the human eye cannot see for itself.

Together, all these
views of Earth teach us
much about our planet,
whether by showing us
the unseen or by taking
us sight-seeing with the
astronauts.

Astronauts sometimes look down at giant storms, such as the eye of Typhoon Pat over the Pacific.

They also see signs of human activities that worry them. This golden haze over the Indian Ocean near Madagascar is not natural but man-made, a sign of air pollution. The sun is glinting off smoke particles in the air.

Islands glide by, tiny outposts in the seas that cover
two-thirds of Earth. Most of them grew from undersea
volcanoes. Eruptions built mountains so high that they
broke through the surface of the sea and became islands.

Once an island is born, life arrives. Seeds and plants
wash up on its shores. Insects and seeds arrive on the
winds. Birds find the island, bringing more seeds in their
feathers and on their feet. In time the island may become
a place where people can live and which they settle. That
is what happened with this island, Santa Cruz de Tenerife,
which is one of the Canary Islands, in the Atlantic Ocean.
At its center, with a light dusting of snow, is Tiedi, an
inactive volcano.

The Hawaiian Islands were also built by undersea volcanoes. The big island of Hawaii was originally two islands, one built by the volcano Mauna Loa, the other by Mauna Kea. Huge lava flows from Mauna Loa linked the two islands and made them one. The clouds in this photograph are moving from right to left. Those to the left were disturbed and broken up as they passed over the islands.

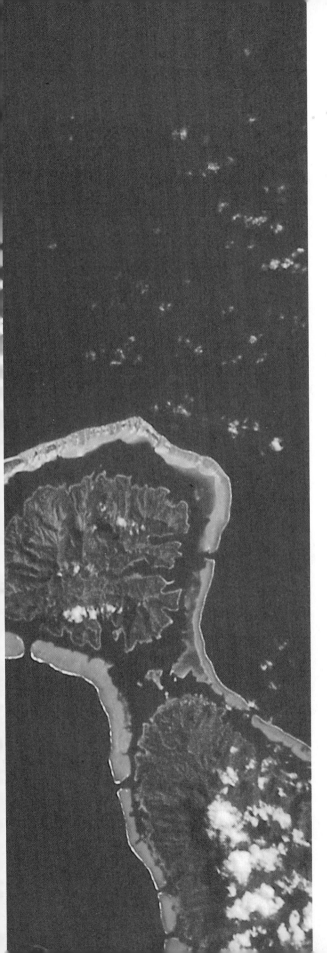

Bora-Bora, center in the picture at left, is a Pacific island that is changing. The middle of the island was built by a volcano. Where the shores of the island shelved off into the ocean, the waters were warm and shallow. Here colonies of corals took hold. Each coral was a tiny animal with a hard skeleton on the outside of its body. At first corals attached themselves to rocks, later to the skeletons of earlier generations. As time passed, they formed a reef around the island. The photograph shows the reef, as well as the lagoon that circles the island inside the reef. Now the volcano is cold and dead. It is slowly sinking back into the Earth. In time it will disappear, leaving a ring of coral and sand with a lagoon at the center. The ring of coral will be the kind of island called an atoll. The same thing is happening to the islands of Raiatea and Tahaa (lower right). Tapai (upper left) has already become an atoll.

The islands of Tarawa (partly cloud-covered) and
Abaiang, shown below, also became atolls many years ago.

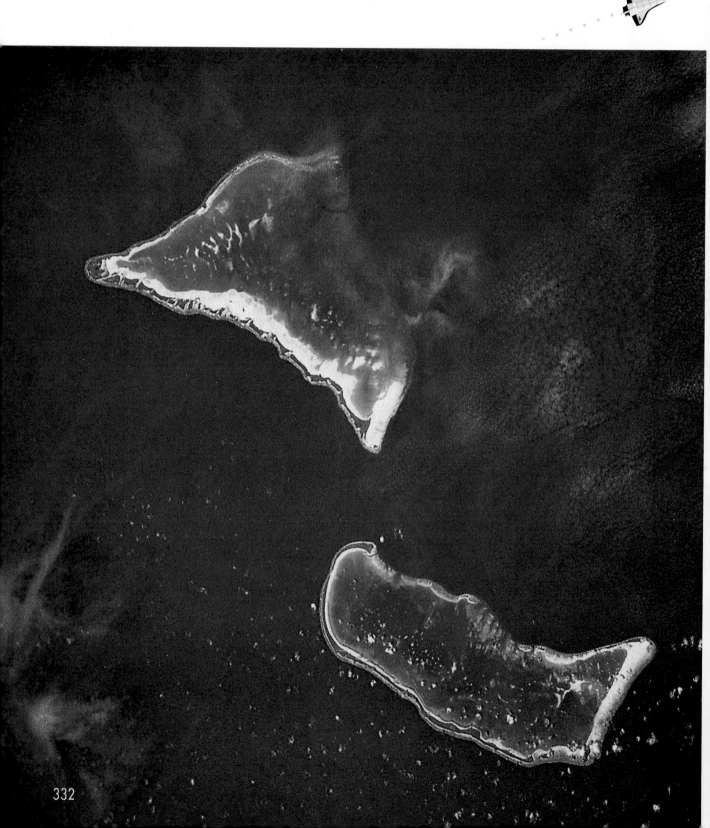

The Earth's crust is broken into huge pieces, or plates, that are in motion. Moving at a rate of an inch or two a year, they carry along whatever is on top of them—ocean floor, islands, whole continents. Millions of years ago, the plate carrying India collided with the plate carrying Asia. When the two land masses were pressed together, the Himalaya Mountains began to crumple out of the crust. As the plates went on pressing together, the mountains grew taller and taller. Today they are still among the Earth's young, growing mountains, and their folded, tilted rock tells of an ancient, great collision.

The ability to see Earth from space helps scientists to understand both how the planet works and how human activities are affecting the Earth. It helps all of us to share the feelings of the men and women who have gone into space.

SPACESHIP EARTH

The Apollo astronauts who landed on the moon found themselves in a strange new world. No one had walked this ground before; the only footprints were their own. Nowhere was there a trace of life other than their own, only craters, seas of hardened lava, hills, and rocks. Above them stars and planets shone with a brilliance never seen on Earth, for the moon has no atmosphere to dim their light. Yet for the astronauts the most exciting sight was Earth. It was more than home.

Seen from the surface of the airless, barren moon or from the orbiting spacecraft, Earth was an island of life in the black sea of space, the only outpost of life to be seen.

All the men and women who have flown in space—
Americans, Soviets, foreign guests—have been awed by
the beauty of the Earth. They have also been surprised
by its size. To a person standing on its surface, the Earth
appears both large and sturdy. From space it seems
small and fragile.

These men and women are often concerned by the
man-made changes they see on the Earth. They look down
at the island of Madagascar (below), where tropical forests
are being felled. They see that the ocean around it is red-
brown, colored by soil eroding from land without trees and
carried to the sea by rivers.

They look down and see the slick of an oil spill in the sea.
They think about the birds and fishes and mammals and
plants that will die and about beaches with tarry sands.

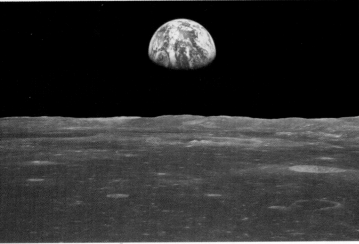

They know that from Earth the atmosphere seems to be boundless, an ocean of air that we take for granted and breathe without thinking about it. From space they see that the atmosphere is only a thin shell surrounding the Earth. Just before sunrise and just after sunset they can see it—the red layer is the air we breathe; above it is the stratosphere; the blue layer is the ionosphere. Beyond the shell is space, black and empty.

Space travelers often return with their thinking changed. On Earth we think of boundaries. The view from space is different. Rivers meander or rush from country to country without stopping, on their way to the sea. Forests reach from one country into another.

Sand and dust from the Sahara spread across the Atlantic (left) and blow toward the Americas. Smoke travels hundreds of miles on the winds. An ocean stretches from continent to continent, and the same waters wash the shores of both.

Space travelers see that the Earth is one planet, small and fragile, wondrous and lovely. It is the spaceship in which we journey around the sun, and our life-support system is its air and waters and lands. We are all, every person in the world, aboard the same ship. And so we must all, in ways large and small, treasure and protect it.

Think and Respond

❶ Which of the main points in this selection are facts? Which are the author's opinions?

❷ Why did the author divide the text into two sections?

❸ How do photographs taken from space help us understand features of Earth such as a **reef**, a **lagoon**, or an **atoll**?

❹ Do you think it would be a good idea for adults, as well as students, to read this selection? Explain your answer.

❺ What reading strategies did you use to help you understand this selection? When did you use them?

What inspired you to write "Seeing Earth from Space"?

This book grew out of my fascination with images of Earth as seen from space. It is one thing to read that Earth is a planet. It is quite something else to *see* Earth from space—to *see* that Earth is a planet.

How did you write the book?

First, I spent several years collecting information from newspapers, magazines, books, and NASA. I wanted to learn how images from space are used by scientists who study weather and climate, the oceans, crops, geology, forests, and ancient civilizations. Then I began to write and to collect images to illustrate what I was saying.

What did you want readers to learn from this book?

My hope was that readers would share the wonder astronauts feel as they look at our planet. I wanted them to see Earth as a place to be treasured and cared for.

Visit *The Learning Site!*
www.harcourtschool.com

Little O, small earth, spinning in space,
face covered with dizzy clouds, racing,
chasing sunlight through the Milky Way,
say your secrets, small earth, little O,
know where you lead, I follow. I go.

Patched together
With land and sea,
I am earth,
Great earth.
Come with me!

EARTH

MYRA COHN LIVINGSTON, POET

Huge continents lie on me, dry land,
sand grained from crumbled rock, now drifted,
sifted to powder. Silt, sand, red clay
weigh down my crust in layers of loam.
Roam everywhere—I am earth, your home.

Mountains rise above me, their slopes white,
bright with fresh snow, tall peaks glistering.
Blistering brown domes bend over, hunched,
bunched together. Some, chained in deep folds,
molded in waves, sleep, wrinkled and old.

SONGS

LEONARD EVERETT FISHER, PAINTER

Hot volcanoes breathe in me, my back
blackened with cinders, scars of old fires,
pyres of ash. My red mouth and throat burn,
churn with hot, liquid lava. Below
flow molten rivers. Turn away! Go!

Forests live on me. Tall evergreens
lean against my mountains. Stands of beech
reach to the sky. Huge timber and bark
darken my leaf-strewn floors. Oak, teak, and pine,
vine-twisted rain forests—all are mine.

Waters bathe me, splash over my shores.
Pouring down from springs, ribboned streams
gleam with rills, hurry downwards, dashing,
plashing. Rivers rise. Blue swells leap high.
Dry up my waters and I will die.

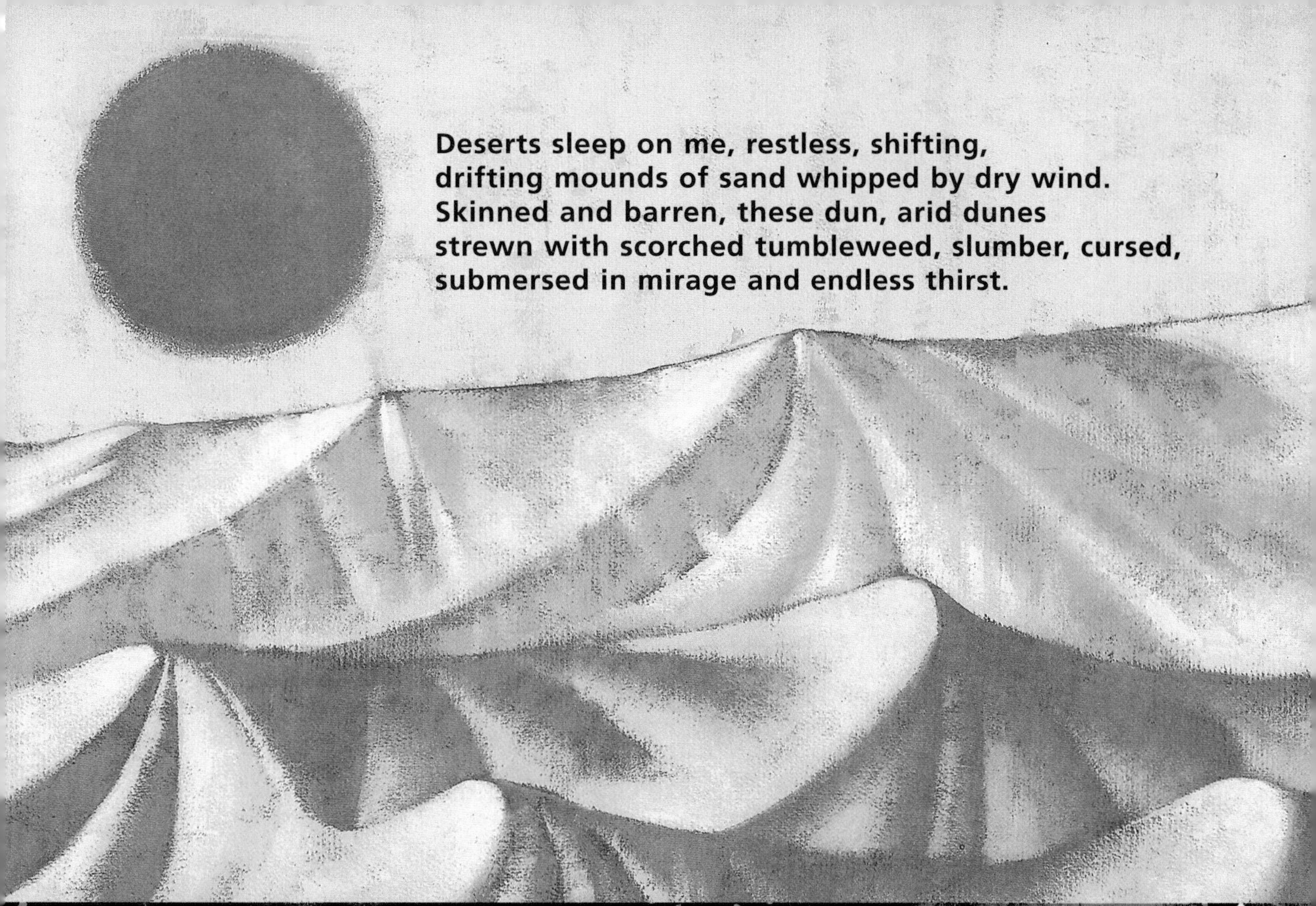

Deserts sleep on me, restless, shifting,
drifting mounds of sand whipped by dry wind.
Skinned and barren, these dun, arid dunes
strewn with scorched tumbleweed, slumber, cursed,
submersed in mirage and endless thirst.

Big O, great planet, spinning in space,
face covered with dizzy clouds, racing,
chasing sunlight through the Milky Way,
say your secrets again, giant O.
Know where you lead, I follow. I go.

Patched together
With land and sea,
I am earth,
Little O.
Come with me!

Making Connections

Compare Texts

1 What changes on Earth can be seen from space in the photo essay "Seeing Earth from Space"?

2 Why does the author call the first section "Planet Earth" and the second section "Spaceship Earth"?

3 Compare the viewpoints of the authors of "Seeing Earth from Space" and the poem "Earth Songs."

4 Compare "Earth Songs" with another poem you have read. How are the two poems alike and different?

5 What else would you like to know about natural features and how they form?

Write a Fictional Narrative

A little over 500 years ago, when Columbus sailed to America, some people believed that Earth was flat. Imagine that you could go back to those days and show people photographs like the ones in "Seeing Earth from Space." Write a narrative about what you think would happen and how people might react. Use a graphic organizer to plan your narrative.

Writing CONNECTION

Characters	Setting
Main Events	

344

Create a Pamphlet

The last lines of "Seeing Earth from Space" point out that every person in the world is aboard the same ship, Spaceship Earth. The author urges us all to treasure and protect our planet. Choose a specific topic, such as oceans, rain forests, or air pollution. Use the Internet to find out about some ways that Earth is being protected. Use the information to create a pamphlet about one way our planet is being helped.

Social Studies CONNECTION

Harcourt

Back   Forward   Home   Reload   Search   Mail   Print   Folder

Protecting Our Earth

Plan a Presentation

The photographs in "Seeing Earth from Space" were taken by scientists for scientific purposes, but they are also beautiful. Is photography an art or a science? Research the topic that interests you more, the science of photography or the art of photography. Prepare a paper on your topic.

Science/Art CONNECTION

▲ Seeing Earth
from Space

Graphic Aids

You have learned that graphic aids help you to "see" and understand information in a selection. You may recall that in "Seeing Earth from Space," the author used a photograph of Bora Bora, taken from space, to help explain how atolls form.

Authors often use photographs and other types of graphic aids, such as maps, charts, diagrams, and graphs, to make complicated explanations easier for you to understand. The following diagram shows how an atoll forms. Compare the diagram to the photograph. What new information does the diagram add to what you already know?

Formation of an Atoll

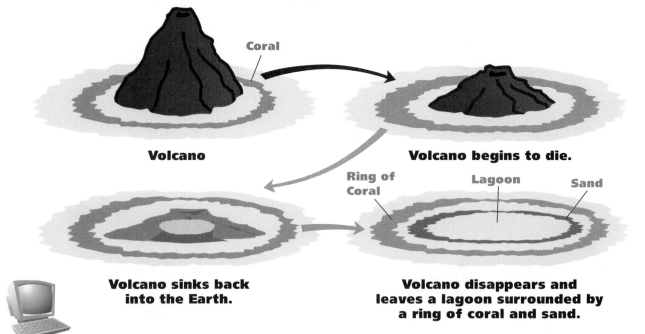

Coral

Volcano

Volcano begins to die.

Ring of Coral

Lagoon

Sand

Volcano sinks back
into the Earth.

Volcano disappears and
leaves a lagoon surrounded by
a ring of coral and sand.

Visit *The Learning Site!*
www.harcourtschool.com

See *Skills* and *Activities*

346

Test Prep
Graphic Aids

▶ **Read the passage and study the diagram. Then answer the questions.**

> A volcano starts to erupt when melted rock inside the Earth, known as *magma*, produces a great amount of gas. The gas and the magma combine and start to rise. The gas-filled magma collects in the *magma chamber* that is formed when the rising hot magma melts a hole in the Earth's crust.

Volcanic Eruption

Rocks — Gas and dust
Central vent — Lava
Crust — Conduit
Magma chamber
Mantle

1. **What information in the passage does the diagram clarify?**

   A the force of a volcano

   B how much gas is produced by magma

   C the location of the magma chamber

   D the temperature of magma

Tip

Ask yourself which detail in the passage the diagram helps you "see" and understand.

2. **Which of these is explained by the diagram but not by the passage?**

   F Melted rock creates gas.

   G Magma melts surrounding rock.

   H Pressure causes magma to move up.

   J Lava is what magma is called after it erupts.

Tip

Find the detail on the diagram that adds new information to what you learned in the passage.

347

▲ The Case of the
Flying-Saucer People

features

piercing

advanced

translation

publicity

Vocabulary Power

A character in the next selection claims to have met people from another planet. Of course, people have many questions about his story. In the following scene, a character named Eddie has some questions about someone his friend Annie met.

ANNIE: I had an encounter
   with a Bullfrog this morning.

EDDIE: You had an unexpected
   meeting with a bullfrog? How
   big was it?

ANNIE: Oh, it wasn't a real bullfrog. It was Mr. Simms.

EDDIE: I don't know Mr. Simms. Why do you call him a bullfrog? Does he have a bullfrog's **features** ? I mean, do his eyes, nose, and mouth look like a bullfrog's?

ANNIE: Of course not! He has **piercing** blue eyes, which give him a strong, powerful look, and a perfectly normal nose and mouth.

EDDIE: Well, then, does he think like a bullfrog?

ANNIE: For your information, Mr. Simms is very **advanced** , or ahead of others, in his thinking. He even speaks Chinese and does **translation** . He changes books written in Chinese into English. I never heard of a bullfrog who could do that!

EDDIE: *I* know! I bet he has a voice like a bullfrog's. Right?

ANNIE: Wrong, Eddie. Mr. Simms plays second base for a baseball team called the Bullfrogs.
He was wearing his Bullfrog uniform today to get some **publicity** , or public attention, for the team.

EDDIE: That was going to be my next guess!

Vocabulary–Writing CONNECTION

What is the most unusual animal, either a pet or a wild animal, that you have seen? Write a paragraph describing the animal's **features.**

The Case of the Flying

Mystery

A mystery is a story built on suspense.

In this selection, look for

- A problem that challenges the reader to find an answer

- Information based on scientific principles

Saucer People

by Seymour Simon
illustrated by Wil Terry

351

Einstein had just come home from the beach when his mother phoned him from her office at the Sparta *Tribune*.

"I'm glad you're home, Adam," said Mrs. Anderson. "I have a favor to ask you."

"Sure, Mom," Einstein said. "What can I do you for?" Einstein liked to mix up his words. It was unfortunate, he felt, that nobody else liked it.

"Adam, there's someone visiting Sparta I want to interview for the newspaper. I'm going to invite him to the house for dinner this evening. And I'd like you to be around when I do the interview."

"Who's the person? And why do you want me to be around? Is there something wrong?"

"His name is Mr. Janus," Mrs. Anderson answered. "He's writing a book about something that happened to him. Or at least that he claims happened to him."

"What happened to him? What do you want me to do when he comes? Do you think he's not telling the truth? Is it something about science?" Einstein asked all the questions in a rush.

"Just hold on a minute and I'll tell you," his mother said with a laugh. "Janus says he was walking along a country road just outside of Sparta when he saw a flying saucer. The saucer landed, and some little people with big heads came out and greeted him."

"Wow!" Einstein exclaimed. "A close encounter of the third kind. What else happened?"

"Janus says that the saucer people were able to talk to him in English with some kind of translation machine they carried. They asked him to go aboard their ship and took him to their base on the far side of the moon. They kept him there for a few days and then took him back and released him."

"That really sounds weird," Einstein said. "Do you believe his story?"

"That's why I'd like you to be around," Mrs. Anderson answered. "He sounds sincere, but he may just be trying to get publicity for his book. I'd like you to listen to what he has to say and then tell me in private whether he's made any scientific mistakes."

Einstein readily agreed. He loved reading science-fiction stories, though he had his doubts about flying saucers.

Mr. Janus turned out to be a long, thin man with sharp features. His eyes were black and piercing. All through dinner he talked about his experiences with the saucer people. He said that they were about

three feet tall with the general shape of humans. They had a head, two arms, and two legs. Their skin was a faint greenish color that seemed to glow. Their eyes were very round with no pupils, and their ears were pointed.

Einstein listened closely, but he could not make up his mind one way or another. If you believed in saucers, he thought, then there was nothing scientifically wrong in anything Mr. Janus was saying.

After dinner Dr. Anderson said that he and Dennis would do the dishes. Dennis seemed to be about to protest, but Dr. Anderson gave him a look. Then Mrs. Anderson led Mr. Janus and Einstein into the den and shut the door.

"Would you continue with your story, Mr. Janus?" asked Mrs. Anderson. "You had just gotten to the part where the saucer people had given you a space suit and you were walking on the moon."

"The moon's surface was dusty and rocky," Mr. Janus said. "You know that there's no water or air on the moon. The temperature in the sunlight was over a hundred degrees Celsius. That's hot enough to boil water, if there was any. It's a good thing that the suit's air-conditioning was working so well.

"The saucer people walked me over to a hill. When we got closer, I could hear a hammering going on behind the hill. It was not difficult climbing the hill, because of the moon's low gravity."

"Did you see what was going on behind the hill?" asked Mrs. Anderson.

"Yes," answered Mr. Janus. "When we got to the top of the hill, I could see that the saucer people were knocking down part of their base.

They asked me to tell the people of the world their reasons
for leaving. They had decided that the people on Earth were
not advanced enough to be welcomed into the Galaxy
Federation of Intelligent Beings."

"That's too bad," Einstein said. But I can see why they felt
that way, he thought. "Mom, would it be O.K. if I went outside
to play now?"

"Would you excuse me for a second, Mr. Janus?" asked Mrs.
Anderson. "I'll be back in a minute."

Einstein and Mrs. Anderson went outside the den. "Well,
what do you think?" Mrs. Anderson asked. "Did Janus make any
scientific errors?"

"As far as I can tell, just one," Einstein said. "But that
error is enough of a whopper to make me think his whole story
is fiction."

Can You Solve the Mystery?

What was the scientific error in the story of the saucer people?

"Was the error in his story that the temperature on the moon was hot enough to boil water?" Mrs. Anderson asked. "That seemed wrong to me. I always thought the moon's surface was very cold."

"The moon's surface is either cold or hot," Einstein said. "Because the moon has no atmosphere, the surface temperatures are very extreme. In the shade, the temperature is lower than the coldest spot on Earth. In the sun, the temperature is higher than the hottest spot here."

"Then what was the error, Adam?"

"The mistake that Janus made had to do with the lack of atmosphere on the moon," explained Einstein. "Mr. Janus said that he heard a hammering going on behind a hill. But sound must travel through air to be heard. How could Janus have heard the sound of hammering in a place that has no air?"

"Thanks, Adam. I knew I could count on you."

"Well, you can certainly count on what I expect to be in two years."

"What?" Mrs. Anderson asked.

"Fourteen," Einstein said.

"Don't press your luck," Mrs. Anderson said.

Think and Respond

1 Why does Einstein's mom ask for his help?

2 Why does the author wait until the very end of the story to give Einstein's explanation?

3 Why does Mr. Janus want **publicity** for his book?

4 What do you like or dislike about reading mysteries like "The Case of the Flying-Saucer People"?

5 When did you use reading strategies to help you understand "The Case of the Flying-Saucer People"?

Making Connections

Compare Texts

1 How does "The Case of the Flying-Saucer People" relate to a theme about our planet?

2 How is Einstein's behavior around Mr. Janus different from the way he acts when he speaks with his mother?

3 How are the space creatures that Mr. Janus describes similar to and different from other imaginary beings you have read about?

4 Think of another short story you have read about a young person who solves a problem or mystery. Which story is more believable, and why?

5 How would you find more information on how sound waves travel through air?

Write Paragraphs

Einstein Anderson's knowledge of science comes in handy in solving "The Case of the Flying-Saucer People." List three facts that you have learned recently in science. Write a paragraph for each fact, telling what you learned and how you think it could be useful to you. Use a graphic like this one to organize your ideas.

Writing CONNECTION

Scientific Fact	Real-Life Situation
1.	
2.	
3.	

Perform a Dramatization

Mr. Janus did not really walk on the moon, but astronauts have. Find out about landings on the moon. You might use science websites, encyclopedias, or other nonfiction books. Prepare a dramatization in which you are an astronaut on the surface of the moon. Tell what you are doing and what you see. Perform your dramatization for classmates.

Science CONNECTION

Make a Time Line

Space travel began in the second half of the twentieth century and developed at a rapid pace. Research major events in the history of space travel using online or print sources. Make a time line that shows the dates and some information about these important events.

Social Studies CONNECTION

October 1958

U.S. creates NASA
(National Aeronautics and Space Administration)

Text Structure:
Main Idea and Details

Focus
Skill

Writers often organize or structure their ideas in the **main idea** and **supporting detail** formats. The main idea may be stated directly in a topic sentence. Often, however, the main idea is only implied, or suggested. You have to identify the important details and use them to figure out what the selection is mainly about. Then you can develop your own main idea statement.

The graphic that follows shows some of the important details in "The Case of the Flying-Saucer People." See how these details help to identify the main idea of the story.

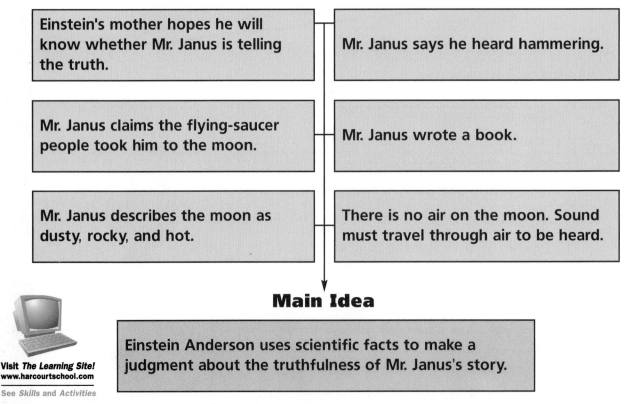

Details

Einstein's mother hopes he will know whether Mr. Janus is telling the truth.

Mr. Janus claims the flying-saucer people took him to the moon.

Mr. Janus describes the moon as dusty, rocky, and hot.

Details

Mr. Janus says he heard hammering.

Mr. Janus wrote a book.

There is no air on the moon. Sound must travel through air to be heard.

Main Idea

Einstein Anderson uses scientific facts to make a judgment about the truthfulness of Mr. Janus's story.

Visit *The Learning Site!*
www.harcourtschool.com

See *Skills* and *Activities*

Test Prep
Text Structure: Main Idea and Details

▶ **Read the passage. Then answer the questions.**

"It's true!" Anthony told his brother James. "I saw them. There were eight of them—five men and three women. They were only two inches tall and bald. They wore silver suits, and they could flatten themselves like cartoon characters. They slipped under the door right after you fell asleep. Then they climbed onto the bed and marched right over your head. I couldn't believe you didn't wake up! They hopped from your head to the night table and then climbed up the lamp and onto the bureau. They jumped over to the windowsill and flattened themselves again. Then they slipped under the window and were gone into the night. Poof!"

1. **What is the implied main idea of this passage?**

   A James doesn't believe Anthony.

   B Anthony can prove visitors came.

   C James was not asleep.

   D Anthony describes the visit of eight tiny people to their room.

Tip

Think about the important details in the passage. Choose the statement that covers most of these details.

2. **Which of these does *not* support the main idea statement you chose?**

   F There were eight of them.

   G They could flatten themselves like cartoon characters.

   H I couldn't believe you didn't wake up!

   J They jumped over to the windowsill and flattened themselves again.

Tip

Look for the detail that does not give more information about the main idea.

365

Express Yourself

CONTENTS

Vocabulary Power

homestead

undeniable

despair

rations

perch

concocted

brooded

Spencer McClintic and his sister Hattie, characters in "Hattie's Birthday Box," recall events that happened a long time ago. This work of fiction includes accurate details about a particular time in American history.

THE HOMESTEAD ACT

The first law giving people the right to **homestead** was passed by the United States Congress in 1862. Under this law, a citizen could become the owner of a piece of land by farming and improving it for five years.

It is **undeniable**, plainly true, that homesteading was good for the homesteaders. People who might have been in **despair**, feeling there was no hope for them, now had a way to own their own farms. Some had to work hard and live on slim **rations**. Although the homesteaders had to survive on such limited amounts of food and other items, they had a way to fulfill their dreams. A homesteader might find a **perch**, a high place to sit or stand on, and look with pride at land that would soon be his or her very own.

The homestead law was good for the country, too. It is unlikely that anyone could have **concocted**, or devised, a better plan for settling the vast open lands west of the Mississippi. Anyone who had **brooded** over that problem did not have to think deeply and worry about it after homesteading began.

**Vocabulary–Writing
CONNECTION**

Think about a problem you have **brooded** over. Write a paragraph about how you solved your problem.

Notable Trade Book for the Language Arts

Genre

Short Story

A short story is a fictional narrative that is not part of a novel.

In this selection, look for

- A plot with a beginning, a middle, and an ending
- One problem or main event

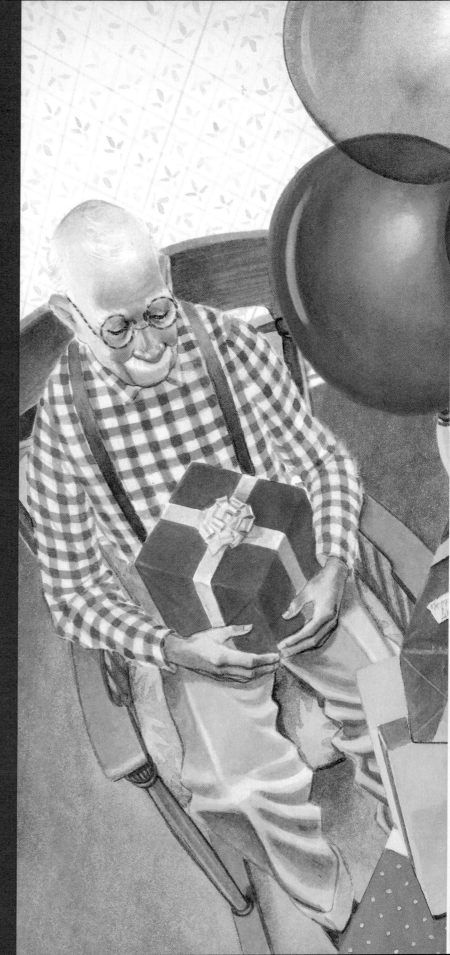

HATTIE'S BIRTHDAY BOX

written by *Pam Conrad*
illustrations by *Tim Ladwig*

The sign stretching across the ceiling of the nursing home's rec room says HAPPY ONE HUNDREDTH BIRTHDAY, SPENCER McCLINTIC, and on the wall in bright numbers and letters it says JULY 5, 1847 to 1947. Spencer McClintic is my great-great-grandfather, and our whole family is coming to celebrate.

Momma and I got here early because Momma wanted me to help her blow up balloons and tack up the decorations before everyone arrived. She says now that the war is over and most everyone is back home and rations are a thing of the past, we're going to *really* celebrate.

But Grandaddy's nervous. He sits in his chair by the window, rubbing his hands together and asking my mother over and over, "Now who-all is coming, Anna?"

And she keeps reciting the list of everyone who's coming, and he ticks them off on his fingers, but before she's even through, he asks impatiently, "But is Hattie coming? My baby sister? Are you sure she's coming?"

"Hattie's coming, Grandaddy. Don't you worry. Hattie will be here."

Momma doesn't hear, but I hear him. He mumbles, "Oh, no, oh, no, not Hattie. She's gonna skin me alive."

I pull up a stool near Grandaddy. "Don't you like Aunt Hattie, Grandaddy?"

"Oh, I love her to pieces," he answers. "But she's gonna have my hide. Last time I saw Hattie, she was a bride of sixteen, heading out in a wagon with her new husband to homestead in Nebraska. And I did a terrible thing, a terrible thing."

All the decorations are up, and now that Momma's sure everything is all set, she tells me to stay with Grandaddy and keep him calm while she runs home to get the cake and soda.

But there is no way to keep Grandaddy calm. "What'd you do that was so bad, Grandaddy? What was it?"

I watch Grandaddy wringing his hands and tapping his slippered feet nervously. He keeps glancing out the window to the road outside, like he's waiting for some old lynch mob to come riding over the hill. This is the story I finally got out of him.

It had been a warm May morning in 1873, and Grandaddy's sister Hattie McClintic Burden was a new bride ready to set out for a life on the distant, promising plains of Nebraska. The sun hadn't quite risen yet, and she and her new husband, Otto, were loading the final things into the wagon. While it was a happy occasion in that Hattie and her husband were heading out for a new life, it was also a sad day, because no one knew when they'd ever see them again. Grandaddy, who was a young man at the time, didn't know it would be seventy-four years before he would finally see her. But no one ever knew that back then. No one knew how long it would be before they saw each other or if they would ever see each other at all. There were no telephones, no airplanes, just the U.S. mail, slow but reliable, carrying recipes for pumpkin bread and clippings of hair from new babies, and sad messages of deaths.

The night before Hattie and Otto left, everyone had tried to smile and be happy for them. There was a combination going-away party and birthday party for Hattie, who was just sixteen. Everyone brought special gifts — blankets and lanterns and bolts of cotton, a pair of small sewing scissors, a bottle of ink, and even a canary in a shiny cage.

My grandaddy, who was then a young man of twenty-six, had stewed and brooded. He had been ten years old when Hattie was born, and she had always been his favorite. More than once he had carried her out into the barn on crystal-clear nights to show her a calf being born. He had taught her to swim in the cool spring. And he had chased away the young boys when they had first started to come sniffing around. His heart was breaking that his little sister was going away, and he had wanted to give her the most special gift. The best gift of all. So she would always remember him and know how much he had loved her.

He would have given her a gold necklace, or a bracelet with diamonds, or earrings with opal jewels, but it had been a rough year, with a few of the cattle dying in a storm and a few others lost to a brief sickness. He had no money, nothing to trade, no real gift to give her. Not knowing what the gift would be, he had lovingly hammered together a small wooden box and carved her initials in it, thinking that whatever it would be, it would be about this size.

It was at the party that night that he realized there was nothing to give her and he concocted his tale. Finding her alone at the punch bowl, Spencer had clasped Hattie's small shoulders in his rough hands, looked straight in her face, and lied boldly.

"I got you something special, Hattie, something so special I think you'd better not open it right away. I want you to just hold on to the box, and don't open it unless times get hard, not unless things get to be their very worst, you hear me? And it will see you through."

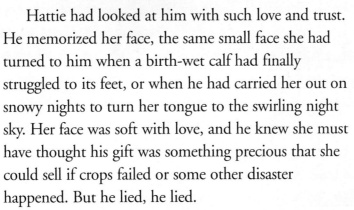

Hattie had looked at him with such love and trust. He memorized her face, the same small face she had turned to him when a birth-wet calf had finally struggled to its feet, or when he had carried her out on snowy nights to turn her tongue to the swirling night sky. Her face was soft with love, and he knew she must have thought his gift was something precious that she could sell if crops failed or some other disaster happened. But he lied, he lied.

So that morning before the sun rose, he helped Otto hook up the team to the wagon, and once Hattie was high on her perch beside her husband — looking for all the world like a little child playing farmhouse — my young grandaddy had slipped the sealed and empty wooden box into her lap and backed away. He waved goodbye and never saw her again.

Until today. Aunt Hattie's flying in from Nebraska with cousin Harold and his wife, Mary. Since she was sixteen, Hattie has never set foot off Nebraska soil.

"I meant to finally buy her something to put in the box, I really did," Grandaddy keeps saying. "I thought that as soon as things got a little better, as soon as I had a little money, I'd buy those earrings or that necklace and send it right off to her, explaining everything. But then I don't know. Soon I got married myself, and then there were my own children, and Hattie just never mentioned it in any of her letters." Grandaddy groans and lowers his head into his upturned hands. "Oh, mercy, Hattie's coming."

People are starting to arrive now, and the room is filling with children, laughter, and presents. Many of the people are my relatives who live right nearby, and a few came up from Jersey and Washington, people I'd normally see on holidays and such but never all together like this in one place.

And Grandaddy won't even look at them. He just gets up and walks slowly to another seat far from the window. Out the window I see an airport taxi pull up.

I post myself behind Grandaddy and watch. His hands are

trembling more than usual, and I can tell he's not paying attention as little babies are brought to him to kiss and my father keeps taking flash pictures of him with everybody.

Suddenly a hush falls over everyone. Even the littlest children grow wide-eyed and still. The name "Hattie" is whispered across the room, like prairie wind over the flute of a stovepipe.

"It's Hattie."

"Hattie's here."

"Hattie!"

I put my hand on Grandaddy's shoulder. "Don't worry, Grandaddy. She'll have to get through me first."

Grandaddy takes a deep breath, and his shoulders slump. He doesn't turn toward the door. He just waits in the silence that falls over the room. We can hear footsteps, Harold's and Mary's, and Hattie's. They stand in the doorway with Hattie in the middle, as though they support her, but when she sees Grandaddy sitting with his back to her, she gently withdraws her arms from them and comes toward us.

She doesn't look like she could swat a fly, and she's not packing a shotgun. The tiny thin net on her hat trembles as she takes tiny steps toward us. "Spencer?" she says softly.

"Grandaddy," I say more sharply, poking him in the arm. "Grandaddy, it's Hattie."

He turns then, ready to meet his Maker, I guess, but I'm right there, right next to them, able to see both their faces, and there is nothing but pure love, pure and powerful and undeniable love.

"Why, Spencer, they told me you were an old man."
She holds out her hands to him, and he takes them.

Tears stream down his cheeks and drip from his chin.
"But no one told me you were still such a pretty young
lady," he says. Still lying, my grandaddy.

"Oh, Spencer, Spencer," she says, "there's been too
much time and space." And I watch her gather him
into her skinny little arms, and he lays his face against
her shoulder. No one in the room is breathing. Then
all of a sudden, one of the cousins starts to clap, and
everyone, one at a time, joins in, until everyone is
laughing and wiping tears, patting Grandaddy on the
shoulder, and hugging Hattie.

I'm not about to leave Grandaddy's side. If
she's ever going to give him the business about
the empty box, I want to hear it. Someone
brings her a chair and sits her down right next
to him, and no one stops me so I sit down
between them right at their feet. And then I
notice it. On her lap is a small wooden box,
and the lid is off. Delicately carved into its
varnished top are the initials HMcB. She
holds the box in her hands, and I can see the
varnish worn dull in spots where her fingers
touch and must have touched for years.

Grandaddy sees it, too, and groans. "Oh,
Hattie, do you hate me? Can you ever forgive me?"

"Forgive you for what?"

"For the empty box."

"Forgive you? Why, Spencer, it was the best present
I've ever gotten."

"An empty box?" Grandaddy is stunned.

"It wasn't an empty box. It was a box full of
good things."

"How d'you figure that?" Grandaddy asks.

"Well, I put it in a safe place, you know. First I hid it under the seat in the wagon, and when we finally got our soddy built, I had Otto make a special chink in the wall where I hid it and where it stayed for years. And I always knew it was there if things got really bad.

"Our first winter, we ran out of food, and I thought to open the box then and see if it would help us, but there were kind neighbors who were generous with us, and I learned to let people be neighborly.

"And then one summer we lost our whole crop in a prairie fire, and I thought of the box, but Otto was sure we could make it on our own, and I learned to let him have his pride. Then when our son drowned, just out of despair I almost opened it, but you had said to open it only if things got their worst, and I knew I still had my daughter, and there was another baby already stirring in me.

"No matter how bad things got, Spencer, they never got their worst. Even when Otto finally died a few years ago. Your box taught me that."

"But you did open it." He points to the box, open and empty in her lap.

"I opened it when I knew I'd be seeing you. I always thought maybe there'd be a brooch or a gold stickpin or something." Hattie smiles. I can almost imagine her with her open face turned up to a snowy sky. She laughs. "I was going to wear it for you!"

"I always meant to fill it, Hattie—"

"Hush now," she says. "They're bringing your cake."

And sure enough, Momma's wheeling over a metal table that has a big iced sheet cake on it. Hattie slips the cover back on her empty box and places it on the floor beside her feet, beside me. I stand to get out of the way of the rolling table and take the box.

Grandaddy and Aunt Hattie hold hands while everyone sings "Happy Birthday." Their hands are like old wisteria vines woven into each other. I hold the empty box. I bring it to my face. I look inside. Nothing. It is empty. And then I smell it. At first I think it smells like wood, and then I smell all the rest—a young farmer's stubbornness, a pioneer mother's sorrow, and a wondrous wild and lasting hope.

Think and Respond

1 How and why do Grandaddy's feelings change from the beginning of the story to the end?

2 What does the author do to create a feeling of suspense?

3 How does the empty box help Hattie get through hard times and feelings of **despair**?

4 Why do you think Hattie brings the box to the party?

5 How did you use reading strategies to help you better understand the story?

About the Author

Pam Conrad was an award-winning author who wrote picture books and novels. She said that even though her books are not autobiographies, "they are each about my life in one disguise or another." She also said that her books for young readers are based on her own children's lives and are her gifts to them.

Pam Conrad published more than two dozen books and won many national awards before she lost her life to cancer at the age of forty-eight.

Visit *The Learning Site!*
www.harcourtschool.com

PANDORA'S BOX

by Anne Rockwell
illustrations by Rafael López

THE ROBBER BABY
STORIES FROM
THE GREEK MYTHS

BY ANNE ROCKWELL

*P*andora was made, not born as other people are. Hephaestus[1] modeled her out of clay. He made her a young woman as beautiful as his wife, Aphrodite[2], the goddess of love and beauty.

Each of the gods and goddesses gave Pandora a gift. Then Athene, the goddess of wisdom, breathed life into her. Most of the gifts the gods gave her were good ones. But unfortunately Hermes[3], as always full of tricks and mischief, gave her more curiosity than was good for her.

Pandora was sent to live on earth. She had no trouble finding a good husband, for the gods and goddesses had given her the gifts of smiles and sweetness and wit and winning ways. Besides that, she was rich, for as a wedding gift the gods and goddesses gave her a box that had been made by Hephaestus. It was as beautiful as Pandora and very valuable, too.

"Never, never open that box!" all the gods and goddesses warned Pandora. She promised to obey them, but as time went on Pandora grew more and more curious about what was in the box that she had promised never to open.

In those days, there was no sadness among the mortals on earth. And why should it have been otherwise? There was no sickness, no hunger, no jealousy, no laziness, no greed, no anger, no cruelty. Even death was like a long and gentle sleep when people were very tired. There was no suffering of any kind.

Perhaps things would have remained that way if tricky Hermes had not given Pandora so much curiosity. But every day Pandora grew more and more curious about just what was in that box. At last, when she could no longer sleep for wondering what her box contained, she said to herself early one morning, "I will just take a little peek!"

---

[1] hə•fes´təs   [2] af•rə•dī´tē   [3] hər´mēz

So she opened the box, just to take a little peek. And out of that box flew dreadful things. Greed and Envy came out first and soared up into the clean, bright air. Pandora tried to slam the box shut, but she could not. Out flew Hatred and Cruelty with terrible force. Hunger and Poverty followed. Then Sickness came, and Despair, and all the other terrible things that the gods and goddesses knew should remain safely hidden in that box.

Pandora had set them all free.

"Come back! Come back where you belong!" Pandora called out to the terrible things as they flew around her. She grabbed at them in the air, but they soared out of her reach and up into the sky. None came back. They are still out there bringing misery and trouble to people on earth.

But the gods and goddesses had not put only dreadful things in Pandora's box. Hidden in among the terrible things was something small and fragile-winged and good. This thing was Hope. Who was the kindly god or goddess who thought to put Hope in among all the miseries and misfortunes? No one knows.

But because Hope was hidden in Pandora's box, whenever there is too much trouble and sadness among us mortals, Hope makes us think that tomorrow will be better.

And soon Pandora dried her tears.

"I hope I will never be too curious again!" she said.

And she never was.

Think and Respond

The myth "Pandora's Box" offers a creative explanation for how bad things came into our world. What is that explanation?

HUNGER DESPAIR POVERTY ENVY HATRED

Making Connections

Compare Texts

1 How do characters in "Hattie's Birthday Box" express themselves in creative and individual ways?

2 Why are there picture frames around the text on pages 373–375?

3 How is the box in "Pandora's Box" different from the one in "Hattie's Birthday Box"?

4 Think of another realistic fiction story you have read in which one character gives another a gift. Which gift would you rather have, and why?

5 Imagine that Hattie opened her "present" when she first arrived in her new home. How do you think she might have reacted?

Write a Journal Entry

Imagine that Hattie kept a journal of her adventures while traveling and settling out West. Think about an event in the story, and write the journal entry that Hattie might have written. Use a graphic like the one shown here to choose details to include in your journal entry.

Writing
CONNECTION

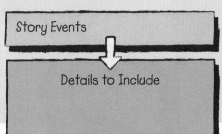

Story Events

Details to Include

Create an Illustrated Report

Carving wood and other materials is an art form that is found in cultures all over the world. Use reference sources to find out about different types of carving. Then choose a specific type to research. Create an illustrated report to share the results of your research.

Art CONNECTION

Create a Diorama

Use an encyclopedia, a social studies text, or another reference source to research the experiences of the pioneers who settled the American West. Then create a diorama to show something that you learned. Write a short explanation of the scene.

Social Studies CONNECTION

Word Relationships

Focus Skill

Authors choose particular words and arrange them in a certain order to make effective sentences. Their words and sentences must convey, or communicate, their ideas.

As you were reading "Hattie's Birthday Box," you may have come across some unfamiliar words. If you used the surrounding words or sentences to figure out their meanings, you used context clues. When you use context clues, you think about the relationships between familiar words and unfamiliar words.

Read the sentence pairs in the box below.

---

1. Grandaddy talked about the <u>great</u> times he and Hattie had together when they were young.
2. To keep warm, he put logs on the <u>grate</u> and started a fire in the fireplace.

---

1. Grandaddy taught Hattie how to swim in the cool <u>spring</u>.
2. When the boys came around, Grandaddy would <u>spring</u> into action.

Use context clues to figure out the correct meaning of the underlined multiple-meaning words. If you know one meaning of the word, but the spelling does not look familiar or the familiar meaning does not make sense in the sentence, try to identify how the word is used in the sentence—is it a noun or a verb? Also look for nearby words, phrases, or sentences that give clues to the meaning of the word or that give an example.

Visit *The Learning Site!*
www.harcourtschool.com

See Skills and Activities

Test Prep
Word Relationships

▶ **Read the passage. Then answer the questions.**

> The wagon train left long before sunrise. Now the sun was directly overhead in the sky. Will's arms grew tired, but he held <u>fast</u> to the reins. Soon the mountains would <u>loom</u> in the distance. Will's pioneer family had accomplished many difficult things, but getting the wagons over the steep mountain trail would be the most challenging feat of all.

1. **In which sentence does the word *fast* have the same meaning as in the passage?**

   A I had to *fast* for twelve hours, and now I'm very hungry.

   B The troops would stand *fast* and not surrender.

   C No one runs as *fast* as Florence.

   D I arrived early because my watch is *fast*.

Tip

In the passage, read the sentence that contains the word *fast*. Figure out the meaning of *fast* in that sentence.

2. ***Loom* means —**

   F to appear in a large or threatening manner

   G a machine used to weave cloth

   H to disappear from sight

   J a circular or oval pattern

Tip

Read the sentence in which the word appears. Choose the meaning that could replace the word and still make sense.

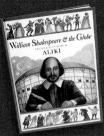

Vocabulary Power

dismantle
adornment
lavish
congested
patron
critical
shareholder

William Shakespeare became a famous playwright. It can be very hard for writers, painters, and other artists to become well known.

*S*ome months ago, the owners of the Two Rivers Art Gallery decided to **dismantle**, or take apart, the gallery and completely rebuild it. Last night I attended its reopening. The new **adornment**, or decoration, is very simple, not too **lavish** or fancy. The owners didn't want to take attention away from the art.

So many people were there that the place was quite crowded, even **congested**. I was lucky enough to be introduced to Mrs. Constance Appleby, who has been the **patron**, or strong supporter, of several young artists. She is a **critical** art lover, commenting thoughtfully about each artist's work. She also is a **shareholder** in the gallery. She owns part of the company in the form of shares of stock.

Here's the best news. Mrs. Appleby has asked to see some of my paintings. She said she'd heard that I was a promising artist, and she'd like to see for herself. I'm very hopeful that she'll like my work!

Mrs. Appleby

Vocabulary–Writing CONNECTION

Suppose you were asked to plan a **lavish** dinner to celebrate a very special occasion. Make a menu of what you would serve at the meal.

Genre

Biography

A biography is the story of a person's life written by another person.

In this selection, look for

- **Events in time-order**

- **Information about why the person is important**

WILLIAM SHAKESPEARE & THE GLOBE

WRITTEN AND ILLUSTRATED BY ALIKI

WILLIAM SHAKESPEARE

1564–1616
Poet • Playwright • Actor • Gentleman

THE GLOBE

1599–1613 • 1614–1644
The "Wooden O" Playhouse

Prologue

William Shakespeare.

Sooner or later, everyone learns that name. It belongs to one of the greatest storytellers who ever lived. Comedy, tragedy, history, fairy tales—Shakespeare wrote about them all, in words that dance off the tongue. We learn about the Globe, too—the playhouse where Shakespeare's plays were performed by the greatest actors of his time.

ACT ONE
SCENE 1

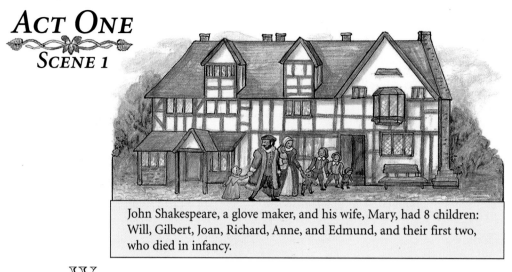

John Shakespeare, a glove maker, and his wife, Mary, had 8 children: Will, Gilbert, Joan, Richard, Anne, and Edmund, and their first two, who died in infancy.

Will was born in Stratford-upon-Avon, England, more than four hundred years ago. He lived with his big family, crowded in a house on Henley Street.

He went to the local grammar school, where he studied Latin, Greek, and subjects he would write about one day.

Will spent long days reading and memorizing drama, poetry, and history. His classmates were all boys, as girls did not go to grammar school in those days.

When he was eighteen, Will married Anne Hathaway, who was eight years older. Anne joined the Shakespeare household, too.

Before long their daughter Susanna was born, and then twins, Hamnet and Judith. Now, with a bulging house and a new family to support, young Will set off to find work in London.

396

ACT TWO

SCENE 1

The hub of London life was London Bridge—a city unto itself. There were nearly 200 houses and shops on it, and even a church. Its narrow passageway was congested with animals, wagons, and crowds, and Will would join them, too.

London. There it was. A noisy, overcrowded city, built on the edge of a river—with only one way to walk across: London Bridge. Shoppers, traders, beggars, animals, and carts clattered along slippery cobblestone streets crammed with houses.

Boats and ships swarmed along the smelly, polluted River Thames. Barges hauled cargo to and fro, and wherries rowed passengers across for a penny. It was faster and easier than walking across the bridge.

London Bridge was a marvel of its time. Over the centuries, it housed merchants and famous people. It survived floods, fires, and rebuildings for 800 years, until it finally "fell down."

SCENE 2

ELIZABETH I
QUEEN OF ENGLAND
1534–1603
Poet
Musician
Linguist
Patron of the Arts

Yet with the noise, smells, and sickness, there was music in the air, and actors performing everywhere.

This was because Elizabeth I was Queen.

She cherished the arts.

She loved music, dance, poetry, and plays.

She encouraged the artists who created them, and even invited them to the palace to entertain her court. One day Will would be one of them.

In Elizabethan England plays were popular afternoon entertainment among nobility and ordinary folk.
Locals and visitors flocked to see their favorite company present a new play. Traveling actors toured around London and the countryside. They set up a stage and performed wherever they could—in city or village inns and inn yards, or in wealthy summer residences. Perhaps as a boy, Will saw them perform in Stratford when they toured there.

Clowns, masked actors, and acrobats entertained and delighted audiences.

RICHARD BURBAGE
1567–1619
Actor • Painter

James Burbage's son Richard became one of the finest actors of his time.

SCENE 3

Traveling actors were not always respected and were often treated like vagabonds.

One actor, James Burbage, decided that players needed a home of their own to gain more dignity.

James leased land, assembled a company of actors, and built the very first public playhouse in England.

It was called The Theatre—the name given to all playhouses after that.

The Theatre was a huge success, and by the time Will Shakespeare arrived in London, more playhouses had sprung up.

THE THEATRE
1576

THE ROSE
1587

THE SWAN
1595

Each playhouse had its own playwright and acting company, named for its noble patron. One playhouse competed with another for its audience.

ACT THREE
SCENE 1

No one knows when Will's interest in the theater world began, or what he did when he first came to London.

Because of that, these are called the "lost years."

He eventually joined the Theatre as an actor and valued playwright.

Its new company, the Lord Chamberlain's Men, was the best in London.

Will wrote parts in his plays with these actors in mind.

Audiences loved Will's plays. They squeezed into the Theatre with their food, drink, and rowdy chatter.

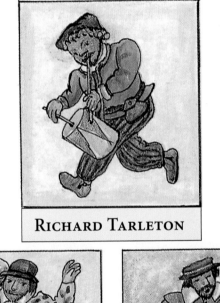

RICHARD TARLETON

WILLIAM KEMPE   **ROBERT ARMIN**

The three most famous clowns in Elizabethan times
were also poets, playwrights, and musicians.

SCENE 2

A deadly plague interrupted the Theatre's success.
For two years all playhouses were closed.
People fell ill, and thousands died.
During this time Will wrote two long poems and dedicated them to a dashing young nobleman, the Earl of Southampton.
The Earl was so honored, he became Will's patron.
Some say he paid Will generously.
By now Will was earning enough for his family to live in comfort.

Will wasted no time. In those two years he also wrote several plays.

SCENE 3

For twenty-one years the Theatre prospered.
Then unexpected trouble hit when the landowner, Giles Allen,
refused to renew their lease.
He had other plans for the land.
James Burbage had recently died, and his sons, Richard and
Cuthbert, became managers.
For two years they pleaded with Allen while their homeless company
struggled in a rented playhouse, the Curtain.
Though Allen owned the land, they owned the Theatre,
and they wanted their valuable timber.
In desperation, the brothers decided to act.
They leased land across the river near the Rose, and waited until
Christmastime, when Allen was away.
At night they secretly began to dismantle the Theatre and
floated it across the Thames piece by piece.

Widow Burbage looked on as Peter Street, their builder-carpenter, led the brave team of twelve—including her sons. They started on 28 December 1598, and it took them nearly a month to complete the task.

With the timber they started to build a new playhouse.
And because all the world's a stage, they would call it the Globe.
By spring they were discovered—but it was too late.
Half the building was up.

The raised flag–depicting Hercules shouldering the globe–announced the opening play. Perhaps it was Henry V. An open-air playhouse like the Globe was for the summer months. In winter the company used an indoor playhouse, the Blackfriars.

By mid-1599 the Globe opened to instant success.

It was so popular, it soon drove the Rose company away to build another playhouse.

Audiences packed into "the house with a thatched roof," sometimes three thousand at a time.

For sixpence the well-off sat in the Lords' Rooms to see—and especially to be seen.

For threepence they sat on cushions in the Gentlemen's Rooms.

For twopence they perched less comfortably on gallery benches.

But most were "groundlings," who paid a penny to stand in the yard beneath the open roof.

When it rained, they knew it.

- Ⓐ *Entrances*
- Ⓑ *Yard*
- Ⓒ *Groundlings*
- Ⓓ *Galleries (benches)*
- Ⓔ *Gentlemen's Rooms*
- Ⓕ *Two-penny Rooms*
- Ⓖ *Stage*
- Ⓗ *Heavens*
- Ⓘ *Underworld (trap to below)*
- Ⓙ *Musicians' Gallery and Lords' Rooms*
- Ⓚ *Hut (contains cannon)*
- Ⓛ *Frons Scenae (stage wall)*
- Ⓜ *Tiring House/Dressing Rooms (backstage)*
- Ⓝ *Thatched Roof*
- Ⓞ *Raised flag shows play is on*

Elizabethan playhouses had no scenery and few props. The glory of the Globe was the adornment of the stage—the richly painted Heavens, columns, and stage wall, and the hangings covering the central opening. Special effects were provided by musicians and a stage cannon that shot blanks. Often the elaborate costumes were discarded clothes—gifts from noblemen to their servants, who sold them to the company.

The Merry Wives of Windsor

Much Ado About Nothing

As You Like It

Henry V

Julius Caesar

Hamlet

Twelfth Night

Troilus and Cressida

All's Well That Ends Well

Measure for Measure

Othello

King Lear

Macbeth

Coriolanus

Timon of Athens

Cymbeline

The Winter's Tale

The Tempest

Henry VIII

Will brings each character and every human experience to life with his wit and the rich, beautiful language of his writing.
Elizabethans were critical and demanding.
They valued words more than scenery.
They used their imaginations to "see" the forests, seas, and battlefields in his plays.
They loved the melodious verse Will wrote. He was their bard.

Scene 2

In the next twelve years Will wrote his greatest plays.
Some were sad years, and the dark, complex tragedies he wrote
reflected his mood.

Will's only son, Hamnet, died of illness at age eleven.
In 1603 the queen died and was succeeded by a new king, James I.
The success of Will's plays and the Globe—of which he was a
shareholder—made him a prosperous gentleman.
He bought his family New Place, the second-finest house in Stratford,
and invested in other properties.
He would soon move back to his family and the countryside for good.

Scene 3

Then disaster struck the Globe.
During a performance of *Henry VIII,*
a spark from the stage cannon acciden-
tally set fire to the thatched roof.
In one blazing hour the glorious Globe
burned down to the ground.
Miraculously, everyone escaped unhurt.
It was a dark time for all.
Yet within a year a second Globe was
built on the original foundations.
It was even more glorious than the first,
and its roof was tile instead of thatch.
They weren't taking any chances.

Costume design by Inigo Jones for
Ben Jonson's *Masque of Blackness*

SCENE 4

The London drama scene was changing, supported by the new King.
He enjoyed plays and entertainment even more than the Queen had.
He admired Will's players and became their patron.
They were called The King's Men and often performed at court.
At the Globe, Ben Jonson was delighting audiences with his plays, and at
court with his elaborate masques—musical dance-dramas.
Inigo Jones was designing a new kind of indoor playhouse and creating
lavish sets and costumes for the masques.

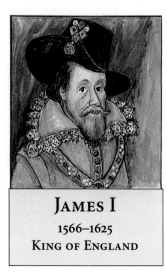

JAMES I
1566–1625
KING OF ENGLAND

INIGO JONES
1573–1652
ARCHITECT • DESIGNER

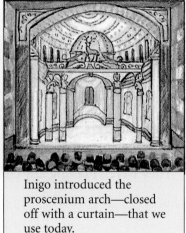

Inigo introduced the
proscenium arch—closed
off with a curtain—that we
use today.

Will kept in touch with friends and events in London, but it was time to rest. In the quiet of Stratford, surrounded by the garden flowers he had woven into his writing, he wrote his last plays.

A few years later, Will died on his fifty-second birthday.

He was buried in Holy Trinity Church.

As his friend Ben Jonson said:

He was not of an age, but for all time!

All the world's a stage,
And all the men and women merely players:
They have their exits and their entrances;
And one man in his time plays many parts.

AS YOU LIKE IT, II, 7

WORDS & EXPRESSIONS

Knock, knock!　　　　　　　　　Who's there?

Shakespeare invented some 2000 words and expressions.
We use many of them without even knowing it. Here are some of them.

mountaineer	schoolboy	shooting star	alligator
fortune-teller	football	moonbeam	critic
bandit	bump	dew-drop	lady-bird
employer	worm hole	glow	luggage
manager	anchovies	radiance	eyeball
watch-dog	fair play	dawn	love-letter
	horn-book		

mimic	farm-house	gloomy	blushing
partner	bed-room	useless	dauntless
zany	birth-place	quarrelsome	soft-hearted
excitement	fairy land	fretful	motionless
shudder	lonely	worthless	noiseless
puppy-dog			

to elbow	long-legged	flea-bitten	upstairs
to outgrow	pale-faced	green-eyed	downstairs
to hurry	hot-blooded	snail-paced	forward
to blanket	well-behaved	never-ending	lower
to cake	successful	full grown	far-off
		laughable	

And this our life . . .
Finds tongues in trees, books in the running brooks.
Sermons in stones, and good in every thing.

AS YOU LIKE IT, II, I

THINK AND RESPOND

1 Why was the Globe important to William Shakespeare?

2 Why are the illustrations and captions important to this selection?

3 Why does the author tell you that Elizabethans were **critical** and demanding?

4 What do you think Ben Jonson meant when he said Shakespeare "was not of an age, but for all time"?

5 What reading strategies did you use to help you understand this selection? When did you use them?

MEET THE AUTHOR/ILLUSTRATOR

ALIKI

Award-winning artist Aliki knew she wanted to be an artist from the time she was in kindergarten. She drew all through school and took art classes on Saturdays. She then went on to graduate from the Philadelphia College of Art.

Aliki has illustrated and written many books, including the *Story of William Tell* and *A Medieval Feast*. She says, "I have always felt close to children and books and feel fortunate that I can direct my creativity to both."

Aliki writes both fiction and nonfiction. Many of her ideas for fiction have come from the places she has visited, including Switzerland and Greece. Her favorite nonfiction areas are science, biography, and history. She says, "I write fiction out of a need to express myself. I write nonfiction out of curiosity and fascination. And I draw in order to breathe."

 Visit *The Learning Site!*
www.harcourtschool.com

AFRICAN PROVERBS

retold and illustrated by Ashley Bryan

I grew up in a household of proverbs. My mother had a proverb ready for any situation, attitude, or event. As a child, I was soon able to anticipate and finish any proverb that she would start. I heard, "Well begun is half-done," "Don't count your chickens before they hatch," "Beauty is what beauty does," "Rome was not built in a day," "Practice makes perfect," "Never weary in doing good," and many more. You probably have heard some of them.

African proverbs have also become familiar to me through my research of African tales. In making this selection, I have chosen proverbs from a number of tribes and have indicated them with the text. But none of the proverbs is exclusive to the tribe named. Many occur in other tribes as well. This is no surprise, for proverbs dramatize experiences common to all. It is therefore likely that you will find among them equivalents to proverbs you already know. —Ashley Bryan

A log may lie in the water for ten years,
but it will never become a crocodile.

—Songhai

As a crab walks, so walk its children.

—Kpelle

416

No one knows the story of tomorrow's dawn.

—Ashanti

Think and Respond

In your own words, tell what you think each proverb means.

Making Connections

Compare Texts

1 Why does the selection "William Shakespeare and the Globe" belong in the theme Express Yourself?

2 What heads and subheads does the author use to divide the biography into sections, and why?

3 How are some of the familiar words and expressions first used by Shakespeare like the proverbs in "African Proverbs"?

4 Name another biography you have read. How does this biography of William Shakespeare compare with that one? Which gives you a better understanding of its subject, and why?

5 If you could ask William Shakespeare a question, what would you ask him? How else might you find out the answer to your question?

Write a Descriptive Paragraph

The captions under the illustrations in "William Shakespeare and the Globe" mostly explain what the pictures show. Choose one of the illustrations from the story. Then write a paragraph that describes it. Jot down a list of descriptive details to help you plan your paragraph.

Illustration
1.
2.
3.
4.

Writing CONNECTION

Write a One-Page Biography

William Shakespeare lived during a time that we now call the Renaissance. Use an encyclopedia or another resource to find the name of someone else who was important during the Renaissance. Then research that person and prepare a one-page biography that tells why this person is remembered in history.

Social Studies CONNECTION

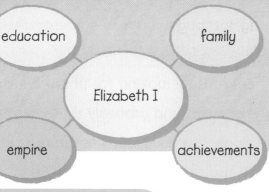

- education
- family
- Elizabeth I
- empire
- achievements

Create a Diagram

The Renaissance saw many advances in science and technology. Research the scientific advances during the Renaissance, and choose a discovery or invention that was made during this time. Create a diagram or another graphic that shows the discovery or invention.

Gutenberg printing press

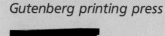

Science CONNECTION

▲ **William Shakespeare & the Globe**

Fact and Opinion

In "William Shakespeare and the Globe," you read about the life, times, and works of William Shakespeare. The author included both facts and opinions in the selection. A **fact** is a statement that can be proved. It is based on valid evidence. An **opinion** expresses the feelings, thoughts, or beliefs of the writer. Often it cannot be proved to be right or wrong, although you may agree or disagree with it.

You can often identify opinions by looking for phrases such as *I think* or for words such as *perhaps* and *probably* that indicate the possibility of other opinions. Adjectives such as *greatest* and adverbs such as *comfortably* also can signal an opinion. Some opinions include facts, but they are still opinions.

The chart shows facts and opinions from the selection.

Statement	Fact or Opinion	Can I Prove It?
Traveling actors toured around London and the countryside.	Fact	Yes. I can look it up in a book about the history of English theater or in an encyclopedia.
It belongs to one of the greatest story-tellers who ever lived.	Opinion	No. The word *greatest* tells me that this is the author's opinion.

Test Prep
Fact and Opinion

▶ **Read the passage. Then answer the questions.**

Theater audiences have long loved the plays of William Shakespeare. He was the greatest writer of his time. These plays were first performed in Elizabethan times. The characters spoke directly to the audience in soliloquies. A soliloquy is a speech in which a character thinks out loud. Shakespeare wrote the finest soliloquies. Hamlet, Shakespeare's most tragic character, delivers the most famous soliloquy of all. It begins, "To be or not to be: that is the question."

1. **Which of these is a *fact* stated in the passage?**

   A Hamlet is Shakespeare's most tragic character.

   B These plays were first performed in Elizabethan times.

   C He was the greatest writer of his time.

   D Shakespeare wrote the finest soliloquies.

Tip

Look for a statement that you can prove by checking it in an encyclopedia, a textbook, or another reliable source.

2. **Which of these is an *opinion* stated in the passage?**

   F A soliloquy is a speech.

   G The characters spoke directly to the audience.

   H Hamlet delivers the most famous soliloquy.

   J It begins, "To be or not to be: that is the question."

Tip

Look for a word or phrase that suggests that the statement gives the writer's feelings about the subject.

421

▲ The World of
William Joyce
Scrapbook

charcoal

encouraged

pastels

illustrating

series

Vocabulary Power

William Joyce is a well-known writer and artist who has created many popular children's books. Artists use a wide range of materials and techniques.

The Shell, 1934, by Georgia O'Keeffe

Artists sometimes use a black substance called **charcoal** to make sketches and drawings. The drawing above is by a famous artist named Georgia O'Keeffe. She used charcoal to create heavy, dark shapes. Art students may be **encouraged** by their teachers to find success with this technique, too.

An artist may draw with **pastels**. These colored crayons are somewhat similar to chalk.

This artist is **illustrating** a book about trees. She will create the pictures that go with the text of the book. The picture she is drawing now is the fourth in a **series** of pictures that show how a tree grows. When the series is finished, it will consist of five illustrations showing how the tree changes from the time it is a seedling until it is very old.

Vocabulary–Writing CONNECTION

Your teacher has **encouraged** you to participate in this year's art fair. Write a description of the work of art that you will enter.

Genre

Autobiography

An autobiography is a person's story of his or her own life.

In this selection, look for

- The author's personal thoughts and feelings

- First-person point of view

THE WORLD OF WILLIAM JOYCE SCRAPBOOK

TEXT AND ART BY WILLIAM JOYCE

PHOTOGRAPHS BY PHILIP GOULD

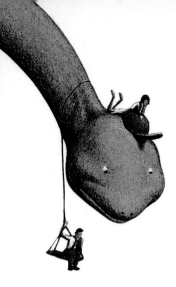

I wake up every day (pretty early, now that I have kids) and draw and think until I get an idea for a story or a picture. That's my job. On the best days, writing and illustrating is like getting paid for recess. Where do I get my ideas? They're all smushed up inside my head. How'd they get inside my head? Well, it started when I was a kid. . . .

When I was a kid, I didn't

have many books, just a Mother Goose book, a fairy-tale book, and a book called *Where the Wild Things Are*.

But I did play with my toys and watch TV a lot. TV was different then. There were only three channels and all the shows were in black and white, but there was plenty of cool stuff to watch. On summer nights, my sisters and I would watch cartoons, westerns, and monster movies all night long (or until we fell asleep).

I loved the stories in those old movies and I loved the drawings in *Where the Wild Things Are*. They really got my imagination going. So I started making up my own stories and drawing pictures to go with them. At first they were just about monsters and cars and spaceships and dinosaurs eating my sisters.

My first drawings were pretty

simple. But I kept drawing and painting and telling
stories with my pictures. My parents let me have art
lessons, and I had a couple of teachers and librarians
who encouraged me. I read lots of books and tried
all different mediums—watercolors, oils,
pencils, pastels, charcoal, crayons,
felt-tipped pens, pen and ink—you
name it. The older I got, the more I
learned. I had favorite artists that I
studied and even copied. I didn't copy
them to make it easier to draw a picture.
I copied them to learn how they drew. My
favorite artists were Maurice Sendak, who did *Where
the Wild Things Are*, Beatrix Potter, who did *Peter
Rabbit*, and N.C. Wyeth, who did lots of famous
stories like *Robin Hood* and *Treasure Island*. There
were times when my drawings looked too much like
theirs, but in time I found my own style.

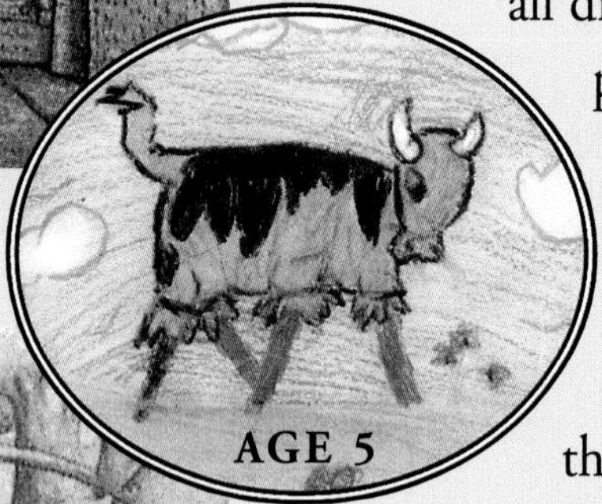

AGE 5

AGE 17

AGE 8

AGE 9

BOOK BEGINNINGS

I had even learned to draw realistically, but drawing real life wasn't very exciting for me. I missed doing spaceships, bugs, dinosaurs, and monsters. I wanted to draw places that I'd never seen, adventures I'd never had, and people I'd always wanted to meet. I didn't care if they were real or not, because making them up was the most fun and made me happy.

So when I was in high school I decided I wanted to write and illustrate books about all the stuff I liked. Once I decided to do that, I had plenty of ideas.

How I Do a Book

It takes a long time to do a book, so I have to like the story or the idea a whole lot. The shortest time I spent on a book was two months. That was on my first book, *Tammy and the Gigantic Fish*. But I spent almost two years on my book *Santa Calls*.

First I plan the whole book with a series of pencil drawings. I figure out what the people and places will look like and where the words will fit. These first drawings are often very loose, but they help me figure out how to do my paintings. The color paintings take the most time to do, so the more I plan, the less likely I am to make a mistake. If you look closely and compare the sketches and paintings, you can see that I change my mind a lot. I move people around and make their hair or clothes different.

I usually paint using very watery layers. First I do yellow, then red, then blue, and then brown or black. Using these four colors, I can mix any color there is.

Red   blue   black

GEORGE SHRINKS

The first book that I both wrote and drew the pictures for was *George Shrinks*. Ever since I was a little kid I loved stories about people who were the wrong size. King Kong was way too big for everything, and Stuart Little was way too small. One day I found some of my old toys in a box. Mixed up with all the dinosaurs and army men was a little airplane that had a tiny pilot, and that got me thinking.

What if a boy named George (George is my Dad's middle name) shrank one day while his parents were away? What would he do? Would it be fun? Would it be scary? What would he eat?

So that's what I made *George Shrinks* about—how fun and scary and neat it would be if, just for a day, you were the same size as your toys. And of course I had George fly in that toy airplane.

But I don't make *everything* up. I used some real toys in the book like my old teddy bear—he's on the title page. I even used some of my real books and other stuff like my desk and a table fan and a potted plant.

GEORGE IS SHRINKING...

SHRINKING...

SHRINKING...

SHRINKING...

SHRINKING...

SHRINKING...

stardust crooner

Bill

DINOSAUR BOB

Sorrowful

Bob ARRIVES

Base ball Bob

the Rescue

Since I'd always liked drawing dinosaurs, I decided I wanted to do a dinosaur book. When I was a kid I wished dinosaurs weren't extinct and that I could have one of my very own, like a really big pet dog. So I thought I'd write a story where a family finds not a stray dog, but a stray dinosaur.

DINOSAUR BOB
AND HIS ADVENTURES WITH THE FAMILY LAZARDO
by William Joyce

I thought about King Kong and the American tall tales like "Paul Bunyan," which was the story of a giant, and "Mighty Casey at the Bat," which was about a baseball player. I sort of combined them all and came up with a dinosaur named Bob who could play baseball and the trumpet and dance the Hokey Pokey.

So that's sort of the story of how I do what I do. I still draw all the time, just like when I was a kid. I sit at my desk, and I never know where the page will take me, or who I'll meet, or what adventure we may go on.

THE END

THINK AND RESPOND

1 Why does William Joyce enjoy writing and **illustrating** books?

2 Why does the author call this autobiography a scrapbook?

3 Why do you think William Joyce includes drawings he made when he was young as well as illustrations from his books?

4 Which of the photographs and drawings in the scrapbook do you like best? Explain your answer.

5 When did you use reading strategies to help you understand this selection?

MEET THE AUTHOR
WILLIAM JOYCE

William Joyce talks about why he wrote "The World of William Joyce Scrapbook."

When I go to schools, I get asked a lot of questions. *How do you do a book? Where do you get your ideas? How did you learn to draw? How long does it take to do a book? Do you put your family in your books? Do you get to sleep late? What was the first book you ever wrote?* Most people don't know any author/illustrators, and you can't find them listed in the phone book like doctors or plumbers or landscape architects.

Every author has his own way of doing a book. On these pages, I've tried to answer the questions about how I do mine.

Making Connections

Compare Texts

1 Do you think "The World of William Joyce Scrapbook" is a good selection for the theme Express Yourself? Explain your answer.

2 Why are the first several words in the first paragraphs on pages 426, 427, 428, 430, 431, and 432 in larger type than the words that follow them?

3 Why are there words in other typestyles and sizes on pages 430 and 431?

4 Think of another autobiography that you have read. What features does it have in common with "The World of William Joyce Scrapbook"? What are the main differences?

5 William Joyce mentions which artists were his favorites when he was young. If you want to see illustrations by these artists, how can you locate them?

Write an Advertisement

Write an advertisement to persuade people to buy a book by William Joyce. Use a graphic like the one shown here to organize the information to include in your advertisement.

Book Title	
Author and Illustrator	
Brief Description of Book	
Who Might Enjoy This Book and Why	

Writing CONNECTION

436

Make a Time Line

William Joyce was born in 1957. He tells about his childhood, when there were only three channels on TV and the shows were in black and white. Brainstorm other inventions that have influenced William Joyce's generation and your own. Find out when and where each item was invented and who invented it. Create a time line to show the results of your research.

1935   1937   **1939**   1941   1943

regular TV broadcasts
began in the United States

Create Book Pages

In his autobiography, William Joyce tells about trying different mediums for his artwork. Research different mediums to learn about artists who are known for their work in those areas. Use the results of your research to create pages for a book about art and artists.

Artists and Their Art

437

Word Relationships

Focus Skill

When you use context to figure out the meaning of an unfamiliar word, you think about the relationships between familiar words and the unfamiliar word. It is important to know how words are related. **Synonyms** are words that have the same or nearly the same meaning. **Antonyms** are words that have opposite meanings.

Authors choose words and put them in a certain order in a sentence to convey an idea. As you read, notice where in the text the author has used a synonym or an antonym to explain a word that might be unfamiliar.

Read the sentences that follow. Look for a nearby synonym or antonym to figure out the meaning of each underlined word.

- As a child, William Joyce did not <u>possess</u> a lot of illustrated books, but he did own a few.

- The drawings in *Where the Wild Things Are* excited Joyce's imagination and <u>stimulated</u> his creative spirit.

- Joyce was encouraged by teachers, but probably nothing would have <u>deterred</u> him from becoming an artist.

Test Prep
Word Relationships

▶ **Read the passage. Then answer the questions.**

> As a child, I loved to write about nature. All plants and animals <u>fascinated</u> me, but I was especially interested in insects. For hours, I would watch tiny ants carry grains of sand to their hill. I would observe how some of them worked together. Then I would write about how determined they seemed. Each day, I was <u>content</u> to look closely at nature and write about it in my own words. I was never dissatisfied with the way I spent my time or the things I learned. Today, I write books and articles about insects of all kinds. These books and articles contain more facts than my childhood stories, but the words are still all mine.

1. **Which word from the passage is a synonym for *fascinated*?**

   A especially

   B interested

   C determined

   D contain

   Tip

   Look at the sentence. Find a familiar word that you can substitute for *fascinated*. Does it make sense?

2. **Which word from the passage is an antonym for *content*?**

   F determined

   G learned

   H dissatisfied

   J spent

   Tip

   Read the sentence that contains the word *content* and the sentence that follows. Look for a word with the opposite meaning.

Vocabulary Power

produce

numerous

international

errands

gravelly

pawnshop

"Satchmo's Blues" tells about experiences in the life of a young boy who grew up to be a famous jazz musician. The place where he lived and the people around him were important influences in his life. Read what another young boy writes about his neighborhood and the people who live there.

Sometimes after school I stop in to see Mr. Gemelli, who owns the **produce** market on the corner. He sells all kinds of fresh vegetables and fruits in his store. There are so many different kinds of lettuce and squash and apples and other kinds of produce that they're just too **numerous** to name.

People from many nations live in our neighborhood. They like to shop at Mr. Gemelli's market because he has the produce they need to cook dishes from their different countries. Mrs. Wu says it is an **international** produce market.

Sometimes Mr. Gemelli asks me to run **errands** for him. For example, he asks me to go down the street and buy him something like a roll of tape or a newspaper. He always thanks me in his rough, **gravelly** voice and tells me to keep the change. Once, he asked me to carry a bag of peaches to his friend Mr. Crabb, who owns the **pawnshop** on the next block. People bring things like watches and musical instruments to the pawnshop to exchange them for money. Mr. Gemelli didn't want money for the peaches, though. They were a gift for Mr. Crabb.

**Vocabulary-Writing
CONNECTION**

Produce appears twice in the dictionary—as a verb and as a noun. Write a paragraph using both forms of *produce*.

Satchmo's BLUES

Genre

Informational Narrative

Informational narrative gives information, but the events themselves might not be real.

In this selection, look for

● Elements of nonfiction and fiction

● Some made-up events

The city of New Orleans sits along the mighty Mississippi River in southeastern Louisiana. It is home to red beans and rice, jazz music, and a musician named Louis Armstrong.

On hot summer nights, young Louis sat outside Economy Hall and listened to the Eagle Band play some of the best jazz music in town. He watched his favorite musician, Bunk Johnson, blow his cornet until the roof trembled. Louis hoped that someday he could blow his own horn that way and send the stars spinning.

Satchmo's BLUES

by Alan Schroeder illustrated by Floyd Cooper

Louis and his family lived on Perdido Street, "back o' town." It was a tough neighborhood, full of broken bottles and mangy dogs and kicked-in fences. But Louis didn't mind. At night when the lanterns were lit and Willie Reed brought out his fiddle, it was just like being at Economy Hall, with everyone clapping and dancing on boards:

"Mr. Jefferson Lord—

Play that barbershop chord!"

"Back o' town," everyone had a musical instrument of some kind—a clarinet, or a banjo, or maybe just an old pot someone had turned into a drum. But Louis didn't want a clarinet or a banjo. He wanted to blow a horn, just like Bunk Johnson. A real cornet, brass, with valves so quiet they whispered. But that took money, and Mama didn't have any. Not enough for a cornet anyway.

"You're gonna have to wait," she told Louis. "Now come on, help me hang up this washin'."

One day, right off Bourbon Street, Louis saw a horn sitting in a pawnshop window. It was a humdinger, all bright and sassy, just begging to be bought. The cardboard sign said $5. Louis turned away. He could never come up with that much money.

"It's not fair!" he thought. Everyone else had a musical instrument. Even Santiago, the pie man, had a little horn hanging from his wooden cart. People came flocking when they heard his familiar *toot-toot-ta-toot-toot*.

The next time Santiago came "back o' town," Louis ran up and tugged on his sleeve.

"Can I blow that horn, mister?" he asked eagerly.

The pie man handed it to him with a grin. Louis whipped the horn up to his lips and blew.

Nothing happened. Just a flat, spitting sound. *Ppphhhh. . . .*

Everybody laughed, especially Santiago. Louis tried again. This time, the noise was even worse.

Santiago reached down and took the horn away.

"I thought you said you could blow it, Louis."

Louis frowned. "I thought I could."

That made everyone laugh even harder.

But Louis didn't give up. He wanted to turn that awful *ppphhhh* into something wonderful—something so hot and jazzy that everyone would come running.

"And I'm gonna do it, too," he said to himself.

Two weeks later, the horn was still in the pawnshop window. Louis wanted to go inside, but the man behind the counter didn't look any too friendly. The cardboard sign still said $5.

"That horn is mine," Louis whispered, pressing his nose against the window. "It's gotta be mine!"

Every afternoon, when he got home from school, Louis stood in front of the mirror and practiced his blowing. He pretended he was Bunk Johnson, raising the roof with his high C's.

"What's you doin' with your lips?" Mama asked. "You look like a fish."

"I'm blowin' my horn," Louis told her.

Mama shook her head. "I don't see any horn."

But Louis could—and it was a beauty.

Anytime there was a parade in New Orleans, Louis joined right in.

"Go on, get out of here, boy," the marchers told him, but that didn't stop Louis. He'd kick out his legs and fall in right behind the Excelsior Brass Band. One time, Bunk Johnson saw him from the sidewalk and waved. Louis's grin must have stretched from ear to ear. He didn't have a uniform—he didn't even have a horn—but Louis just had to be the proudest stepper in the whole parade.

That spring, he did everything he could to earn five dollars. He sold rags and coal, and ran errands for the neighbors. Twice a week, he went "front o' town" to the produce markets and poked through the trash barrels.

"You're not going to find a horn that way," his sister Beatrice said, laughing.

"Go away," Louis said. He wasn't looking for a horn—he was hunting for spoiled onions. Using a little knife, he'd cut out the rotten parts, dump the good parts in a sack, and sell them to the restaurants on Perdido Street. Five cents a bag.

"Where'd you get these onions, boy?" a man asked suspiciously.

"I grow 'em," Louis said. "I eat 'em, too. Want to smell my breath?"

The man stared at him for a moment, then laughed. "Why, you're sassier'n blazes! I like that! I'll take two bags."

Every Sunday, Mama took Louis and Beatrice to Elder Cozy's church. Louis could hardly sit still, listening to the rich gospel music around him. Mama closed her eyes and rocked back and forth, clapping her hands. During the sermon, Louis pretended he was messing with his horn.

"Quit makin' that fish face!" Mama whispered.

But Louis couldn't quit. Blowing that horn was all he could think about. Any week now, he'd walk into that pawnshop and plunk down his money. He had four dollars now—only one dollar to go.

Still, that was a lot of onions to sell.

On Decoration Day, Louis took the trolley to the Girod Cemetery. There, he pulled weeds and polished the tombstones for tips. He earned fifty-five cents that day. Heading home, Louis felt tired but happy. He'd have his horn by the end of the week!

He was surprised to see Mama waiting for him out on the front stoop. She looked worried.

"Today is your sister's birthday," she said quietly. "You know every year I make a mess of jambalaya, but that costs money, and right now I'm low. I need a quarter, Louis."

She held out her hand. For a second, Louis felt like bursting into tears. Why was she asking for a whole quarter? Didn't she know he was trying to save his money? Didn't she care?

"But Mama—"

"It's not for me, it's for your sister."

Louis pointed to his mother's apron pocket, where she kept her money. "You have enough," he said.

"I may and I may not. I think you need to chip in, Louis. You can't always be thinkin' about yourself and what you want." She touched his shoulder gently. "And, Louis . . . you know how much you love my jambalaya."

It was a hard choice. Louis stuck his hand in his pants pocket and fished around for a quarter. Why, why was Mama asking him to do this?

"Here," he said, quickly handing her the money. And before Mama could say thank you, Louis ran into the house, tears streaming down his cheeks.

That evening, Mama fixed a huge pot of her best jambalaya: shrimp and crab, and thick slices of spicy Cajun sausage.

"This'll keep your jaws a-jumpin'." She laughed, spooning the jambalaya into three big soup bowls.

Louis ate till his stomach was fixing to burst. He was glad now he'd given Mama the quarter. There was nothing "back o' town" to beat the taste of good jambalaya.

An hour later, after the dishes had been washed, Mama came out onto the stoop. Louis was sitting there quietly, looking up at the sky.

"I 'preciate what you did," Mama told him. "I know you were savin' that quarter for somethin' else." She paused, like she wasn't sure what to say next. "Here, I have something to give you. Hold out your hand."

Louis did. Mama dropped a silver dollar into his palm.

"I'm tired of seein' that fish face," she said to him, grinning. "It's time you got a real horn."

At last, Louis had his five dollars! He didn't even wait to put on his shoes. He ran as fast as he could down to the pawnshop and flung his money on the counter. The nickels spun like crazy on the wood.

"What do you want?" the owner asked. "I'm closin'."

"I want that horn in the window," Louis said.

The man grunted. "That horn is five dollars, sonny."

"That horn is mine!" Louis said proudly.

Leaving the pawnshop, Louis felt ten feet tall. Underneath a streetlamp, he got a good look at his horn. Sure, it was full of dings and dents, but he didn't care. A little elbow grease and it'd be as good as new.

The air that night was rich with honeysuckle and jazz. Louis leaned up against an old packing crate, pressed his lips to the mouthpiece, and blew.

A moment later, a wonderful sound filled the alley: music. One note, then two, three, four, then a whole cluster, all tripping out over each other. Louis' cheeks puffed out like air bags. He loved the sound he was hearing. It wasn't "Dixie Flyer," but it wasn't *ppphhhh*, either.

"Lou-is!" Mama was calling him in the distance. But he wasn't ready to go home yet. Not by a long shot. He'd waited a long time for this moment.

Leaning back, Louis pointed his horn straight up at the moon.

"Hold on, stars," he whispered. "Someday, I'm gonna blow you right out of the sky."

He propped his elbows on his knees, closed his eyes, and began to play.

Think and Respond

1 What chain of events begins when Louis sees the horn in the **pawnshop** window?

2 Why is it important to know where Louis lived?

3 Why do you think Louis's mother took his quarter and then gave him a silver dollar?

4 Do you admire Louis for what he did? Why or why not?

5 What reading strategies did you use to help you understand "Satchmo's Blues"? When did you use them?

LOUIS ARMSTRONG

ALAN SCHROEDER

Louis Armstrong went on to become the most famous trumpeter in the history of popular music.

Leaving New Orleans at the age of twenty-one, he traveled north to Chicago, where he began his long and successful recording career. The public loved Louis. Over the years, his string of hits included "Ain't Misbehavin'," "Tiger Rag," "West End Blues," and "Hello, Dolly!" The film industry was quick to spot Louis's remarkable talent. He appeared in numerous musicals, and by the 1950s he had become an international celebrity, known around the world as Satchmo or Ambassador Satch.

Louis was also a talented composer, writing, among other pieces, "Coal Cart Blues," "Cornet Chop Suey," and "Struttin' with Some Barbecue." His autobiography, *Satchmo: My Life in New Orleans*, appeared in 1954.

Louis Armstrong, the Trumpet King of Swing, died in New York City on July 6, 1971. His gravelly voice and dynamic trumpet playing will never be forgotten.

FLOYD COOPER

❝When I was three years old, my father added extra rooms to our house and had huge pieces of Sheetrock to use for the walls. I thought the Sheetrock looked like big chalkboards and drew a very large duck on one sheet. My duck lasted through repeated washings with soap and water. But I wasn't discouraged that my father tried to get rid of my artwork. I kept right on drawing. When I was nine, I sold my first painting. A family friend paid me $16.00 for artwork and hung it in his place of business. I began to paint and draw more than ever.

After college I worked for a greeting card company, but I didn't feel that I could be creative. Then I discovered the world of children's book illustrating. I like that it allows me to be creative. As I read a story that I am going to illustrate, I try to imagine it. I ask myself: What is the weather like? What time of day is it? What sounds can I hear? What are the smells? Then I try to make the story look as real as possible.❞

ALAN SCHROEDER

FLOYD COOPER

Visit *The Learning Site!*
www.harcourtschool.com

457

Brass Instruments

from *Oxford Children's Encyclopedia*

Brass instruments are long, funnel-shaped tubes with a mouthpiece, coiled to make them easier to hold. The longer and wider the funnel, the deeper the notes it can produce.

To play a note on a brass instrument, you have to make your lips vibrate on the mouthpiece: it is a bit like trying to blow a raspberry. On simple instruments like the bugle, you play different notes by changing the shape of your lips. Instruments like the trumpet and trombone have valves or slides that open up extra lengths of tubing, so that you can play more notes.

A good brass player can fit a mouthpiece to any tube—for example a garden hose, or even a kettle spout—and play it.

◀ The French horn is always held by the player with one hand inside the bell. The sound the French horn makes can be changed by removing the hand from the bell.

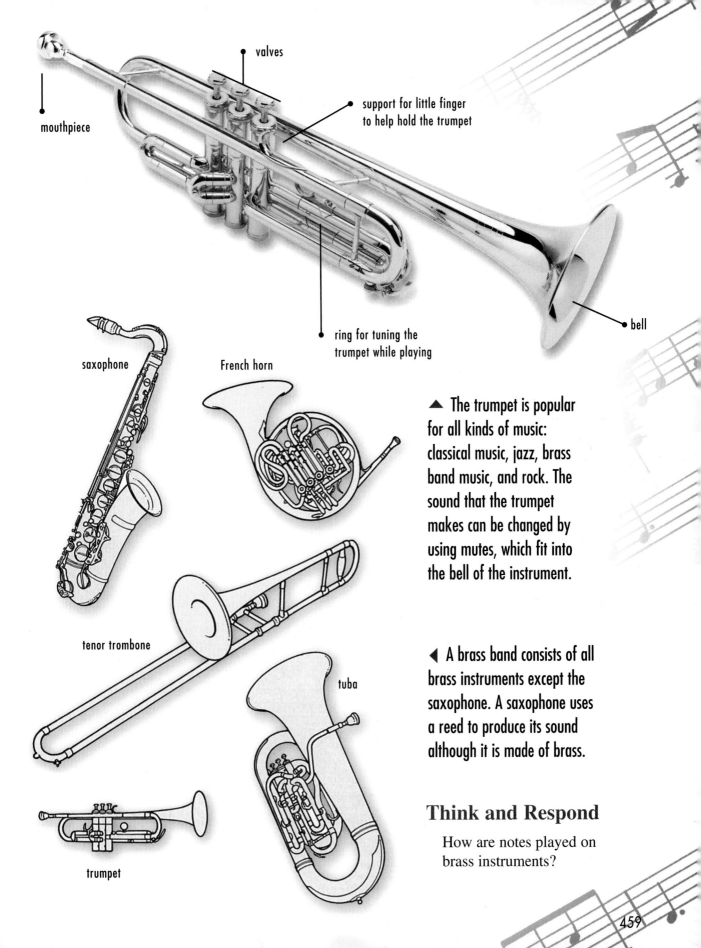

mouthpiece

valves

support for little finger
to help hold the trumpet

ring for tuning the
trumpet while playing

bell

saxophone

French horn

tenor trombone

tuba

trumpet

▲ The trumpet is popular
for all kinds of music:
classical music, jazz, brass
band music, and rock. The
sound that the trumpet
makes can be changed by
using mutes, which fit into
the bell of the instrument.

◀ A brass band consists of all
brass instruments except the
saxophone. A saxophone uses
a reed to produce its sound
although it is made of brass.

Think and Respond

How are notes played on
brass instruments?

Making Connections

Compare Texts

1 What can readers learn about self-expression from "Satchmo's Blues"?

2 How does the author show a change in Louis's mother's attitude over the course of the story?

3 Compare and contrast the authors' purposes for writing "Satchmo's Blues" and "Brass Instruments."

4 How would the biography "Satchmo's Blues" be different if the author had included only facts that could be shown to be true?

5 Suppose you wanted to hear Louis Armstrong's music for yourself. How could you do that?

Write a Conversation

Imagine that you live in New Orleans and Louis is a friend of yours. Think about what you might say the first time you see his horn and hear him play. What do you think Louis would say to you? Write your conversation as if for a scene in a movie or a play.

Writing CONNECTION

(YOUR NAME): ————————————————
LOUIS: ————————————————
(YOUR NAME): ————————————————
LOUIS: ————————————————

Create a Poster

In "Satchmo's Blues," you learned about the great jazz musician Louis Armstrong. Use the Internet and other resources to learn more about jazz. Look for information to answer questions such as these: What is jazz? How and where did jazz begin? What do the terms *ragtime, blues, scat singing, swing, bop,* and *cool jazz* mean? What and when was the Golden Age of Jazz? After you have completed your research, create a poster to share something you have learned about jazz or about a specific performer.

Social Studies CONNECTION

Create a Diagram or Cross-Section

"Satchmo's Blues" tells how young Louis Armstrong tries to blow the pie man's horn. He can't blow it because he doesn't know the proper technique for playing a cornet or trumpet. Use encyclopedia articles to learn about sound waves and how musicians make the tones of different instruments. Then create and label a diagram or cross-section of a musical instrument.

Science CONNECTION

461

Fact and Opinion (Focus Skill)

A **fact** is a statement that can be proved by checking it in a reliable source such as an encyclopedia or textbook. Look for facts that may support the main idea of a paragraph or of a selection.

An **opinion** is a statement that reflects someone's interpretation of facts. Writers may state an opinion in such a way that it sounds like a fact, or they may include a fact within a statement of opinion.

As you read each sentence below, ask yourself, "Can this statement be proved by checking it in a reliable source?" If the answer is yes, then the statement is a fact. Look for words that signal opinions—for example, *I think* and *I believe*.

Fact or Opinion	Louis and his family lived on Perdido Street.
Fact or Opinion	The man thought that Louis was "sassier'n blazes."
Fact or Opinion	Bunk Johnson played the coronet.

Visit *The Learning Site!*
www.harcourtschool.com

See *Skills* and *Activities*

462

Test Prep
Fact and Opinion

▶ **Read the passage. Then answer the questions.**

> Last summer our family took a trip to New Orleans, Louisiana. My dad is the biggest fan of jazz music in our entire town. I think it had always been his dream to see the city where jazz was born. After we checked into our hotel, we got a map of the French Quarter from the desk clerk. This district was settled by French colonists. That's how it got its name. The architecture has a lovely Spanish flavor. This part of town had to be rebuilt after fire destroyed it. Jazz music seemed to be coming from every doorway and window that we passed.

1. **Which of these is a *fact* stated in the passage?**

   A Our family took a trip to New Orleans, Louisiana.

   B My dad is a fan of jazz music.

   C I think it had always been his dream to see the city where jazz was born.

   D Jazz music seemed to be coming from every doorway and window.

Tip

Look for a statement that tells something that can be proved.

2. **Which of these is an *opinion* stated in the passage?**

   F The French Quarter was settled by French colonists.

   G That's how it got its name.

   H The architecture has a lovely Spanish flavor.

   J This part of town had to be rebuilt.

Tip

Opinions can't be proved. Eliminate answer choices that can be proved by looking in a reliable resource.

Vocabulary Power

▲ Evelyn Cisneros

The selection "Evelyn Cisneros: Prima Ballerina" tells how a great dancer achieved her goals through talent and hard work. Many people believe that both talent and dedication are needed to achieve success.

devote

scholarship

timid

migrant

apprentice

flexibility

thrived

The Leonard Building in downtown Southton is the latest project of the Vargas Construction Company.

Vargas Is a Winner

Mr. Manuel T. Vargas, president and CEO of the Vargas Construction Company, is a busy man these days. In addition to running his booming business, he makes it a point to **devote** as much time as he can to helping young people achieve their dreams. Recently, he set up a **scholarship** to award money for college to students who cannot pay for their education.

"I was a **timid** youngster," says Vargas, "too shy to speak up for myself. My parents were **migrant** workers who traveled from place to place to find work harvesting crops. As a result, I changed schools often."

Mr. Vargas was eighteen years old when he went to work as a carpenter's **apprentice**. He was glad to have the chance to work for and learn from a skilled carpenter. "I had to crawl into all sorts of tight places," Mr. Vargas recalls. "I was the youngest one on the crew and the only one with the **flexibility** to bend and twist my body in and out of narrow spaces."

Young Manuel Vargas had to work very hard, but he **thrived** as a carpenter, progressing steadily toward his goal of owning his own construction firm. He hopes that by giving scholarships to deserving young people, he can help others achieve success in life as he did.

Vocabulary–Writing CONNECTION

What kinds of activities or hobbies do you **devote** your time to? Write for five minutes about your favorite activities, and tell why you enjoy them.

Award-Winning
Author

Genre

Biography

A biography is a story
about a person's life
written by another person.

In this selection, look for

- Information about why
  the person is important

- Opinions and personal
  judgements based on facts

466

Evelyn Cisneros

Prima Ballerina

by Charnan Simon

*Evelyn dances
the role of
Sleeping Beauty.
Prince Charming
is performed by
Anthony Randazzo.*

Prima Ballerina

As the curtain fell, the audience rose to its feet, clapping wildly. The San Francisco Ballet had just finished a performance of *Sleeping Beauty*. The princess found her prince and lived happily ever after. The audience, however, wasn't ready to let their princess go.

"Brava!" they shouted, throwing flowers to the stage. "Brava! Brava!"

The curtains rose, and Sleeping Beauty herself came to the center of the stage. She bowed gracefully and smiled. Evelyn Cisneros looked exactly like a princess.

Evelyn Cisneros is the prima ballerina for the San Francisco Ballet. She has danced on stages around the world. It is hard to imagine that she was once so shy she wouldn't even talk in school.

Evelyn Cisneros was born in Long Beach, California, on November 18, 1958. The Cisneros family soon moved to the seaside town of Huntington Beach. Evelyn, her younger brother Robert, and her parents were a warm and close-knit family. They were also the only Mexican American family in Huntington Beach for a

> As the curtain fell, the audience rose to its feet, clapping wildly.

long time. Evelyn's father was a precision machinist whose parents had come to America from Mexico as migrant workers. Evelyn's mother's family had come to the United States from Durango, Mexico, in 1910 after the outbreak of the Mexican Revolution.

Belonging to such a loving family helped when neighborhood children teased Evelyn about how "different" she looked. Evelyn's dark skin, hair, and eyes made her stand out from her friends. Evelyn grew more and more timid. By the time she was seven, she was

> Evelyn grew more and more timid.

afraid to even raise her hand or speak out in class.

Evelyn's mother thought perhaps dance classes would help cure her daughter's shyness. At first, Evelyn didn't like ballet class. She remembers, "I was very shy, and it was hard for me to stand in front of everyone in tights and leotard."

Evelyn's mother encouraged her to go to class for at least a year. By the end of the year, Evelyn had met Phyllis Cyr, who would be her first real ballet teacher. Phyllis Cyr taught Evelyn how to enjoy ballet. She showed Evelyn how to move to different kinds of music and to see the beauty of dance.

Evelyn worked hard at being a good dancer. She was naturally graceful, and turns and jumps came easily to her. But her left foot turned slightly inward, and Evelyn worked hours on stretching exercises to get the foot to turn out. Then, too, Evelyn's shoulders were naturally somewhat rounded. Again, Evelyn worked many long hours to develop flexibility and strength in her shoulders and back.

Hard work didn't bother Evelyn. With her family's support, Evelyn learned all that she could about dance. And not just ballet, either. Evelyn quickly mastered jazz, tap, and other styles of dancing.

Dance lessons were expensive, and for a long time the Cisneros family could afford only one

*Evelyn's first
toe dance at age 9.*

The San Francisco Ballet School requires the dancers to practice long hours every day.

A Decision to Make

class a week. To help pay for more lessons, Evelyn taught tap dancing and demonstrated ballet positions for younger students. Mrs. Cisneros helped, too, by working at the front desk of the dance studio.

By the time she was fourteen, Evelyn knew she had a decision to make. She was enjoying school. In junior high she played softball, basketball, and volleyball—and held the long distance track record for her school district. Evelyn knew it would be hard to give up her school activities and devote herself to ballet. But it would be even harder to give up ballet. Evelyn chose dance.

From 7:30 in the morning until 2:30 in the afternoon, Evelyn went to junior high with her friends. After school she headed straight to the ballet studio. All afternoon she attended ballet class, demonstrated steps for other teachers, and taught tap class herself. After a quick dinner at home, she would go to the Pacific Ballet Theatre in Los Angeles. Evelyn danced at least five nights a week.

When she was fourteen, Evelyn's dance teachers encouraged her to try out for the San Francisco Ballet School. The teachers in San Francisco were impressed by Evelyn. To her surprise and delight, she was offered a full scholarship for the summer session.

Evelyn thrived under her new challenge. She practiced new and harder steps, and began acting some of the characters from famous ballets. More and more Evelyn was convinced that this was where she was meant to be.

> By the time she was fourteen, Evelyn knew she had a decision to make.

The San Francisco Ballet

The next year both the San Francisco Ballet School and the School of American Ballet in New York City offered Evelyn scholarships for their summer sessions. As much as she had loved San Francisco, Evelyn and her parents thought she should go to New York.

473

The summer proved to be scary, exciting—and disappointing. Fifteen-year-old Evelyn had never been away from her family for so long. She had never lived in such a huge, confusing city as New York. Still, she looked forward to studying with some of the finest dancers in the world. But when ballet school started, Evelyn was put in a very slow class. Evelyn recalls, "By the end

> ## "I was just about ready to quit dancing."

of the summer, I was very discouraged. I felt very depressed, and so unsure of the talent I had that I was just about ready to quit dancing."

Evelyn's parents again helped. They suggested that she call the San Francisco Ballet School. The company invited her to join them for the last

week of their summer session and to come back the following summer as well.

Evelyn worked hard at school all winter and returned to San Francisco the summer she was sixteen. At the end of that summer, the company offered to make her an apprentice. This would mean she would have to move to San Francisco and dance full time. At the end of the year, if she were good enough, she would be invited to join the company.

On February 1, 1976, Evelyn Cisneros moved to San Francisco. Within a year, she had joined the company as a full-fledged member of the ballet. She was just eighteen years old.

Evelyn quickly attracted the attention of the company's artistic director, Michael Smuin. In 1979 he created a major role for her in his ballet titled *A Song for Dead Warriors*. This ballet was broadcast nationally and turned out to be very controversial.

Helgi Tomasson, artistic director of the San Francisco Ballet, oversees rehearsals of Sleeping Beauty *with Evelyn and Anthony Randazzo.*

The ballet told about the mistreatment of Native Americans. Some people loved the ballet, and others hated it. Critics everywhere, however, praised Evelyn Cisneros's dancing ability.

Evelyn Becomes Famous

In 1980, while the company was performing in New York City, the leading ballerina was injured. Evelyn was called on to take her place. Important writers from newspapers and magazines saw her dance and praised her performance. Almost overnight Evelyn Cisneros became a very famous dancer.

Triumph followed triumph in the next few years. In 1981,

Evelyn again appeared on television in the ballet *The Tempest*. In 1982, she danced both ballet and tap in a live telecast from the White House. Later that same year, she received more praise from both audiences and critics for her lead role in a new version of *Romeo and Juliet*.

Not everything went smoothly for the young ballerina, however. In 1978, when she was just nineteen, she married fellow dancer David McNaughton. Less than two years later, Evelyn and David were divorced. It was a sad time. Evelyn's close family hadn't prepared her for a personal upset such as this.

There were professional upsets as well. In 1985, Michael Smuin was replaced by Helgi Tomasson as director of the San Francisco Ballet. During his years in San Francisco, Smuin had worked closely with Evelyn. He had created some of his finest roles for her, and she had grown under his direction.

Helgi Tomasson, however, also appreciated Evelyn's talent and her popularity as a leading ballerina. He has continued to give her important roles and has even created two new ballets especially for her. "In the

> Evelyn Cisneros has truly earned the title of prima ballerina.

beginning it was very difficult," Evelyn admits. "But now we have a very reliable working relationship."

Evelyn Cisneros has truly earned the title of prima ballerina. One night she is the lovely, playful Princess Aurora in *Sleeping Beauty*. The next night she dazzles in the double role of Odette/Odile in *Swan Lake*. She shows off her brilliant technique in difficult modern ballets, and sparkles as the Sugar Plum Fairy in the Christmas favorite, *The Nutcracker Suite*.

An Award-Winning Career

Evelyn's dark Hispanic beauty, which was once a source of childhood teasing, is now admired by audiences everywhere. Today, Evelyn Cisneros is an international dancing star; she has never forgotten her roots. Evelyn is proud of her cultural heritage. Young Hispanics look up to her as an inspiration. She takes her

Evelyn is proud of her cultural heritage.

responsibilities as a spokesperson for the Hispanic community seriously.

Evelyn Cisneros received awards from Hispanic Women Making History in 1984 and the Mexican American Legal Defense Fund in 1985. In 1987, she was honored as an outstanding member of the Hispanic community by the National Concilio of America. The next year, in 1988, she was honored for her outstanding achievement in the performing arts by the California State League of United Latin American Citizens. That same year she also was a spokesperson for a Latino youth conference held at California State University.

Evelyn also talks often to school children about what her life is like. She tells young dancers, "When you do anything athletic—and ballet is very hard on your body—you have to take good care of yourself. You have to make sure you eat properly and get enough rest."

When Evelyn is not dancing she and her husband, former dancer Robert Sund, share their home with two cats, Chatito and Boris. They like to walk on the beach, invite friends over for dinner, and go to the movies. For vacations, she and Robert go to Hawaii, or to visit Evelyn's parents in Baja California.

The San Francisco Ballet production of Swan Lake.

479

. . . she is applauded wherever she goes.

Evelyn Cisneros has traveled a long way from being a shy little Mexican American girl in Huntington Beach. Today, she is comfortable on dance stages around the world. Instead of being teased and left out, she is applauded wherever she goes. Through hard work and determination, she has turned her talent into a treasure.

Think and Respond

❶ How has Evelyn Cisneros changed from the time she was a **timid** little girl?

❷ Why does the author tell about the events of Evelyn's life in time order?

❸ Why do you think the author uses direct quotes from Evelyn Cisneros?

❹ What quality about Evelyn Cisneros do you most admire? Why?

❺ What reading strategies were useful in helping you better understand this biography?

Meet the Author
Charnan Simon

Charnan Simon grew up in Ohio, Oregon, and Washington. She holds a B.A. degree in English Literature from Carleton College in Northfield, Minnesota, and an M.A. in English Literature from the University of Chicago. Ms. Simon worked for a children's book company in Boston after college and then spent five happy years editing *Cricket* magazine. It was during her *Cricket* years that she began studying ballet and tap. She loved it—and it was great preparation for writing about Evelyn Cisneros. Ms. Simon has written dozens of books and articles for young people and especially likes writing—and reading— history, biography, and fiction of all sorts. She wrote *Jane Addams: Pioneer Social Worker* and won the Notable Social Studies Trade Book award in 1997. Today Ms. Simon lives in Madison, Wisconsin, with her husband and two daughters.

Visit *The Learning Site!*
www.harcourtschool.com

Celebration

I shall dance tonight.
When the dusk comes crawling,
There will be dancing
 and feasting.
I shall dance with the others
 in circles,
  in leaps,
   in stomps.
Laughter and talk
 will weave into the night,
Among the fires
 of my people.
Games will be played
And I shall be
 a part of it.

—Alonzo Lopez
Illustrated by Tomie dePaola

Eagle Flight

An eagle wings gracefully
through the sky.
On the earth I stand
and watch.
My heart flies with it.

—*Alonzo Lopez*

Illustrated by Tomie dePaola

Making Connections

Compare Texts

1 What art form does Evelyn Cisneros use to express herself? How does she use her creativity to overcome difficulties?

2 How is the information on the last few pages of "Evelyn Cisneros, Prima Ballerina" different from the information in the rest of the biography?

3 How is Charnan Simon's purpose for writing about Evelyn Cisneros different from Alonzo Lopez's purpose for writing the poems "Celebration" and "Eagle Flight"?

4 Compare and contrast "Evelyn Cisneros: Prima Ballerina" with another biography you have read.

5 How could you find out the country in which ballet began?

Write an Informative Paragraph

The photographs in "Evelyn Cisneros, Prima Ballerina" add to your enjoyment of the selection. Think about which photograph best conveys to you the spirit and personality of Evelyn Cisneros. Write a paragraph explaining which photograph you chose and why. Use a graphic organizer like the one shown here to collect your ideas.

Writing CONNECTION

Page Number of Photo	
What the Photo Shows	
Why I Chose This Photo	

Create a Booklet

Use the Internet to research one of the following famous ballets: *Sleeping Beauty*, *The Nutcracker*, or *Swan Lake*. Look for information about the music, story, characters, or other interesting details. Take notes, and use them to help you create a booklet about your ballet.

Harcourt

Back Forward Home Reload Search Mail Print Folder

Ballet Performance

Give an Oral Presentation

Use encyclopedias and other resources to learn about the Mexican Revolution. Find out the answers to questions like these:
- What events led to the Mexican Revolution?
- What was the outcome?

Create an oral presentation to share your information. You may want to display a map of Mexico to point out where key events in the Revolution took place.

Durango   Mexico

Text Structure:
Main Idea and Details

Focus Skill

In this selection, the author presents events in the life and career of Evelyn Cisneros. Each event in her life becomes the focus, or main idea, of a passage within the biography. Details provide information about each event.

In the diagram below notice that the main idea of each passage is also a supporting detail for a larger main idea—the main idea of the selection. How are all the main ideas in the diagram related to the main idea of the selection?

Main Idea of Selection

With the support of her family, Mexican American Evelyn Cisneros overcame extreme shyness, worked hard, and made many sacrifices to become a prima ballerina.

Main Idea of Passage	**Main Idea of Passage**	**Main Idea of Passage**
In Huntington Beach, California, Evelyn's mother enrolled her in dance classes to help her overcome her shyness.	Shyness kept Evelyn from enjoying ballet at first, but teacher Phyllis Cyr taught her how to see the beauty of dance.	Evelyn worked hard to become a good dancer, but hard work never bothered her.

Think about how the main ideas in the selection are related, and use them to identify the main idea of the entire selection.

Visit *The Learning Site!*
www.harcourtschool.com

See Skills and Activities

486

Test Prep

Text Structure: Main Idea and Details

▶ **Read the passage. Then answer the questions.**

> Alvin Ailey was a famous African American dancer and the founder of the Alvin Ailey American Dance Theater. Alvin tried tap dancing but found he was not good at it. Still, he was fascinated by music and dance and attended theater performances whenever he could. Alvin was in high school when a friend introduced him to Janet Collins, a famous African American ballerina. Through Collins, he met dance instructor Lester Horton. Alvin got up the nerve to start taking dance classes himself. These dance classes led him to a career as one of the most important figures in modern dance.

1. **Which sentence could support the main idea?**

   A Alvin attended ballet performances.

   B Alvin composed dances for TV.

   C Alvin Ailey stopped dancing in 1965.

   D Alvin Ailey's dance company has performed in forty-five countries.

Tip

Identify the important details in the passage to determine what the passage is mainly about.

2. **Choose one sentence that best states the main idea of the passage.**

   F Alvin Ailey knew Janet Collins.

   G Alvin Ailey was fascinated by music.

   H Alvin Ailey founded the Alvin Ailey American Dance Theater.

   J Alvin Ailey's interest in the arts led him to a career in dance.

Tip

Ask yourself, "Would this statement make sense in this passage?"

CONTENTS

489

Vocabulary Power

graffiti

obnoxious

campaign

endorse

residence

People of all ages, like Miata Ramirez in "Off and Running," may wish their schools, streets, or neighborhoods were cleaner or more attractive. Sometimes people decide to do something about it.

Walking home from school today, Kyle and I decided we were tired of seeing **graffiti** everywhere. Names, slogans, drawings, and other graphic images are painted on the sides of buildings, on walls and fences, and even on the sidewalk! Sometimes graffiti can be funny or interesting. As Kyle says, however, most of the time it's **obnoxious**. I agree that it's very disagreeable and unpleasant.

We decided to start a **campaign** to clean up the graffiti. Here's what we plan to do.

---

1. Talk to other students in school, and invite them to join our Graffiti Group.

2. Ask our parents and teachers to **endorse** our plans. We'll need their support and approval.

3. Print flyers to distribute in our neighborhood. Here's how our flyers will look.

Tired of graffiti?

The Graffiti Group can help. Let's erase graffiti from the walls of the **residence** where you live or from your place of business. You supply the cleaning materials, paint, or whatever is needed. We'll supply the energy and hard work.

Call the Graffiti Group today!

Vocabulary–Writing CONNECTION

Think about the kind of **residence** you would like to live in some day. Write a few sentences to describe it.

491

OFF AND RUNNING

Off a

Realistic Fiction

Realistic fiction tells about
characters and events that
are like people and events
in real life.

In this selection, look for

● Characters that have
feelings that real people
have

● A setting that is familiar to
most readers

M iata Ramirez is running
for fifth grade president
against Rudy, the class clown.
Miata promises to plant flowers
and clean up the school if
elected. Rudy promises extra
ice cream days and more
recess time. When Rudy
appears to be winning,
Miata considers what
she can do to get back
in the race.

nd Running

by Gary Soto   illustrated by Jerry Tiritilli

493

Saturday morning. There were only a few days to go until election day. Miata sat before the cluttered desk in her bedroom, surrounded by campaign posters and buttons. She stirred the water of her five-gallon aquarium with a pencil. One of the guppies darted and blew out a single bubble that rose to the surface and popped.

"Come on," Miata said into the telephone cradled between her ear and neck. She was calling a classmate to remind her to vote on Tuesday. She had called Dolores, Alma, Sandra, and Apple, whose real name was Apolonia.

"Belinda?" Miata asked when a voice answered.

"No, it's her mom," the thick voice replied. "She's still asleep."

"Would you please remind her to vote for me—this is Miata Ramirez."

The woman said that she would give the message to her daughter and hung up.

Then Miata's telephone rang.

Miata answered in an official tone, "The Ramirez residence." Then she heard that *quack-quack* of duck laughter. Miata sat up straight and pulled some loose ends of hair behind her ear.

"Who is this?"

"*Quack-quack.*"

"You think you're cute!"

"No. Rudy's cute. *Quack-quack.*"

"Are you a friend of Rudy's?"

"Better than a friend."

With this, the person hung up, leaving Miata repeating to herself, "Better than a friend. What does that mean?" Miata stared at the telephone. She picked up the receiver again and expected to hear the obnoxious *quack-quack* of laughter but got only the usual long *buzzzzzzzzz.*

When she heard her name being called, she left her bedroom and sniffed in the delicious scent of *chorizo con huevos*. She tried to get into a better mood. She skipped to the kitchen, where her father was already at the table.

"*Buenos días*," he greeted her, the sports page folded in front of him. "You been on the phone a lot, *mi'ja*." He sipped his coffee and asked, "*Pues*, so who's your *novio*?"

"Papi, I don't have a boyfriend! I was calling some girls to vote for me." She sat down, stomach growling, and clutched her napkin. She liked Saturday mornings. That was when her mother made tortillas.

"Dad," she asked, "you ever know anyone important?"

"Ever know anyone important?" her father repeated slowly. His eyes floated up to his wife, who was cracking an egg into the frying pan. "How 'bout your mommy? She's important."

Miata got up and hugged her mom's waist. "Mom is the best." She looked down at the eggs, now brownish red from the *chorizo*, and inhaled the flavorful smells of fried *papas*.

Her father sipped his coffee and said, "You mean someone well known?"

"Yeah." Miata returned and sat down, scooting her chair along the linoleum floor.

"Someone like a rock star or an actor?"

"Yeah, like that!"

"Someone like Eddie Olmos or Carlos Santana?"

"Yeah, Dad!"

"Like those *vatos* called Culture Clash?"

"Exactly!"

Miata's father tapped his wrench-thick finger on the table as he searched his memory. He finally shook his head and said, "Nah, can't say I have."

Miata's heart sank. She wanted to see if someone famous would endorse her campaign.

Joey came into the kitchen, still in his pajamas. His eyes were thick with sleep. He said, "Hi," and climbed into his chair.

Breakfast was now on the table. As Miata's family tore into the morning feast, her mom told her about a woman who had been mayor of a town in Mexico. It was Miata's *abuela's* sister-in-law. The woman had been mayor three times and was responsible for educating the young people.

"A real mayor?" Miata said with her mouth full. She swallowed and drank from her milk glass. Her mind began to turn. She thought that maybe that woman could tell her something about winning an election.

"Yeah, in a *pueblecito* near Aguascalientes. That was way before she moved here." Her mother wiped her plate with a piece of tortilla.

"Can you call her for me?" Miata asked.

"If you want, *mi'ja*," Miata's mother said. "I think I have her number. But she's really old." Mrs. Ramirez got up and cleared away some of the dishes from the table.

Miata's father asked, "We're going to the *quinceañera, ¿que no?*" as he picked up his own plate. They had been invited to celebrate the fifteenth birthday of a friend's daughter.

"Of course, but I'll let Miata visit with *la señora* for a little bit first."

After breakfast Miata and her father did the dishes, soapsuds climbing to their elbows. By the time they were finished, Miata's mother had arranged to see the woman, who lived nearby. Her name was Doña Carmen Elena Vasquez. Miata's mother said the woman was very happy to talk with Miata but would she please buy her some bread and Doña Carmen would pay her later.

"What should I ask her?" Miata asked. Now she was uncertain about meeting the woman.

"I don't know, *mi'ja,*" her mother said. She was standing in front of the mirror in the hallway, dabbing her puckered mouth with peach-colored

lipstick. "Come on. I'll give you a ride and you can walk home."

"Where are you going, Mom?" Miata asked. She pushed her face toward the mirror and glanced at her curls. She was starting to like her new hairdo.

"To Kmart."

Miata and her mother left, pulling away from the curb in their new used car, a Ford Thunderbird. They drove slowly up the street, the tires sweeping the fall leaves. They stopped at a convenience store to buy the bread.

499

They arrived at Doña Carmen's house.

"Don't let her pay you for the bread," Miata's mother told her. "Tell her it's a gift."

Miata got out of the car and eyed the small house, which was white with a toppled TV antenna on the roof. Geraniums, potted in coffee cans and milk cartons, lined the steps of the porch. A ceramic statue of *la Virgen de Guadalupe* stood in the middle of the lawn. On the bumper of Doña Carmen's old Ford LTD gleamed a sticker: YO ♥ JALISCO.

"Do I have to go by myself?" Miata asked.

"Yes. You wanted to meet someone important," Miata's mother replied through the window.

"Is she nice?"

"Of course she's nice. She's your *abuela's* sister-in-law. She's family."

Miata looked at the house. A cat was now stretching on the steps.

"When you're done talking, I want you to go straight home," her mother continued. "We have to be at the *quinceañera* at three." She touched a button and the window slowly rolled up with a sigh. The Thunderbird pulled away, scattering some leaves and an orange-colored cat washing itself in the middle of the street.

Miata approached the house, kicking at the fall leaves. She walked up the steps, knocked on the screen door, and peered in. An old woman was sitting on the edge of the couch. She was holding a lamp in one hand and a screwdriver in the other. A toolbox sat on the coffee table.

"Hello," Miata called brightly. "Am I disturbing you?"

501

"*¿Quién es?* Who is it?" the woman asked. She rose from the couch and unlatched the screen door.

"It's me—Miata Ramirez." She held up the loaf of bread. "I got it for you, Doña Carmen."

"*¡Ven acá, mi'ja!* Come in," Doña Carmen said in a singsong voice. She was a short woman, an inch taller than Miata, and walked with a slow shuffle. Her face was as soft as a pear, but her hair was steel gray.

Miata entered the house. A yellowish shaft of sunlight entered the corner of the living room, where a bookshelf sat. Portraits of the Kennedys and Cesar Chavez hung on the wall. A crucifix, made of bronze, hung on the wall.

"*¿Cómo te llamas?* What's your name?" Doña Carmen asked.

"Miata."

"Miata?" Doña Carmen regarded the young girl. "You gotta lot of curls."

Miata touched her hair. She wanted to explain the perm but thought the story was too complicated.

Doña Carmen told Miata in Spanish to sit down and apologized for the messiness of the house. She gestured to the toolbox on the coffee table.

"I'm fixing the lamp," Doña Carmen said. "It wouldn't close."

"You mean turn off?"

"*Sí.*" She sighed and said, "So you want to be *la jefa*, the leader, at your school?"

When Miata nodded her head, the curls bounced about her ears.

"Your *mami* probably told you. I used to be the mayor of *mi pueblo.*" She sat up straight, hands on the lap of her print dress. "Yes, I beat *mi esposo*, my husband."

"You . . . ran against your husband?" Miata asked.

"*Sí, muchacha.*" Doña Carmen's eyes sparkled as she recalled her husband, dead now eight years. They had loved each other but had seldom thought the same way.

"*Pues*, he would argue, '*Vieja*, today is Tuesday,' and I would say, '*No, hombre*, it's Wednesday.' Then we would spend all week arguing if

Tuesday was really Wednesday. That's how we were. We went round and round. Imagine! We lived like that for forty-six years until God took him away."

"So you ran against him for mayor?" Miata was now more than curious. She had spied a portrait of the couple on top of the television. They were as young as fruit on a tree.

"Yes. The man didn't want to advance. When we had a chance to hire some smart young women from Mexico City to teach in the school, he was against it. He said that the young women had city ideas that would make the children bad." Doña Carmen laughed and slapped her lap. "But you know what? Our children were already bad!" She laughed again and said, "No, they weren't *really* bad. They just liked to play."

Immediately Miata pictured Rudy and Alex. They just liked to play, too.

Doña Carmen explained how she had run against her husband because she had seen the future. She knew that one day the children of her town

would need to advance, not stay in place.

"The days of working like donkeys were gone, *mi'ja*," Doña Carmen said. "And the *gente*—the people—could see this. So I won! I was the mayor for three terms!"

"That's great," Miata said. She was impressed and full of fire as she listened to Doña Carmen tell her

recess." Miata clicked her tongue. "Doesn't that sound ridiculous?"

Doña Carmen looked right into Miata's eyes and, it seemed to her, right into her heart. "*¿Y tú?* What are you promising?"

Miata looked away for a moment and bit her bottom lip. After listening to the old woman's story, Miata was afraid that she had nothing really to offer.

"I just want to do little things," Miata said.

"*¿Cómo?*"

Miata told her that her school was run-down. There was graffiti, broken equipment, a poor, muddy lawn, and no flowers in the flower beds. Her promise was to make things pretty.

"Good. I will help you."

"How?"

"I'll give you all the flowers and little snippings you need." Doña Carmen rose from the couch and pulled Miata by her arm. She led her through the kitchen and out the back door. They stood on the small porch overlooking hundreds of plants— geraniums, azaleas, rosebushes,

about the new school they had constructed and the numbers who had gone on to the university.

"You're running against a *muchacho* at school, *¿que no?*" Doña Carmen asked.

"Yeah, this boy named Rudy Herrera."

"What is he promising?"

"Ice cream every day and more

hydrangeas, and jasmine.

"It's almost winter, but in spring, *pues*, we'll have *muchas flores*!"

"Yeah," Miata whispered to herself, as she pictured in her mind the

fragrant jasmine waving in the wind. She also pictured the azalea she had planted, dotted with white flowers. "We're going to have a sweet-smelling school."

Think and Respond

1 How does meeting Doña Carmen make a difference in Miata's **campaign**?

2 How does the author's use of Spanish words add to the selection?

3 What traits does Miata have that might make her a good school leader? Why are these traits important?

4 If Miata and Rudy were running for office in your school, who do you think would win? Tell why you think so?

5 How did you use reading strategies to help you understand this story?

Meet the Author

Gary Soto

"I think I'm very childlike," says Gary Soto. "I like the *youth* in my poetry. For me that's really important."

It was Soto's youthful outlook on life that led him to start writing poetry and stories for young people. Most of his stories are about experiences he had growing up. He believes he can write best about the things he knows. The fun that he had pops up in many of his stories. The things that were not fun are there too—things such as chopping cotton and cutting grapes under the hot California sun. In Gary Soto's stories you can share these experiences.

Making Connections

Compare Texts

1 How does the selection "Off and Running" fit into a theme about being part of a school community?

2 What does the picture on page 496 show you about the Ramirez family? How does this fit with what you learn about them from reading the story?

3 When Miata and her mother arrive at Doña Carmen's house, Miata asks if she has to go by herself and if Doña Carmen is nice. Why does the author have Miata ask these questions?

4 Think of another realistic fiction story you have read about a main character your own age. Would you rather have Miata or the other character as a classmate? Explain.

5 If you wanted information about the best types of flowers to plant in your area, where might you find it?

Write a Thank-You Note

Imagine that Miata decides to write a note to Doña Carmen to thank her for her help. Think about specific events in the story that Miata might mention, and write the note. If you know Spanish, you may want to include Spanish words and phrases that Miata might use.

Date

Dear Doña Carmen,
_____
_____
Your friend,
Miata

Writing CONNECTION

Create a Fact Sheet

In "Off and Running," Miata learns that Doña Carmen had been the mayor of her town in Mexico. Who is the mayor of your town? Use local newspapers and other sources to find out about the mayor. Make up a fact sheet telling about your mayor and what he or she has done for your community.

Fact Sheet

Name of Mayor:
Background:

When First Elected:
Major Accomplishments:

Create a Display

Doña Carmen has hundreds of plants growing in her yard. Find out how plants grow and about the process called photosynthesis. Use resources such as encyclopedias, science texts, or science websites to research this subject. Create a display to share the information you find. Include diagrams, flow-charts, other graphics, or written explanations.

Text Structure:
Compare and Contrast

Authors often show the relationships between characters, ideas, or events in a story by pointing out how things are alike and how they are different. Words such as *like, both*, and *similarly* signal information that is being compared. Words such as *different from*, *although*, and *nevertheless* signal information that is being contrasted.

Authors organize text in different ways. "Off and Running" is organized in the compare and contrast format. The chart below shows the similarities and differences between characters.

	Characters	**Information**
Compare	Miata and Doña Carmen	Both run for office against a male candidate. Both try to do something positive for the future.
Contrast	Miata and Rudy	Miata wants to clean up the school and make it pretty. Rudy wants the school to offer ice cream every day and more recess.

Miata's present life experiences are compared and contrasted with Doña Carmen's past life experiences. These relationships allow Miata to examine what is important to her and to find a solution to her problem.

**Visit *The Learning Site!*
www.harcourtschool.com**

See *Skills* and *Activities*

510

Test Prep
Text Structure: Compare and Contrast

▶ **Read the passage. Then answer the questions.**

> Chan and Corey were chosen to be student representatives at the mayor's youth council meeting. The mayor hoped to find out how young people felt about city youth programs. Mrs. Alvarez, the fifth-grade teacher, chose Chan and Corey because both had run for class president and both were interested in school government.
>
> Before the meeting, Chan researched the city's youth programs and talked to other students to find out what kinds of programs they wanted the city to provide. Corey made a list of his complaints about the city programs, to share with the mayor. Unlike Chan, Corey had no interest in what other students wanted.

1. The passage points out similarities between Chan and Corey. How are Chan and Corey alike?

Tip

Look for words that signal a comparison—for example, *also*, *and*, and *both*.

2. The passage explains how Chan and Corey prepare for the mayor's meeting. How are their preparations different?

Tip

Look for words that signal a contrast—for example, *different*, *but*, and *unlike*.

Vocabulary Power

Author Jean Little was in fifth grade in the 1940s during World War II. How do you think people's daily lives have changed since then?

What do you suppose these people would have thought of today's clothing fashions? Would they have **despised**, or hated, our styles? How would you feel if you opened your closet tomorrow and found it filled with clothing that was in style during the 1940s? You might be filled with **dismay**, a feeling of disappointment, uneasiness, and confusion.

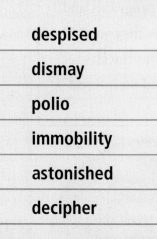

Years ago, some children and young adults came down with an infectious disease called **polio**. It was caused by a virus and was often followed by paralysis. President Franklin D. Roosevelt was unable to move his legs after having polio. Yet the **immobility** of his legs did not keep him from being an active and energetic leader.

Can you imagine being a student in this fifth-grade classroom? Students in the 1940s would have been **astonished** and amazed by our classrooms today. They would probably not be able to **decipher**, or figure out, the meaning of phrases and terms such as *surfing the Net*, *VCR*, and *CD-ROM*.

Vocabulary–Writing CONNECTION

Think about a time when you were truly **astonished**. Write a rhyming poem about what surprised you.

ALA Notable Book
Boston Globe—Horn
Book Honor

In this selection look for

- The author's personal thoughts and feeling

- First-person point of view

Little by Little

by Jean Little

illustrated by Allen Garns

Nine-year-old Jean Little enjoys reading, though she has problems with it. The words jiggle before her eyes and are badly blurred. To make matters worse, some children are mean to her about these problems. But Jean is determined to fit in, especially today, the first day in fifth grade.

I looked up from my grade five reader and smiled. I liked Miss Marr a lot. And, even though we had only met an hour ago, I thought she liked me, too.

She was young and pretty and she had a gentle voice. But that was not all. Like Mr. Johnston, she had had polio. As I listened to her passing out books behind me, I could hear limping, first a quick step, then a slow one. The sound made me feel a little less lonely. My teacher would understand how it felt to be the only cross-eyed girl in Victory School.

"This is your desk, Jean," she had said.

It sat, all by itself, right up against the front blackboard. I was supposed to be able to see better there. I had not yet managed to make anyone understand that if I wanted to read what was written on the board, I would have to stand up so that my face was only inches away from the writing. Then I would have to walk back and forth, following the words not only with my eyes but with my entire body. If the writing were up at the top of the board, I would have to stand on tiptoe or even climb on a chair to be able to decipher it. If it were near the bottom, I would have to crouch down.

I remembered Miss Bogart printing large, thick, yellow letters on a green chalkboard. That had been so different. These dusty grey boards looked almost the same colour as the thin, white scratches Miss Marr's chalk made. Her small, neat words were composed of letters that flowed into each other, too, which made reading them even harder.

I would not explain. How could I? She might make me climb and crouch to read the words.

I stood out far too much as it was. All the desks except mine were nailed to the floor in five straight rows. The seats flipped up when you slid out of them. They were attached to the desk behind. On top was a trough for your pencil, and in the right-hand corner, an inkwell which Miss Marr kept filled from a big ink bottle with a long spout. All the desk lids were a dark wine colour.

My desk was new and varnished a shiny golden brown. It had been provided for me because, in theory, it could be moved to wherever I could see best. It was, however, far too heavy and unwieldy for Miss Marr or me to shift. All that special desk did was single me out even more.

I turned sideways in my new desk so that I could watch Miss Marr and caught sight of Shirley Russell instead. If only she would notice me!

Shirley had about her the magic of a story. She and her brother Ian had

517

come from England to stay with their aunt and uncle and be safe from the bombing. She had joined our class near the end of grade four. Shirley had a lovely voice, with an accent like the child movie actress Margaret O'Brien's. She also had golden ringlets, longer and fairer than Shirley Temple's. She was a War Guest. She was different, too, but everybody wanted to be her friend.

"Face front, Jean," Miss Marr said. "Here are your spelling words."

She had typed them for me on a big print typewriter. I bent over them, drawing each letter on the roof of my mouth with the tip of my tongue. I had discovered that this helped me to remember them. It also helped fill in time.

When the bell rang for recess, Miss Marr astonished me by saying to Shirley Russell, "This is Jean Little, Shirley. She can't see well. Would you be her friend and help her get into the right line when it's time to come back inside?"

Shirley smiled sweetly and nodded her golden head. I could not believe this was really happening. Shirley Russell was actually going to be my friend. At last I was going to have a girl to do things with, and not just any girl. The War Guest herself!

We marched down the stairs and went out into the girls' side of the playground. I turned to Shirley, my smile shy, my heart singing.

Shirley scowled. Just under her breath, so that nobody but me could hear, she snarled, "You keep away from me. Get lost!"

Then she turned and ran.

"Be my partner, Shirley, and I'll give you my Crackerjack prize," I heard one girl call out.

There was a hubbub of offered bribes and vows of eternal friendship. Nobody looked in my direction.

I stood where I was, stunned into immobility. I should have guessed, perhaps, that our teacher had asked the impossible of the English girl. She was popular at the moment, but if she had me trailing after her, her accent might suddenly cease to be interesting and just be weird. She was a foreigner, after all, and she knew it.

Before any of them had time to notice me watching them, I walked away to the far side of the playground. I leaned up against a tall tree and stared off into the distance, as though I had my mind on things other than silly grade five girls. To keep myself from crying, I began talking to the tree that was supporting me.

"Are you lonely, too, tree?" I murmured. "If you are, I'll come every day and talk to you. We could be friends."

As I drew a shaking breath, much like a sob, I heard a gentle rustle above my head. I glanced up. The leafy branches seemed to nod to me.

You can count on a tree, I told myself. A tree is better than a person.

But I knew it was not true.

When we were supposed to line up to march in again, I heard Shirley's laugh and tagged on the end of the right line. I counted my steps on the way in. I'd find it tomorrow without any help from Shirley Russell.

Back at my desk, I heard Miss Marr ask two people to pass out pieces of paper. Staring down at the blank sheet, I hoped we were going to draw or write a composition.

"We're going to have a mental arithmetic test," Miss Marr said.

"Write down the numbers 1 to 10 on your paper."

I bent my arm around my sheet, shielding it from prying eyes, even though the others were not close to me. I had a sinking feeling the test she was talking about would involve those horrible times tables everybody but me had mastered in grade three. I picked up the special fat pencil Miss Marr had given me and did as I had been told. As I waited for the first question, I clutched the pencil so tightly that my knuckles whitened.

"Question one," said Miss Marr. "8 × 3."

I began to add. Eight and eight were . . . sixteen? Or was it fourteen?

Three and three are six, I muttered inside my head, changing my method of attack. I turned down two fingers so that I would know when I reached eight.

"Question two," Miss Marr said. "6 × 4."

I gave up on question one and began to add fours. I had reached twelve and four are sixteen when she went on to question three.

When she reached question ten, I stared down at my paper in dismay. All that was written on it were the numbers 1 to 10 in a neat column. I had not managed to get even one answer.

"Since this is the first day, you can each mark your own paper," she said. "What is it, Ruth?"

"Can I sharpen my pencil?" Ruth Dayton's voice asked.

"Yes. But hurry up. You are keeping us all waiting."

As she passed behind me, Ruth glanced over my shoulder. I did not notice her small hiss of astonishment as she took in the fact that I had not answered a single question.

"The answer to question one is twenty-four," the teacher said as Ruth regained her seat.

I knew that behind my back, forty pencils were checking the answer. I had to do something to look busy. With painstaking neatness, I pencilled in 24 beside the number 1.

"If you have 24 beside the number 1," said my new teacher, "check it right."

I stared down at my page. There, right next to the 1 was written 24. Feeling a little like a sleepwalker, unable to stop herself, I put a check mark next to the answer my teacher had just dictated. After all, she had *not* said, "If you got the answer right . . ." She had said, "If you have the number 24 beside the number 1 . . ." And I did.

"The correct answer for Number 2 is also 24," she said then. I wrote that down.

"If you have the answer 24 beside the number 2, check it right."

We worked our way down the sheet. First she would tell us the answer. I would write it down. Then she would instruct us to "check it right," and I would put a neat check mark on the paper.

When the others had finished marking their answers right or wrong, Miss Marr said, "Raise your hand if you have ten answers checked right."

I looked at my arithmetic paper. There they were, all ten answers checked right. I raised my hand. As I did so, I expected something dramatic to happen, a thunderbolt to strike me dead or a huge voice to roar, *"Jean Little, what have you done?"* Nothing of the kind disturbed Miss Marr's classroom. The teacher looked around at the eight or nine raised hands.

"Good for you," she said.

I snatched my hand down and stared hard at a broken piece of chalk lying in the chalk trough. I did not check to see whether anybody admitted to having none checked right. I was sure I was the only one who would have missed them all.

As she began a geography lesson, I felt relief wash over me. Mental arithmetic was at an end, for that day, at least. Perhaps everything was going to be all right.

My happiness lasted until noon.

Ruth and Stella came marching up to my desk while I was putting away my books. They stared at me with contempt.

"I saw you," Ruth said.

"What a cheat!" Stella put in. Her eyes were gleaming.

"Saw me what?" I said feebly. "I don't know what you're talking about. I didn't cheat."

"You might as well save your breath," Stella sneered. "Ruth *saw* you and so did I. You copied down the answers after she said them out loud."

"Are you going to tell on me?" I heard, and despised, the bleat of panic in my voice. They had me at their mercy and we all knew it.

"Do you think we would tattle?" Stella said, as though such a thing had never been known to happen. "We won't tell."

I cheered up too soon. She had not finished.

"But if you don't tell her yourself what a cheater you are, nobody in this class will ever speak to you again. We don't intend to be friends with a cheater."

I had no choice. I longed for friends. In spite of Shirley's snub, I still hoped that someday it might happen. I couldn't risk turning the entire class against me.

Miss Marr was at her desk. I walked up to stand beside it, moving slowly, trying hard to think of a way to confess that would satisfy my class and not make Miss Marr hate me.

Ruth and Stella lurked near enough to hear what I said. I stood by my teacher's elbow until she looked up. Then I took a deep breath and began. I stammered and stuttered, but at last she took in what I was mumbling. She told me to sit down. Then she waved Stella and Ruth away.

"You two are supposed to be on your way home," she said, her voice a little sharp. "Run along."

They went as slowly as they dared, but until they were well out of earshot, Miss Marr ignored me. She sharpened a pencil, then two. Finally she turned and looked at me.

"I saw what you did, Jean," she said.

I gasped. Had she watched me cheat and said nothing? I could not believe it.

She sat down near me and went on quietly.

"I don't think you meant to cheat, did you? It just happened . . . when you could not get the answers fast enough to keep up. Wasn't that the way it was?"

"Yes. That's just what happened," I told her, staring at the floor and trying not to cry. "I'm no good at my times tables . . ."

"You won't ever do it again, will you?"

I shook my head violently.

"Never ever!"

"Then we'll just forget it this time," she told me. "And you'd better get busy learning your tables."

"I will," I promised. "Oh, I will."

Think And Respond

1 What problems does Jean face, and what does she learn?

2 Why do you think the author called her autobiography "Little by Little"?

3 Why doesn't Jean tell her teacher that she can't **decipher** the writing on the board?

4 If you were a classmate of Jean's and had seen her cheating, as Ruth and Stella did, what would you have done?

5 How did using reading strategies help you understand the selection?

Meet the Author
Jean Little

When did you decide to become a writer? I always wanted to become a writer, but I thought writers had a difficult time making a living. So I became a teacher. After teaching for a while, I decided to give writing a try. I wrote a book, *Mine for Keeps*, which was a story about a young girl with cerebral palsy.

Do you use any special tools to help you when writing? Yes. I write on a talking computer, and I use a scanner that magnifies print.

How do you try to capture the interest of your readers? I like to start a story at a point where the main character is facing a change or a challenge of some sort. I never start with the main character cozily waking up. He or she is usually puzzled, afraid, irritated, or sad.

Visit *The Learning Site!*
www.harcourtschool.com

527

About Notebooks

from *Hey World, Here I Am!* by Jean Little
illustrated by Jennie Oppenheimer

I love the first page of a new notebook.
I write the date crisply.
My whole name marches exactly along the line.
The spaces are always even.
The commas curl just so.
I never have to erase on the first page.
Never!

When I get to the middle, there are lots of eraser holes.
The corners are dog-eared.
Whole paragraphs have been crossed out.
My words slide off the lines and crowd together.
I wish it was done.

I have a dream that, someday, someone will say,
"Here, give me that beat-up old notebook.
You needn't bother filling in all those other zillion pages.
Start a new one this instant
— Because it's February, because today's not Wednesday,
Because everybody deserves beginning again more often."

Yet, crazy as it sounds,
I always like to write the number 8,
Even on the third last page of a messy notebook.
It meets itself so neatly it's almost magic.
And I love swooping big E's and looping small z's.
If, for some reason, I get to write a word
Like "quintessence" maybe or something with lots of m's
or "balloon" or "rainbow" or "typhoon" or "lollipop"
I forget I'm sick of the book with its stupid margins
And, while I'm writing, I hum inside my head.

Making Connections

Compare Texts

1 What can readers learn about the theme School Rules from "Little by Little"?

2 Compare the illustrations on pages 515 and 525. How do these pictures show Jean's feelings?

3 How are the emotions that Jean Little expresses in "Little by Little" different from the emotions expressed in her poem "About Notebooks"?

4 If another person had written a biography of Jean Little, how might it have been different from this autobiography?

5 After reading "Little by Little," would you like to learn more about the time period in which the events took place? How could you find that information?

Write an Autobiographical Narrative

Jean Little wrote a true account of a day at school when something memorable happened to her. Think about an important event you would like to write about that happened to you at school one day. Use a graphic organizer like the one shown here to help you gather your ideas.

Writing CONNECTION

Details of the Event	How I Felt	Why It Was Important

Prepare a Report

More than fifty years have passed since Jean Little was in fifth grade. Since then, many scientific advances have been made in the treatment of various conditions that affect vision. Use the Internet to research advances in vision care that have been made in the last fifty years. Prepare a written report on your research. You may want to include diagrams or illustrations.

Science CONNECTION

Harcourt

Advances in Eye Care

Give an Oral Presentation

Like Jean Little, many people have faced challenges that have not prevented them from achieving their goals. Choose one of these famous people to research: Itzhak Perlman, Helen Keller, Jorge Luis Borges, Pierre-Auguste Renoir, Ethel Mary Smith, Louis Braille, or Jacqueline du Pré.

Use print, CD-ROM, or online encyclopedias to do your research. Find information about what the person accomplished and the challenges he or she faced, as well as other interesting facts. Use your information to prepare an oral presentation.

Social Studies CONNECTION

▲ **Little by Little**

Author's Purpose and Perspective

Focus Skill

The reason an author writes is called the **author's purpose**. The most common purposes are to entertain, to persuade, and to inform.

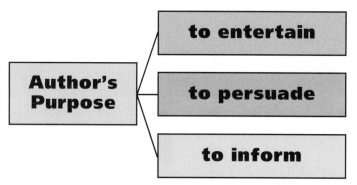

Authors often have an opinion about a subject. This is called the **author's perspective**, or viewpoint.

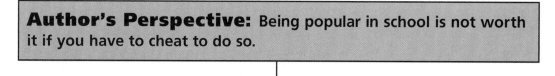

Author's Perspective: Being popular in school is not worth it if you have to cheat to do so.

Evidence: Jean fills in the answers on the mental arithmetic test to impress Miss Marr. She gets caught and just makes matters worse.

The author's perspective influences his or her choice of details to include in the text. It also influences the author's choice of language to use in presenting those details.

By identifying the author's purpose and noticing what details he or she uses, you can determine that author's perspective.

Visit *The Learning Site!*
www.harcourtschool.com

See *Skills* and *Activities*

Test Prep

Author's Purpose and Perspective

▶ **Read the passage. Then answer the questions.**

> No matter how hard I try to be on time, something happens to make me late. In my opinion, people are too concerned about being on time.
>
> One Saturday, I was about to leave for soccer practice when I remembered I hadn't fed my fish. I ran upstairs to look for the fish food, but it wasn't on my shelf. As I searched for the fish food, I noticed I had left my card collection out on the floor. I decided to put it away. Suddenly I realized soccer practice was about to start.
>
> I ran downstairs. As I passed the fish tank, I saw, right on the table next to it, the container of fish food. A few sprinkles later, I was on my way. I arrived at soccer practice to find Tim dodging balls in my goalie position. I thought I had a good reason to be late. Tim did not agree.

1. **Which of these best expresses the author's purpose?**

   A to persuade readers to be on time

   B to explain why feeding fish is important

   C to entertain readers with a story

   D to describe a list of chores

Tip

Look for details that suggest the tone of the story. Think about the whole story and eliminate choices that don't fit.

2. **Which of these best expresses the author's perspective?**

   F Being on time is very important.

   G Some people worry too much about being on time.

   H People who are late have reasons.

   J Lateness should not matter.

Tip

Look for words that signal the author's opinion, such as *I believe* or *in my opinion.*

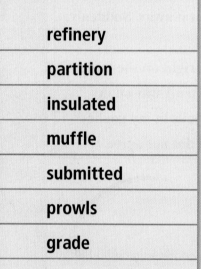

▲ Dear Mr. Henshaw

refinery

partition

insulated

muffle

submitted

prowls

grade

Vocabulary Power

In "Dear Mr. Henshaw," Leigh Botts wants to write a story for the Young Writers' Yearbook. Here are some story ideas that another student had for a writing contest.

Story Ideas

1. I could write about an oil **refinery** like the one where my dad works. I could describe the process by which crude petroleum is refined, or made pure. It's really interesting. A diagram would help show it.

2. Maybe I could write a story about visiting my mother's office. A **partition**, or screen, on each side separates her office from other offices. The partitions are **insulated** with a special material that stops some of the sound from passing through. The material can **muffle** the sound from the other offices.

3. Here's another idea. Suppose I **submitted** a story in rhyme. I could send in a story about a tiger that **prowls** in the forest, roaming quietly and slyly, slipping through the shadows.

4. I could describe how my dad and I made a dirt-bike track in our yard last summer. We even added a **grade** so we'd have a hill to ride up and down.

Vocabulary–Writing CONNECTION

Write a tongue twister about an animal that **prowls** around the jungle. For example: The jumping jaguar juggles jelly jars just for joy.

DEAR

Genre

Realistic Fiction

Realistic fiction tells about characters and events that are like people and events in real life.

In this selection, look for

- Characters with challenges and problems that could happen in real life

- A setting that is familiar to most readers

Leigh Botts has been keeping a diary and writing to his favorite author, Mr. Boyd Henshaw, since second grade. Now, as a sixth grader, Leigh has new problems:

❶ His mother and his father, a truck driver, are divorced.

❷ His father's girlfriend has a son his age that Leigh calls the pizza boy.

❸ Someone at school is stealing the best part of Leigh's lunch every day.

❹ His story for the Young Writers' Yearbook is not going well.

Can Leigh find solutions to any of these problems?

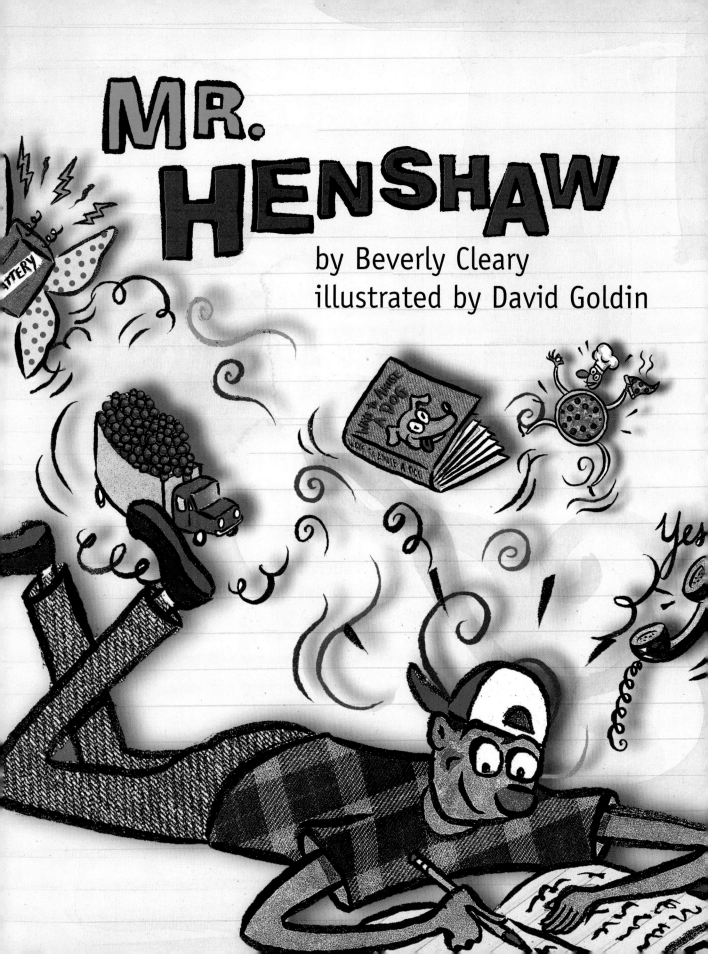

Thursday, March 1

I am getting behind in this diary for several reasons, including working on my story and writing to Mr. Henshaw (really, not just pretend). I also had to buy a new notebook because I had filled up the first one.

The same day, I bought a beat-up black lunchbox in the thrift shop down the street and started carrying my lunch in it. The kids were surprised, but nobody made fun of me, because a black lunchbox isn't the same as one of those square boxes covered with cartoon characters that first and second graders carry. A couple of boys asked if it was my Dad's. I just grinned and said, "Where do you think I got it?" The next day my little

slices of salami rolled around cream cheese were gone, but I expected that. But I'll get that thief yet. I'll make him really sorry he ate all the best things out of my lunch.

Next I went to the library for books on batteries. I took out a couple of easy books on electricity, really easy, because I have never given much thought to batteries. About all I know is that when you want to use a flashlight, the battery is usually dead.

I finally gave up on my story about the ten-foot wax man, which was really pretty dumb. I thought I would write a poem about butterflies for Young Writers because

a poem can be short, but it is hard to think about butterflies and burglar alarms at the same time, so I studied electricity books instead. The books didn't have directions for an alarm in a lunchbox, but I learned enough about batteries and switches and insulated wires, so I think I can figure it out myself.

Friday, March 2

Back to the poem tonight. The only rhyme I can think of for "butterfly" is "flutter by." I can think up rhymes like "trees" and "breeze" which are pretty boring, and then I think of "wheeze" and "sneeze." A poem about butterflies wheezing and sneezing seems silly, and anyway a couple of girls are already writing poems about monarch butterflies that flutter by.

Sometimes I start a letter to Dad thanking him for the twenty dollars, but I can't finish that either. I don't know why.

Saturday, March 3

Today I took my lunchbox and Dad's twenty dollars to the hardware store and looked around. I found an ordinary light switch, a little battery and a cheap doorbell. While I was looking around for the right kind of insulated wire, a man who had been watching me (boys my age always get watched when they go into stores) asked if he could help me. He was a nice old gentleman who said, "What are you planning to make, son?" *Son*. He called me son, and my Dad calls me kid. I didn't want to tell the man, but when he looked at the things I was holding, he grinned and said, "Having trouble with your lunch, aren't you?" I nodded and said, "I'm trying to make a burglar alarm."

He said, "That's what I guessed. I've had workmen in here with the same problem."

It turned out that I needed a 6-volt lantern battery instead of the battery I had picked out. He gave me a couple of tips and, after I paid for the things, a little slap on the back and said, "Good luck, son."

I tore home with all the things I bought. First I made a sign for my door that said

KEEP OUT
MOM
THAT MEANS YOU

Then I went to work fastening one wire from the battery to the switch and from the other side of the switch to the doorbell. Then I fastened a second wire from the battery to the doorbell. It took me a while to get it right. Then I taped the battery in one corner of the lunchbox and the doorbell in another. I stood the switch up at the back of the box and taped that in place, too.

Here I ran into a problem. I thought I could take the wire clamp meant to hold a thermos bottle inside the lunchbox lid and hook it under the switch if I reached in carefully as I closed the box. The clamp wasn't quite long enough. After some thinking and experimenting, I twisted a wire loop onto it. Then I closed the box just enough so I could get my hand inside and push the wire loop over the button on the switch before I took my hand out and closed the box.

KEEP OUT
MOM
THAT MEANS YOU

DOORBELL

BATTERY

CONNECT
TO SWITCH

Monday, March 5

Today Mom packed my lunch carefully, and we tried the alarm to see if it still worked. It did, good and loud. When I got to school, Mr. Fridley said, "Nice to see you smiling, Leigh. You should try it more often."

I parked my lunchbox behind the partition and waited. I waited all morning for the alarm to go off. Miss Martinez asked if I had my mind on my work. I pretended I did, but all the time I was really waiting for my alarm to go off so I could dash back behind the partition and tackle the thief. When nothing happened, I began to worry. Maybe the loop had somehow slipped off the switch on the way to school.

Then I opened the box. My burglar alarm worked! That bell inside the box went off with a terrible racket that brought Mom to my door. "Leigh, what on earth is going on in there?" she shouted above the alarm.

I let her in and gave her a demonstration of my burglar alarm. She laughed and said it was a great invention. One thing was bothering me. Would my sandwich muffle the bell? Mom must have been wondering the same thing, because she suggested taping a piece of cardboard into the lid that would make a shelf for my sandwich. I did, and that worked, too.

I can't wait until Monday.

Lunchtime came. The alarm still hadn't gone off. We all picked up our lunches and went off to the cafeteria. When I set my box on the table in front of me, I realized I had a problem, a big problem. If the loop hadn't slipped off the switch, my alarm was still triggered. I just sat there, staring at my lunchbox, not knowing what to do.

"How come you're not eating?" Barry asked with his mouth full. Barry's sandwiches are never cut in half, and he always takes a big bite out of one side to start.

Everybody at the table was looking at me. I thought about saying I wasn't hungry, but I was. I thought about taking my lunchbox out into the hall to open, but if the alarm was still triggered, there was no way I could open it quietly. Finally I thought, here goes. I unsnapped the two fasteners on the box and held my breath as I opened the lid.

Wow! My alarm went off! The noise was so loud it startled everybody at the table including me and made everyone in the cafeteria look around. I looked up and saw Mr. Fridley grinning at me over by the garbage can. Then I turned off the alarm.

I began to feel like some sort of **HERO**. Maybe I'm not so medium after all.

L U N C H B O X   H E R O

Suddenly everybody seemed to be noticing me. The principal, who always prowls around keeping an eye on things at lunchtime, came over to examine my lunchbox. He said, "That's quite an invention you have there."

"Thanks," I said, pleased that the principal seemed to like my alarm.

Some of the teachers came out of their lunchroom to see what the noise was all about. I had to give a demonstration. It seems I wasn't the only one who had things stolen from my lunch, and all the kids said they wanted lunchboxes with alarms, too, even those whose lunches were never good enough to have anything stolen. Barry said he would like an alarm like that on the door of his room at home. I began to feel like some sort of hero. Maybe I'm not so medium after all.

One thing bothers me, though. I still don't know who's been robbing my lunch.

Tuesday, March 6

Today Barry asked me to come home with him to see if I could help him rig up a burglar alarm for his room because he has a bunch of little sisters and stepsisters who get into his stuff. I thought I could, because I had seen an alarm like that in one of the electricity books from the library.

Barry lives in a big old house that is sort of cheerful and messy, with little girls all over the place. As it turned out, Barry didn't have the right kind of battery so we just fooled around looking at his models. Barry never uses directions when he puts models together, because the directions are too hard and spoil the fun. He throws them away and figures out how the pieces fit by himself.

I still don't know what to write for Young Writers, but I was feeling so good I finally wrote to Dad to thank him for the twenty dollars because I had found a good use for it even if I couldn't save it all toward a typewriter. I didn't say much.

I wonder if Dad will marry the pizza boy and his mother. I worry about that a lot.

Thursday, March 15

This week several kids turned up with lunchboxes with burglar alarms. You know that song about the hills ringing with the sound of music? Well you might say our cafeteria rang with the sound of burglar alarms. The fad didn't last very long, and after a while I didn't even bother to set my alarm. Nobody has robbed my lunchbox since I set it off that day.

I never did find out who the thief was, and now that I stop to think about it, I am glad. If he had set off the alarm when my lunchbox was in the classroom, he would have been in trouble, big trouble. Maybe he was just somebody whose mother packed bad lunches—jelly sandwiches on that white bread that tastes like Kleenex. Or maybe he had to pack his own lunches and there was never anything good in the house to put in them. I have seen people look into their lunches, take out the cookies and throw the rest in the garbage. Mr. Fridley always looks worried when they do this.

I'm not saying robbing lunchboxes is right. I am saying I'm glad I don't know who the thief was, because I have to go to school with him.

Friday, March 16

Tonight I was staring at a piece of paper trying to think of something to write for Young Writers when the phone rang. Mom told me to answer because she was washing her hair.

It was Dad. My stomach felt as if it was dropping to the floor, the way it always does when I hear his voice. "How're you doing, kid?" he asked.

"Fine," I said, thinking of the success of my burglar alarm. "Great."

"I got your letter," he said.

"That's good," I said. His call took me so by surprise that I could feel my heart pounding, and I couldn't think of anything to say until I asked, "Have you found another dog to take Bandit's place?" I think what I really meant was, Have you found another boy to take my place?

"No, but I ask about him on my CB," Dad told me. "He may turn up yet."

"I hope so." This conversation was going no place. I really didn't know what to say to my father. It was embarrassing.

Then Dad surprised me. He asked, "Do you ever miss your old Dad?"

I had to think a minute. I missed him all right, but I couldn't seem to get the words out. My silence must have bothered him because he asked, "Are you still there?"

"Sure, Dad, I miss you," I told him. It was true, but not as true as it had been a couple of months ago. I still wanted him to pull up in front of the house in his big rig, but now I knew I couldn't count on it.

"Sorry I don't get over your way more often," he said. "I hear the sugar refinery in Spreckels is closing down."

"I read about it in the paper," I said.

"Is your mother handy?" he asked.

"I'll see," I said even though by then she was standing by the phone with her hair wrapped in a towel. She shook her head. She didn't want to talk to Dad.

"She's washing her hair," I said.

"Tell her I'll manage to send your support check sometime next week," he said. "So long, kid. Keep your nose clean."

"So long, Dad," I answered. "Drive carefully." I guess he'll never learn that my name is Leigh and that my nose is clean. Maybe he thinks I'll never learn that he drives carefully. He doesn't really. He's a good driver, but he speeds to make time whenever he can avoid the highway patrol. All truckers do.

After that I couldn't get back to thinking about Young Writers, so I picked up *Ways to Amuse a Dog* and read it for the thousandth time. I read harder books now, but I still feel good when I read that book. I wonder where Mr. Henshaw is.

Saturday, March 17

Today is Saturday, so this morning I walked to the butterfly trees again. The grove was quiet and peaceful, and because the sun was shining, I stood there a long time, looking at the orange butterflies floating through the gray and green leaves and listening to the sound of the ocean on the rocks. There aren't as many butterflies now. Maybe they are starting to go north for the summer. I thought I might write about them in prose instead of poetry, but on the way home I got to thinking about Dad and one time when he took me along when he was hauling grapes and what a great day it had been.

Tuesday, March 20

Yesterday Miss Neely, the librarian, asked if I had written anything for the Young Writers' Yearbook, because all writing had to be turned in by tomorrow. When I told her I hadn't, she said I still had twenty-four hours and why didn't I get busy? So I did, because I really would like to meet a Famous Author. My story about the ten-foot wax man went into the wastebasket. Next I tried to start a story called *The Great Lunchbox Mystery*, but I couldn't seem to turn my lunchbox experience into a story because I don't know who the thief (thieves) was (were), and I don't want to know.

Finally I dashed off a description of the time I rode with my father when he was trucking the load of grapes down Highway 152 through Pacheco Pass. I put in things like the signs that said STEEP GRADE, TRUCKS USE LOW GEAR and how Dad down-shifted and how skillful he was handling a long, heavy load on the curves. I put in about the hawks on the telephone wires and about that high peak where Black Bart's lookout used to watch for travelers coming through the pass so he could signal to Black Bart to rob them, and how the leaves on the trees along the stream at the bottom of the pass were turning yellow and how good tons of grapes smelled in the sun. I left out the part about the waitresses and the video games. Then I copied the whole thing over in case neatness counts and gave it to Miss Neely.

Saturday, March 24

Mom said I had to invite Barry over to our house for supper because I have been going to his house after school so often. We had been working on a burglar alarm for his room which we finally got to work with some help from a library book.

I wasn't sure Barry would like to come to our house which is so small compared to his, but he accepted when I invited him.

Mom cooked a casserole full of good things like ground beef, chilies, tortillas, tomatoes and cheese. Barry said he really liked eating at our house because he got tired of eating with a bunch of little sisters waving spoons and drumsticks. That made me happy. It helps to have a friend.

Barry says his burglar alarm still works. The trouble is, his sisters think it's fun to open his door to set it off. Then they giggle and hide. This was driving his mother crazy, so he finally had to disconnect it. We all laughed about this. Barry and I felt good about making something that worked even if he can't use it.

Barry saw the sign on my door that said KEEP OUT MOM THAT MEANS YOU. He asked if my Mom really stays out of my room. I said, "Sure, if I keep things picked up." Mom is not a snoop.

Barry said he wished he could have a room nobody ever went into. I was glad Barry didn't ask to use the bathroom. Maybe I'll start scrubbing off the mildew after all.

Sunday, March 25

I keep thinking about Dad and how lonely he sounded and wondering what happened to the pizza boy. I don't like to think about Dad being lonesome, but I don't like to think about the pizza boy cheering him up either.

Tonight at supper (beans and franks) I got up my courage to ask Mom if she thought Dad would get married again. She thought awhile and then said, "I don't see how he could afford to. He has big payments to make on the truck, and the price of diesel oil goes up all the time, and when people can't afford to build houses or buy cars, he won't be hauling lumber or cars."

I thought this over. I know that a license for a truck like his costs over a thousand dollars a year. "But he always sends my support payments," I said, "even if he is late sometimes."

"Yes, he does that," agreed my mother. "Your father isn't a bad man by any means."

Suddenly I was mad and disgusted with the whole thing. "Then why don't you two get married again?" I guess I wasn't very nice about the way I said it.

Mom looked me straight in the eye. "Because your father will never grow up," she said. I knew that was all she would ever say about it.

Tomorrow they give out the Young Writers' Yearbook! Maybe I will be lucky and get to go have lunch with the Famous Author.

Monday, March 26

Today wasn't the greatest day of my life. When our class went to the library, I saw a stack of Yearbooks and could hardly wait for Miss Neely to hand them out. When I finally got mine and opened it to the first page, there was a monster story, and I saw I hadn't won first prize. I kept turning. I didn't win second prize which went to a poem, and I didn't win third or fourth prize, either. Then I turned another page and saw Honorable Mention and under it:

A DAY ON DAD'S RIG
by
LEIGH M. BOTTS

There was my title with my name under it in print, even if it was mimeographed print. I can't say I wasn't disappointed because I hadn't won a prize, I was. I was really disappointed about not getting to meet the mysterious Famous Author, but I liked seeing my name in print.

Some kids were mad because they didn't win or even get something printed. They said they wouldn't ever try to write again which I think is pretty dumb. I have heard that real authors sometimes have their books turned down. I figure you win some, you lose some.

Then Miss Neely announced that the Famous Author the winners would get to have lunch with was Angela Badger. The girls were more excited than the boys because Angela Badger writes mostly

about girls with problems like big feet or pimples or something. I would still like to meet her because she is, as they say, a real live author, and I've never met a real live author. I am glad Mr. Henshaw isn't the author because then I would *really* be disappointed that I didn't get to meet him.

Friday, March 30

Today turned out to be exciting. In the middle of second period Miss Neely called me out of class and asked if I would like to go have lunch with Angela Badger. I said, "Sure, how come?"

Miss Neely explained that the teachers discovered that the winning poem had been copied out of a book and wasn't original so the girl who submitted it would not be allowed to go and would I like to go in her place? Would I!

Miss Neely telephoned Mom at work for permission and I gave my lunch to Barry because my lunches are better than his. The other winners were all dressed up, but I didn't care. I have noticed that authors like Mr. Henshaw usually wear old plaid shirts in the pictures on the back of their books. My shirt is just as old as his, so I knew it was OK.

Miss Neely drove us in her own car to the Holiday Inn, where some other librarians and their winners were waiting in the lobby. Then Angela Badger arrived with Mr. Badger, and we were all led into the dining room which was pretty crowded. One of the

librarians who was a sort of Super Librarian told the winners to sit at a long table with a sign that said Reserved. Angela Badger sat in the middle and some of the girls pushed to sit beside her. I sat across from her. Super Librarian explained that we could choose our lunch from the salad bar. Then all the librarians went off and sat at a table with Mr. Badger.

There I was face to face with a real live author who seemed like a nice lady, plump with wild hair, and I couldn't think of a thing to say because I hadn't read her books. Some girls told her how much they loved her books, but some of the boys and girls were too shy to say anything. Nothing seemed to happen until Mrs. Badger said, "Why don't we all go help ourselves to lunch at the salad bar?"

What a mess! Some people didn't understand about salad bars, but Mrs. Badger led the way and we helped ourselves to lettuce and bean salad and potato salad and all the usual stuff they lay out on salad bars. A few of the younger kids were too short to reach anything but the bowls on the first rows. They weren't doing too well until Mrs. Badger helped them out. Getting lunch took a long time, longer than in a school cafeteria, and when we carried our plates back to our table, people at other tables ducked and dodged as if they expected us to dump our lunches on their heads. All one boy had on his plate was a piece of lettuce and a slice of tomato because he thought he was going to get to go back for roast beef and fried chicken. We had to straighten him out and explain that all we got was salad. He turned red and went back for more salad.

I was still trying to think of something interesting to say to Mrs. Badger while I chased garbanzo beans around my plate with a fork. A couple of girls did all the talking, telling Mrs. Badger how they wanted to write books exactly like hers. The other librarians were busy talking and laughing with Mr. Badger who seemed to be a lot of fun.

Mrs. Badger tried to get some of the shy people to say something without much luck, and I still couldn't think of anything to say to a lady who wrote books about girls with big feet or pimples. Finally Mrs. Badger looked straight at me and asked, "What did you write for the Yearbook?"

I felt myself turn red and answered, "Just something about a ride on a truck."

"Oh!" said Mrs. Badger. "So you're the author of *A Day on Dad's Rig*!"

Everyone was quiet. None of us had known the real live author would have read what we had written, but she had and she remembered my title.

"I just got honorable mention," I said, but I was thinking, She called me an author. *A real live author called me an author.*

"What difference does that make?" asked Mrs. Badger. "Judges never agree. I happened to like *A Day on Dad's Rig* because it was written by a boy who wrote honestly about something he knew and had strong feelings about. You made me feel what it was like to ride down a steep grade with tons of grapes behind me."

"But I couldn't make it into a story," I said, feeling a whole lot braver.

"Who cares?" said Mrs. Badger with a wave of her hand. She's the kind of person who wears rings on her forefingers. "What do you expect? The ability to write stories comes later, when you have lived longer and have more understanding. *A Day on Dad's Rig* was splendid work for a boy your age. You wrote like *you*, and you did not try to imitate someone else. This is one mark of a good writer. Keep it up."

I noticed a couple of girls who had been saying they wanted to write books exactly like Angela Badger exchange embarrassed looks.

"Gee, thanks," was all I could say. The waitress began to plunk down dishes of ice cream. Everyone got over being shy and began to ask Mrs. Badger if she wrote in pencil or on the typewriter and did she ever have books rejected and were her characters real people and did she ever have pimples when she was a girl like the girl in her book and what did it feel like to be a famous author?

I didn't think answers to those questions were very important, but I did have one question I wanted to ask which I finally managed to get in at the last minute when Mrs. Badger was autographing some books people had brought.

She called me an author. A real live author called **me** an author.

553

"Mrs. Badger," I said, "did you ever meet Boyd Henshaw?"

"Why, yes," she said, scribbling away in someone's book. "I once met him at a meeting of librarians where we were on the same program."

"What's he like?" I asked over the head of a girl crowding up with her book.

"He's a very nice young man with a wicked twinkle in his eye," she answered. I think I have known that since the time he answered my questions when Miss Martinez made us write to an author.

On the ride home everybody was chattering about Mrs. Badger this, and Mrs. Badger that. I didn't want to talk. I just wanted to think. A real live author had called *me* an author. A real live author had told me to keep it up. Mom was proud of me when I told her.

The gas station stopped pinging a long time ago, but I wanted to write all this down while I remembered. I'm glad tomorrow is Saturday. If I had to go to school I would yawn. I wish Dad was here so I could tell him all about today.

Think and Respond

❶ What events help Leigh feel happier about himself?

❷ Leigh writes that he's glad he doesn't know the lunch thief's identity. What does this tell you about his character?

❸ Why do you think the author wrote this story in the form of a diary?

❹ From what Leigh tells about the story he **submitted** to the contest, do you think it is a good piece of writing? Why or why not?

❺ How did you use reading strategies to help you understand this story?

Meet the Author
Beverly Cleary

Did you know that you were going to write _Dear Mr. Henshaw_ in journal style when you began?

Yes. I prefer to write in the third person, but I know that first-person books are popular with children. I decided that presenting this book in the form of a diary and letters might be an interesting change of pace for me.

There is a scene in _Dear Mr. Henshaw_ in which a well-known author goes to lunch with several writing students. Did anything like this ever happen to you?

Even though I usually don't write so specifically from life, this incident did happen. I was asked to go to lunch with a group of about 20 children who had won a reading contest. We were only allowed to eat from the salad bar. One boy did not understand this and took just one piece of lettuce and tomato because he thought he was going back for roast beef and fried chicken. We had to set him straight, and the children had a good laugh.

Visit _The Learning Site!_
www.harcourtschool.com

THE
CHINESE
LANGUAGE
PUZZLE

BY KAREN E. HONG

Did you know that there is more than one *spoken* Chinese language? For thousands of years, someone who spoke only Cantonese (a dialect, or variation, of Chinese) could not understand someone who spoke Mandarin (a different dialect). Yet both could read the same writing. But if each read the same writing aloud, it sounded like two differen lan- guages. Puzzling, isn't it? This happened because the Chinese language has evolved to include hundreds of dialects. These dialects sound as different from each other as English sounds from German. Yet *written*, they are all the same.

In Chinese, changing the tone of a word can change its entire mean- ing. Depending on how the word *ma* is said, for example, it can mean four completely different things: mother, hemp, horse, and scold. To make matters even more com- plicated, each dialect uses different pronunciation and tones.

Today, most Chinese people speak *putonghua*, which means "common spoken language." Also known as Mandarin, putonghua is the official national language taught in schools.

Chinese writing uses characters that represent words. Characters often have built-in clues to the sound or meaning of a word. Learning to read the traditional characters is quite a challenge, though. There are about 50,000 different characters. How were all these characters created?

The earliest characters were simple pictures of things and ideas: A ⊡ represented the sun; ☽ represented the moon. After the Chinese invented paper and began to write with small brushes, characters changed somewhat. The sun became 日, the moon became 月.

Sometimes, combining two or more characters made new words. The characters suggest the meaning of the new word.

In the past, Chinese was written from top to bottom and from right to left on a page. Today books in China are written in the same order as English books.

Combining sun 日 and moon 月, for instance, made the word bright 明.

To those who do not know the language, Chinese looks difficult to read and write. But if we look closely and use our imagination, we can see patterns from the world around us.

A few pen strokes form each character. Usually, strokes are drawn from left to right and from the top down, lifting the pen between strokes.

人 Here is a person. Do you see the sideways view of someone walking? The legs form the legs of the character.

Today, Chinese characters have been simplified so that fewer strokes are used. The Chinese also created pinyin (meaning "spell-sound"), a way of using the alphabet to spell Chinese words.

大 The person turns to face us and opens his arms. Like a small child, he tells us "big."

小 By drawing his arms and legs close to his body, he tells us "small."

天 Do you see the person in this character? Above the person is a line. And what is above a person but the sky?

晶 Remember the character for the sun? With three suns together, we get the word *sparkling*.

木 Do you see the tree trunk and branches? This character means "tree" or "wood." Two trees together means "forest." 林

Can you see the meaning of these characters?

山
mountain

火
fire

炎
blaze, blazing

火山
volcano

THINK AND RESPOND

Explain how Chinese characters were created.

Making Connections

Compare Texts

1 What lesson or lessons about getting along in school does Leigh learn in "Dear Mr. Henshaw"?

2 Why do you think the illustrator used cartoon doodles and diagrams to illustrate the story?

3 How are the types of writing and the authors' purposes different for "The Chinese Language Puzzle" and "Dear Mr. Henshaw"?

4 Think of another realistic fiction story you have read that is told in the first person by the main character. Does that main character seem more real to you than Leigh Botts? Explain.

5 Do you think Leigh's relationship with his father will improve as time goes on? Why or why not?

Write a How-to Paragraph

Leigh and Barry invent a burglar alarm for Barry's room, but Barry's mother can't stand the noise. Think of a way that Barry might keep out unwanted visitors without bothering his mother. Use a graphic like the one shown here to plan your paragraph. Add as many steps as you need.

Writing CONNECTION

My Invention: _____

Step 1: _____

Step 2: _____

Step 3: _____

Write an Article

In "Dear Mr. Henshaw," Leigh uses a doorbell, a switch, insulated wire, and a battery to invent his lunchbox alarm. Brainstorm a list of other common inventions. Then choose one invention to research in depth. Do online research to answer these questions: Who was the inventor? When and where was the invention created? Why was the invention needed? Use the results of your research to write and illustrate a magazine article about your invention.

Science CONNECTION

Create a Poster

Leigh's father is a trucker. Do research, using encyclopedias and nonfiction books and articles, to learn more about what truck drivers do. Look for information about the training, the kind of equipment, and the licenses needed to be a trucker. Create a poster that presents your research findings.

Social Studies CONNECTION

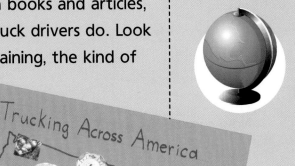
Trucking Across America

561

Text Structure:
Compare and Contrast

You know that authors sometimes compare and contrast information as a way of organizing text. In "Dear Mr. Henshaw," the story is told through a series of diary entries that compare and contrast the characters, settings, and events.

This Venn diagram shows how the author compares and contrasts Leigh and Barry in "Dear Mr. Henshaw."

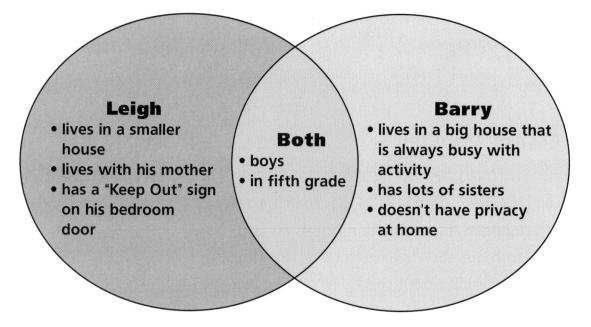

Leigh
• lives in a smaller house
• lives with his mother
• has a "Keep Out" sign on his bedroom door

Both
• boys
• in fifth grade

Barry
• lives in a big house that is always busy with activity
• has lots of sisters
• doesn't have privacy at home

Now compare and contrast some other elements in "Dear Mr. Henshaw." Think about how the characters, the settings, and the themes are alike and different.

**Visit *The Learning Site!*
www.harcourtschool.com**

See *Skills* and *Activities*

Test Prep

Text Structure: Compare and Contrast

▶ **Read the diary entries. Then answer the questions.**

Dear Diary,

    I am so excited! Today Mr. Coe asked for ideas for a class science project. Lin raised her hand confidently. She always has good ideas. She had read about a fifth-grade class in our state that spent three days on the Cape at the Oceanside Nature Preserve. Those students raised all the money for the trip themselves. Everyone in our class loved the idea.

Your friend, Pete

Dear Diary,

    Today Mr. Coe asked for suggestions for a class science project. I had an idea, but I didn't raise my hand at first. What if everyone thought that a three-day science field trip was a dumb idea? But guess what? When I finally did raise my hand, Mr. Coe smiled as if he really liked the idea. The other kids did, too.

Lin

1. **What do the two diary entries have in common? State two similarities.**

2. **What different images of Lin do you get from the two diary entries? Support your answer with references to the diary entries.**

Tip

Focus on details that give the same information in both entries.

Look at the way each writer describes the scene you are contrasting.

▲ Frindle

Vocabulary Power

Did you ever wonder why words mean what they do? Some people, such as the teacher in the next selection, are fascinated by words and their meanings. Even at a movie, someone can get caught up in words.

ZACK: I was so **absorbed** in the movie that I forgot to eat my popcorn! It took my full attention.

ALEXIS: Did you know that the word *absorb* also means "to take up," the way a sponge takes up water?

ZACK: No, I didn't know that, but I do know your **reputation** for being a human dictionary. That's what most people think about you.

CHAD: I bet you know more about words than anybody else, Alexis. You probably know more than all the people in this **aisle** put together.

ALEXIS: Well, I do know that an aisle is a passageway that separates one section from another.

ZACK: Wasn't that a great movie? I loved the ending, when the hero was **beaming**, smiling that great big smile.

ALEXIS: Are you trying to **sidetrack** me, or distract me, from the subject of words? By the way, *sidetrack* originally meant "a railroad siding." To sidetrack a train was to move it off the main track.

CHAD: Don't you remember taking an **oath** to talk about something besides words once in a while? You said you truly meant to keep your promise.

ALEXIS: Oh, all right. I'm sorry.

ZACK: I was just thinking about the word *beaming*. It means "smiling warmly," and it also means "sending out beams of light," like the sun.

CHAD: Oh, no! Now she's got *you* doing it!

Vocabulary–Writing CONNECTION

Have you ever been totally **absorbed** in a book or a movie? Write a paragraph about the book or movie, and tell why you liked it so much.

Genre

Realistic Fiction

Realistic fiction tells about characters and events that are like people and events in real life.

In this selection, look for

- The effect of the characters' actions on the plot

- A setting that is familiar to most readers

Nicholas Allen is known for his ideas. In third grade he transformed his classroom into a tropical island. In fourth grade he chirped like a blackbird during class and made the other students giggle. But now it's fifth grade and Nick knows he has to be very careful. He's in Mrs. Granger's language arts class, and she is as clever as she is strict. She loves the dictionary and she posts a "Word of the Day" on the blackboard each day. When Nick tries to avoid a homework assignment by asking a difficult question, she gives him an extra task—an oral report on where words come from. Nick presents an unusual report, but Mrs. Granger surprises him with an even more unusual reaction.

by ANDREW CLEMENTS

illustrated by Sheila Bailey

rs. Granger was beaming at him. Nick sank lower in his chair. This was worse than writing the report, worse than standing up to give it. He was being treated like — like the teacher's pet. And he had the feeling she was doing it on purpose. His reputation was in great danger. So he launched another question.

He raised his hand, and he didn't even wait for Mrs. Granger to call on him. "Yeah, but, you know, I still don't really get the idea of why words all mean different things. Like, who says that d-o-g means the thing that goes 'woof' and wags its tail? Who says so?"

And Mrs. Granger took the bait. "Who says *dog* means dog? You do, Nicholas. You and me and everyone in this class and this school and this town and this state and this country. We all agree. If we lived in France, we would all agree that the right word for that hairy four-legged creature was a different word—*chien*—it sounds like 'shee-EN,' but it means what d-o-g means to you and me. And in Germany they say *hund*, and so on, all around the globe. But if all of us in this room decided to call that creature something else, and if everyone else did, too, then that's what it would be called, and one day it would be written in the dictionary that way. *We* decide what goes in that book." And she pointed at the giant dictionary. And she looked right at Nick. And she smiled again.

Then Mrs. Granger went on, "But of course, that dictionary was worked on by hundreds of very smart people for many years, so as far as we are concerned, that dictionary is the law. Laws can change, of course, but only if they need to. There may be new words that need to be made, but the ones in that book have been put there for good reasons."

Mrs. Granger took a look at the clock, eight minutes left. "Now then, for today you were to have done the exercises beginning on page twelve in your *Words Alive* book. Please get out your papers. Sarah, will you read the first sentence, identify the mistake, and then tell us how you corrected it?"

Mrs. Granger jammed the whole day's work into the last eight minutes, a blur of verbs and nouns and prepositions, and yes, there was another homework assignment.

And Nick didn't try to sidetrack Mrs. G. again. He had slowed her down a little, but had he stopped her? No way.

She was unstoppable . . . at least for today.

Three things happened later that same afternoon.

Nick and Janet Fisk had missed the bus because of a school newspaper meeting, so they walked home together. They were seeing who could walk along the curb without falling. It took a lot of concentration, and when Janet stepped off into the street, Nick said, "That's three points for me."

But Janet said, "I didn't fall. I saw something. . . . Look." She bent down and picked up a gold ballpoint pen, the fancy kind.

That was the first thing—Janet finding the pen.

They got back on the curb, and Nick followed Janet, putting one foot carefully in front of the other on the narrow concrete curb. And while he stepped along, he thought back over the school day, especially about his report. And what Mrs. Granger had said about words at the end of the period finally sank in.

That was the second thing—understanding what Mrs. Granger had said.

She had said, "Who says *dog* means dog? You do, Nicholas."

"You do, Nicholas," he repeated to himself.

I do? Nick thought, still putting one foot in front of the other, following Janet. *What does that mean?* And then Nick remembered something.

When he was about two years old, his mom had bought him one of those unbreakable cassette players and a bunch of sing-along tapes. He had loved them, and he played them over and over and over and over. He would carry the tape and the player to his mother or his big brother or his father and bang them together and say, "Gwagala, gwagala, gwagala," until someone put the cassette in the machine and turned it on.

And for three years, whenever he said "gwagala," his family knew that he wanted to hear those pretty sounds made with voices and instruments. Then when Nick went to preschool, he learned that if he wanted his teacher and the other kids to understand him, he had to use the word *music*. But *gwagala* meant that nice sound to Nick, because Nick said so. Who says *gwagala* means music? "You do, Nicholas."

"No fair!" yelled Janet. They were at the corner of their own street, and Nick had bumped into her, completely absorbed in his thoughts. Janet stumbled off the curb, and the gold pen in her hand clattered onto the street.

"Sorry . . . I didn't mean to, honest," said Nick. "I just wasn't watching. . . . Here . . ." Nick stooped over and picked up the pen and held it out to her. "Here's your . . ."

And that's when the third thing happened.

Nick didn't say "pen." Instead, he said, "Here's your . . . frindle."

"Frindle?" Janet took her pen and looked at him like he was nuts. She wrinkled her nose and said, "What's a *frindle*?"

Nick grinned and said, "You'll find out. See ya later."

It was there at the corner of Spring Street and South Grand Avenue, one block from home on a September afternoon. That's when Nick got the big idea.

And by the time he had run down the street and up the steps and through the door and upstairs to his room, it wasn't just a big idea. It was a plan, a whole plan, just begging for Nick to put it into action. And "action" was Nick's middle name.

The next day after school the plan began. Nick walked into the Penny Pantry store and asked the lady behind the counter for a frindle.

She squinted at him. "A what?"

"A frindle, please. A black one," and Nick smiled at her.

She leaned over closer and aimed one ear at him. "You want *what*?"

"A frindle," and this time Nick pointed at the ballpoint pens behind her on the shelf. "A black one, please."

The lady handed Nick the pen. He handed her the 49¢, said "thank you," and left the store.

Six days later Janet stood at the counter of the Penny Pantry. Same store, same lady. John had come in the day before, and Pete the day before that, and Chris the day before that, and Dave the day before that. Janet was the fifth kid that Nick had sent there to ask that woman for a frindle.

And when she asked, the lady reached right for the pens and said, "Blue or black?"

Nick was standing one aisle away at the candy racks, and he was grinning.

Frindle was a real word. It meant *pen*. Who says frindle means pen? "You do, Nicholas."

Half an hour later, a group of serious fifth graders had a meeting in Nick's play room. It was John, Pete, Dave, Chris, and Janet. Add Nick, and that's six kids — six secret agents.

They held up their right hands and read the oath Nick had written out:

From this day on and forever, I will never use the word PEN again. Instead, I will use the word FRINDLE, and I will do everything possible so others will, too.

And all six of them signed the oath — with Nick's frindle.
The plan would work.
Thanks, Mrs. Granger.

Think and Respond

❶ What is Nick's idea, and how does he make it work?

❷ What **reputation** does Nick have in school?

❸ Why is Mrs. Granger an important character in the story?

❹ If you were a friend of Nick's, would you want to help him carry out his plan? Why or why not?

❺ How did you use reading strategies to help you understand this story?

Meet the Author
Andrew Clements

When Andrew Clements visits schools and talks to students, he gives the same speech his character Mrs. Granger gives to her students. "I tell kids that the dictionary is a work in progress, that words mean what they mean because we agree. If we stopped calling pens 'pens' and started calling them 'frindles,' eventually the dictionary would change." Then he asks the students to think about hooking words together. He explains, "A word is a word because it has meaning, and when we hook words together we're dealing with larger and larger chunks of meaning." He reminds young writers that their work will have an audience, so their written ideas must make sense. He also says, "Storytelling is the artistic exploration of an idea. And the best stories are honest."

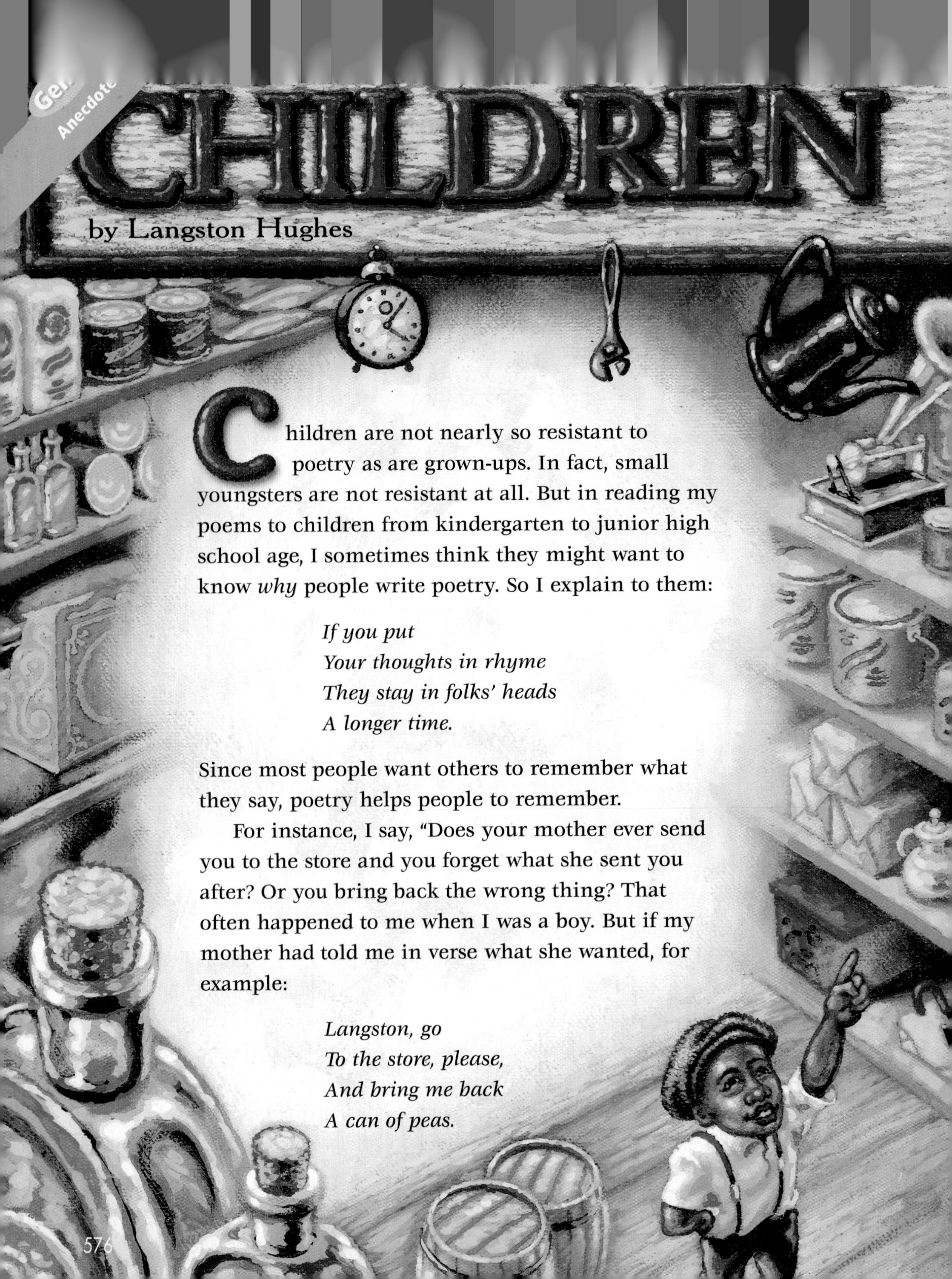

CHILDREN

by Langston Hughes

Children are not nearly so resistant to poetry as are grown-ups. In fact, small youngsters are not resistant at all. But in reading my poems to children from kindergarten to junior high school age, I sometimes think they might want to know *why* people write poetry. So I explain to them:

If you put
Your thoughts in rhyme
They stay in folks' heads
A longer time.

Since most people want others to remember what they say, poetry helps people to remember.

For instance, I say, "Does your mother ever send you to the store and you forget what she sent you after? Or you bring back the wrong thing? That often happened to me when I was a boy. But if my mother had told me in verse what she wanted, for example:

Langston, go
To the store, please,
And bring me back
A can of peas.

illustrated by Eric Westbrook

"I wouldn't have brought back a can of corn. *Please* and *peas* rhyme, which makes it easy to remember. Or if my mother had said:

> *Sonny, kindly*
> *Do me a favor*
> *And go get a bottle*
> *Of vanilla flavor.*

"Then I am sure I would not have gotten a bottle of vinegar. The word *flavor*, not simply *bottle*, would have stuck in my head because of its sound tag with *favor*. That is one reason why:

> *To make words sing*
> *Is a wonderful thing—*
> *Because in a song*
> *Words last so long.*

Think and Respond

In what other situations could you use rhyming poetry to help you remember something?

577

▲ Frindle

Making Connections

Compare Texts

1 How does "Frindle" fit into the theme School Rules?

2 How does the author show a change in Nick's attitude toward Mrs. Granger from the beginning to the end of the story?

3 What viewpoint is shared by Andrew Clements, the author of "Frindle," and Langston Hughes, the author of "Children and Poetry"?

4 Do you agree that "Frindle" is realistic fiction, or do you think it should be called something else? Explain your answer.

5 How do you think Mrs. Granger will feel about Nick's new word? Why do you think so?

Write an Informational Paragraph

Imagine that in the future everyone uses a *frindle* instead of a *pen*. Think about how the word came into the English language. Then write to explain the origin of the word *frindle*. Use a graphic like the one shown here to plan your paragraph. Add other steps as needed to explain the process.

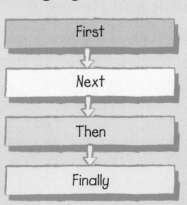

First

Next

Then

Finally

Writing CONNECTION

578

Create a Chart or Poster

Social Studies CONNECTION

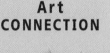

In "Frindle," Nick and his friends sign an oath that is written in words. At other times and places, however, people have used very different methods of writing. Choose a writing system to research. Here are some ideas: Native American ideograms, Egyptian hieroglyphics, Sumerian cuneiform writing, or Aztec pictographic writing. Use encyclopedias or search the Internet for information about the writing system you chose. Then create a chart or poster to share information you have learned.

Research and Draw

Art CONNECTION

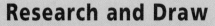

The ballpoint pens in "Frindle" were used for writing, but pens can be used for drawing as well. Research information about the techniques used in pen drawings, and study how artists have used those techniques. You may find information in an encyclopedia or in books on art. Then use pens and scrap paper to experiment with drawing techniques. Create a finished drawing to display in your classroom.

▲ Frindle

Author's Purpose and Perspective

When you identify the author's purpose for writing a piece, and also his or her perspective on the subject, you are better able to make judgments about what you are reading.

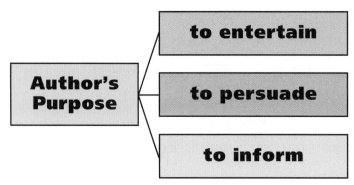

Author's Purpose
- to entertain
- to persuade
- to inform

This chart shows how to determine the author's perspective for "Frindle."

Author's Perspective: People create language and decide what goes in dictionaries.

↓

Evidence: Nick creates a new word, <u>frindle</u>, and gets all the students to use it as a synonym for <u>pen</u>.

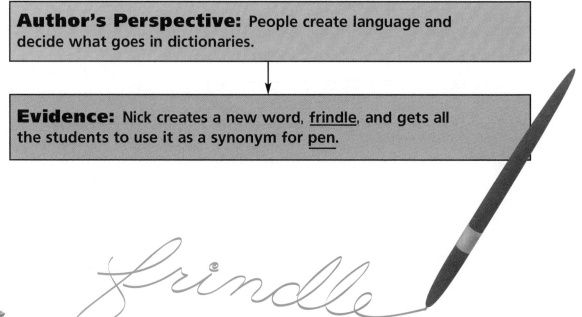

Visit *The Learning Site!*
www.harcourtschool.com

See *Skills* and *Activities*

Test Prep
Author's Purpose and Perspective

▶ **Read the passage. Then answer the questions.**

> Cal was in line at the movies when he first heard someone talk about X. "It will change our lives," one girl said. "I'm buying one, no matter what it costs," the boy announced. Cal smiled. These kids planned to spend money for a product they had never even seen.
>
> Actually, X did not really exist. Cal and his brother had made it up. "People will buy anything if the advertising is good," Cal said. "Let's find out," his brother had challenged. They persuaded their teacher to allow them to include several ads in the school newspaper about a new and secret product called X. "If our plan works, we can write an editorial about the power of advertising," they told the teacher.

1. **Which of these best expresses the author's purpose?**

   A to entertain

   B to inform

   C to explain

   D to persuade

Tip

Think about your reaction to the story. What was the author trying to achieve?

2. **Which of these best expresses the author's perspective?**

   F People need to be more aware of persuasion.

   G People believe everything that they read.

   H Young people watch too much television.

   J People should not believe anything.

Tip

Decide what the key ideas tell you about the author's opinions and feelings.

Vocabulary Power

dispute

nonchalantly

sorrowfully

loftily

adjusted

"**T**he Fun They Had" tells about students in the future who find an old book. What do you suppose people of the future would think if they found a photo album about life in your school?

Doesn't Lara look scornful? She looks full of anger and disgust. She always wants to **dispute**, or argue against, having her picture taken.

Tim does things so **nonchalantly** that he seems not to have a care in the world. In fact, he seems too cool to pose for a picture.

Maria looks down **sorrowfully**, as if she is very sad. She thought everyone had forgotten her birthday. Her surprise party really cheered her up.

Steve posed **loftily** for the camera. He thought he was better than the rest of us because he **adjusted**, or changed, Mr. Day's computer to make it work better.

Vocabulary-Writing CONNECTION

Every year, you have **adjusted** to new teachers. Write for five minutes about one of your most memorable teachers.

Genre

Science Fiction

A science fiction story is set in the future and is based on scientific ideas.

In this selection look for

- Characters that are like real people

- Technology that takes place in the future

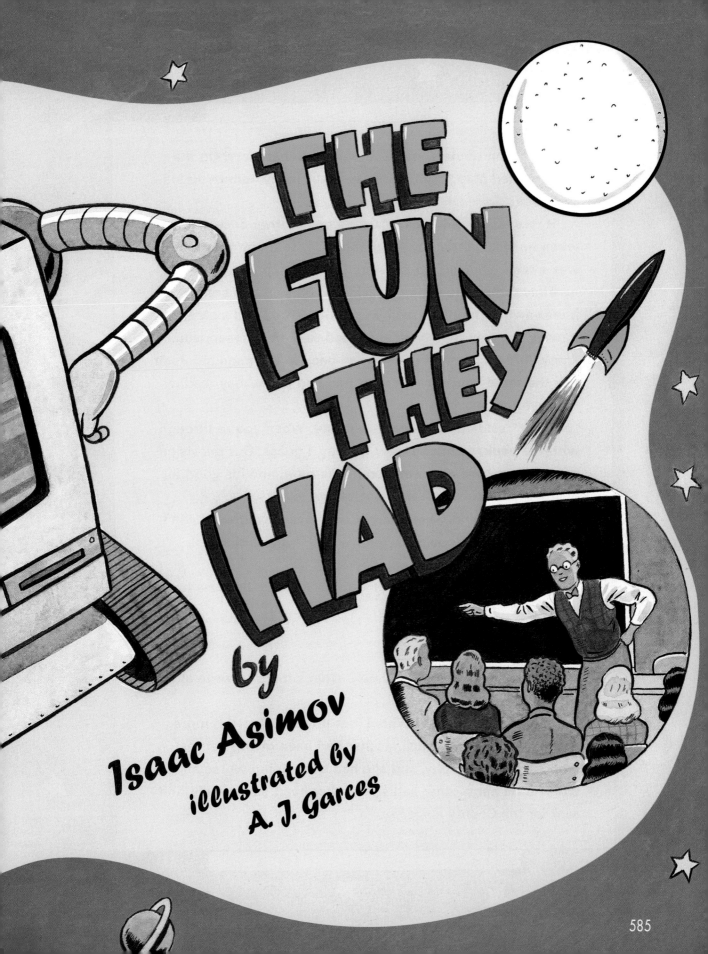

Margie even wrote about it that night in her diary. On the page headed May 17, 2157, she wrote, "Today Tommy found a real book!"

It was a very old book. Margie's grandfather once said that when he was a little boy *his* grandfather told him that there was a time when all stories were printed on paper.

They turned the pages, which were yellow and crinkly, and it was awfully funny to read words that stood still instead of moving the way they were supposed to — on a screen, you know. And then, when they turned back to the page before, it had the same words on it that it had had when they read it the first time.

"Gee," said Tommy, "what a waste. When you're through with the book, you just throw it away, I guess. Our television screen must have had a million books on it, and it's good for plenty more. I wouldn't throw it away."

"Same as mine," said Margie. She was eleven and hadn't seen as many textbooks as Tommy had. He was thirteen.

She said, "Where did you find it?"

"In my house." He pointed without looking, because he was busy reading. "In the attic."

"What's it about?"

"School."

Margie was scornful. "School? What's there to write about school? I hate school."

Margie always hated school, but now she hated it more than ever. The mechanical teacher had been giving her test after test in geography, and she had been doing worse and worse until her mother had shaken her head sorrowfully and sent for the County Inspector.

He was a round
little man with a red face and a
whole box of tools with dials and wires.
He smiled at Margie and gave her an apple,
then took the teacher apart. Margie had hoped
he wouldn't know how to put it together again, but
he knew how all right, and, after an hour or so, there it
was again, large and black and ugly, with a big screen on
which all the lessons were shown and the questions were
asked. That wasn't so bad. The part Margie hated most was the
slot where she had to put homework and test papers. She always
had to write them out in a punch code they made her learn when
she was six years old, and the mechanical teacher calculated the
mark in no time.

The Inspector had smiled after he was finished and patted
Margie's head. He said to her mother, "It's not the little girl's fault,
Mrs. Jones. I think the geography sector was geared a little too
quick. Those things happen sometimes. I've slowed it up to an
average ten-year level. Actually, the overall pattern of her progress is
quite satisfactory." And he patted Margie's head again.

Margie was disappointed. She had been hoping they would take
the teacher away altogether. They had once taken Tommy's teacher
away for nearly a month because the history sector had blanked
out completely.

So she said to Tommy, "Why would anyone write
about school?"

Tommy looked at her with very superior eyes.
"Because it's not our kind of school, stupid. This is
the old kind of school that they had hundreds
and hundreds of years ago." He added
loftily, pronouncing the word carefully, "*Centuries* ago."

589

Margie was hurt. "Well, I don't know what kind of school they had all that time ago." She read the book over his shoulder for a while, then said, "Anyway, they had a teacher."

"Sure they had a teacher, but it wasn't a regular teacher. It was a man."

"A man? How could a man be a teacher?"

"Well, he just told the boys and girls things and gave them homework and asked them questions."

"A man isn't smart enough."

"Sure he is. My father knows as much as my teacher."

"He can't. A man can't know as much as a teacher."

"He knows almost as much, I betcha."

Margie wasn't prepared to dispute that. She said, "I wouldn't want a strange man in my house to teach me."

Tommy screamed with laughter. "You don't know much, Margie. The teachers didn't live in the house. They had a special building and all the kids went there."

"And all the kids learned the same thing?"

"Sure, if they were the same age."

"But my mother says a teacher has to be adjusted to fit the mind of each boy and girl it teaches and that each kid has to be taught differently."

"Just the same, they didn't do it that way then. If you don't like it, you don't have to read the book."

"I didn't say I didn't like it," Margie said quickly. She wanted to read about those funny schools.

They weren't even half-finished when Margie's mother called, "Margie! School!"

Margie looked up. "Not yet, Mamma."

"Now!" said Mrs. Jones. "And it's probably time for Tommy, too."

Margie said to Tommy, "Can I read the book some more with you after school?"

"Maybe," he said nonchalantly . He walked away whistling, the dusty old book tucked beneath his arm.

Margie went into the schoolroom. It was right next to her bed-room, and the mechanical teacher was on and waiting for her. It was always on at the same time every day except Saturday and Sunday, because her mother said little girls learned better if they learned at regular hours.

The screen was lit up, and it said, "Today's arithmetic lesson is on the addition of proper fractions. Please insert yesterday's home-work in the proper slot."

Margie did so with a sigh. She was thinking about the old schools they had when her grandfather's grandfather was a little boy. All the kids from the whole neighborhood came, laughing and shouting in the schoolyard, sitting together in the same school-room, going home together at the end of the day. They learned the same things, so they could help one another on the homework and talk about it.

And the teachers were people...

The mechanical teacher was flashing on the screen: "When we add the fractions $\frac{1}{2}$ and $\frac{1}{4}$ —"

Margie was thinking about how the kids must have loved it in the old days. She was thinking about the fun they had.

Think and Respond

① Why is Margie so curious about the book Tommy finds in his attic?

② If the story didn't give the date in Margie's diary, could you tell that it takes place in the future? Explain.

③ Why is Margie **scornful** at first when Tommy tells her the book is about school?

④ Do you think Margie is right when she says that schools today are more fun than her school? Why or why not?

⑤ What reading strategies did you use as you read this story?

Isaac Asimov

Read this true-false quiz about Isaac Asimov (1920–1992), one of the most active science fiction writers ever. (He wrote *hundreds* of books!)

1. Asimov started writing science fiction stories because he liked science fiction television shows as a boy.

Answer: *False. Most families in the United States did not own televisions until after Isaac was grown up. As a boy, Isaac loved reading the science fiction magazines that were sold in his father's candy store.*

2. Asimov's first science fiction stories were not published.

Answer: *True. The editor of* Astounding Science Fiction *magazine did not accept them, but he gave the young writer many helpful suggestions. Later on, the magazine did publish his work.*

3. Asimov liked to use scientific ideas in his science fiction.

Answer: *True. He often based his stories on one interesting scientific idea.*

Visit *The Learning Site!*
www.harcourtschool.com

593

Making Connections

Compare Texts

1. How can reading "The Fun They Had" help students appreciate their own school experience?

2. Contrast how Margie feels about her own school with how she thinks students felt about "old" schools, in the days of her grandfather's grandfather.

3. What advantages might you point out to Tommy about our books today compared with his books?

4. Name one or more science fiction stories that you have read besides "The Fun They Had." What qualities do these science fiction stories share that make them different from other kinds of fiction?

5. How might you learn about the kind of schools your grandfather's grandfather went to?

Write a Letter to the Editor

Suppose that Margie writes a letter to the editor of her local newspaper, expressing her opinion about school. Think about how Margie might suggest making school more enjoyable. Write to persuade newspaper readers to agree with Margie's opinion.

Writing CONNECTION

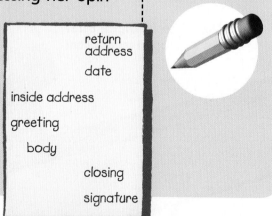

return address
date
inside address
greeting
body
closing
signature

Create a Web Page

Social Studies
CONNECTION

Margie and Tommy were interested in finding out about people who lived long before their own time. You can do research to learn about people who lived long ago in what is now the United States. Choose one of these groups: cliff-dwellers, pueblo people, or Eastern woodland peoples.

Research the culture of the group you chose. You can use encyclopedias, social studies texts, or online resources to find out how these people adapted to their environment, what their homes were like, their customs, and other interesting information. Use the information you find to create a web page, either on the computer or on paper.

Construct a Math Machine

Math
CONNECTION

In "The Fun They Had," Margie puts her math homework in a slot in her mechanical teacher. Her lesson for the day is on the addition of proper fractions. Design and construct a math machine that shows fraction problems and gives the correct answers. Challenge classmates to answer the math problems correctly.

$$\frac{1}{2} + \frac{1}{4}$$

3/4

Draw Conclusions

Focus Skill

Good readers use their personal knowledge and experience, in addition to story clues, to make inferences, draw conclusions, and make generalizations.

Use the following information from "The Fun They Had" to draw a conclusion, make an inference, and make a generalization:

Margie says that she hates school. She especially hates writing the codes for homework and test papers. She writes in her diary about finding a book. Words did not move on the book as they are supposed to. Her grandfather has told Margie that all stories were on once paper.

Inference	Conclusion	Generalization
(reading between the lines to supply information the author omitted)	(evidence from the text and your own experiences)	(evidence from the text, interpreted more broadly)
In the story, books are no longer printed on paper and have not been for a long time.	Margie lives in the future, but she is not different from the children of today.	There will probably always be things that some students will not like about their learning situations.

Visit *The Learning Site!*
www.harcourtschool.com

See *Skills* and *Activities*

Test Prep
Draw Conclusions

▶ **Read the passage. Then answer the questions.**

> Seth and his mechanical history teacher, Voltage, took a field trip back to the days of school buildings, live teachers, and paper textbooks. Voltage assured Seth's parents that the trip would be educational and safe. Even so, they allowed him to go only after Voltage agreed to transmit a live broadcast of the journey to his mother's laboratory.
>
> The trip *was* educational. For one thing, Seth discovered something about himself he would never have known. Every time he picked up a paper textbook, he sneezed. Voltage told him that before the PureAirSystem was invented, many people with allergies had to take medicines.

1. **Which sentence is an inference you could make about the story?**

   A   Time travel is possible.

   B   Seth is afraid of field trips.

   C   Seth's mother does not like Voltage.

   D   People no longer read.

   Tip

   Choose an inference that makes sense based on what you know and on what the characters say and do.

2. **Which statement about the passage is a generalization?**

   F   Field trips are educational and safe.

   G   Seth discovered many things about the past.

   H   The future is an interesting place.

   J   Most people in the future no longer have books.

   Tip

   Choose a very broad conclusion. Look for clue words that signal a generalization, such as *usually*, *most*, and *often*.

THEME
6

AMERICAN
ADVENTURE

CONTENTS

Vocabulary Power

| settlement |
| lurked |
| vast |
| rigging |
| furl |
| huddled |
| beams |

"**A**cross the Wide Dark Sea" tells about the journey of the *Mayflower* from Europe to North America in 1620. Even earlier than that, other colonists had sailed here from England.

A scene of colonial life in Jamestown, Virginia

English colonists started a new **settlement**, or village, in Jamestown, Virginia, in 1607. They didn't know then that dangers **lurked**, or lay hidden. These dangers would cause the colony to fail by 1699. The colonists did not give up, though. They moved to the place that is now Williamsburg, Virginia. The original colonists had come a **vast** distance across a huge ocean to start a new life, and the colonies continued.

Models of early sailing ships in Jamestown, Virginia

Colonists sailed to America on ships like these. The tall masts hold the **rigging**, the arrangement of sails and other gear. In high winds and storms, the sailors would **furl**, or roll up and fasten, the sails. Passengers on the ships would stay **huddled** below deck, crowded together in a small space. They could listen to the creaking of the long, horizontal wooden **beams** that made up a ship's frame. It took a lot of courage to undertake a long journey by sea in those days.

Vocabulary-Writing CONNECTION

Picture a small town long ago. Describe the needs of the people who lived in the **settlement**. List the different kinds of items they would need.

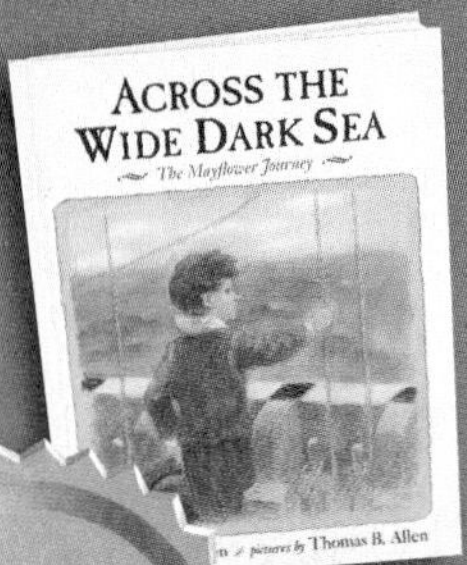
ACROSS THE
WIDE DARK SEA
The Mayflower Journey
pictures by Thomas B. Allen

Award-Winning Author

Genre

Historical Fiction

Historical fiction is a story that is set in the past and portrays people, places, and events that did or could have happened.

In this selection, look for

- **A real time and place in the past**
- **Some made-up events**

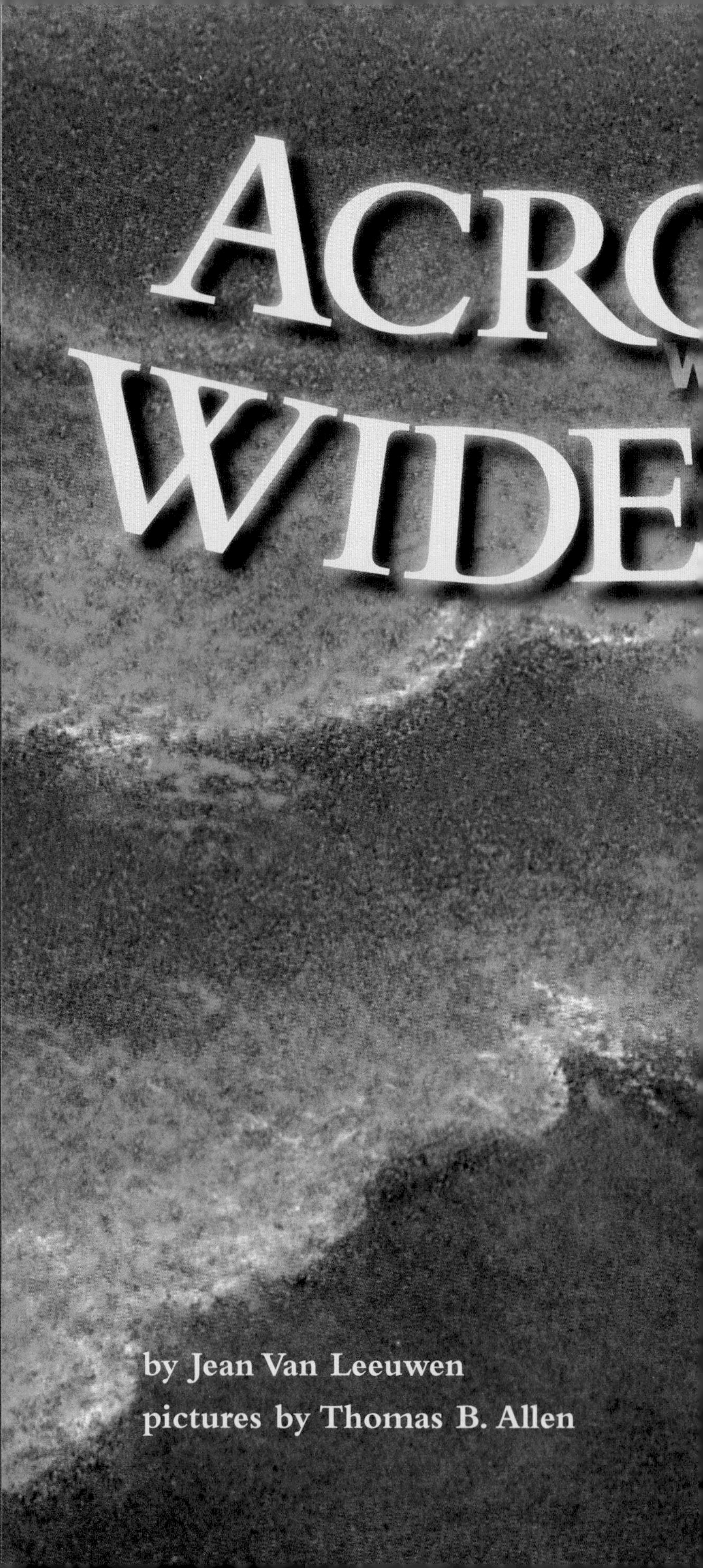
ACR
WIDE

by Jean Van Leeuwen

pictures by Thomas B. Allen

OSS THE
DARK SEA

THE MAYFLOWER JOURNEY

E

S

603

Plymouth, England, 1620

I STOOD CLOSE TO MY FATHER as the anchor was pulled dripping from the sea. Above us, white sails rose against a bright blue sky. They fluttered, then filled with wind. Our ship began to move.

My father was waving to friends on shore. I looked back at their faces growing smaller and smaller, and ahead at the wide dark sea. And I clung to my father's hand.

We were off on a journey to an unknown land.

The ship was packed tight with people—near a hundred, my father said. We were crowded below deck in a space so low that my father could barely stand upright, and so cramped that we could scarcely stretch out to sleep.

Packed in tight, too, was everything we would need in the new land: tools for building and planting, goods for trading, guns for hunting. Food, furniture, clothing, books. A few crates of chickens, two dogs, and a striped orange cat.

Our family was luckier than most. We had a corner out of the damp and cold. Some had to sleep in the ship's small work boat.

The first days were fair, with a stiff wind.

My mother and brother were seasick down below. But I stood on deck and watched the sailors hauling on ropes, climbing in the rigging, and perched at the very top of the mast, looking out to sea.

What a fine life it must be, I thought, to be a sailor.

One day clouds piled up in the sky. Birds with black wings circled the ship, and the choppy sea seemed angry.

"Storm's coming," I heard a sailor say.

We were all sent below as the sailors raced to furl the sails.

Then the storm broke. Wind howled and waves crashed. The ship shuddered as it rose and fell in seas as high as mountains. Some people were crying, others praying. I huddled next to my father, afraid in the dark.

How could a ship so small and helpless ever cross the vast ocean?

The sun came out.
We walked on deck
and dried our clothes. But
just when my shoes felt
dry at last, more clouds
gathered.

"Storm's coming,"
I told my father.

So the days passed,
each one like the last.
There was nothing to do
but eat our meals of salt
pork, beans, and bread,
tidy up our cramped
space, sleep when we could, and try to keep dry. When it was not
too stormy, we climbed on deck to stretch our legs. But even then
we had to keep out of the sailors' way.

How I longed to run and jump and climb!

Once during a storm a man was swept overboard. Reaching
out with desperate hands, he caught hold of a rope and clung to it.

Down he went under the raging foaming water.

Then, miraculously, up he came.

Sailors rushed to the side of the ship. Hauling on the rope,
they brought him in close and with a boat hook plucked him
out of the sea. And his life was saved.

Storm followed storm. The pounding of wind and waves caused one of the main beams to crack, and our ship began to leak.

Worried, the men gathered in the captain's cabin to talk of what to do. Could our ship survive another storm? Or must we turn back?

They talked for two days, but could not agree.

Then someone thought of the iron jack for raising houses that they were taking to the new land. Using it to lift the cracked beam, the sailors set a new post underneath, tight and firm, and patched all the leaks.

And our ship sailed on.

For six weeks we had traveled, and still there was no land in sight. Now we were always cold and wet. Water seeping in from above put out my mother's cooking fire, and there was nothing to eat but hard dry biscuits and cheese. My brother was sick, and many others too.

And some began to ask why we had left our safe homes to go on this endless journey to an unknown land.

Why? I also asked the question of my father that night.

"We are searching for a place to live where we can worship God in our own way," he said quietly. "It is this freedom we seek in a new land. And I have faith that we will find it."

Looking at my father, so calm and sure, suddenly I too had faith that we would find it.

Still the wide dark sea went on and on. Eight weeks. Nine.

Then one day a sailor, sniffing the air, said, "Land's ahead." We dared not believe him. But soon bits of seaweed floated by. Then a tree branch. And a feather from a land bird.

Two days later at dawn I heard the lookout shout, "Land ho!"

Everyone who was well enough to stand crowded on deck. And there through the gray mist we saw it: a low dark outline between sea and sky. Land!

Tears streamed down my mother's face, yet she was smiling. Then everyone fell to their knees while my father said a prayer of thanksgiving.

Our long journey was over.

The ship dropped anchor in a quiet bay, circled by land. Pale yellow sand and dark hunched trees were all we saw. And all we heard was silence.

What lurked among those trees? Wild beasts? Wild men?
Would there be food and water, a place to take shelter?

What waited for us in this new land?

A small party of men in a small boat set off to find out. All day
I watched on deck for their return.

When at last they rowed into sight, they brought armfuls of
firewood and tales of what they had seen: forests of fine trees,
rolling hills of sand, swamps and ponds and rich black earth. But
no houses or wild beasts or wild men.

So all of us went ashore.

My mother washed the clothes we had worn for weeks beside a shallow pond, while my brother and I raced up and down the beach.

We watched whales spouting in the sparkling blue bay and helped search for firewood. And we found clams and mussels, the first fresh food we had tasted in two months. I ate so many I was sick.

Day after day the small party set out from the ship, looking for just the right place to build our settlement.

The days grew cold. Snowflakes danced in the wind. The cold and damp made many sick again. Drawing his coat tightly around him, my father looked worried.

"We must find a place," he said, "before winter comes."

One afternoon the weary men returned with good news. They had found the right spot at last.

When my father saw it, he smiled. It was high on a hill, with a safe harbor and fields cleared for planting and brooks running with sweet water. We named it after the town from which we had sailed, across the sea.

✸ Think and Respond ✸

1 What problems arose on the journey, and how did the *Mayflower* passengers solve them?

2 How is the author's account of these events different from what you might read in a social studies text?

3 What did the people name their new **settlement**? How do you know?

4 Do you think the Mayflower passengers were courageous or foolish to sail off on such a dangerous journey? Explain your answer.

5 How did you use reading strategies to help you understand this story?

MEET THE AUTHOR
JEAN VAN LEEUWEN

As a child, Jean Van Leeuwen loved to read. She says, "Anytime, anywhere, I was likely to be found with a book in my hand. I read while riding in the car, even though it made me dizzy. I read late at night under the covers, by flashlight, when I was supposed to be asleep." She would read anything, "just as long as it had a story."

Jean Van Leeuwen has continued her enjoyment of books as an adult. She edited children's books for nearly ten years and has been writing her own books for almost three decades. She says, "I write to rework childhood experiences. And I write in the hope of touching the life of another person." ✦

MEET THE ILLUSTRATOR
THOMAS B. ALLEN

Thomas B. Allen was born in Nashville, Tennessee, and spent much of his childhood playing in woods and creeks. He started art lessons when he was nine and later studied painting at the Art Institute of Chicago. He says, "I spent three summers and three winters living life in a cabin on a pond near Cold Spring, New York. I drew, painted, illustrated, and wrote poetry. I think of those three years as a journey." Thomas B. Allen has since won numerous awards, and his artwork can be found in many magazines and children's books. ⚙

Visit *The Learning Site!*
www.harcourtschool.com

619

▲ Across the Wide
Dark Sea

Making Connections

Compare Texts

 1 How does the selection "Across the Wide Dark Sea" fit into the theme American Adventure?

2 How does the narrator's tone change during the first storm at sea?

3 How does the illustration on page 612 aid readers in understanding the text?

4 Think of another historical fiction story that you have read. Which story, "Across the Wide Dark Sea" or the other, gave you a better understanding of history? Explain your answer.

5 What subject or subjects would you like to learn more about as a result of reading "Across the Wide Dark Sea"? How could you find information about these subjects?

Write a Paragraph to Compare and Contrast

The journey of the *Mayflower* might be compared to taking a trip in a spaceship to explore a distant planet. Think about how the journeys would be alike and how they would be different. Write to compare and contrast the two journeys. Use a Venn diagram to plan your paragraph.

Writing CONNECTION

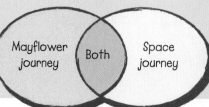

Present a News Broadcast

In "Across the Wide Dark Sea," you read about the *Mayflower* voyage that carried the Pilgrims to America. Imagine that you are presenting a live news broadcast from Plymouth when the *Mayflower* arrives. Search the Internet for information about the *Mayflower* passengers. Use the information you find to write and answer interview questions such as these:

- What is your name? Where are you from?
- Why did you leave your home?
- What was the journey like for you?
- What do you plan to do in this new land?

After you have written your news broadcast, practice and perform it for your classmates.

Social Studies CONNECTION

Write a Report

What causes storms at sea? How and where do they originate? What effects do they have on weather patterns on land? Use resources such as encyclopedias and science texts to research this topic. Then write a report to share the information. Include diagrams and illustrations.

STORMS AT SEA

Science CONNECTION

Connotation/ Denotation

The **denotation** of a word is its dictionary definition. Multiple-meaning words have more than one denotation, or meaning. The **connotation** of a word refers to the feelings and ideas that the word suggests to readers. Writers choose words for both their denotations and their connotations.

The sets of words below have similar denotations but different connotations. Discuss the shades of meaning of the words. Then read the sentences below them. Why do you think the author chose *clung* and *weary*?

Weaker ←	Connotation	→ Stronger
held tired	gripped fatigued	clung weary

I. And I <u>clung</u> to my father's hand.
2. One afternoon, the <u>weary</u> men returned with good news.

Words that create pleasant feelings and images have positive connotations. Words that create unpleasant feelings and images have negative connotations.

Test Prep
Connotation/Denotation

▶ **Read the passage. Then answer the questions.**

> We had been in Plymouth scarcely six months when John got lost in the woods. He and his brother Francis were quite <u>mischievous</u>. At first John's parents thought it was another one of his jokes. When John did not return by nightfall, they grew frantic. Five long days had passed when Aspinet, with at least one hundred natives, brought John home. Unconcerned about the fright he had caused, John stood there <u>beaming</u>. He had had a great adventure! We later learned that John had eaten only berries for days.

1. **Which word has a more positive connotation than <u>mischievous</u>?**

   A   mean

   B   adventurous

   C   naughty

   D   dishonest

Tip

Look for a word that has a meaning similar to mischievous but that suggests a lighter feeling.

2. **Which word has a more negative connotation than <u>beaming</u>?**

   F   laughing

   G   smiling

   H   grinning

   J   smirking

Tip

Say each word to yourself and pay attention to how it makes you feel. Choose the word that creates an unpleasant feeling.

Vocabulary Power

anthem

guarantee

misleading

stumps

indebted

suffrage

distinguished

interpreter

The next selection is filled with famous characters from American history. People who run for office today hope that they will be part of tomorrow's history.

Senate candidate Adela Santiago speaks to crowd at rally

Adela Santiago made several stops in our area yesterday in her run for the state senate. Each rally began with the singing of our national **anthem**, "The Star-Spangled Banner," in praise of our country.

Ms. Santiago told voters, "I **guarantee**, I give you my promise, that I will work for new programs to benefit our schools and our students." She said it would be **misleading**, or false, to claim that she has the solution to every problem at her fingertips. "Nobody has all the answers," she told the crowd, "but when something **stumps** me, I work on it until I'm no longer baffled or confused."

Governor Harris, who appeared with Ms. Santiago, said we are all **indebted** to her. "We owe her many thanks for her years of hard work in our state government," he said. Ms. Santiago replied that all Americans should be most thankful for our **suffrage**, our right to vote. She added that she is proud to have the support of our **distinguished** governor, who has set himself apart by his great wisdom and courage.

"I promise"

Cindy Wilson, an American Sign Language **interpreter**, was on hand to present the speeches in sign language for citizens with impaired hearing.

Vocabulary-Writing CONNECTION

Think about a **distinguished** person. Write a list of the qualities that set this person apart.

Name This American

by Hannah Reinmuth
illustrated by Russ Wilson

Quiz show keeps panelists guessing.

TIME: *Present.*

SETTING: *The stage of a quiz program. Podium is center. Next to it is music stand. Long table with blindfolds on it and six chairs are right. Desk and chair are left.*

AT RISE: SIX PANELISTS *are seated at long table.* UNCLE SAM *stands at podium.* MISS LIBERTY *stands behind music stand.*

Characters

UNCLE SAM

MISS LIBERTY

WALTER HUNT

GUTZON BORGLUM

MARIA MITCHELL

DOLLEY MADISON

SACAGAWEA (sometimes spelled SACAJAWEA)

ELIZABETH CADY STANTON

BABE RUTH

LILIUOKALANI

SIX PANELISTS

UNCLE SAM: Good afternoon, everyone, and welcome to Name This American! We are honored to have as our guests a number of remarkable Americans. Some you may know, and some you may not know, but I guarantee you'll know them all by the time the show's over. To help us identify these special guests is our panel of distinguished scholars. Let's give them all a hand. (*He and LIBBY clap. PANELISTS wave and smile.*) Now, my assistant, Miss Liberty, will explain how the game works. (*Gesturing*) Libby?

LIBBY: Thank you, Uncle Sam. The panel will question our guests and the guests will answer yes or no. If a question has a yes answer, the panelist may continue the questioning. If the answer is no, we move on to the next panelist, and the mystery guest receives $50. If our guest stumps all the panelists, he or she wins $500.

SAM: Thank you, Libby. Now, let's begin by bringing in our first guest. (*LIBBY beckons offstage and WALTER HUNT enters and sits at desk.*) Welcome to our show.

HUNT: Thank you.

SAM: Panelist number one, please begin the questioning.

1ST PANELIST: Are you famous?

HUNT: No, not really.

SAM: Mystery guest, you've already won $50. (*LIBBY puts $50 sign on stand. Throughout game, LIBBY props scores up on stand.*) Let's continue with the next panelist.

2ND PANELIST: Did you discover something?

HUNT (*Giving SAM questioning look*): I suppose you could say so.

SAM: Actually, I'm afraid a yes would be misleading, so we will have to say no and move on to our third panelist.

3RD PANELIST: Let me see. . . . Were you the first to do something?

HUNT: Yes.

3RD PANELIST: Did you, perhaps, invent something?

HUNT: Yes.

SAM: Now we're on the right track.

3RD PANELIST: Is it something you would find around the house?

HUNT: Yes.

3RD PANELIST: Is it electrical?

HUNT: No.

SAM: That's another $50. Panelist four, your turn.

4TH PANELIST: Is it bigger than a bread box?

HUNT: No.

5TH PANELIST: Is it small enough to carry in your pocket?

HUNT: Yes.

5TH PANELIST: Is it a comb?

HUNT: No.

SAM: Panelist six, you're our last chance.

6TH PANELIST (*Pleased*): I think I've got it. Did you invent the pen?

HUNT: No, I did not.

SAM: Mystery guest, congratulations. You stumped our panel of experts. (*All applaud as* LIBBY *puts out the $500 card.*) We are all eager to hear about your invention. Please tell us who you are and what you invented.

HUNT: My name is Walter Hunt. Few people have heard of me, but everyone has used my invention. I am quite proud of my safety pin. (PANELISTS *express surprise.*) I had thought about it for a long time, but it took me only about three hours to make. I had it patented in April, 1849.

SAM: We are certainly honored to meet you, Mr. Hunt. Thank you for playing Name This American.

HUNT: Thank you. (*All applaud as he exits.* GUTZON BORGLUM *enters and sits.*)

SAM: Here's our next challenger, so let's begin.

1ST PANELIST: Are you not very well known?

BORGLUM: Yes, that's true. Few people know my name.

1ST PANELIST: Oh, another hard one! (*Thinks a moment*) Are you involved in the scientific field?

BORGLUM: No.

SAM: That's your first no, panel, and our guest's first $50. Next panelist.

2ND PANELIST: Are you an artist?

BORGLUM: Yes.

2ND PANELIST: Are you a painter?

BORGLUM: I've done some painting, but that's not what I'm known for.

SAM: We'll have to count that as a no and go on to the next panelist.

3RD PANELIST: Are you a musician?

BORGLUM: No.

4TH PANELIST: An entertainer?

BORGLUM: No.

5TH PANELIST (*Thinking, at a loss*): Are you — a sculptor?

BORGLUM: Yes, I am.

5TH PANELIST (*Pleased*): Have I seen your work?

BORGLUM: I'm sure you have.

5TH PANELIST: Have you sculpted any of our presidents?

BORGLUM: Yes.

5TH PANELIST: Do you have any work displayed in Washington, DC?

BORGLUM: Yes.

5TH PANELIST (*Knowingly*): And at Mt. Rushmore?

BORGLUM: Yes.

5TH PANELIST: Then you must be Gutzon Borglum.

OTHER PANELISTS (*Ad lib; surprised, to* 5TH PANELIST): Who? I've never heard of him. (*Etc.*)

SAM: Yes, this is Gutzon Borglum, the artist who designed and carved Mt. Rushmore. Mr. Borglum, please tell us more about yourself.

BORGLUM: My full name is John Gutzon de la Mothe Borglum. I was born in 1867 in Idaho. In 1916, I completed plans to make a Confederate memorial on Stone Mountain near Atlanta, Georgia, but I had a disagreement with my sponsors and by the time it was settled, I had begun the Mt. Rushmore Memorial. I died before it was finished, so my son completed it.

SAM: We certainly admire your work. Now more of us will remember your name. Thank you for joining us.

BORGLUM: I enjoyed it. (*All applaud as he exits and MARIA MITCHELL enters, sits.*)

SAM (*To* MITCHELL): Welcome to Name This American. Are you ready to play?

MITCHELL (*Smiling*): I'm ready.

SAM: Panelist number one, begin.

1ST PANELIST: We've had an inventor and an artist. Could you be in politics?

MITCHELL: No. Politics never interested me.

2ND PANELIST: Were you involved in something related to science?

MITCHELL: Yes, I was.

2ND PANELIST: Are you in the field of medicine?

MITCHELL: No.

3RD PANELIST: Are you involved in the earth sciences?

MITCHELL: No.

4TH PANELIST: Astronomy?

MITCHELL: Yes.

4TH PANELIST: I can't think of any astronomers. (*Thinks a moment, then gets an idea*) Did you, by any chance, grow up on Nantucket Island, Massachusetts?

MITCHELL: Yes.

4TH PANELIST: Are you Maria Mitchell?

MITCHELL: Yes, I am. (*All applaud.*)

SAM: Congratulations, panel. Miss Mitchell, please tell us about your interest in astronomy.

MITCHELL: It was unusual for a woman in the mid 1800s to become an astronomer, but I was always interested in the stars — and in the sun, too. I did a lot of research on sun spots. (*Enthusiastically*) In 1847 I discovered a new comet, which was very exciting!

SAM: Thank you, Miss Mitchell. You were way ahead of your time. I'm sorry you didn't win more from our panel.

MITCHELL (*Rising*): I'm sorry, too. (*All applaud. She exits as* DOLLEY MADISON *enters.*)

SAM: Welcome to Name This American.

MADISON: Thank you, Uncle Sam.

SAM: Panelist one, let's start right in.

1ST PANELIST: Your dress makes me think you may have lived about 200 years ago. Is that correct?

MADISON: Yes, that's correct.

1ST PANELIST: Were you involved in the Revolutionary War?

MADISON: I was very young, but yes, I remember it.

SAM: I'm afraid I must count that as a no, since she was only a child at the time.

2ND PANELIST: Were you a seamstress who worked on our first flag?

MADISON: No.

3RD PANELIST: Were you married to one of our presidents?

MADISON (*Smiling*): Yes, I was.

3RD PANELIST: Are you Martha Washington?

MADISON (*Slightly offended*): No, she was much older than I am.

4TH PANELIST: Are you Abigail Adams, the wife of the second president, John Adams?

MADISON: No.

5TH PANELIST: Let's try the next president. Are you Mrs. Jefferson?

MADISON: No.

6TH PANELIST (*Embarrassed*): I can't remember who was the fourth president. Are you Mrs. Monroe?

MADISON: No.

SAM: Too bad, panel. Our fourth president was James Madison. Let me present that famous first lady, Dolley Madison. (*All applaud.*) Tell us about yourself, Mrs. Madison.

MADISON: I was born in North Carolina in 1768 but grew up in Virginia. My first husband, John Todd, was a lawyer. We had two sons, but one of them and my husband died in 1793. I met and married Congressman James Madison a year later and was thrilled to become the first lady in 1809. (*Enthusiastically*) I loved entertaining at the White House. One of my favorite days was when I introduced ice cream to my guests for the first time. What a party! (*More seriously*) I suppose my greatest accomplishment was during the War of 1812. I managed to save a lot of my husband's papers and a portrait of George Washington before the British burned down the White House.

SAM: Mrs. Madison, our country is indebted to you. Thank you for coming today.

MADISON: It was my pleasure. (*All applaud as she exits.*)

633

Sam: Now, Libby, why don't you explain how the second part of our program works?

Libby: I'd be glad to, Uncle Sam. This is the time we ask our panelists to wear blindfolds, as we welcome special celebrities who would be too easy to identify by sight. (PANELISTS *put on blindfolds.*)

Sam: Thank you, Libby. Panel, no peeking, and, audience, no hints. Blindfolds in place? (PANELISTS *nod.*) Then let's bring in our next guest. (LIBBY *motions offstage and* SACAGAWEA *enters.*) Welcome, mystery guest. Are you ready to play?

Sacagawea (*Sitting; in deep voice throughout following*): I'm ready.

1st Panelist: Are you from the 20th century?

Sacagawea: No.

2nd Panelist: The 19th century?

Sacagawea: Yes and no.

Sam: Actually only part of this person's life took place in the 1800s.

2nd Panelist: Then, I assume, the other part was in the 1700s?

Sacagawea: Yes.

2nd Panelist: And with that voice, I assume you're a man.

Sacagawea (*In regular voice*): No, I'm not.

2nd Panelist (*Surprised*): What? You tricked us.

Sacagawea (*Laughing*): I'm sorry. I really am a woman.

3rd Panelist: If you lived around 1800, did you have anything to do with the westward movement?

Sacagawea: Yes.

3rd Panelist: I can't think of any women of the West except Annie Oakley and Calamity Jane. Are you either of them?

Sacagawea: No.

4th Panelist: Did you move west with the settlers?

Sacagawea: No.

5th Panelist (*Thinking*): Were you an explorer?

Sacagawea: No.

6th Panelist (*Shaking head*): This is a hard one! (*Pause*) Did you help an explorer?

Sacagawea: Yes.

6th Panelist (*Pleased*): Oh good, now we're getting somewhere! (*Thoughtfully*) Are you an Indian?

SACAGAWEA: Yes.

6TH PANELIST: Are you Sacagawea?

SACAGAWEA: Yes.

SAM: Good work, panel. You may remove your blindfolds (*They do so.*) and take a look at the famous Indian guide for Lewis and Clark, Sacagawea. (*All applaud.*) Please tell us about yourself.

SACAGAWEA: My name, Sacagawea, means Bird Woman in Shoshone. I was captured by enemy Indians and sold to a French-Canadian trader. We joined Lewis and Clark's famous expedition to explore the Louisiana Territory in 1804. I helped as an interpreter with the local Indians and was their principal guide.

SAM: And they would not have made it without you. That's why a river, a mountain peak, and a mountain pass have been named after you, not to mention numerous monuments and memorials. (SACAGAWEA *smiles and nods modestly.*) Thank you for joining us today. (*All applaud, as* PANELISTS *put on blindfolds and* SACAGAWEA *exits.* ELIZABETH CADY STANTON *enters and sits.*) Panelist number one, you may begin.

1ST PANELIST: Are you a woman?

STANTON (*Strongly*): Absolutely!

1ST PANELIST (*Taken aback*): Well, that was emphatic! Are you interested in women's rights?

STANTON: Yes, most assuredly I am.

1ST PANELIST: Are you a famous woman suffrage leader?

STANTON: Yes, definitely.

1ST PANELIST: I can think of several women's rights leaders—Lucretia Mott, Susan B. Anthony, and Matilda Gage. Are you any of those?

STANTON: No.

2ND PANELIST: Did you help organize the first women's rights convention held in Seneca Falls, New York, in 1848?

STANTON: Yes, I made the first formal demand for the right to vote to be extended to women.

2ND PANELIST: Were you the first president of the National Woman Suffrage Association?

STANTON: Yes.

2ND PANELIST: In 1868, didn't you even run for Congress?

STANTON (*Angrily*): Yes, and I'd have won if it weren't for the fact that there were only men voting. That was so unfair. Do you realize that women still couldn't vote until the 19th Amendment to the Constitution was passed in 1920!

2ND PANELIST: You're Elizabeth Cady Stanton, aren't you?

STANTON (*Proudly*): Yes, I am! (*Applause. PANELISTS remove blindfolds.*)

SAM: If it weren't for women like you, where would we be today?

STANTON: I was hoping to win $500 for my latest cause, but I suppose I'll be able to get it elsewhere.

SAM: Yes, I'm sure you will.

STANTON: Good day. (*She waves to crowd. Applause as she exits and PANELISTS put on blindfolds. BABE RUTH enters.*)

SAM: Welcome, challenger. (*BABE sits.*) Let's begin.

1ST PANELIST: Are you in politics?

BABE: No, I am not a politician.

2ND PANELIST: Are you involved in sports in any way?

BABE: Yes.

2ND PANELIST: Is that sport football?

BABE: No.

3RD PANELIST: Is it basketball?

BABE: No.

4TH PANELIST: What about baseball?

BABE: That's the one.

4TH PANELIST: Two great players come to mind when I think of baseball, Babe Ruth and Lou Gehrig. Are you one of them?

BABE: Yes.

4TH PANELIST: Well, I have a 50-50 chance. Are you Babe Ruth?

BABE: Yes. (*All applaud.* PANELISTS *remove blindfolds.*)

SAM: Good work, panel. Babe, tell us about some of the highlights of your amazing baseball career.

BABE: I love everything about the game. I set records both from the mound and at the plate. For years I held the record with my total of 714 career homeruns. And in 1936 I was among the first ballplayers elected to the Baseball Hall of Fame.

SAM: Thank you for being part of our show. (*Applause.* PANELISTS *restore blindfolds.* BABE *exits and* LILIUOKALANI *enters.*) It's time for our final contestant. (*To* LILIUOKALANI) Welcome. Are you ready? (*She nods, sits.*) I'm going to help you out, panel, by telling you this is a woman. Now you won't waste any questions on that, and I'm going to give her $50 to start with. (LIBBY *puts up $50 card.*) Panelist number six, let's begin with you.

6TH PANELIST: Thank you. Mystery guest, do we need blindfolds because we would recognize your face or would the clothes you are wearing give you away?

LILIUOKALANI: Which question do you want me to answer?

6TH PANELIST: I'm sorry. Would your clothes give us a clue to your identity?

LILIUOKALANI: Yes, I'm sure they would.

6TH PANELIST: Would a man wear the same outfit?

LILIUOKALANI (*Giggling*): I certainly hope not.

5TH PANELIST: Are you an entertainer?

LILIUOKALANI: No.

4TH PANELIST: Let's get back to the clothes idea. Do they have anything to do with the part of the United States where you live?

LILIUOKALANI: Yes.

4TH PANELIST: Are you from the western part of our country?

LILIUOKALANI: Yes.

4TH PANELIST: The northwest?

LILIUOKALANI: No.

3RD PANELIST: Then it must be the southwest, maybe New Mexico, California, or Arizona.

LILIUOKALANI: No — farther southwest.

2ND PANELIST (*Knowingly*): Are you a famous Hawaiian?

LILIUOKALANI: Yes.

2ND PANELIST: Are you Queen Liliuokalani?

LILIUOKALANI: Yes, I am.

SAM: Good work, panel. (*Applause. PANELISTS remove blindfolds.*) Tell us a little about yourself.

LILIUOKALANI: As a child, I loved to write songs. When I got older I wrote the national anthem of Hawaii, but it was never as popular as my song "Aloha Oe." My older sister was supposed to be queen, but she married an American and decided to give up the throne. Then my brother became King Kalakaua. When he died in 1891, I became Queen Liliuokalani, ruling until 1893, when the United States took over. Hawaii became the 50th state in 1959.

SAM: And a beautiful state it is!

LILIUOKALANI (*Graciously*): It is only one of many.

SAM: Ladies and gentlemen, I'm afraid our time is up, but we are glad you could join us in honoring a few famous Americans. After all, it takes special people to make a great nation like ours. Before we go, we would like to bring out all our contestants. (*Everyone enters.*) Please join us in singing "This Land Is Your Land." (*All sing. Curtain*)

THE END

Production Notes

NAME THIS AMERICAN

CHARACTERS: *4 male; 6 female; 6 male or female for panelists.*

PLAYING TIME: *25 minutes.*

COSTUMES: *Walter Hunt, Gutzon Borglum, Maria Mitchell, Dolley Madison, and Elizabeth Cady Stanton wear period dress. Sacagawea, Indian outfit. Liliuokalani, colorful Hawaiian outfit and lei. Babe Ruth, baseball uniform. Uncle Sam wears red, white, and blue. Liberty, green dress and crown. Panelists, everyday clothes.*

PROPERTIES: *Large cards marked: $50, $100, $150, $200, $250, and $500; six blindfolds.*

SETTING: *The stage of a quiz program. Podium is center. Next to it is music stand. Long table and six chairs are right. Desk and chair are left.*

LIGHTING AND SOUND: *No special effects.*

Think and Respond

 What do all the mystery guests on the quiz show have in common?

 What might have been the author's purpose in writing a play about a quiz show including these characters?

 Why would it be **misleading** for Walter Hunt to say he had discovered something?

 If your class were going to perform this play, which character would you like to portray? Why?

 What reading strategies did you use to help make this selection easier to understand?

SALLY ANN
THUNDER ANN WHIRLWIND
CROCKETT

A TALL TALE RETOLD AND ILLUSTRATED BY
STEVEN KELLOGG

Sally Ann Thunder Ann Whirlwind astonished folks throughout her childhood. When she was one year old, she beat the fastest runners in the state.

At four she flipped the strongest arm wrestlers.

At seven she was the champion tug-of-war team.

On her eighth birthday Sally Ann decided she was grown-up and ready for new challenges. "I'm off to the frontier!" she announced.

For several years she lived with different animals and learned their habits. She loved life in the wilderness during every season except winter.

Finally, the fierce cold drove her underground to hibernate with the bears. Deep in a cave that bristled with stalactites and stalagmites Sally Ann snuggled close to a large warm grizzly.

Suddenly the bear awakened, and Sally Ann felt a blast of terrible heat from his great ovenlike mouth. It was clear that the bear was more interested in a snack than a roommate.

But before the monster could swallow her, Sally Ann stunned him with a grin as bright as a flash of lightning.

Over backward he went, rolling among razor-sharp stalactites and stalagmites that skinned him from his ears to his toes. Naked and embarrassed, the creature scrambled out of sight. "That was a close shave for both of us!" cried Sally Ann.

She wrapped herself in the bear's fur and set off in search of new adventures.

That bearskin kept Sally Ann cozy for many winters, and she grew tall and strong. But as the years rolled by she became tired of living alone.

One day she came upon an unhappy fellow who had dozed off while leaning against a tree and awakened to find himself stuck.

Two eagles were adding to his misery by yanking out his hair to line their nests.

"You're in a pretty predicament, mister!" exclaimed Sally Ann. "Let me give you a hand."

Sally Ann tried to shoo away the eagles, but they fought her like flapping furies. So she let loose a wild scream that blasted the color off their heads and tails and left them as placid as pigeons.

"Well, star spangle my banner!" cried Sally Ann Thunder Ann Whirlwind. "I've just invented bald eagles!"

Unfortunately, the fellow Sally Ann was trying to rescue had been knocked unconscious by her scream. Quickly she hauled six rattlers out of a nearby snake den, knotted them together, and lassoed a branch. One sharp tug and his head popped free.

He's kind of handsome, thought Sally Ann. I'll freshen up and look my best before I nurse him back to health.

Sally Ann grabbed a hornet's nest for a bonnet and fogged herself with the perfume of a passing skunk.

Then she heaved her patient into the creek.

Just as she expected, the minute he hit that icy water he perked right up. "My heart's pounding like a buffalo stampede," he sputtered.

"So's mine," confessed Sally Ann.

"My name is Davy Crockett. Marry me!" he exclaimed.

Sally Ann was astonished to learn that she had rescued the most famous woodsman in America. Lightning flashed between them, and they fell head over heels in love.

The happy couple celebrated their wedding with a batch of eagle-egg eggnog. Then they settled down in a farmhouse with a fine view of the Mississippi River.

The End
of the Tale

Think and Respond

What challenges did Sally Ann find on the frontier? What character traits helped her to meet them?

Making Connections

Compare Texts

1 How does reading about the characters in "Name This American" help you understand the theme American Adventure?

2 How does the author show differences between the characters, in addition to the different facts each character tells?

3 How is Sally Ann in "Sally Ann Thunder Ann Whirlwind Crockett" like the women who are guests in "Name This American"? How is she different?

4 Why do you think the author decided to write "Name This American" as a play, rather than as a story?

5 What resources could you use to find out about famous Americans who lived in your own area?

Write an Opinion Statement

Suppose you could meet one of the remarkable Americans in "Name This American." Think about which one you would choose. Then write about why you would choose this person and what you might like to learn from him or her. Use a graphic like the one shown here to plan your statement.

Person I Would Choose:	
Reasons for My Choice	What I Think I Might Learn

Writing CONNECTION

Make a Quiz Game

In "Name This American," Maria Mitchell says that she did research on sun spots. What are sun spots? What have scientists learned about the causes of sun spots and how they affect Earth? Find answers to these and related questions that interest you. You may find information on the Internet, in encyclopedias, or in nonfiction science books and articles. Use the information to make cards with questions about sun spots on one side and the answers on the other side. Use the cards to play a quiz game with classmates.

Science CONNECTION

What American astronomer discovered in 1908 that sun spots contain strong magnetic fields?

Sun spots appear in cycles of how many years?

Create a Recorded Message

Some important symbols of our nation are featured in "Name This American." They include Uncle Sam, the Statue of Liberty, and the White House. Use print or online sources to research one of these symbols or another of your choice. Imagine that there is an 800 number for people to call about national symbols. Create and tape-record a message about the national symbol you researched.

Social Studies CONNECTION

645

▲ Name This American

Cause and Effect

A cause is why something happens. An **effect** is what happens because of an action. An effect may have many causes, and a cause may have many effects. A causal chain is a series of events in which one event must happen in order for the next event to happen.

This diagram shows the pattern that the author uses to play the game in "Name This American." The arrows show different ways the action could proceed.

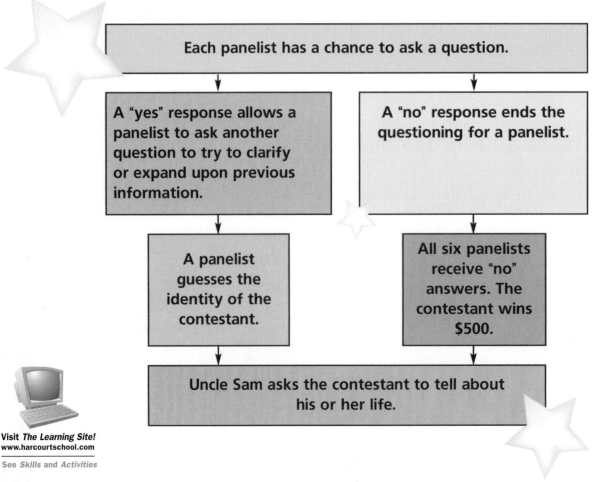

Each panelist has a chance to ask a question.

A "yes" response allows a panelist to ask another question to try to clarify or expand upon previous information.

A "no" response ends the questioning for a panelist.

A panelist guesses the identity of the contestant.

All six panelists receive "no" answers. The contestant wins $500.

Uncle Sam asks the contestant to tell about his or her life.

Visit *The Learning Site!*
www.harcourtschool.com

See *Skills* and *Activities*

646

Test Prep
Cause and Effect

▶ **Read the passage. Then answer the questions.**

> **Setting:** *Boston, the evening of April 18, 1775. Joseph Warren, a patriot leader, knocks on the door of Paul Revere's house.*
>
> Joseph Warren: Paul, the British are headed to Concord. Lieutenant Colonel Smith and 700 of his troops have been commanded to arrest John Adams and John Hancock for treason.
>
> Paul Revere: Adams and Hancock must be warned!
>
> Joseph Warren: I want you and Dawes to ride to Lexington tonight.
>
> Paul Revere: The patriots in Concord must be alerted. Arrange for a signal to be sent from the steeple of the Old North Church in Boston. Flash two lanterns if the British are coming by water. Flash one if they are coming by land. I am off now to find Dawes.

1. **Joseph Warren goes to Paul Revere's house because —**

   A Adams and Hancock have left

   B British troops are on their way to Concord

   C Revere has asked him to warn the patriots

   D the patriots have destroyed British supplies

Tip

Find where Joseph Warren describes his own wishes.

2. **What will the effect of the signal be?**

   F Paul Revere will return to his home.

   G Dawes will ride to Lexington.

   H The patriots will know how the British are coming.

   J Joseph Warren will warn Dawes.

Tip

Think about what will happen right after the signal is given.

▲ What's the Big Idea, Ben Franklin?

honors

edition

contraption

suspended

repeal

treaty

Vocabulary Power

Benjamin Franklin is an important and colorful figure in American history. He had a wide variety of interests and unusual ideas.

My Goals for the Future

I've been reading about Benjamin Franklin and other great people in history. I hope I can grow up to make a difference in the world the way they did. Maybe someday I'll win **honors**, too, like the glory and fame they received. Here is how I will do it.

1. I want to write a book so good that the first **edition**, the books printed at the same time, sells out in a week. I'm not sure yet what the book will be about, but I know it will be great.

2. I'd like to invent a **contraption**, or odd machine, that can read aloud for people who can't see well. It will be able to read books, newspapers, magazines, or anything else with printed words on it. I guess the contraption will have

to be **suspended**, or hung by a support, above whatever it's supposed to read. I'm still working on the details.

3. I'll get Congress to **repeal**, or cancel, all laws that are written in complicated language. Lawmakers should write laws so that people like me can read and understand them.

4. The most important goal I hope to achieve is to get all the countries of the world to sign a **treaty**. This will be a formal agreement between nations to guarantee world peace forever. I bet I can get lots of other people to help me work on that one!

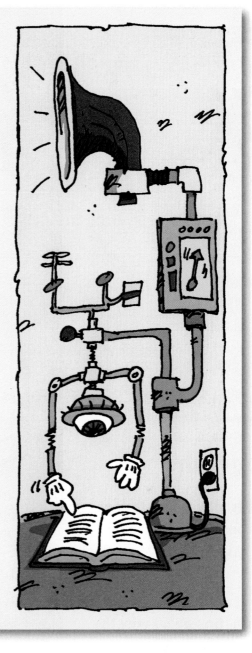

Vocabulary–Writing CONNECTION

Think of a **contraption** that we use today that would impress Benjamin Franklin. Write three sentences telling why.

What's the Big Idea, Ben Franklin?

by JEAN FRITZ

illustrated by Margot Tomes

ALA
Notable Book
Children's
Choice

WHAT'S

THE BIG IDEA, BEN FRANKLIN?

by *Jean Fritz*

ILLUSTRATED BY MARGOT TOMES

In 1732, when he was 26 years old, Benjamin Franklin had one of his best ideas. He decided to publish an almanac. Every family bought an almanac each year. People read it to find out the holidays, the weather forecasts, the schedule of tides, the time the sun came up and went down, when the moon would be full, when to plant what. It was just the kind of book that Benjamin loved—full of odd pieces of information and bits of advice on this and that. It was, in addition to being a calendar, a grand how-to book and Benjamin figured he knew as many how-to's as anyone else. Besides, he knew a lot of jokes.

He put them all in his almanac, called it *Poor Richard's Almanack*, and published the first edition in 1733. His specialty was short one-line sayings.

Sometimes these one-liners were quick how-to hints for everyday living: "Eat to live, not live to eat"; "A penny saved is a

penny earned"; "Half Wits talk much but say little."

Sometimes his one-liners were humorous comments on life: "Men and melons are hard to know"; "Fish and visitors smell in 3 days."

In a few years Franklin was selling 10,000 copies of his almanac every year. (He kept it up for 25 years.)

This was certainly a good idea, but it was not Benjamin Franklin's Big Idea. He was 40 years old when he first became interested in the idea that would become the Big one. By this time he had 2 children—William Temple, who was 17, and Sarah, who was 2. (A third child, Francis, died in 1736 when he was 4 years old.)

The idea had to do with electricity, which had become a new fad. For some time it had been known that electricity could be generated by rubbing glass tubes with silk. Now a Dutch scientist had found that this electricity could be stored in specially equipped bottles, then drawn from them by applying wires (or conductors) to the 2 sides of the bottle. All over Europe people were meeting in darkened rooms to see these sparks and the tricks that could be performed. Wires twisted into the shape of giant spiders were electrified. Sparks were drawn from a cake of ice and even from the head of a boy suspended from the ceiling by a silk rope. Electrical performers traveled from town to town selling shocks to curious people. Once, before a large audience in Spain, 180 grenadiers were linked together by wire, then given a shock to make them jump into the air at the same time.

Franklin bought electrical equipment and began writing to European scientists. He learned to perform the usual tricks and made up some of his own. Once he gave an electrical picnic. He planned to kill a turkey by an electrical shock, roast it in a container connected to electrical circuits, on a fire lit by an electrical bottle. He was, however, so carried away by his performance in front of his guests that he was careless. He took the whole shock through his own arms and body and was knocked unconscious. When he came to, he was embarrassed. "What I meant to kill was a turkey," he said. "Instead I almost killed a goose."

His Big Idea was that electricity and lightning were the same. Up to that time most people had thought lightning was (and always would be) as mysterious as heaven itself. And here was Franklin saying it was the same stuff that you saw in parlor tricks—only on a grander scale. What was more, Franklin believed he could prove it. Let a sentry box be built on the top of a high tower, he wrote a scientist in Europe. Put a pointed rod in

the tower and let a man stand in the box during a storm. Franklin knew that electricity was attracted to pointed iron rods; if the man in the sentry box could find that lightning was also attracted to a rod, that would prove they were the same. The only reason Franklin didn't make the experiment himself was that Philadelphia didn't have a high enough tower or even a high hill.

In the spring of 1752 three scientists in Europe tried the experiment and all three proved that Franklin's Big Idea was right. (One scientist was killed, but that was because he was careless.) Meanwhile Benjamin thought of a way to prove the Idea himself. One stormy day he raised a kite with a long pointed wire at the tip and felt the electric shock come through a key he had tied to the kite string near his hand. So he already had his own proof when the news reached him about the experiments in Europe. Still, he was surprised to hear how excited people were about his Idea. He was suddenly famous. Indeed, he was becoming the most celebrated man in America. The King of France sent him congratulations; the Royal Society of England presented him with a medal; universities gave him honors and called him Dr. Franklin; newspapers praised him. Benjamin was pleased. He felt secretly as proud, he said, as a girl wearing a new pair of garters.

A Big Idea, however, meant little to Benjamin Franklin unless he could put it to everyday use. So he invented the lightning rod, a pointed iron rod that could be

raised from the roof of a house or barn to attract lightning and lead it harmlessly through a wire and into the ground. For his own lightning rod, he also fixed up a contraption that would ring a bell in the house whenever lightning hit. (Debbie hated that bell.*)

Benjamin would have liked to do nothing but experiment with his ideas, but people had discovered that he was more than an inventor. Whatever needed doing, he seemed able and willing to do it. He was made Postmaster General and organized a new system so that it took only 3 weeks instead of 6 weeks for a letter to go from Boston to Philadelphia. (Later he cut the time to 6 days.) He helped organize a fire insurance company, a hospital, and an expedition to seek the

*Ben's wife

Northwest Passage. And because he was so good at talking people into doing what he wanted them to do, in 1757 he was sent to London. He was to do what he could to further the interests of the people of Pennsylvania.

*I*n London Benjamin began right away to live in style and comfort. He bought new shoes, new wigs, new shirts, a new watch, 2 pairs of silver shoe and knee buckles, new candlesticks, new chinaware, and a new carriage. He had his sword blade repaired and ordered new spectacles because he'd left his best pair at home. He rented 4 large rooms in a house owned by a Mrs. Stevenson, who treated him like a king. When his back itched, she gave him an ivory backscratcher; she warmed his shirts before he put them on;

she even trained her cat not to sit in his favorite chair. Of course she served only the foods he liked best (*never* beef, which upset him), and as if this were not enough, Benjamin received a regular supply of American cornmeal, venison, cranberries, and bacon from his wife, Debbie. (He sent Debbie presents in return, including a crimson satin coat and an apple corer.)

With the exception of 2 years back in America, Benjamin lived in London for 18 years, from the time he was 51 until he was 69. (Debbie, afraid to cross the ocean, died the year before he finally returned.) Benjamin was in London when George the Third was crowned King of England. He was

there in 1765 when England began laying down taxes and making trouble for America. He did his best to keep the two countries friendly, but over the years England became more and more stubborn. First one tax. Then another. Sometimes England would repeal a tax, but it would never, never give up its right to tax America. Benjamin discovered that all his rules for arguing which had

worked so well in the past were of no use against such stubbornness. He finally gave up arguing altogether one day in 1774 when he was called before the British government to explain his activities in behalf of America. For 2 hours he stood before the government's Privy Council. He was shouted at, laughed at, insulted, and condemned. Franklin, white with rage, said not one word. He was being treated like an apprentice. Indeed, England was treating America as if it were a country of apprentices instead of a country of free men. And Franklin could stand it no longer. In the spring of 1775 he returned to America, only to find that America and England were already at war. The Battle of Lexington had been fought while he was at sea.

Franklin was so mad that he told Americans if there wasn't enough gunpowder to go around they should use bows and arrows against the English. He was so mad that he would have swum out into the ocean with electric bolts to shoot at the English, if he could have. But America had other uses for him. Right away he was put in the Continental Congress and placed on 10 different committees. When the time came to write the Declaration of Independence, he was one of those asked to do it. As it turned out, Thomas Jefferson did the writing, but Franklin made changes. The "truths" that Jefferson held to be "sacred and undeniable" became "self-evident" truths when Franklin had finished.

But these jobs were small compared to the big one Congress had for him. Benjamin Franklin was still America's best arguer and America's most famous citizen. So, in the fall of

1776, he was sent to France to try to talk the French into entering the war on America's side. George Washington would run the war in America, but Benjamin Franklin would run it in Europe, getting all the help and money from any country he could.

Benjamin was 70 years old now and found the ocean trip hard. The seas were rough; the weather was freezing. He had boils on his body, gout in his legs, and a skin disease on his head that bothered him so much that he wore a loose fur hat instead of his usual wig. When he arrived in France he was rumpled, crumpled, and weak— not the stylish, famous-looking figure the French had expected. Of course Benjamin planned to dress up as soon as he felt better, but to his surprise he discovered the French liked him as he was, fur hat and all. Indeed, he was an immediate sensation. A plain man in the most fashionable country in the world! Within a month the French had made him their hero. French ladies found him charming. They fussed over him and called him Papa; they hung his picture over their mantels and wore his picture in their rings.  Frenchmen cleared the way for him when he appeared in the streets. So Benjamin never did dress up. He never wore a wig or carried a sword the whole time he was in France, not even when he went to see the King. If being plain made him popular, Benjamin Franklin had the good sense to stay plain.

Paris suited old Benjamin perfectly. On one side he had the River Seine when he wanted a swim; on the other side he had friends when he wanted company. Altogether, Benjamin had such a good time in Paris that he couldn't always be bothered with his old rules for good behavior. Frequently he ate too much. But rather than worry, he carried a bottle of oil of wormwood for indigestion and he gained weight. (Sometimes he called himself Dr. Fatsides.) Occasionally he went to extremes. If he became interested in a game of chess, he'd stay up all night playing. And he wasn't neat. His desk was a mess. A Scottish visitor once pointed out the danger of leaving important state papers scattered so carelessly over his desk. There might be spies in the household, the Scotsman said. (And there really were spies.)

But the important thing was that Benjamin did what he'd set out to do. He talked France into joining America in the war and he took good care of America's business in Europe. And when peace came in 1783, he helped to write the peace treaty.

When Franklin (79 years old now) finally returned to Philadelphia, he was given a wildly enthusiastic welcome. Cannon were fired, bells rung, parades formed, speeches made. His daughter, Sarah, was so excited that she fell into a wheelbarrow. But the people of Pennsylvania put Franklin right back to work. Three years in a row they elected him president of their government, and when Franklin was 82, they asked him to help write the Constitution of the United States. For 4 months he attended meetings of the Constitutional Convention. Sometimes he dozed off during a speech; often he disagreed with what was being done. But in the end he was satisfied with the Constitution. With so many different opinions, he said this was the best they could do.

Now at last Benjamin Franklin was finished with public life. He did not have long to live,

but even when he couldn't get out of bed, he still read and he still wrote. And every afternoon his 9-year-old granddaughter, Deborah, would come to his bedside and he would hear her spelling lesson for the next day. If she did well, he would give her a spoonful of fruit jelly that he kept beside him.

At 11 o'clock on the night of April 17, 1790, Benjamin Franklin died. He was 84 years old—a man who had not only had a Big Idea of his own but had played a large part in one of the Biggest Ideas of his time—the idea of an independent United States.

Think and Respond

1. What were some of Ben Franklin's big ideas, and why have they been important?

2. How is the beginning of each new topic or section indicated in this biography?

3. Why do you think the author includes bits of everyday information about Ben Franklin, as well as important historical facts?

4. Do you think Ben Franklin deserved the fame and **honors** he received in his lifetime? Why or why not?

5. What reading strategies did you use as you were reading this selection? When did you use them?

Meet the Author
JEAN FRITZ

Why did you begin writing?

I was born in Hankow, China, where I attended an English school until I was twelve. I was an American, but I didn't feel like a real American because I was so far away. When I returned to the United States, I read many history books and began writing about Americans of the past.

Why do you choose to write about Benjamin Franklin and other historical people?

I think Benjamin Franklin was a very human American hero that students should know about. I want students to know that historical figures were real people and that humorous things happened to them. Most often, historical figures are treated like statues—frozen in one position. I want to show students that these people were once truly alive.

When people ask me how I find ideas, I tell them that I don't. Ideas find me. A character in history will suddenly step right out of the past and demand a book from me. Once I decide to take him or her on, I begin my detective work. I read old books, old letters, and old newspapers. I visit the places where my character lived and worked. I try to figure out as much as I can about the person and the period in which he or she lived. Often I turn up surprises and, of course, I pass these on to my readers.

THE MANY LIVES OF
★ ★ ★ ★ ★ ★ ★ ★
Benjamin Franklin

BY MARY POPE OSBORNE

Almanacs were a favorite form of reading in colonial America. They were small books that forecast the weather and told about the tides and changes of the moon. They also contained calendars, jokes, poems, and odd facts. In 1732 Ben Franklin began publishing his own almanac which he called *Poor Richard's Almanack.*

Poor Richard, 1733
AN
Almanack
For the Year of Chrift
1733,
Being the Firft after LE'AP YEAR;

Wherein is contained
The Lunations, Eclipfes, Judgement of
the Weather, Spring Tides, Planets Motions &
mutual Afpects, Sun and Moon's Rifing and Setting, Length of Days, Time of High Water,
Fairs, Courts, and obfervable Days.
Fitted to the Latitude of Forty Degrees,
and a Meridian of Five Hours Weft from London,
but may without fenfible Error, ferve all the ad-
jacent Places, even from Newfoundland to South-
Carolina.

By RICHARD SAUNDERS, Philom.
PHILADELPHIA
Printed and fold by B. FRANKLIN, at the New
Printing Office near the Market.
The Third Impreffion.

Poor Richard was a gold mine for Ben—after the Bible, it became the most popular reading in the colonies. It came out once a year and was sprinkled with useful information about the weather and stars. The almanac also gave Ben the chance to share his philosophy of self-improvement. He took many of the sayings from ancient writers and rewrote them to make them simple and clear. Today historians believe that the philosophy expressed in *Poor Richard* helped mold the American character, ideas such as:

God helps those who help themselves.

Early to bed and early to rise makes a man healthy, wealthy, and wise.

When you're good to others, you are best to yourself.

There are no gains without pains.

At the working man's house hunger looks in, but dares not enter.

For the next twenty-five years, as "Poor Richard," Ben Franklin preached his ideals to the American people—the value of hard work, common sense, and self-sufficiency. Today people might think that his methods of trying to solve human problems were a bit too simple, but Franklin himself seemed to know that. Though he didn't put it on his list, one of his most outstanding virtues was humor. And he seems to be laughing at himself when he writes in *Poor Richard:*

Who is wise? *He that learns from every one.*
Who is powerful? *He that governs his passions.*
Who is rich? *He that is content.*
Who is that? *Nobody.*

★ ★ ★ ★ ★ ★ ★

Think and Respond

What needs did Benjamin Franklin's almanacs fill for the people in his day? How do people fill the same kinds of needs today?

INK

Making Connections

Compare Texts

1 Why is Ben Franklin a good subject to include in the theme American Adventure?

2 How does the tone of the writing change when the author discusses matters such as the reasons for the American Revolution or the Declaration of Independence?

3 Compare and contrast how the authors of "What's the Big Idea, Ben Franklin?" and "The Many Lives of Benjamin Franklin" treat the subject of *Poor Richard's Almanack*.

4 How would the selection be different if it had been written as a history book rather than as a biography?

5 Where might you find more information about Ben Franklin?

Write a Journal Entry

Writing CONNECTION

Pick an event from the selection. How might Benjamin Franklin's daughter, Sarah, have reacted to it? Write a journal entry to express what Sarah Franklin might have thought and felt about that event. Use this chart to help you plan your journal entry.

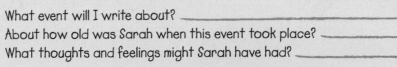

What event will I write about? _____
About how old was Sarah when this event took place? _____
What thoughts and feelings might Sarah have had? _____
_____

Plan an Experiment

Many scientists have experimented with electricity, as Benjamin Franklin did. Research simple, safe experiments that demonstrate principles of electricity. You might find experiments on educational websites about science projects, in books about science fair projects, or in science texts. Choose an experiment, practice it, and perform it for your classmates. Explain the scientific principles that your experiment demonstrates.

Science CONNECTION

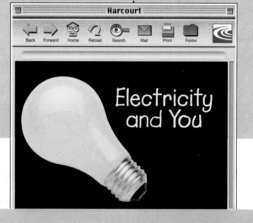

Harcourt

Electricity and You

Give a Presentation

Benjamin Franklin played an important role in the American Revolution. Use encyclopedias and social studies texts to research another patriot

Thomas Jefferson

who helped the United States become an independent nation. Share your information in an oral presentation by role-playing the patriot speaking about his or her experiences.

Social Studies CONNECTION

▲ What's the Big Idea, Ben Franklin?

Connotation/ Denotation

Focus Skill

A word's **denotation** is its dictionary meaning. A word's **connotation** is the feeling or idea that you associate with that word. Writers choose words for what they mean. They also choose words for the mood, or feeling, the words create and for the effect the words have on readers.

Think about the connotations, or shades of meaning, in the group of words below. Then read the sentences.

Weaker ← Connotation → Stronger		
pleased	delighted	elated

1. Franklin was <u>pleased</u> with the praise he received.
2. Franklin was <u>delighted</u> with the praise he received.
3. Franklin was <u>elated</u> with the praise he received.

Notice how the image of Ben Franklin changes when the underlined word changes. Why do you think the author of the selection chose *pleased* instead of *delighted* or *elated*?

Visit *The Learning Site!*
www.harcourtschool.com

See *Skills* and *Activities*

Test Prep
Connotation/Denotation

▶ **Read the passage. Then answer the questions.**

> Theodore Roosevelt is remembered as America's twenty-sixth President. As a boy, however, a <u>determined</u> Roosevelt studied animals and insects for hours at a time and wanted to be a naturalist. At the age of nine, he started the "Roosevelt Museum of Natural History" in his bedroom in his parents' New York City apartment. By the age of ten, he had written an essay titled "About Insects and Fishes, Natural History, by Theodore Roosevelt, 1869." Roosevelt's boyhood diaries reveal that his <u>keen</u> interest in nature was encouraged by his family.

1. **Which word would change the feeling the author creates if it replaced <u>determined</u> in the passage?**

   A serious

   B dedicated

   C bored

   D persistent

Tip

Substitute each word choice for *determined*. Choose the word that creates in your mind a different image of young Roosevelt.

2. **Which word could replace <u>keen</u> in the passage and not change the feeling the author creates?**

   F everyday

   G intense

   H passing

   J slight

Tip

Say each word. Pay attention to how it makes you feel. Choose the word that creates a feeling similar to *keen*.

Vocabulary Power

esteem

terrain

ordeal

peril

profusely

dismal

Have you ever heard of Lewis and Clark? They were explorers who set out on an important journey of discovery. Scientists, too, sometimes set out on special journeys to make discoveries.

These scientists are setting off on a mission, a scientific expedition. The purpose of their journey is to study plants that live high up in the mountains. Although this is not the first expedition of its kind, the scientists **esteem**, or value, it as the best organized.

All the scientists have to be expert climbers to tackle this rocky **terrain**, or area of land. It is quite an **ordeal**, or difficult adventure. They could find themselves in real **peril** when they climb the dangerous cliffs.

It is raining **profusely**, coming down hard and without stopping. It's only the weather, though, that's **dismal**. The scientists aren't gloomy. They're very pleased with their boxes full of samples and photographs.

Vocabulary–Writing CONNECTION

Write a paragraph describing a recent trip. What was the **terrain** like?

Nonfiction

Nonfiction tells about people, things, events or places that are real.

In this selection, look for

- **An interesting historical event**
- **Characters who help each other**
- **Illustrations with captions**

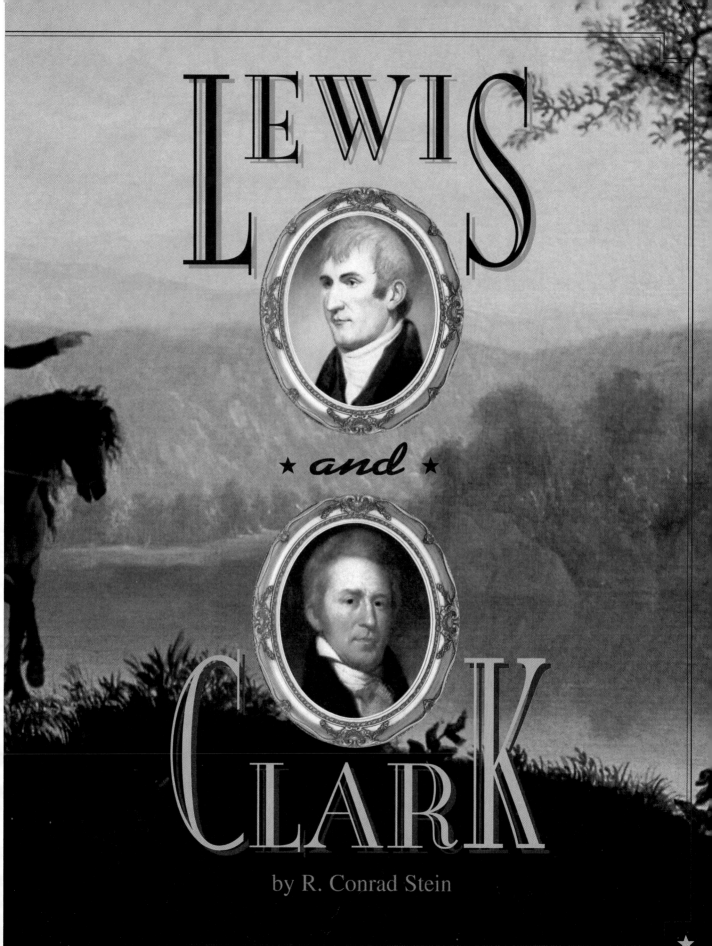

LEWIS

★ *and* ★

COOK

CLARK

by R. Conrad Stein

In 1803, President Thomas Jefferson doubled the size of the United States through an agreement known as the Louisana Purchase. Then Jefferson decided that American explorers should take a journey through the Louisiana Territory, which stretched from St. Louis, Missouri, to the Pacific. He enlisted Meriwether Lewis to lead a group called the Corps of Discovery. Lewis then selected William Clark to help lead the expedition. In 1804, Lewis and Clark began their journey from St. Louis. They traveled through the Great Plains and then stopped for the winter season. A trader and his wife, an American Indian named Sacagawea [sak•ə•jə•wē′ə], decided to travel with the expedition when it resumed its journey in April 1805 into territory never before seen by outsiders.

William Clark had perhaps the best eyesight of any crew member. On May 26, he saw the outline of a great mountain range to the west. In the next few days, all of the explorers could see the snow-covered Rocky Mountains on the horizon. The sight was inspiring as well as troubling. The explorers knew that they would have to find a way to cross the incredible barrier.

Before they could cross the Rockies, the Corps of Discovery faced the Great Falls of the Missouri River in present-day Montana. Here the river tumbled

◄ *Lewis considered the Mandan Indians' stories about huge bears to be fanciful tales until one of the explorers was chased by a grizzly bear.*

down a bluff that was as high as a modern six-story building. The roar of the water was deafening. Lewis called it, "the grandest sight I ever beheld." But the waterfall meant that the explorers had to carry their boats and supplies up steep cliffs before they could set out again on quieter waters upstream. Traveling around the falls took the party twenty-four days, and left everyone exhausted.

Carrying her baby boy on her back, Sacagawea [sak•ə•jə•wē′ə] won the admiration of the crew. She carefully scanned the riverbank to find edible roots and fruit. These foods provided a welcome relief from the customary diet of meat and water. And in the mountain country, the Missouri River became a crooked stream that split into many small tributaries. Sacagawea pointed out landmarks that

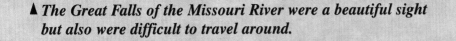

▲ *The Great Falls of the Missouri River were a beautiful sight but also were difficult to travel around.*

she remembered from a journey as a slave child, and she helped the captains choose the correct river branches on which to travel.

Soon the members of the party began to wonder why they had not yet seen any Shoshone [shō•shō′•nē] or other American Indians. They had seen signs of Indian settlement-hunters' trails and abandoned campsites— but since they left the Mandan [man′dən] and Hidatsa [hē•dät′sə] villages, the Corps of Discovery had not encountered any other people at all.

In mid-August, Meriwether Lewis, hiking ahead of the party with a few other explorers, came upon three Shoshone women and several children. Lewis had carried an American flag in his pack for just such a meeting. He waved the banner and walked slowly toward the group. One of the children fled. The women sat very still as if frozen in fear. Lewis explained that he was an explorer, and the women led him to their village.

Sacagawea quickly ► *proved to be a valuable asset to the expedition.*

▲ *At first, the Shoshone were cautious of Lewis and Clark, but the explorers soon realized that they were fortunate to encounter the Indians.*

The Shoshone were a small tribe who were almost always at war with their powerful neighbors, the Blackfeet. They had never seen white people, but constant warfare made the Shoshone suspicious of all outsiders. Lewis hoped to buy horses from the tribe. Now that the rivers had all but disappeared, he needed horses to cross the peaks of the Rocky Mountains. But the chief, Cameahwait [kə•mē′ə•wāt], would not part with any of the animals. Lewis did persuade Cameahwait to send a few Shoshone to find Clark and the rest of the party and bring them to the village.

The next morning, Clark and the others arrived at the village, and a meeting was held with Chief Cameahwait. Sacagawea prepared to serve as the translator. When the meeting began, Sacagawea stared intently at the chief. Then she broke into tears of joy. Lewis wrote, "she jumped up, ran, and embraced him, and threw her blanket over him, and cried profusely." Sacagawea recognized Cameahwait as her brother, whom she had not seen in six years. Cheers and laughter rose from the village. The Shoshone hailed Sacagawea as a lost daughter who had come home.

On September 1, 1805, the Corps of Discovery left the Shoshone territory. Chief Cameahwait not only provided the party with horses, he also gave them a guide to show them the best route through the mountains. Crossing the Rockies proved to be a difficult ordeal. The trails were too rugged to ride on, so the party walked and used the horses as pack animals.

In mid-September, a blinding snowstorm struck. Even the Shoshone guide got lost. Worst of all, the once-abundant wild game could not be found on the high mountain peaks. The explorers were forced to kill some of their pack animals for meat. The explorers' journals report that the men laughed out loud when they finally crossed the mountains and reached grasslands on level terrain.

The Lewis and Clark expedition emerged from the Rocky Mountains into the lovely valley of the Clearwater River in present-day Idaho. The waters were so clear that the river bottom and schools of fish were visible despite the river's depth. In the Clearwater country, Lewis and Clark abandoned their pack horses and built new canoes. They reasoned that the streams on this side of the Rockies would all eventually flow into the Columbia River, the major river of the Pacific Northwest. American Indians called the Columbia River the *Ouragon* or *Origan*. The land around it was later called the Oregon Territory.

Traveling the rivers, the voyagers met the Nez Perce [nes pûrs'] Indians, who taught them valuable techniques for building and sailing log canoes. Less friendly were the Chinook [shi•nŏŏk'], who drove hard bargains when trading for goods. But encountering the Chinook meant that the Pacific Ocean was not far away. One

Crossing the Rocky Mountains was one ► *of the most difficult parts of the expedition. Part of the trail (in Montana) the explorers used still exists.*

of the Chinook wore a black navy coat that he may have bought from a North American or European sailor.

A dismal rain pelted the travelers in early November as they sailed down the Columbia River. They made a camp near an Indian village and spent a restless night. On the morning of November 7, 1805, the rain stopped and the fog cleared. A chorus of shouts suddenly went up from the camp. William Clark scribbled in his notes, "Ocean in view! O! the joy." On the horizon, still many

The expedition crossed ►
the Rockies on foot,
using the horses to carry
their equipment and
supplies.

▲ *Upon reaching the Clearwater River Valley, the expedition built new canoes to continue their journey west.*

miles to the west, lay the great Pacific Ocean. Upon seeing the ocean, some of the explorers wept, and others said prayers of thanksgiving.

But arriving at the Pacific Ocean did not end the Lewis and Clark expedition. The party still had to return home to St. Louis. President Jefferson had provided Meriwether Lewis with a letter of credit guaranteeing payment to any ship captain who would take the explorers to the eastern coast. The party made a winter camp at the mouth of the Columbia River near present-day Astoria, Oregon, and kept a watch for ships. No vessels were spotted. Finally, on March 23, 1806, the crew broke camp and began the long trek east toward St. Louis.

To the explorers, the six-month return journey seemed to be easier than their first journey because they knew what to expect in the river and mountain country. When the crew reached the Mandan village, they said good-bye to Sacagawea and her husband and continued back to St. Louis.

On September 23, 1806, the Lewis

and Clark expedition arrived safely back in St. Louis, Missouri, where their journey had begun more than two years earlier. The travelers had gone a distance of just less than 4,000 miles (6,400 km) from St. Louis to the mouth of the Columbia River and back. But the twisting rivers and mountain trails meant that the Corps of Discovery had actually covered about 8,000 miles (13,000 km) on the history-making trip. Throughout the explorers' travels, they encountered more than fifty American-Indian tribes. The expedition returned with numerous samples of plant and animal life that had never before been seen by American scientists. Before the expedition, President Jefferson had hoped that the explorers would find a broad river that ships could use to sail directly to the Pacific Ocean. Lewis and Clark failed to find such a river, and the expedition was final proof that an

▼ *The explorers experienced some difficulty in dealing with the Chinook Indians, but their encounter brought signs that the Pacific Ocean was near.*

Jefferson's letter of credit survived the journey west, but it was never used because the explorers returned home over land, instead of by ship. ▼

Washington. U.S. of America. July 4. 1803.

Dear Sir

In the journey which you are about to undertake for the discovery of the course and source of the Missouri, and of the most convenient water communication from thence to the Pacific ocean, your party being small, it is to be expected that you will encounter considerable dangers from the Indian inhabitants. should you escape those dangers and reach the Pacific ocean, you may find it imprudent to hazard a return the same way, and be forced to seek a passage round by sea, in such vessels as you may find on the Western coast. but you will be without money, without clothes, & other necessaries; as a sufficient supply cannot be carried with you from hence. your resource in that case can only be in the credit of the U.S. for which purpose I hereby authorise you to draw on the Secretaries of State, of the Treasury, of War & of the Navy of the U.S. according as you may find your draughts will be most negociable, for the purpose of obtaining money or necessaries for yourself & your men: and I solemnly pledge the faith of the United States that these draughts shall be paid punctually at the date they are made payable. I also ask of the Consuls, agents, merchants & citizens of any nation with which we have intercourse or amity, to furnish you with those sup- plies which your necessities may call for, assuring them of honorable and prompt retribution. and our own Consuls in foreign parts where you may happen to be, are hereby instructed & required to be aiding & assisting to you in whatsoever may be necessary for procuring your return back to the United States. And to give more entire satisfaction & confidence to those who may be disposed to aid you, I Thomas Jefferson, President of the United States of America, have written this letter of general credit for you with my own hand, and signed it with my name.

Th: Jefferson

To Capt Meriwether Lewis.

The explorers saw the Pacific Ocean ▲
for the first time near present-day
Astoria, Oregon.

inland waterway in North America did not exist.

From St. Louis, Lewis and Clark traveled to Washington, D.C. Almost every town they passed through brought out bands to welcome them as heroes. In Washington, D.C., the explorers delighted President Jefferson with tales of grizzly bears and high mountain passes. The president said, "Lewis and Clark have entirely fulfilled my expectations. . . . The world will find that those travelers have well earned its favor."

To Meriwether Lewis and William Clark, the mission itself was their greatest reward. Traveling through virtually unexplored lands was an exhilarating experience that they would cherish for the rest of their lives. Although they faced many dangers, the thrill—not the peril—of the expedition bursts from the pages of the journals they kept. As Lewis wrote the day he left the Indian village to enter the Western wilderness, "I could but esteem this moment of my departure as among the most happy of my life."

Sacagawea is remembered ▶ as a vital reason for the success of the Lewis and Clark expedition. This statue of Sacagawea stands in Bismarck, North Dakota.

HISTORY

OF

THE EXPEDITION

UNDER THE COMMAND OF

CAPTAINS LEWIS AND CLARK,

TO

THE SOURCES OF THE MISSOURI,

THENCE

ACROSS THE ROCKY MOUNTAINS

AND DOWN THE

RIVER COLUMBIA TO THE PACIFIC OCEAN.

PERFORMED DURING THE YEARS 1804—5—6.

By order of the

GOVERNMENT OF THE UNITED STATES.

PREPARED FOR THE PRESS

BY PAUL ALLEN, ESQUIRE.

IN TWO VOLUMES.

VOL. I.

PHILADELPHIA:
PUBLISHED BY BRADFORD AND INSKEEP; AND
ABM. H. INSKEEP, NEWYORK.
J. Maxwell, Printer.
1814.

▲ *The journals kept by Captains Lewis, Clark, and several members of their expedition have been compiled into many published accounts since the journey ended in 1806. This one, published in 1814, was printed in two volumes.*

LEWIS AND CLARK EXPEDITION

The Cascades of the Columbia

CAPTAINS MERIWETHER LEWIS AND WILLIAM CLARK AND THEIR PARTY OF 31 MEN AND SACAGAWEA AND HER PAPOOSE NAVIGATED THE 15 MILES OF THE CASCADES ON THEIR WAY WEST, DURING THE THREE DAYS OF OCTOBER 30 TO NOVEMBER 1, 1805. THE UPPER PORTION WAS THE MOST HAZARDOUS: OF THIS CLARK WROTE: "THIS GREAT SHUTE OF FALLS IS ABOUT ½ A MILE, WITH THE WATER OF THIS GREAT RIVER COMPRESSED WITHIN THE SPACE OF 150 PACES... GREAT NUMBER OF BOTH LARGE AND SMALL ROCKS, WATER PASSING WITH GREAT VELOCITY FORMING & BOILING IN A HORRIABLE MANNER, WITH A FALL OF ABOUT 20 FEET..."

Think and Respond

1 Why was the Lewis and Clark **expedition** important?

2 How does the author organize information in the article?

3 Why were Lewis and Clark welcomed as heroes in nearly every town they passed through on their way to Washington, D.C.?

4 Do you think Lewis and Clark could have succeeded without the help of Sacagawea? Why or why not?

5 What reading strategies did you use to help you understand "Lewis and Clark"? When did you use them?

691

AMERICA THE

O beautiful for spacious skies,
For amber waves of grain,
For purple mountain majesties
Above the fruited plain!
America! America!
God shed His grace on thee,
And crown thy good with brotherhood
From sea to shining sea!

O beautiful for pilgrim feet,
Whose stern, impassioned stress
A thoroughfare for freedom beat
Across the wilderness!
America! America!
God mend thine every flaw,
Confirm thy soul in self-control,
Thy liberty in law!

O beautiful for heroes proved
In liberating strife,
Who more than self their country loved,
And mercy more than life!
America! America!
May God thy gold refine
Till all success be nobleness
And every gain divine!

O beautiful for patriot dream
That sees beyond the years
Thine alabaster cities gleam
Undimmed by human tears!
America! America!
God shed His grace on thee
And crown thy good with brotherhood
From sea to shining sea!

Valley of the Yosemite by Albert Bierstadt, 1864.

BEAUTIFUL
by Katharine Lee Bates

Making Connections

Compare Texts

1 Do you think the Lewis and Clark Expedition is a good example of an American adventure? Explain your answer.

2 How does the author's description of the journey change after the party crosses the Rocky Mountains?

3 Based on the words of her song "America the Beautiful," how do you think Katherine Lee Bates might have felt about the Lewis and Clark Expedition?

4 What is another nonfiction selection you have read that tells about events in history? How is that selection similar to "Lewis and Clark"? How is it different?

5 In "Lewis and Clark," you read that, along the route, there are many historic sites that commemorate the expedition. How could you find information about them?

Write an Explanation

Primary sources of information about historical events include diary entries, letters, and similar documents from the time of the actual events. Think about the primary sources that the author refers to in "Lewis and Clark." Write an explanation of why authors may prefer to use primary sources. Use a web to help you plan your explanation.

Writing CONNECTION

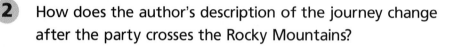

reasons for using primary sources

694

Make a Map

The territory that Lewis and Clark explored was later divided into areas that became states of the United States. Do research to find out the names of these states. Make a map that shows the states, their capitals, mountains, rivers, and other important features. Show the routes that Lewis and Clark followed.

Social Studies CONNECTION

Create a Pamphlet

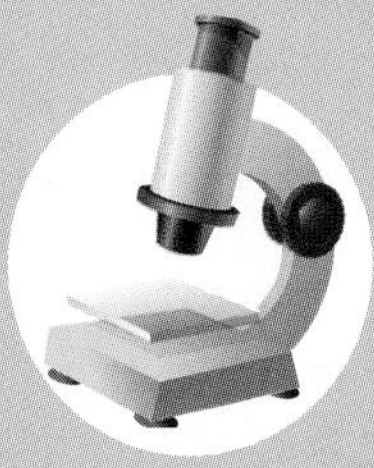

In "Lewis and Clark," the Clearwater River is described as *so clear that the river bottom and schools of fish were visible despite the river's depth.* Today, keeping our nation's rivers clean and clear is a major concern. What efforts have been made to prevent and reverse pollution of rivers and other freshwater systems? Who is working on this problem today, and what are they doing about it? Do a web search or use other resources to find out. Create a pamphlet to share your information.

Science CONNECTION

The SIERRA CLUB

Cause and Effect Focus Skill

The reason something happens is the **cause**. The things that happen are the **effects**. In a fiction selection, a change of setting may cause several new things, or new effects, to happen.

In a nonfiction selection, the author may use causes and effects to organize the information. For example, the influence of a parent may have been the cause for a famous person to enter a certain career. What that person accomplished in that career would be an effect.

This diagram shows a cause and some of its effects.

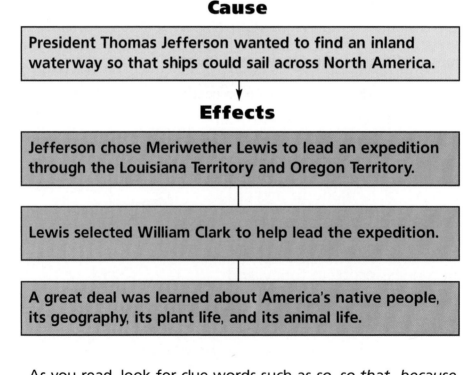

Cause

President Thomas Jefferson wanted to find an inland waterway so that ships could sail across North America.

Effects

Jefferson chose Meriwether Lewis to lead an expedition through the Louisiana Territory and Oregon Territory.

Lewis selected William Clark to help lead the expedition.

A great deal was learned about America's native people, its geography, its plant life, and its animal life.

Visit *The Learning Site!*
www.harcourtschool.com

See *Skills* and *Activities*

As you read, look for clue words such as *so, so that*, *because*, and *then*, which signal cause-and-effect relationships.

696

Test Prep
Cause and Effect

▶ **Read the passage. Then answer the questions.**

Elizabeth Cady Stanton was interested in women's rights. Stanton believed that women should have the right to vote. In 1848 she and Lucretia Mott organized the nation's first women's rights convention in Seneca Falls, New York. Stanton lived in Seneca Falls at the time. She used the Declaration of Independence as a model to write a Declaration of Sentiments, stating that "all men and women are created equal."

In 1878 Stanton persuaded Senator Aaron A. Sargent of California to sponsor a women's suffrage amendment to the Constitution of the United States. The amendment giving women the right to vote was finally approved in 1919 and became the nineteenth Amendment in 1920.

1. **What caused Elizabeth Cady Stanton to work for women's rights?**

    A She wanted to be the president.

    B She believed that women needed organizations to help them.

    C She believed women should vote.

    D She wanted to be a senator.

> **Tip**
>
> Figure out what Elizabeth Cady Stanton believed and hoped to do.

2. **Which of these events was *not* an effect of Stanton's work?**

    F A Declaration of Sentiments was written.

    G A women's rights convention was held.

    H The nineteenth amendment was passed.

    J Stanton made her home in Seneca Falls.

> **Tip**
>
> Look back to see what Stanton did. Read each item to see if it is a result of what she believed.

Vocabulary Power

migrated

exodus

burrowed

installments

designated

In frontier America, strong and hardy people traveled great distances. Read about some other creatures, much smaller and more delicate, that travel long distances.

   From the first time I saw a monarch butterfly, I was fascinated. I found out that monarchs in California have **migrated** hundreds of miles from places where winter temperatures are extremely cold. Every year, there is a great **exodus**, or departure, of monarchs from states in the northern and central United States. They migrate from there to California, Florida, or the mountains of Mexico. That's a long way for these small butterflies to travel!

Each monarch butterfly began its life as a larva, or caterpillar, hatched from an egg attached to the leaf of a milkweed plant. Each larva **burrowed**, or dug, its way far enough into the plant to feed on a chemical that made the larva taste bad. The bad taste prevents birds and other creatures from eating the monarchs.

I dream of going to Pacific Grove, one of the places where huge numbers of monarch butterflies gather to spend the winter. I made a deal with my mother. If she would pay for the trip, I would pay her back in **installments**. That means I have to pay her smaller amounts at definite times until my debt is paid off. I was so happy when she said yes!

We agreed to set aside a special day for our butterfly trip. I'm very excited because tomorrow is the **designated** day!

Vocabulary–Writing CONNECTION

Design a colorful creature that might have **burrowed** into your schoolyard. What did it look like? What special characteristics did it have?

BLACK

Genre

Expository Nonfiction

Expository nonfiction presents and explains information or ideas.

In this selection, look for

● **Sections divided by headings**

● **Paragraphs with main ideas and supporting details**

FRONTIERS

A History of African American Heroes in the Old West

BY LILLIAN SCHLISSEL

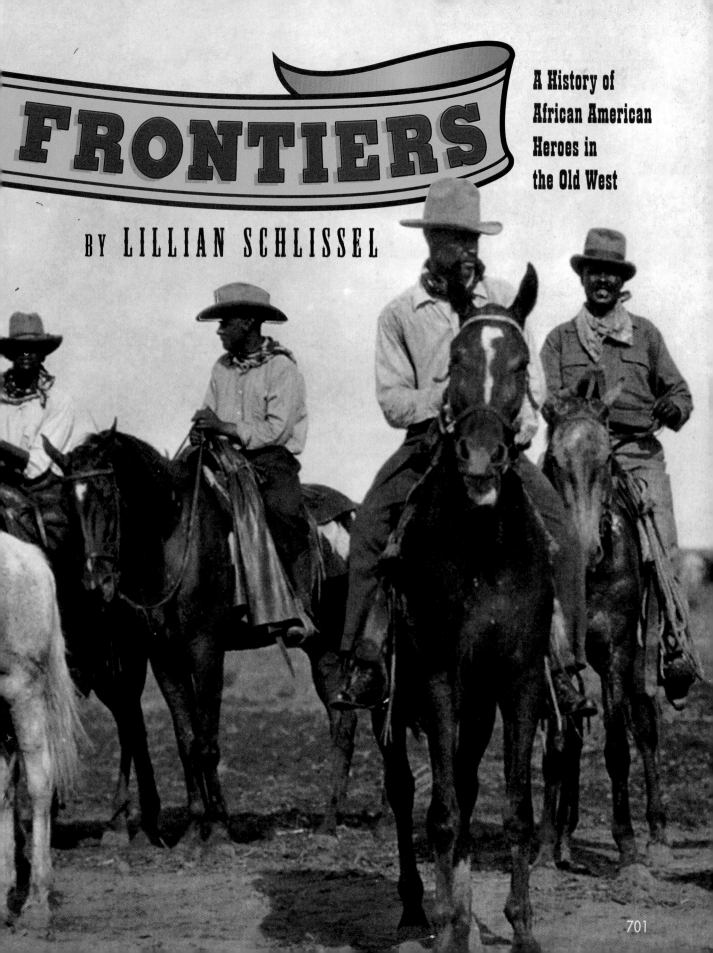

BLACK HOMESTEADERS

Homesteading was not easy for black or white settlers. Rocks, grass, and trees had to be cleared before crops could be planted. A farmer needed a horse, a mule, and a plow. He needed seed to plant and food for his family until the crops were ready to harvest. Most of all a pioneer needed a home.

Loading sod for a house on the Dismal River, Thomas County, Kansas

Dugout on the South Loup River, near Virge Allen's homestead, Custer County, Nebraska, 1892. A wagon load of sod stands by to repair the roof.

In regions where there were trees, pioneers built log cabins. But in Kansas and Nebraska, there was only tall grass, as high as a man's shoulder. Pioneers learned that tough root systems under the grass held the dirt firmly, and sod could be cut like bricks and piled, layer upon layer, until it took the shape of a house. These homesteaders were called sod busters, and their homes were called soddies.

Sod homes could be warm and comfortable. Some were two stories high, with glass windows and chimneys. But in heavy rain, smaller sod houses leaked, and some families remembered being surprised by a snake slithering through a wall.

In North and South Dakota, where the land was rocky and winter temperatures fell to 30 degrees below zero, early pioneers burrowed into the ground and covered themselves with an earthen roof. They brought their small animals into the house in the winter, while cows and goats huddled on the roof, warming themselves on the house that was under their feet.

During the first seasons in a new settlement, a pioneer woman might have no stove. She dug a hole in the ground and fed the fire with weeds, adding small rocks, like coals, to keep in the fire's heat. Buffalo chips, the droppings of buffalo, provided the fuel. When the great animals migrated across the land, women and children gathered chips for the family's cooking fires.

In the hot and dry climate of the Southwest, pioneers built homes with thick walls made of mud and straw. The mud walls, called adobe, kept the houses cool in the summer and warm in the winter. In desert regions, women learned from the Indians to brew teas out of wild grasses and to make soap and shampoo from the yucca plant.

Even youngsters helped settle the West. These are the children of homesteaders who lived near Brownlee, Cherry County, Nebraska.

In the early days of settlement, there were few black families homesteading. For them, loneliness was part of being a pioneer. But black pioneer families held on, and in sticking it out, they made the way easier for those who came after.

Unidentified child on the Maurice Brown homestead in Nebraska

For black pioneer families, homesteading was a desolate life.

Benjamin Singleton, founder of the black community of Dunlap, Kansas.

Ho for Kans

Brethren, Friends, & Fellow C

I feel thankful to inform you t

REAL ESTAT

AND

estead   Associa

Will Leave Here the

h of April, 1

n pursuit of Homes in the Sout
Lands of America, at Transp
Rates, cheaper than eve
was known before.

For full information inquire of

Benj. Singleton, better known as

NO. 5 NORTH FRONT STR

Beware of Speculators and Adventurers, as it is a

THE EXODUSTERS

Men and women who had been slaves read in the Bible about the ancient Israelites who were brought out of bondage and delivered into freedom. Benjamin Singleton, born a slave in Tennessee, was determined that he would bring his people to free soil if it was the last thing he ever did.

After the Civil War, Singleton visited Kansas and over a period of years, he and his friends managed to buy part of a Cherokee reservation. In 1877 they advertised for homesteaders to start an all-black community there. They hoped to attract two hundred families. Fliers promised that settlers who paid one dollar "in installments of 25 cents at a time or otherwise as may be desired" could be part of the new community. By 1879 an exodus of black families out of the Old South began, and before long there were eight hundred homesteaders in the new Kansas communities of Dunlap and Nicodemus. Benjamin Singleton said, "My people that I carried to Kansas came on our own resources. We have tried to make a people of ourselves. . . ." They were known as the Exodusters.

Handbills encouraged black families to move to Kansas. Notice the warning at the bottom of the flier.

Ho for Kansas!

Brethren, Friends, & Fellow Citizens:
I feel thankful to inform you that the
REAL ESTATE
AND
Homestead Association,
Will Leave Here the
15th of April, 1878,
In pursuit of Homes in the Southwestern Lands of America, at Transportation Rates, cheaper than ever was known before.
For full information inquire of
Benj. Singleton, better known as old Pap,
NO. 5 NORTH FRONT STREET.
Beware of Speculators and Adventurers, as it is a dangerous thing to fall in their hands.
Nashville, Tenn., March 18, 1878.

[Beware of Speculators and Adventurers, as it is a dangerous thing to fall in their hands.]

Schoolhouse in Dunlap,
Kansas. Pupil in foreground
carries a sign that reads,
"God Bless Our School."

Farmers in Nicodemus
owned only three horses. One man plowed
with a milk cow, and others broke ground
with shovels and spades. White farmers saw
how hard their new neighbors worked and
lent the new settlers a team of oxen and a
plow. Black farmers planted their first crops
and in time they prospered. By the turn of the
century there were about eight thousand black
homesteaders in Nicodemus and Dunlap.

Some black settlers moved farther west to
Nebraska and Oklahoma where they built
three new black communities—Taft, Langston,
and Boley. George Washington Bush went
all the way to Oregon Territory where he
introduced the first mower and reaper into
the area around Puget Sound.

The Shores family in front of their sod house near Westville, Custer County, Nebraska, 1887. The Shores became famous as musicians.

The Moses Speese family — neighbors of the Shores family — outside their sod house near Westville, Custer County, Nebraska

709

Kansas City
Monarchs, 1908 ▶

Satchel Paige,
one of baseball's
greatest pitchers,
playing for the
Kansas City
Monarchs, 1908

▼

▲
This black baseball team
played for the Pullman Club
in Tonopah, Nevada, 1907.

Of all the black communities, however, Nicodemus and Dunlap remained the most famous. Each year they celebrated the Fourth of July, and they had their own special holiday, Emancipation Day. On July 31 and August 1, a square mile of land was set aside as a carnival fairground. There were boxing matches and baseball games. In 1907 the town formed one of the nation's first black baseball teams—the Nicodemus Blues. The Blues played black teams as far away as Texas, Nevada, and Louisiana. Satchel Paige, one of the greatest black pitchers in American baseball history, played ball in Nicodemus.

In 1976 Nicodemus was designated a National Historic Landmark. The town's history is being recorded and buildings restored. It marks the proud legacy of black homesteaders in America.

THINK AND RESPOND

1. What do you think it took to be a successful homesteader? Explain your answer.

2. Why do you think the author uses photographs to illustrate this selection?

3. Why do you think the author includes the information about the Emancipation Day and the Nicodemus Blues?

4. Do you think that the people who joined the **exodus** out of the Old South found what they were looking for? Explain.

5. What reading strategies did you use to help you understand the selection?

Lillian Schlissel

Lillian Schlissel remembers that as a schoolgirl, she visited the public library as often as she could. "There was no television," Schlissel says. "So after homework, there were piles of books to read."

Now Schlissel has written a pile of books for others to read. In 1994 she wrote her first children's book — *The Way West: Journal of a Pioneer Woman*. "I wanted to give modern children some idea of what it was like to travel more than a thousand miles in a wagon pulled by oxen, moving only thirteen miles a day, with no motels or restaurants."

Schlissel began collecting photographs for *Black Frontiers* while writing *Women's Diaries of the Westward Journey*. She enjoys reading about the West and uncovering stories that have never been told. She says, "Being a historian and a writer is the best of jobs."

Visit *The Learning Site!*
www.harcourtschool.com

▲ Black Frontiers

Making Connections

Compare Texts

1 Why does "Black Frontiers" belong in the theme American Adventure?

2 Why is "Black Frontiers" divided into sections?

3 Why did pioneers in different regions build different kinds of houses?

4 Think of another photo essay that you have read. Which do you think makes more dramatic use of the photographs, "Black Frontiers" or the other photo essay? Explain your answer.

5 Suppose you wanted to know more about the National Historical Landmark status of Nicodemus. Where might you find that information?

Write Paragraphs That Contrast

"**B**lack Frontiers" tells about the lives of black homesteaders. Think about life in your own city or town today and how it is different from the lives of the homesteaders. Write a paragraph to tell one way that you think life is better now. Write another paragraph to tell one way that life was better then. Use a graphic like the one shown here to organize your ideas.

Writing CONNECTION

How Life Was Better Then	How Life Is Better Now
Reasons:	Reasons:

Write a Report

Satchel Paige, whose photograph appears on page 710 of "Black Frontiers," is considered one of the greatest baseball players of all time. He played in what was then called the Negro Leagues. Research another player from the Negro Leagues. You might look for websites about the Negro Leagues, or use an encyclopedia. Use your information to write a report.

Social Studies CONNECTION

Negro League Players

James Thomas Bell
Oscar Charleston
Ray Dandridge
Leon Day
Martin Dihigo
Rube Foster
Willie Foster
Josh Gibson
Monte Irvin
Judy Johnson
Buck Leonard
John Henry Lloyd
Willie Wells

Give an Oral Description

Some photographers of the frontier era are well known and remembered. Using an encyclopedia or books on photographers and photography, examine nineteenth-century photographs. Choose a photograph that you especially like. Present an oral description of the photograph to your classmates. Include information about the photographer and about the subject of the photograph.

Art CONNECTION

▲ **Black Frontiers**

Summarize and Paraphrase

Focus Skill

When you **summarize**, you retell only the most important points in a selection. When you **paraphrase**, you restate parts of the selection in your own words, without changing the meaning. You summarize and paraphrase to help you remember and understand what you have read.

This web shows the important points in the first part of "Black Frontiers." Use the information in the web to summarize.

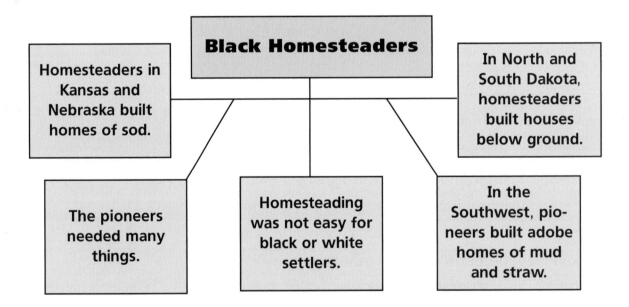

Black Homesteaders

Homesteaders in Kansas and Nebraska built homes of sod.

In North and South Dakota, homesteaders built houses below ground.

The pioneers needed many things.

Homesteading was not easy for black or white settlers.

In the Southwest, pioneers built adobe homes of mud and straw.

Reread "The Exodusters," the second part of "Black Frontiers," and select a passage to paraphrase. Focus on the important points. Use synonyms to replace key words, and leave out unimportant details. As you paraphrase, be sure you do not change the meaning of the text.

Visit *The Learning Site!*
www.harcourtschool.com

See *Skills* and *Activities*

714

Test Prep

Summarize and Paraphrase

▶ **Read the passage. Then answer the questions.**

> Cowboys played a major role in the development of the Western frontier. One of the most famous African American cowboys was Nat Love. He was only fifteen when he headed to Kansas to become a cowboy. For the next twenty years, he worked on cattle drives. On a cattle drive cowboys helped move great herds of cattle long distances. During his days on the trail, Nat Love became renowned for his excellent riding skills. He also earned a reputation for being able to recognize specific cattle brands.

1. **Which of these would *not* belong in a summary of the passage?**

   A Nat Love was a famous African American cowboy.

   B Love was a cowboy for many years.

   C Cowboys moved cattle long distances.

   D Nat was famous for his riding skills.

Tip

The passage is mostly about Nat Love. Look for a sentence that does not contain information about the main idea.

2. **How could the last two sentences *best* be combined for a paraphrase?**

   F Nat's riding skills made him valuable.

   G Nat Love could identify cattle brands.

   H Nat's talent for identifying brands and his riding helped make him famous.

   J Long days on the trail made Nat Love a skilled rider.

Tip

Identify the sentence that has the same meaning as the last two sentences but uses different words.

Writer's Handbook

Purposes for Writing

People write for different purposes and for different audiences. You may be asked to write to inform, to respond to something you read, to persuade, or to entertain. You may write for more than one purpose.

Expository Writing

Expository writing gives information or directions. **Research reports** contain information about a topic. **How-to essays** give directions for doing or making something. **Comparison and contrast essays** show similarities and differences.

Sample prompt: *Some people live in the city and others live in the country.*
Think about *the differences between living in each type of place.*
Now write *an essay that compares and contrasts the city and the country.*

> ### Tips for Expository Writing
>
> - Begin with a sentence that tells the main idea of what you are explaining.
>
> - Organize details or steps in a logical or sequential order.
>
> - Use transitions or time-order words, such as *first*, *next*, and *finally*.
>
> - Write a conclusion that includes a summary of the main idea.

Expressive Writing

Through **expressive writing,** you can tell about your thoughts and feelings. Expressive writing may be a personal narrative, a made-up story, a description, or poetry. When you write to express, you are writing to share an experience or to entertain.

Sample prompt: *Write about your favorite activity. Use descriptive details to show the reader why you enjoy that activity.*

Tips for Expressive Writing

- Introduce yourself or the characters.

- Introduce the problem or conflict that must be solved, and describe the characters' or your thoughts and feelings.

- Include details about the experience or the story in sequential order.

- Tell what you learned from the experience or how the characters solved the conflict.

Persuasive Writing

The goal of **persuasive writing** is to change the way people think about something and, usually, to get them to take action. The writer of a persuasive essay might show readers another way of looking at a problem and its solution or might try to persuade readers to behave in a certain way.

Sample prompt: *Your teacher wants your class to choose between a class trip to the planetarium or to the history museum.*
Think about *which place you like best.*
Now write *to convince your classmates which place to visit.*

Tips for Persuasive Writing

- Begin by getting your audience's attention and stating your opinion.

- Give reasons to support your opinion.

- Write a conclusion that restates your opinion and calls readers to take action or to agree with your opinion.

Try This

Find examples of all of these types of writing. Explain what you think the author's purpose is.

The Writing Process

Although there is no one correct way to write, most writers go through similar steps in composing any kind of writing.

Most students find that writing a composition is easiest when they divide the writing job into parts. The following steps show the main parts of the writing process. Following the bulleted directions will make the process easier.

Prewriting

Before you begin a writing assignment, you need to think about the assignment and plan what you will write.

- Make sure you understand the assignment. Make sure you know how long your composition needs to be and how you will present it.

- Think about the audience and the purpose of the assignment.

- Brainstorm ideas and do research if you need to.

- Organize notes, make an outline, or use graphic organizers.

Drafting

This is the step in which your writing begins to take shape.

When you draft, you actually write your composition.

- Begin with an idea that will catch your audience's attention.

- In the main part of your composition, state your major points. Add details and facts that support these points.

- Write a concluding paragraph that summarizes the main points.

- Be sure to write in paragraphs and sentences and to follow your writing plan.

Revising

Revising is the first step in the editing process. When you edit, you find and correct problems in your composition. Revise your writing by adding, deleting, combining and rearranging words to clarify meaning. Ask yourself these questions to make sure your writing accomplishes its purpose:

- Does it fulfill all parts of the assignment?

- Will the audience understand it?

- Are the story events or steps in a process in the correct order?

- Does it have an appropriate ending?

Make changes in any areas that need improvement. You may want to trade papers with a classmate and share ideas about each other's writing.

Proofreading

Proofreading is the second step of the editing process.

- When you proofread, you check your composition for errors in grammar, punctuation, capitalization, and spelling.

- After you have corrected all the errors, make a final copy of your composition.

Publishing

In this step, you share your writing with an audience. Here are some suggestions for publishing your work:

- Use your composition to make a video or a speech.

- Make a book by collecting in a notebook the compositions written by your classmates.

- Publish your writing in a school newspaper or a class literary magazine.

How to Get Ideas

Writers need ideas to write. There are many activities you can do that will help you get ideas for your writing. You may want to use some of the following activities to get and develop ideas for writing.

Keep a Journal of Your Experiences

Keeping a daily journal of the things you do and the people you meet can help you build a file of ideas for writing. While writing in your journal, think about the new things you have learned. Good writers write every day, and keeping track of their experiences helps them come up with interesting subjects to write about.

Make a Web Diagram

A **web diagram** is another way to get ideas. Begin by writing a word or phrase that is related to your assignment in an oval in the center of a sheet of paper. Then use spokes to connect the center oval with other ovals that contain words about your topic. One student made this web diagram to explore ideas about camping.

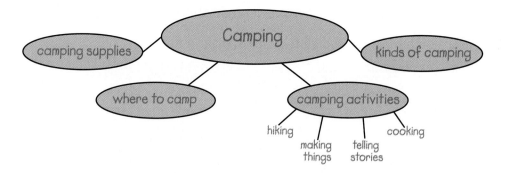

Read About Your Topic

It may help you to read what other people have written about your topic. Sometimes you can get ideas by exploring encyclopedias and other reference books. Look through newspapers and magazines for articles on your topic. Take notes so that you can give credit to others for their ideas.

Ask Questions

Thinking of questions about your topic will help you get ideas, too. Writing questions that begin with *who, what, where, why, when,* and *how* can help you find new angles to your topic. Here are some questions that a student wrote about camping:

- What are some different kinds of camping sites?

- Why do people like to camp?

- Where can you go camping?

- When can you go camping?

Freewrite

Freewriting is a way of finding out what you know about your topic. Write your topic at the top of a blank sheet of paper. Then very quickly write your thoughts about the topic. Give yourself five or ten minutes to write. Write phrases and important words about your topic. When your time is up, read what you have written. Underline or highlight the ideas that you want to use in your composition.

Try This

Think about a subject area that interests you. Use each suggestion for getting ideas to think of a good writing topic. Then tell which suggestion gave you the most or the best ideas.

Using References and Resources

Encyclopedia

An **encyclopedia** is a set of books that contain information about many subjects. Encyclopedias are arranged alphabetically. Each book, or volume, in a set covers subjects whose names begin with a particular part of the alphabet.

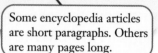

Pottery

Pottery is the name given to items made of clay. Pottery is often shaped by using a potter's wheel, a spinning platform that is controlled by the potter. Clay is put on the center of the platform and is formed by the artist as the wheel spins. The completed form is then air-dried, glazed (if desired), and heated, or fired, in a special oven called a kiln.

See also: ceramics, china, decorative arts

Often an article will **refer** you to other articles in the encyclopedia.

Some encyclopedia articles are short paragraphs. Others are many pages long.

Guide words appear at the top of every page or column. They identify the first and last articles on the page or the first article on a left-hand page and the last article on a right-hand page.

You can find information in an encyclopedia in one of two ways. You can look for an article alphabetically in the proper volume, or you can check the **index.** The index is usually at the end of the last volume of the encyclopedia. The index will show you where to find information about a subject.

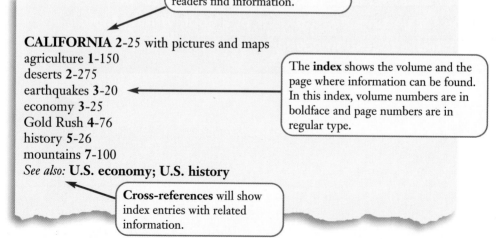

A **large subject** is broken down into **topics** and **subtopics** to help readers find information.

CALIFORNIA 2-25 with pictures and maps
agriculture **1**-150
deserts **2**-275
earthquakes **3**-20
economy **3**-25
Gold Rush **4**-76
history **5**-26
mountains **7**-100
See also: **U.S. economy; U.S. history**

The **index** shows the volume and the page where information can be found. In this index, volume numbers are in boldface and page numbers are in regular type.

Cross-references will show index entries with related information.

Almanac

An **almanac** is a reference book that contains information about many different subjects. An almanac contains important statistics, geographical and historical facts, and summaries of important events. You can also find facts about scientific topics, sports, entertainment, and politics in an almanac. An almanac is revised and published every year.

California: The Golden State

31st state; joined U.S. in 1850. **Capital:** Sacramento. **Area:** 155,973 sq. mi. (ranks 3rd among states). **Highest point:** Mt. Whitney, 14,495 ft. **Lowest point:** Death Valley, 282 ft. below sea level. **Population:** 33,145,121 (1999 est.); 11.2% gain since 1990. **Gross domestic product:** $875.7 billion (1994). **Per capita personal income:** $21,760 (1996).

> Almanacs have information about the countries of the world and the states in the United States. This entry gives facts about California.

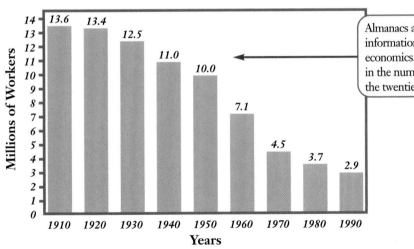

Total Number of U.S. Farm Workers 1910–1990

> Almanacs also contain graphs showing information about business and economics. This graph shows changes in the number of farm workers during the twentieth century.

Try This

Search the pages of a recent almanac for an entry that you find interesting. Then look up the same topic in an encyclopedia to find more information.

Internet

The **Internet** is a valuable resource for research. A wealth of up-to-date information is available online.

You find information on the Internet by using **search engines.** After you type what you are looking for, a search engine matches your information request with websites in its data bank. Because different search engines work differently, you may want to ask a librarian to help you find the best search engine for your research topic.

To use a search engine, type keywords about your subject in the search box. After you click the search button, the search engine will find and list sites about your keywords. If you want to increase or decrease the number of sites listed, follow the directions on the screen to broaden or narrow your search. Here is the result of one student's search:

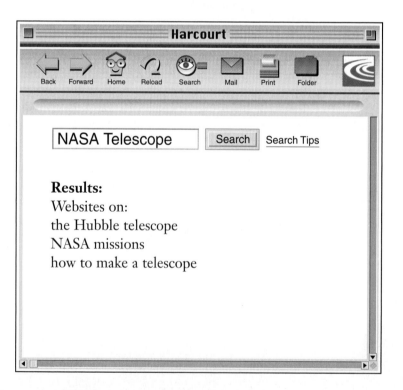

The best matches for your search will appear at the top of the list. Click on the site that interests you the most. Return to the list by using the Back button on the screen.

CD-ROM Resources

Encyclopedias and other reference sources are also available on **CD-ROM.** A CD-ROM must be installed on a computer before you can use it.

The first screen you see after opening a CD-ROM encyclopedia is the *home screen.* Usually, the home screen can direct you to a section that tells how to use the reference source.

You will probably find most of the information you are looking for in the articles section. This section should have a feature that helps you search by using keywords. Your search will usually result in a list of articles that contain the keywords. Click on an article title to display the article.

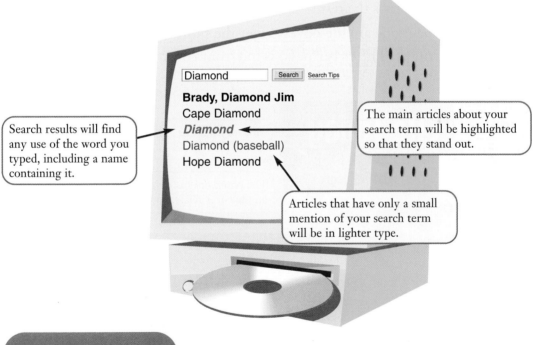

Search results will find any use of the word you typed, including a name containing it.

Diamond — Search — Search Tips

Brady, Diamond Jim
Cape Diamond
Diamond
Diamond (baseball)
Hope Diamond

The main articles about your search term will be highlighted so that they stand out.

Articles that have only a small mention of your search term will be in lighter type.

Try This

With an adult, use a search engine on the Internet to find information on a chosen topic. Then use a CD-ROM encyclopedia to find information on the same topic. Compare and contrast the two resources.

Periodicals

A periodical is a work that is published at regular times. A periodical may be published daily, weekly, or monthly. Some periodicals are published quarterly, or four times a year. The individual publications of a periodical are called **issues. Magazines** and **newspapers** are two kinds of periodicals.

Magazines

Some magazines contain articles about only one subject. Other magazines have articles about many different subjects. The *Readers' Guide to Periodical Literature* will help you locate magazine articles. First, look up the subject. Subjects are in alphabetical order. Articles and their locations are listed under subjects.

The main parts of a magazine are the **cover page,** the **table of contents,** and the **articles.** The **cover page** is the front cover.

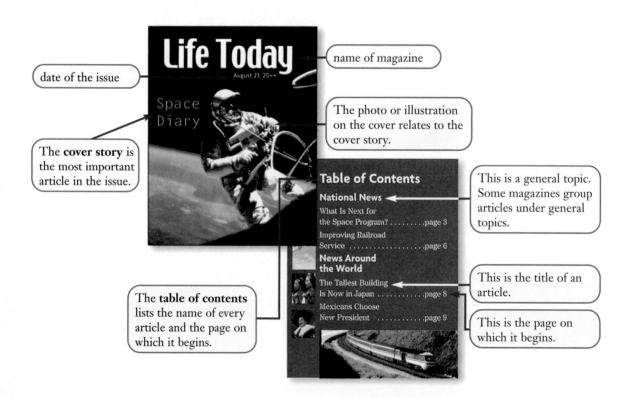

date of the issue

name of magazine

The photo or illustration on the cover relates to the cover story.

The **cover story** is the most important article in the issue.

This is a general topic. Some magazines group articles under general topics.

This is the title of an article.

This is the page on which it begins.

The **table of contents** lists the name of every article and the page on which it begins.

Life Today
August 23, 20--

Space Diary

Table of Contents

National News
What Is Next for
the Space Program? . . . . .page 3
Improving Railroad
Service . . . . .page 6
**News Around
the World**
The Tallest Building
Is Now in Japan . . . . .page 8
Mexicans Choose
New President . . . . .page 9

Newspapers

Newspapers are the most up-to-date of all periodicals. Newspapers are usually published every day, although some are published every week.

The **front page,** the **editorial page,** and the **features** are the main parts of a newspaper. The front page has the most important news articles on it. The editorial page gives the newspaper writers' opinions about people and events in the news. **Features,** found in various sections of the newspaper, are articles that entertain or inform readers about subjects that are not necessarily current events.

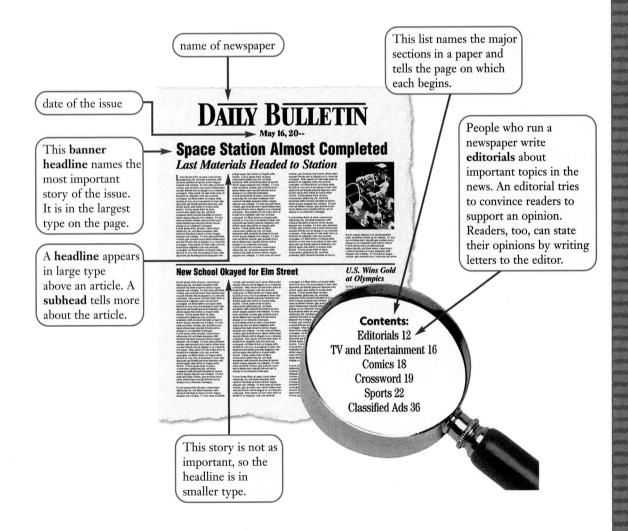

name of newspaper

This list names the major sections in a paper and tells the page on which each begins.

date of the issue

This **banner headline** names the most important story of the issue. It is in the largest type on the page.

People who run a newspaper write **editorials** about important topics in the news. An editorial tries to convince readers to support an opinion. Readers, too, can state their opinions by writing letters to the editor.

A **headline** appears in large type above an article. A **subhead** tells more about the article.

DAILY BULLETIN
May 16, 20--
Space Station Almost Completed
Last Materials Headed to Station

New School Okayed for Elm Street

U.S. Wins Gold at Olympics

Contents:
Editorials 12
TV and Entertainment 16
Comics 18
Crossword 19
Sports 22
Classified Ads 36

This story is not as important, so the headline is in smaller type.

Organizing Information

Note Taking

When you **take notes,** you are recording information so that you can use it later. Your notes will help you when you write a report or study for a test.

This page has an article on birds. Below the article are notes that a student took for a report.

> Birds are animals with feathers. Like mammals, birds are warm-blooded. Unlike mammals, birds hatch from eggs and have feathers. Most birds can fly, because their bones are hollow and fused together for strength.

After taking notes, review what you have written. Look at your source again to be certain that your notes are correct and complete.

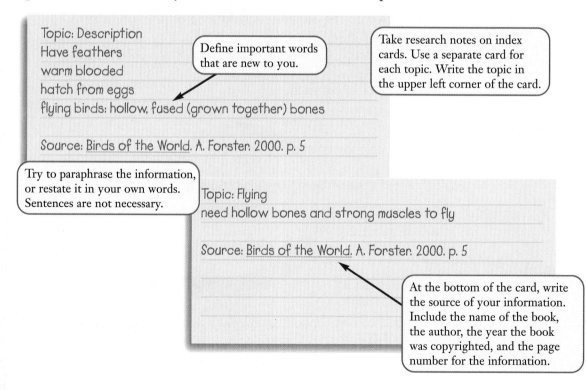

Topic: Description
Have feathers
warm blooded
hatch from eggs
flying birds: hollow, fused (grown together) bones

Source: Birds of the World. A. Forster. 2000. p. 5

Define important words that are new to you.

Take research notes on index cards. Use a separate card for each topic. Write the topic in the upper left corner of the card.

Try to paraphrase the information, or restate it in your own words. Sentences are not necessary.

Topic: Flying
need hollow bones and strong muscles to fly

Source: Birds of the World. A. Forster. 2000. p. 5

At the bottom of the card, write the source of your information. Include the name of the book, the author, the year the book was copyrighted, and the page number for the information.

Citing Sources

When you take notes, you must keep track of your sources. Even if you do not use the exact words of your sources, you still must cite the sources of your information.

At the end of your report, include a **bibliography,** or a list of sources. The bibliography tells readers where to find additional information. **Bibliographic citations** follow certain patterns. The following examples show proper formats for citations.

Book

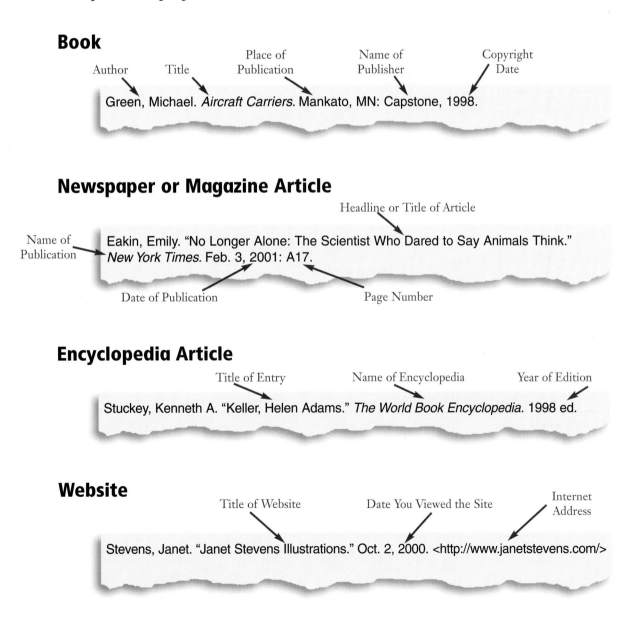

Author → Green, Michael. Title → *Aircraft Carriers.* Place of Publication → Mankato, MN: Name of Publisher → Capstone, Copyright Date → 1998.

Newspaper or Magazine Article

Name of Publication → Eakin, Emily. "No Longer Alone: The Scientist Who Dared to Say Animals Think." ← Headline or Title of Article *New York Times.* Feb. 3, 2001: A17.

Date of Publication, Page Number

Encyclopedia Article

Stuckey, Kenneth A. "Keller, Helen Adams." ← Title of Entry *The World Book Encyclopedia.* ← Name of Encyclopedia 1998 ed. ← Year of Edition

Website

Stevens, Janet. "Janet Stevens Illustrations." ← Title of Website Oct. 2, 2000. ← Date You Viewed the Site <http://www.janetstevens.com/> ← Internet Address

Making Outlines

After you have done your research, you can organize your ideas in an **outline.** Like graphic organizers, an outline shows how ideas relate to one another. An outline is the framework on which a writer can build a composition.

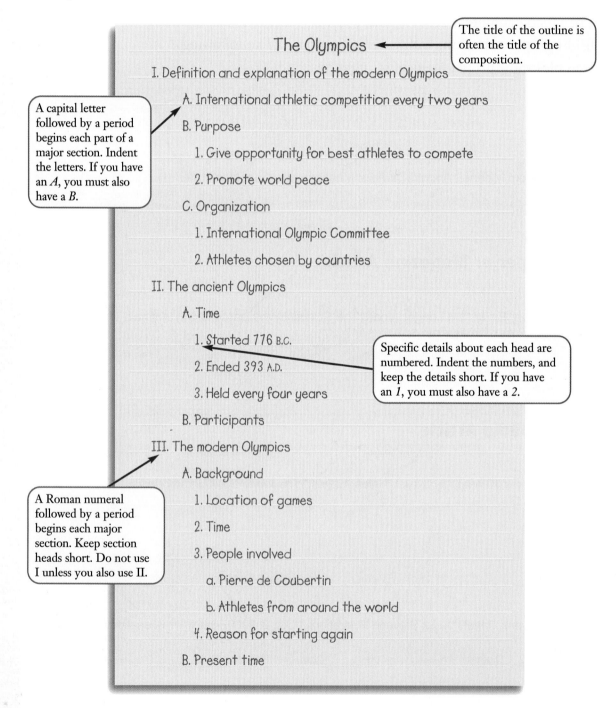

The title of the outline is often the title of the composition.

The Olympics

I. Definition and explanation of the modern Olympics

A capital letter followed by a period begins each part of a major section. Indent the letters. If you have an *A*, you must also have a *B*.

   A. International athletic competition every two years

   B. Purpose

     1. Give opportunity for best athletes to compete

     2. Promote world peace

   C. Organization

     1. International Olympic Committee

     2. Athletes chosen by countries

II. The ancient Olympics

   A. Time

     1. Started 776 B.C.

Specific details about each head are numbered. Indent the numbers, and keep the details short. If you have an *1*, you must also have a *2*.

     2. Ended 393 A.D.

     3. Held every four years

   B. Participants

III. The modern Olympics

A Roman numeral followed by a period begins each major section. Keep section heads short. Do not use I unless you also use II.

   A. Background

     1. Location of games

     2. Time

     3. People involved

       a. Pierre de Coubertin

       b. Athletes from around the world

     4. Reason for starting again

   B. Present time

These are the first two sections of the report written from the outline on the Olympics.

The first paragraph goes with the first Roman numeral of the outline.

The Olympics

Detail A

Every two years, the athletes of the world meet to compete against each other in the Olympic games. Although the athletes come together for sports, the aim of the games is to promote world peace. The International Olympic Committee organizes the games, but individual countries choose the athletes who will represent them in the games.

Detail B

Detail C

The Olympics began in Greece in the year 776 B.C. Greece had a long tradition of athletic games such as wrestling and marathon running. At that time, only Greeks could participate in the Olympics. Other countries weren't allowed to send athletes to compete. These games were held every four years until the year 393 A.D.

Try This

Make an outline of your activities during a single day. Organize your outline in a logical way.

Traits of Good Writing

Good writing involves more than just writing what someone tells you to write. Good writing has special **traits**. These traits are the characteristics that will make your writing shine! The chart below shows the traits of good writing.

Trait	Definition
Focus/Ideas	interesting, focused content
Organization	logical and clear structure
Development	reasons and details
Voice	original personal mood and tone
Effective Sentences	flow, rhythm, variety
Effective Paragraphs	similar ideas grouped together
Word Choice	vivid verbs, strong adjectives, specific nouns
Conventions	correct punctuation, grammar, spelling

Checklist for Good Writing

Good writers practice often. As you practice, ask yourself these questions. If you can say "yes" to most of them, you're doing quite well indeed! Remember, keep practicing!

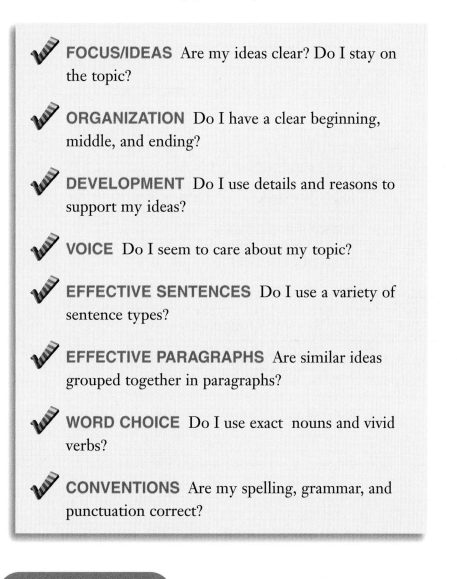

✓ **FOCUS/IDEAS** Are my ideas clear? Do I stay on the topic?

✓ **ORGANIZATION** Do I have a clear beginning, middle, and ending?

✓ **DEVELOPMENT** Do I use details and reasons to support my ideas?

✓ **VOICE** Do I seem to care about my topic?

✓ **EFFECTIVE SENTENCES** Do I use a variety of sentence types?

✓ **EFFECTIVE PARAGRAPHS** Are similar ideas grouped together in paragraphs?

✓ **WORD CHOICE** Do I use exact nouns and vivid verbs?

✓ **CONVENTIONS** Are my spelling, grammar, and punctuation correct?

Try This

Choose a piece of writing from your portfolio. Use the Checklist. What are your strengths? What can you improve? Jot down your ideas in your Writer's Journal.

735

Using a Rubric

A **rubric** is a set of guidelines, or a checklist, that will help you evaluate your writing. Some rubrics are based on specific assignments. Other rubrics are general.

Before writing Look at the checklist to remind yourself of how to make your writing the best it can be.

During writing Check your draft against the list to see how you can make your writing better.

After writing Check your finished work against the list to see if it shows all the points of the best writing.

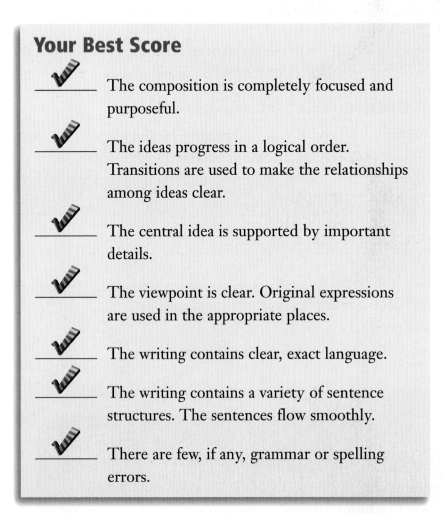

Your Best Score

_____ The composition is completely focused and purposeful.

_____ The ideas progress in a logical order. Transitions are used to make the relationships among ideas clear.

_____ The central idea is supported by important details.

_____ The viewpoint is clear. Original expressions are used in the appropriate places.

_____ The writing contains clear, exact language.

_____ The writing contains a variety of sentence structures. The sentences flow smoothly.

_____ There are few, if any, grammar or spelling errors.

Peer Conferences

A **peer conference** is a special meeting for you and one or more classmates. You read each other's compositions, comment on the writing, and offer suggestions for improvement.

Peer conferences can be very helpful to writers. They can help you find problems in your work. You, in turn, can help your classmates with their writing and can become a stronger editor in the process.

For a peer conference to work well, you and your classmates should follow some simple rules:

1. Trade compositions with other group members. If your teacher has given you a rubric, use it to check the compositions of other group members.

2. Carefully read a composition once to get the general idea. Then read it again to check organization. Look carefully at sentences and word choices. Finally, mark spelling, grammar, and punctuation problems.

3. Talk with your classmates. Be polite, and give positive feedback about their writing. Discuss any problems you found, and make suggestions for correcting them.

Try This

Work with a partner, and read each other's compositions carefully. Use the rubric on page 736 to help you see what your partner has done well and what he or she can improve.

Preparing Multimedia Presentations

Your teacher may ask you to publish your writing by making a multimedia presentation to the class. In a **multimedia presentation,** you combine your writing with other forms of information, such as charts, graphs, diagrams, photographs, maps, drawings, music, objects, film, audio, or video clips. A presentation is an opportunity for you to share what you have learned.

Here are the steps to a successful presentation:

1. Think about your audience. What will make your presentation interesting and helpful to them?

2. Reread your report. Decide what information can be put into graphs, charts, or tables to make it easier to understand.

3. Visit the school or community library to find photographs or maps. Search the Internet and other computer resources for images or sounds that illustrate your research. Choose materials that will be most useful in your presentation.

4. You may want to put maps, pictures, and charts on poster board to make them easy for you to handle and for the audience to see.

5. You may need to make arrangements for special equipment, such as a VCR.

6. Prepare a script based on your report and the materials you have found. Mark the script to show when to use the materials you have prepared.

7. Practice your presentation with the script and your media selections.

8. On the day of the presentation, make certain that all of your materials are in order. Speak clearly and loudly, and look at your audience. Be prepared to answer questions at the end.

Being a Good Listener

While your classmates are making their presentations, it is your job to be a good listener. Here are some suggestions to help you listen well and remember what you have heard:

1. Focus on the speaker's purpose, message, and point of view. Pay attention to the media that the speaker has chosen.

2. Listen to the speaker's main points. Notice how the details support the main points. Write down any questions you may have.

3. If the presentation includes the speaker's opinions, give fair consideration.

4. Ask your questions when the presentation is over.

Try This

Practice giving an oral presentation in front of a mirror. What do you think you do well? What do you think needs improvement?

Using the Glossary

Like a dictionary, this glossary lists words in alphabetical order. To find a word, look it up by its first letter or letters.

To save time, use the **guide words** at the top of each page. These show you the first and last words on the page. Look at the guide words to see if your word falls between them alphabetically.

Here is an example of a glossary entry:

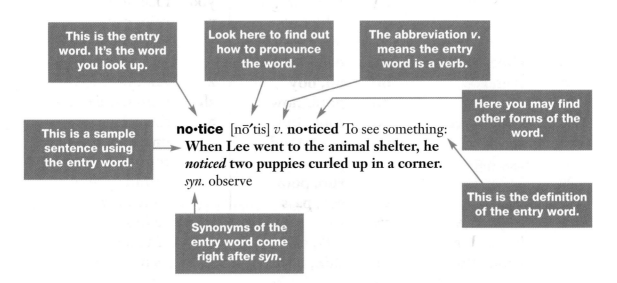

This is the entry word. It's the word you look up.

Look here to find out how to pronounce the word.

The abbreviation *v.* means the entry word is a verb.

Here you may find other forms of the word.

This is a sample sentence using the entry word.

no•tice [nō′tis] *v.* **no•ticed** To see something: **When Lee went to the animal shelter, he *noticed* two puppies curled up in a corner.** *syn.* observe

This is the definition of the entry word.

Synonyms of the entry word come right after *syn.*

Word Origins

Throughout the glossary, you will find notes about word origins, or how words got started and changed. Words often have interesting backgrounds that can help you remember what they mean.

Here is an example of a word-origin note:

> **familiar** At first, *familiar* meant "of the family," from the Latin word *familiaris*. Its meaning grew to include friends and to become "known from being around often." *Familiar* began to be used in English in the 1300s.

Pronunciation

The pronunciation in brackets is a respelling that shows how the word is pronounced.

The **pronunciation key** explains what the symbols in a respelling mean. A shortened pronunciation key appears on every other page of the glossary.

PRONUNCIATION KEY*

a	add, map	m	move, seem	u	up, done
ā	ace, rate	n	nice, tin	û(r)	burn, term
â(r)	care, air	ng	ring, song	yoo	fuse, few
ä	palm, father	o	odd, hot	v	vain, eve
b	bat, rub	ō	open, so	w	win, away
ch	check, catch	ô	order, jaw	y	yet, yearn
d	dog, rod	oi	oil, boy	z	zest, muse
e	end, pet	ou	pout, now	zh	vision, pleasure
ē	equal, tree	ŏŏ	took, full	ə	the schwa, an
f	fit, half	o͞o	pool, food		unstressed vowel
g	go, log	p	pit, stop		representing the
h	hope, hate	r	run, poor		sound spelled
i	it, give	s	see, pass		*a* in *above*
ī	ice, write	sh	sure, rush		*e* in *sicken*
j	joy, ledge	t	talk, sit		*i* in *possible*
k	cool, take	th	thin, both		*o* in *melon*
l	look, rule	t̶h̶	this, bathe		*u* in *circus*

Other symbols
- separates words into syllables
- ´ indicates heavier stress on a syllable
- ˏ indicates light stress on a syllable

Abbreviations: *adj.* adjective, *adv.* adverb, *conj.* conjunction, *interj.* interjection, *n.* noun, *prep.* preposition, *pron.* pronoun, *syn.* synonym, *v.* verb

A

ab·a·lo·ne [ab′ə·lō′nē] *n.* An edible water animal that lives in a shell: **The *abalone* shell has a pearl-like lining.**

abalone

ab·sorb [əb·zôrb′] *v.* **ab·sorbed** To be so interested in something as not to notice anything else: **Jan was so *absorbed* in her book that she didn't hear the doorbell.** *syn.* preoccupy

ac·com·pa·ni·ment [ə·kum′pə·nē·mənt] *n.* Music that is played along with another's performance: **The dancer needs a piano's *accompaniment.***

ac·com·pa·nist [ə·kum′pə·nist] *n.* A person who plays music while another person performs: **The *accompanist* waited for the singer's signal.**

ace [ās] *adj.* Best: **She is the *ace* player on our team.** *syn.* star

ad·just [ə·just′] *v.* **ad·just·ed** To arrange so as to fit or match: **The seamstress *adjusted* the hem of my dress to the length I wanted.** *syn.* alter

a·dorn·ment [ə·dôrn′mənt] *n.* Something that decorates or increases beauty: **The queen's *adornment* included her diamond-and-ruby crown.** *syn.* decoration

ad·vanced [ad·vanst′] *adj.* Ahead of or more difficult than others in progress or thought: **Kim took *advanced* math so that she would be accepted into college.** *syn.* complex

aisle [īl] *n.* A passageway, such as between rows of seats: **Don't block the *aisle* when people are leaving the auditorium.** *syn.* walkway

an·them [an′thəm] *n.* A song in honor of a country, a school, or some other institution: **"The Star-Spangled Banner" is the national *anthem.*** *syn.* theme song

ap·pren·tice [ə·pren′tis] *n.* A person who is in training in a craft or an art under the supervision of an expert: **The sculptor's *apprentice* polished the finished pieces.**

ar·ti·fi·cial [är′tə·fish′əl] *adj.* Manufactured by humans as a substitute for something natural: **Dentures are *artificial* teeth.** *syn.* synthetic

as·sure [ə·shŏŏr′] *v.* **as·sured** To convince someone: **The salesperson *assured* my mom she was getting the best possible price.** *syn.* guarantee

as·ton·ish [ə·stän′ish] *v.* **as·ton·ished** To amaze or shock: **Paul was *astonished* to learn he had won the contest.** *syn.* surprise

a·toll [a′tôl] *n.* A narrow, ring-shaped island: **The *atoll* was made of coral.**

au·di·tion [ô·dish′ən] *n.* A tryout for a performing role or a job: **We wished Ari luck before his *audition* for the play.** *syn.* test

Word Origins

audition At the root of the word *audition* is the Latin base *aud*, which has to do with hearing. Other related words are *audio*—the sound component of electronics; *auditorium*—a place where you go to hear a performance; and *audience*—the people who hear the performance.

au·thor·i·ty [ə·thôr′ə·tē] *n.* A person who knows a lot about a particular subject and is considered to be an expert: **Ray is the class *authority* on baseball.** *syn.* master

B

bar·ren [bar′ən] *adj.* Without the conditions necessary to support life: **The *barren* desert had received no rain for years.** *syn.* desolate

beam [bēm] 1. *n.* **beams** A heavy crosspiece of a ship or building: **The main *beams* gave the ship its structure.** *syn.* crossbar 2. *v.* **beam·ing** To smile in a warm way at someone: **Sally was *beaming* at her best friend.** *syn.* glow

beams

boun·ti·ful [boun′tə·fəl] *adj.* Abundant; plentiful: **The *bountiful* harvest meant that everyone would have enough food for the winter.**

brood [brood] *v.* **brood•ed** To mope and worry for a long time over something: **Lana *brooded* after she had argued with a friend.** *syn.* sulk

bulge [bulj] *n.* A swollen part or place: **The *bulge* in the tire means it needs replacement.** *syn.* protrusion

bulk [bulk] *n.* The largeness of something, including what it weighs or how much room it takes up: **The massive bear threw its *bulk* against the door.** *syn.* mass

burrow [bər′ō] *v.* **bur•rowed** To dig into the ground for protection: **The mouse *burrowed* into a pile of leaves.** *syn.* tunnel

cam•paign [kam•pān′] *n.* The process of running for elected office: **The candidate made speeches during her *campaign*.**

> **Word Origins**
>
> **campaign** The word *campaign* traces its origins back to the French word *campagne*, meaning "countryside." The open country was the site of military maneuvers and battles. *Campaign* also means "the military operations involved in winning a battle." The idea of "winning a battle" carries over to politics.

can•o•py [kan′ə•pē] *n.* A rooflike covering: **The forest *canopy* is made up of the uppermost leaves and branches.** *syn.* awning

char•coal [chär′kol] *n.* A black substance used as a drawing crayon: **Students did their sketches in *charcoal*.**

com•mo•tion [kə•mō′•shən] *n.* A disturbance; confusion: **A *commotion* occurred in the halls on the first day because students didn't know where their classes were meeting.** *syn.* uproar

com•pose [kəm•pōz′] *v.* To calm oneself: **Juan had to *compose* himself before the test.** *syn.* relax

con•coct [kən•käkt′] *v.* **con•coc•ted** To invent or develop something: **Pat *concocted* a delicious shake from five kinds of juice.** *syn.* devise

con•do•lence [kən•dō′ləns] *n.* **con•do•lenc•es** An expression of sympathy: **The judge gave his *condolences* to the grieving family.**

con•gest [kən•jest′] *v.* **con•gest•ed** To make too full or very crowded: **The mall was *congested* with holiday shoppers.** *syn.* packed

con•trap•tion [kən•trap′shən] *n.* A mechanical device, sometimes fanciful: **This *contraption* wakes you up and finds your socks in the morning.** *syn.* gadget

con•trol tow•er [kən•trōl′ tou′ər] *n.* The tower at an airport from which planes are guided to take off and land: **The pilot got clearance form the *control tower* to take off.**

cor•re•spon•dence [kôr′ə•spän′dəns] *n.* Communication by means of writing letters or electronic mail: **The pen pals kept up their *correspondence* for three years before they met in person.**

control tower

coun•sel [koun′sel] *v.* To give advice: **My older brother likes to *counsel* me on how to handle my friends.** *syn.* advise

crit•i•cal [krit′i•kəl] *adj.* Likely to find fault: **My grandmother is *critical* of the music I listen to.** *syn.* disapproving

de•ci•pher [dē•sī′fər] *v.* To make out the meaning of something such as code or illegible handwriting: **My handwriting was hard to *decipher* at first.** *syn.* decode

ded•i•cate [ded′ə•kāt] *v.* **ded•i•cat•ed** To declare—often in writing—that an artwork or a project is in honor of a person: **John *dedicated* his first symphony to his father.** *syn.* inscribe

de•sig•nate [dez′ig•nāt] *v.* **de•sig•na•ted** To set something apart for a special honor: **This day has been *designated* Best Friends Day.** *syn.* appoint

a add	e end	o odd	$\overline{oo}$ pool	oi oil	th this
ā ace	ē equal	ō open	u up	ou pout	zh vision
â care	i it	ô order	û burn	ng ring	
ä palm	ī ice	oo took	yoo fuse	th thin	

ə = { a in *above*, e in *sicken*, i in *possible*, o in *melon*, u in *circus* }

de·spair [di·spâr'] *n.* A feeling of hopelessness: **Mark felt *despair* because he thought he would never understand the work.**

de·spise [di·spīz'] *v.* **de·spised** To dislike intensely: **I *despise* television programs that insult my intelligence.** *syn.* loathe, detest

des·ti·ny [des'tə·nē] *n.* The outcome that is bound to come: **I believe it is my *destiny* to become famous.** *syn.* fate

de·ter·mi·na·tion [di·tûr'mə·nā'shən] *n.* Firmness of purpose: **With *determination* and hard work, you can achieve your goals.** *syn.* courage

de·vote [di·vōt'] *v.* To dedicate oneself to a person, a career, and so on: **Lana knew that she would *devote* herself to achieving her dream.** *syn.* commit

dig·ni·ty [dig'nə·tē] *n.* The state of having pride and self-worth: **Aunt Flo always carried herself with *dignity*.**

dil·i·gence [dil'ə·jəns] *n.* Willingness or ability to work steadily and carefully: **The *diligence* of Susan B. Anthony helped women gain the right to vote.**

dis·en·gage [dis·ən·gāj'] *v.* To unfasten or release: **The spacecraft can *disengage* itself from the space station.** *syn.* detach

disengage

dis·mal [diz'məl] *adj.* Dark, gloomy, and depressing: **Outside it was *dismal* before the storm.** *syn.* dreary

dis·man·tle [dis·man'təl] *v.* To take apart: **The mechanic had to *dismantle* the engine to replace the broken part.**

dis·may [dis·mā'] *n.* Worry; discouragement; a feeling of alarm, uneasiness: **Gwen sighed in *dismay* when so few came to the meeting.**

dis·pute [dis·pyōōt'] *v.* To argue or challenge in debate: **I cannot *dispute* the suggestion that we should eat from the four major food groups each day.**

dis·tin·guished [dis·ting'gwisht] *adj.* Having high position and honor: **The mayor was one of the *distinguished* guests.** *syn.* famous

dwin·dle [dwin'dəl] *v.* **dwin·dled** To shrink in size, value, or quantity: **Joseph's savings *dwindled* because he often bought snacks from vending machines.** *syn.* decrease

e·di·tion [i·dish'ən] *n.* A number of copies of something, such as a book, all printed in the same way and at about the same time: **The first *edition* of her book came out in May.**

em·ber [em'bər] *n.* **em·bers** In a fire, a glowing piece of wood or coal: **We toasted marshmallows over the *embers*.** *syn.* coal

ember

en·cour·age [in·kûr'ij] *v.* **en·cour·aged** To give confidence, praise, or emotional support to another person: **The teacher *encouraged* her students to succeed.** *syn.* inspire

en·dorse [in·dôrs'] *v.* To give support to something or someone, such as a product or a candidate for office: **The company asked famous sports stars to *endorse* its products.** *syn.* recommend

en·er·gy [en'ər·jē] *n.* Power that is used to do work: **Food gives your body *energy* to move and grow.**

en·trust [in·trust'] *v.* **en·trust·ed** To make responsible for something: **King Arthur was *entrusted* with the sword Excalibur.**

e·on [ē'ən *or* ē'on] *n.* **e·ons** An extremely long time; hundreds of thousands of years: **Many *eons* ago dinosaurs roamed the earth.**

er·rand [er'ənd] *n.* **er·rands** A short trip on which someone does something, often a trip for someone else: **Sally's job was to run *errands* for her father's grocery store.**

er·ror [er′ər] *n.* A mistake in thinking or in judgement; in baseball, a mistake in fielding the ball: **Noel was charged with an *error* when he dropped the ball and the runner made it to second base.** *syn.* blunder

es·teem [is·tēm′] *v.* To consider; deem: **I *esteem* it an honor to be given this award.**

ex·ag·ger·ate [ig·zaj′ə·rāt′] *v.* To add to the facts in a way that distorts the meaning: **If you *exaggerate* the facts of the news story, then it is no longer good journalism.** *syn.* overstate

ex·haust [ig·zôst′] *v.* **ex·haust·ed** To make tired: **The mule was *exhausted* from carrying the heavy packs.** *syn.* fatigue

ex·o·dus [ek′sə·dəs] *n.* A large group of people going out from a place: **At first only a few refugees left, but soon an *exodus* began.** *syn.* migration

fea·ture [fē′chər] *n.* **fea·tures** A part of the face, as the eyes, nose, or mouth: **The man's pointed *features* made him look like a bird.**

flex·i·bil·i·ty [flek′sə·bil′i·tē] *n.* The quality of being able to bend without breaking: **Some types of plastic have *flexibility*, but wood does not.** *syn.* malleability

for·lorn [fər·lôrn′] *adj.* Feeling miserable, lost, or abandoned: **Sarah wore a *forlorn* expression when no one played with her.** *syn.* sad

furl [fûrl] *v.* To wrap up tightly and then tie, such as a sail: **Dori had to *furl* the sail after tying the small sailboat to the dock.** *syn.* roll

G

gen·er·ate [jen′ə·rāt] *v.* **gen·er·at·ed** To cause something to happen because of a physical or a chemical change: **The light *generated* a lot of heat.** *syn.* produce

gey·ser [gī′zər] *n.* A spring of water heated by an underground source so that it boils at regular intervals, shooting water and steam into the air: **The tourists were misted with warm water when the *geyser* shot upward through the ground.**

Word Origins

geyser The word *geyser* is the only Icelandic word commonly used in the English language. *Geysir* is the name of a certain geyser in southern Iceland. The word means "gusher." Geysir has quieted in the past 60 years, but other Icelandic geysers are quite active.

geyser

gorge [gôrj] *v.* **gorged** To overeat; to gobble food like an animal: **The hungry lions *gorged* themselves on their prey.** *syn.* stuff

grade [grād] *n.* The steepness of the land; the steepness of an angle: **The road's *grade* grew steeper as it approached the mountain.**

graf·fi·ti [grə·fē′tē] *n.* A kind of vandalism in which people write their names or draw pictures on others' property: **The students who wrote the *graffiti* had to stay after school and scrub it off.** *syn.* scrawl

grav·el·ly [grav′əl·lē] *adj.* Having a rough sound: **Her bad cold made her voice sound *gravelly*.** *syn.* raspy

grav·i·ta·tion·al [grav′ə·tā′shən·əl] *adj.* Having to do with the law in physics that states that two objects exert a pull on each other: **The Earth's *gravitational* pull is one reason objects have weight; the other is the mass of the objects themselves.**

gri·mace [grim′əs] *v.* **gri·maced** To twist one's face, as if in pain: **Cal *grimaced* as he heard the off-key music.**

a	add	e	end	o	odd	o͞o	pool	oi	oil	th	this		*a in above*
ā	ace	ē	equal	ō	open	u	up	ou	pout	zh	vision	ə =	*e in sicken*
â	care	i	it	ô	order	û	burn	ng	ring				*i in possible*
ä	palm	ī	ice	o͝o	took	yo͞o	fuse	th	thin				*o in melon*
													u in circus

745

guar·an·tee [gar′ən•tē′] *v.* To pledge that something will be done as promised: **We *guarantee* that you will like our product, or we will give you back your money.** *syn.* affirm

han·dler [han′dlər] *n.* **han·dlers** A person who trains or manages an animal in a race, a show, or a contest: **The show dogs looked to their *handlers* for instructions.** *syn.* manager

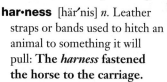

handler

har·ness [här′nis] *n.* Leather straps or bands used to hitch an animal to something it will pull: **The *harness* fastened the horse to the carriage.**

head·quar·ters [hed′kwôr′tərz] *n.* The central office for controlling an operation, campaign, or business: **Lila sent a letter of complaint to company *headquarters* and got a reply.**

┌ **Word Origins**
│ **headquarters** The head, because it houses the brain and contains four major sense organs, is the center of control for all of the body's functions. Some words in our language that expand on this idea are *headline*—the most important part of a news story; *headmaster*—the principal of a school; and *headspring*—the source of a spring of water.

home·stead [hōm′sted] *v.* To develop a substantial piece of land, including building on it and farming it: **The Smith family decided to *homestead* rather than stay in the crowded city.**

hon·or [än′ər] *n.* **hon·ors** Recognition of or respect for someone's achievement: **She received a certificate of *honor* for her high grades.** *syns.* tribute, award

hud·dle [hud′əl] *v.* **hud·dled** To nestle close together, as for protection: **The pigeons *huddled* together under the awning.** *syn.* crowd

il·lus·trate [il′ə•strāt′] *v.* **il·lus·trat·ing** To make pictures that go along with written material, such as books: **Emily enjoys writing and *illustrating* her own books.** *syn.* draw

┌ **Word Origins**
│ **illustrate** The word *illustrate* is derived from the Latin word *illustratus*, "to light up." One meaning of *illustrate* is "to make clear or explain" by using examples and comparisons. Illustrations "shed light on" the words of a book.

im·mo·bil·i·ty [i′mō•bil′ə•tē] *n.* The condition of not being able to move: **An engine problem caused the car's *immobility*.** *syn.* motionlessness

in·cred·i·ble [in•kred′ə•bəl] *adj.* Too unusual to be believed: **Eighty years ago, space travel seemed an *incredible* idea.** *syn.* unbelievable

in·debt·ed [in•det′id] *adj.* Feeling that one owes something in return for a favor: **We are *indebted* to you for your help after the earthquake.** *syn.* obligated

in·let [in′let] *n.* A narrow strip of water; a small bay or creek: **We traveled the *inlet* in a small canoe.** *syn.* passageway

inlet

in·spire [in•spīr′] *v.* To motivate someone to accomplish or feel something: **A good teacher seeks to *inspire* the class.** *syn.* encourage

in·stall·ment [in•stôl′mənt] *n.* **in·stall·ments** One part of a total amount of money that is owed: **Jennie paid her mother back for the broken vase in three *installments*.** *syn.* payments

in·su·late [in′sə•lāt′] *v.* **in·su·lat·ed** To cover, as with a material that does not conduct electricity or a material that does not allow heat or cold to pass through: **The wires were not *insulated* well and so posed a fire hazard.** *syn.* wrap

in·ter·na·tion·al [in·tər·nash′nəl] *adj.* Having to do with many nations: **Antarctica is the site of *international* scientific research.** *syn.* global

in·ter·pret·er [in·tər′prə·tər] *n.* A person who translates spoken words from one language into another: **Kim acted as *interpreter* between her sister and the salesclerk.** *syn.* translator

la·goon [lə·go͞on′] *n.* An area of water that is surrounded by a circular thin strip of land called an atoll: **The water in the *lagoon* was very calm.**

lagoon

lair [lâr] *n.* The home of some kinds of animals: **The bear hibernated all winter in its *lair*.** *syn.* den

lav·ish [lav′ish] *adj.* Generous or too generous: **The prince showered his new bride with *lavish* gifts.**

line·up [līn′up′] *n.* In baseball or softball, the batting order for a team: **Ken batted third in the *lineup*.** *syn.* order

loft·y [lôf′tē] *adj.* **loft·i·ly** *adv.* Proud; arrogant: **James *loftily* announced that he would win the competition.**

lurk [lûrk] *v.* **lurked** To be ready to attack while hiding from view: **The leopard *lurked* in the jungle, quietly searching for food.** *syn.* skulk

me·an·der [mē·an′dər] *v.* To move back and forth in a snakelike fashion: **The cat likes to *meander* through the garden.** *syn.* wind

men·tor [men′tər] *n.* An advisor and tutor who works one-on-one with a young person: **With a *mentor's* help, Cyd improved his music skills.** *syn.* teacher

Fact File

mentor In Greek mythology, Mentor was a friend of Odysseus, the hero of Homer's epic poem *The Odyssey*. Mentor became the helper and teacher of Odysseus' son, Telemachus. Odysseus had been called away to battle, and he encountered many adventures and difficulties during his return journey. Throughout Odysseus' absence, Mentor often helped Telemachus choose the right course of action.

mi·grant [mī′grənt] *adj.* Moving regularly from place to place: **_Migrant_ farmers must often find new homes.** *syn.* nomadic

mi·grate [mī′grāt] *v.* **mi·grat·ed** To move with others of the same group to a place that is far away: **The birds *migrated* south in winter in search of food and warmth.** *syn.* relocate.

mis·lead [mis·lēd′] *v.* **mis·lead·ing** To give a false idea to others: **The robber tried *misleading* the police when he was questioned.** *syn.* deceive

mock [mok] *v.* **mock·ing** To ridicule or deride: **My brother continued his *mocking* even after Mother told him to stop calling me names.**

moss [môs] *n.* A kind of small plant that grows in moist, shaded areas: **_Moss_ grows on the north side of trees in the Northern Hemisphere.**

muf·fle [muf′əl] *v.* To lower the volume by covering or enclosing the source of the noise: **Dina used a pillow to *muffle* the ringing of the alarm clock.** *syn.* deaden

mul·ti·tude [mul′tə·t(y)o͞od′] *n.* Great number of persons or things: **The *multitude* of people made the football stadium overcrowded.** *syn.* crowd

a add	e end	o odd	o͞o pool	oi oil	th this	a in *above*
ā ace	ē equal	ō open	u up	ou pout	zh vision	e in *sicken*
â care	i it	ô order	û burn	ng ring	ə =	i in *possible*
ä palm	ī ice	o͝o took	yo͞o fuse	th thin		o in *melon* / u in *circus*

non·cha·lant [non'shə·länt'] *adj.* **non·cha·lant·ly** *adv.* Not excited or concerned: **The judge** *nonchalantly* **placed the silver medal around the skater's neck.**

nu·mer·ous [noo'mər·əs] *adj.* Consisting of a large group of things or events: **He tried** *numerous* **times to grow plants from seeds in his backyard.** *syn.* many

oath [ōth] *n.* An oral or written promise about a serious matter, such as honesty or faithfulness to an ideal: **At his inauguration, President Washington took the first** *oath* **of office.** *syn.* vow

oath

ob·nox·ious [əb·näk'shəs] *adj.* Extremely unpleasant or offensive: **The landfill gave off an** *obnoxious* **smell.** *syn.* intolerable

> **Word Origins**
> **obnoxious** The word *obnoxious* is from the Latin word *obnoxiosus,* meaning "exposed to danger." It is made up of the word parts *ob,* which means "to" or "toward," and *noxa,* which means "harm." The word is used today with a meaning that is closer to "annoying," such as "an obnoxious attitude." However, the original meaning was more danger-oriented.

or·deal [ôr·dēl', ôr·dē'əl, *or* ôr'dēl'] *n.* A very difficult or trying experience: **Finding our way home through the fog was a frightening** *ordeal.*

over·come [ō'vər·kum'] *v.* To make weak or helpless: **Elizabeth was** *overcome* **by fear because she had to compete.** *syn.* overwhelm

pace [pās] *n.* A rate of walking, running, or doing other activities: **The scouts hiked at a fast** *pace.* *syn.* tempo

par·ti·tion [pär·tish'ən] *n.* A divider; a wall: **A** *partition* **usually divides the big gym into two smaller ones.** *syn.* separation

pas·tel [pas·tel'] *n.* **pas·tels** A chalklike colored crayon, used for art: **The technique for using** *pastels* **often involves blending colors.**

pa·tron [pā'trən] *n.* A person who supports or champions a person or thing: **Queen Elizabeth I was a** *patron* **of the arts and a supporter of artists.** *syn.* sponsor

pawn·shop [pòn'shäp] *n.* A business in which a person is licensed to lend money in exchange for goods, which may be redeemed if the loan is repaid: **In the** *pawnshop* **were cases of watches and jewelry.**

pen·in·su·la [pə·nin's(y)ə·lə] *n.* A piece of land nearly surrounded by water and joined to a larger landmass: **Italy is a** *peninsula* **extending into the Mediterranean Sea.**

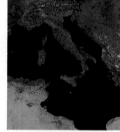

peninsula

perch [pûrch] *n.* A place to sit or stand, especially at a height: **Our parakeet thinks my shoulder is her** *perch.* *syn.* roost

per·il [per'əl] *n.* Exposure to the chance of injury, loss, or destruction: **The firefighter put his life in** *peril* **to save the cat from the burning building.** *syn.* danger

pierc·ing [pir'sing] *adj.* Penetrating; intense: **His** *piercing* **glance made me feel transparent.**

pitch [pich] *v.* **pitched** For a ship to plunge down and rise up again repeatedly: **The ship** *pitched* **violently on the rough waves.** *syn.* dip

plen·i·tude [plen'ə·t(y)ood'] *n.* Condition of being full or abundant: **Such a** *plenitude* **of apples will last the settlers all winter.**

plod [plod] *v.* **plod·ded** To walk with great effort: **The ranger** *plodded* **through the deep snow.** *syn.* trudge

plunge [plunj] *v.* **plunged** To jump, dive, or fall, as into water or a chasm: **The grizzly bear** *plunged* **into the cold water, looking for a salmon.**

point·ed·ly [poin′tid•lē] *adv.* Clearly noticeable; emphatic: **Katie *pointedly* asked Mona why she hadn't been invited.** *syn.* directly

pol·i·cy [pä•lə•sē] *n.* A set of rules for an organization that are in keeping with its philosophical point of view: **The restaurant has a good *policy* toward refunding money to unsatisfied customers.** *syn.* practice

po·li·o [pō′lē•ō] *n.* Short form of *poliomyelitis*, a virus that causes paralysis and deformity, especially in children: **Dr. Jonas Salk developed a vaccine that conquered *polio*.** *syn.* infantile paralysis

┌ **Fact File**
polio Polio was a terrifying killer and a crippler of both children and adults. Franklin D. Roosevelt was paralyzed by polio in 1921. After he returned to public life, he was elected governor of New York State and President of the United States, the office he held from 1932 until his death in 1945. Dr. Jonas Salk's vaccine was introduced in 1955, followed by the Sabin vaccine. These vaccines have practically eliminated polio.

pon·der [pon′dər] *v.* **pon·dered** To think over carefully: **Karen *pondered* the question before giving the correct answer.** *syn.* consider

po·si·tion [pə•zish′ən] *n.* **po·si·tions** The place occupied by a person or thing: **The runners took their *positions* in their lanes before the race began.** *syn.* post

po·ten·tial [pō•ten′shəl] *n.* An ability that has not yet been used: **Zoe has the *potential* to be a great violinist.** *syn.* capacity

pro·duce [prō′dyo͞os] *n.* Something that has been grown, such as fruits and vegetables: **You'll find fresh corn in the *produce* department of the supermarket.** *syn.* harvest

produce

pro·fuse [prə•fyo͞os′] *adj.* **pro·fuse·ly** *adv.* Overflowing; abundant: **The award-winning actress *profusely* thanked her fans.** *syn.* generously

prowl [proul] *v.* **prowls** To search around like an animal hunting prey: **Our cat *prowls* around the backyard searching for mice.** *syn.* stalk

pub·lic·i·ty [pub•lis′ə•tē] *n.* Any information intended to bring a person or thing to the attention of the public: **The story was created by the reporter to get *publicity* for the newspaper.**

qui·ver [kwiv′ər] *n.* A container for arrows: **Sean drew an arrow from the *quiver* and pulled back the bowstring.** *syn.* sheath

quiver

ra·tion [rash′ən] *n.* **ra·tions** A system of distributing goods that would be scarce if they were not controlled: **Rations were a way for both soldiers and civilians to get enough supplies during World War II.** *syn.* quota

┌ **Fact File**
ration During World War II many countries, including the United States, practiced rationing. Basic supplies, like meat, eggs, footwear, gasoline, rubber tires, and butter, were rationed rather than freely available. Each family received a coupon book and then gave stores ration coupons along with money to buy items.

a	add	e	end	o	odd	o͞o	pool	oi	oil	th	this		*a* in *above*
ā	ace	ē	equal	ō	open	u	up	ou	pout	zh	vision		*e* in *sicken*
â	care	i	it	ô	order	û	burn	ng	ring			ə =	*i* in *possible*
ä	palm	ī	ice	o͞o	took	yo͞o	fuse	th	thin				*o* in *melon*
													u in *circus*

ra·vine [rə·vēn'] *n.* Long, narrow, deep depression in the earth, with steep sides, usually cut out by a flow of water: **Over hundreds of years, the river cut a deep *ravine* into the land.** *syn.* gorge

reef [rēf] *n.* A ridge of rock or coral lying near or just above the surface of the water: **Anna and James used snorkels as they explored the coral *reef*.** *syn.* shoal

re·fin·er·y [ri·fīn'ə·rē] *n.* A place where a raw material is processed into a finished product, such as sugar or oil: **All impurities from the sugarcane were filtered out at the *refinery*.** *syn.* plant

re·peal [ri·pēl'] *v.* To cancel or withdraw something, such as a penalty: **The judge will *repeal* the parking fine.** *syn.* annul

rep·u·ta·tion [re'pyə·tā'shən] *n.* The opinion most people have about the character of someone or something: **Our school has a *reputation* for graduating many honor students.**

re·sem·ble [ri·zem'bəl] *v.* **re·sem·bled** To be similar in appearance or character to someone or something else: **This case *resembled* an earlier case the police had solved.** *syn.* parallel

res·i·dence [rez'ə·dəns] *n.* The place where one lives: **Our *residence* was an apartment on the top floor of a three-story house.** *syn.* dwelling

re·tire [ri·tīr'] *v.* **re·tired** To take something out of use because of advancing age: **Andrew *retired* his baseball glove when it became too small for his hand.**

rev·o·lu·tion [rev'ə·lōō'shən] *n.* Overthrow of an established government by those formerly under its authority: **The American *Revolution* freed the thirteen colonies from British control.**

rid·i·cule [rid'ə·kyōōl] *v.* **rid·i·culed** To criticize or make fun of someone in a way that embarrasses him or her: **The boys *ridiculed* the new student for the way she dressed.** *syns.* mock, belittle

rig·ging [rig'ing] *n.* The lines and chains used with sails and masts on a sailing vessel: **Julian found that the hardest part of making a model ship was setting up the *rigging* correctly.**

rigging

schol·ar·ship [skäl'ər·ship] *n.* Money that is awarded to pay for a student's tuition: **Charles was admitted to college with a full *scholarship*.** *syns.* stipend, grant

scur·ry [skûr'ē] *v.* **scur·ried** Run quickly or hastily: **The mouse *scurried* into the hole with a piece of cheese.** *syn.* scamper

sen·sor [sen'sər] *n.* **sen·sors** A device that measures or monitors physical events: ***Sensors* on a seismograph detect and record earth movement.**

se·ries [sir'ēz] *n.* A number of things coming one after another in time or place: **A *series* of concerts will be held at Town Hall this winter.** *syn.* sequence

set·tle·ment [set'əl·mənt] *n.* A place people develop so they can live there: **These ruins show that there was once a large *settlement* here.** *syn.* colony

shal·low [shal'ō] *adj.* Something, such as water, that is not deep: ***Shallow* puddles were all over the parking lot after the rainstorm.**

share·hold·er [shâr'hōl'dər] *n.* Owner of a share or shares of a company's stock: **Every *shareholder* in the company has the right to vote.** *syn.* stockholder

side·track [sīd'trak] *v.* To make something go off the proper course: **The rodeo clown's important job is to *sidetrack* a charging bull.** *syn.* distract

> **Fact File**
> **sidetrack** The word *sidetrack* has a more literal meaning than the one we commonly use. It means to switch a train from its main track to a siding—a short piece of track where the train can wait while it is being loaded or while another train passes.

si·mul·ta·ne·ous·ly [sī'məl·tā'nē·əs·lē] *adv.* At the same time: **The children explained the story *simultaneously*.** *syn.* concurrently

snort [snôrt] *v.* To make a noise by quickly forcing air through the nostrils: **Horses only breathe through their noses, so when they run, they *snort*.**

so·na·ta [sə·nä'tə] *n.* A musical piece written for one or two instruments, consisting of one or more movements, or sections: **Beethoven's "Moonlight Sonata" is a piano piece.**

sor·row·ful [sor'ō·fəl] *adj.* **sor·row·ful·ly** *adv.* Feeling or showing sadness or distress of mind because of some loss or misfortune: **Emily looked *sorrowfully* at the rain-soaked library book.** *syn.* sadly

sou·ven·ir [sōō′və·nir′] *n.* An item that is a reminder of a person, place, or event: **The tourist bought a** *souvenir* **postcard in the gift shop.** *syn.* remembrance

> **Word Origins**
> **souvenir** The word *souvenir* is the French verb meaning "to remember." It contains the root word *venir*, "to come." On Quebec's license plates, the motto "*Je me souviens*" ("I remember") is imprinted.

stern·ly [stûrn′lē] *adv.* In a severe, strict, or scolding manner: **The teacher talked to him** *sternly* **about not listening in class.** *syn.* sharply

stump [stump] *v.* **stumps** To puzzle or baffle someone, as during a quiz: **The spelling word "xyster"** *stumps* **even our best contestants.** *syn.* confuse

sub·mit [səb·mit′] *v.* **sub·mit·ted** To display or show something so that others can judge it or comment upon it in some way: **Jan** *submitted* **her poem to the school magazine, and it was printed.** *syn.* present

suf·frage [suf′rij] *n.* The right to vote for candidates for political office: **Women's** *suffrage* **in the United States became a reality after World War I.**

sus·pend [sə·spend′] *v.* **sus·pen·ded** To hang up and leave dangling: **The fish was** *suspended* **from Libby's line.** *syn.* dangle

tan·gle [tan′gəl] *n.* Something that is snarled or muddled: **There was a** *tangle* **in Melissa's hair that was so stubburn it had to be cut out.** *syn.* knot

ter·rain [tə·rān′] *n.* A type of land: **The rocky** *terrain* **was difficult for the hikers to cross.** *syn.* region

thrive [thrīv] *v.* **thrived** To prosper under the effect of something: **The plant** *thrived* **when it got enough sun and water.** *syns.* flourish, succeed

tim·id [tim′id] *adj.* Lacking self-confidence; fearful; shy: **The** *timid* **child found it hard to make new friends.** *syn.* bashful

tin·der [tin′dər] *n.* Material that catches fire easily because it is very dry, brittle, and thin: **The camper added dry twigs as** *tinder* **to get the campfire started.** *syn.* kindling

tinder

trans·la·tion [trans·lā′shən] *n.* The act of changing something spoken or written into another language: **The class read the English** *translation* **of a Greek book.**

tread [tred] *n.* The act, manner, or sound of walking: **My brother's quiet** *tread* **allowed him to surprise people all the time.** *syn.* footfall

treaty [trē′tē] *n.* An official agreement between peoples or countries, stating what each side will do about a certain issue: **The peace** *treaty* **ended the long war.** *syns.* arrangement, compact

un·de·ni·a·ble [un′di·nī′ə·bəl] *adj.* Something that one is sure of beyond question: **It is** *undeniable* **that Lewis is the best student in class.** *syn.* indisputable

vain [vān] *adj.* **vain·er** Being excessively proud of one's appearance and honor: **The actor had become** *vainer* **and demanded the largest dressing room.** *syn.* conceited

vast [vast] *adj.* Of very large size; enormous; huge: **The Atlantic Ocean is** *vast.* *syn.* great

veer [vir] *v.* **veered** To turn sharply from one direction to another: **The driver** *veered* **sharply to the right.** *syn.* swerve

vow [vou] *n.* A promise about a serious matter: **Ted made a** *vow* **to help his new classmate in any way that he could.** *syn.* pledge

a	add	e	end	o	odd	ōō	pool	oi	oil	th	this	
ā	ace	ē	equal	ō	open	u	up	ou	pout	zh	vision	*a* in *above*
â	care	i	it	ô	order	û	burn	ng	ring			*e* in *sicken*
ä	palm	ī	ice	ŏŏ	took	yōō	fuse	th	thin			*i* in *possible*

ə = { *a* in *above* / *e* in *sicken* / *i* in *possible* / *o* in *melon* / *u* in *circus* }

Page numbers in color refer to biographical information.

Acknowledgments

For permission to reprint copyrighted material, grateful acknowledgment is made to the following sources:

Atheneum Books for Young Readers, an imprint of Simon & Schuster Children's Publishing Division: From *The Night Has Ears: African Proverbs* (Retitled: "African Proverbs"), selected and illustrated by Ashley Bryan. Illustrations copyright © 1999 by Ashley Bryan.

Molly Bang: Illustration by Molly Bang from *Red Dragonfly on My Shoulder*, translated by Sylvia Cassedy and Kunihiro Suetake. Illustration copyright © 1992 by Molly Bang.

Brandt & Brandt Literary Agents, Inc.: From *The Many Lives of Benjamin Franklin* by Mary Pope Osborne. Text copyright © 1990 by Mary Pope Osborne. Published by Dial Books for Young Readers, a division of Penguin Putnam Inc.

Maria Carvainis Agency, Inc.: "Hattie's Birthday Box" by Pam Conrad from *Birthday Surprises: Ten Great Stories to Unwrap*, edited by Johanna Hurwitz. Text © 1994 by Pam Conrad.

Ellen Cassedy: Haiku by Kyoshi from *Red Dragonfly on My Shoulder*, translated by Sylvia Cassedy and Kunihiro Suetake. Text copyright © 1967 by the Estate of Sylvia Cassedy and Kunihiro Suetake.

Childrens Press, a Division of Grolier Publishing: Evelyn Cisneros: Prima Ballerina by Charnan Simon. Text copyright © 1990 by Children's Press®, Inc. From *Lewis and Clark* by R. Conrad Stein. Text copyright © 1997 by Children's Press®, a Division of Grolier Publishing Co., Inc.

Cobblestone Publishing Company, 30 Grove Street, Suite C, Peterborough, NH 03458: "The Chinese Language Puzzle" by Karen E. Hong from *Appleseeds: Beijing*, April 2000. Text © 2000 by Cobblestone Publishing Company.

Coward-McCann, Inc., a division of Penguin Putnam Inc.: From *What's the Big Idea, Ben Franklin?* by Jean Fritz, illustrated by Margot Tomes. Text copyright © 1976 by Jean Fritz; illustrations copyright © 1976 by Margot Tomes.

Dial Books for Young Readers, a division of Penguin Putnam Inc.: From *Across the Wide Dark Sea* by Jean Van Leeuwen, illustrated by Thomas B. Allen. Text copyright © 1995 by Jean Van Leeuwen; illustrations copyright © 1995 by Thomas B. Allen.

Dorling Kindersley Limited, London: "Climate and Seasons" from *DK Guide to Weather* by Michael Allaby. Copyright © 2000 by Dorling Kindersley Limited, London.

Doubleday, a division of Random House, Inc.: "The Fun They Had" from *Earth Is Room Enough* by Isaac Asimov. Text copyright © 1957 by Isaac Asimov. "Celebration" and "Eagle Flight" by Alonzo Lopez from *Whispering Wind*, edited by Terry Allen. Text copyright © 1972 by the Institute of American Indian Arts.

Katherine Froman: "When Birds Remember" from *Seeing Things: A Book of Poems* by Robert Froman, lettering by Ray Barber. Copyright © 1974 by Robert Froman.

HarperCollins Publishers: From *William Shakespeare & the Globe* by Aliki. Copyright © 1999 by Aliki Brandenberg. From *Dear Mr. Henshaw* by Beverly Cleary, cover illustration by Paul O. Zelinsky. Text and cover illustration copyright © 1983 by Beverly Cleary. *Everglades* by Jean Craighead George, illustrated by Wendell Minor. Text copyright © 1995 by Jean Craighead George; illustrations copyright © 1995 by Wendell Minor. From *The Hot & Cold Summer* by Johanna Hurwitz, cover illustration by Gail Owens. Text copyright © 1984 by Johanna Hurwitz; cover illustration copyright © 1984 by Gail Owens. Cover illustration by Michael Garland from *Birthday Surprises: Ten Great Stories to Unwrap*, edited by Johanna Hurwitz. Cover illustration copyright © 1997 by Michael Garland. From *The World of William Joyce Scrapbook* by William Joyce, photographs by Philip Gould. Text and illustrations copyright © 1997 by William Joyce; photographs copyright © 1997 by Philip Gould. From *Sally Ann Thunder Ann Whirlwind Crockett*, retold by Steven Kellogg. Copyright © 1995 by Steven Kellogg. "About Notebooks" from *Hey World, Here I Am!* by Jean Little, cover illustration by Sue Truesdell. Text copyright © 1986 by Jean Little; cover illustration copyright © 1989 by Susan G. Truesdell. "Pandora's Box" from *The Robber Baby: Stories from the Greek Myths* by Anne Rockwell. Text and cover illustration copyright © 1994 by Anne Rockwell. From *Oceans* by Seymour Simon, illustrated by Frank Schwartz. Copyright © 1990 by Seymour Simon. "The Case of the Flying Saucer People" from *Einstein Anderson Science Detective: The Howling Dog and Other Cases* by Seymour Simon. Text copyright © 1980, 1997 by Seymour Simon. "How the Moon Became Ivory" from *Sky Legends of Vietnam* by Lynette Dyer Vuong. Text copyright © 1993 by Lynette Dyer Vuong. "Virtue Goes to Town" from *The Rainbow People* by Laurence Yep, illustrated by David Wiesner, cover illustration by Kam Mak. Text copyright © 1989 by Laurence Yep; illustration copyright © 1989 by David Wiesner; cover illustration © 1992 by Kam Mak.

Holiday House, Inc.: Illustrations by Leonard Everett Fisher from *Earth Songs* by Myra Cohn Livingston. Illustrations copyright © 1986 by Leonard Everett Fisher.

Houghton Mifflin Company: From *Island of the Blue Dolphins* by Scott O'Dell, cover illustration by Ted Lewin. Text copyright © 1960, renewed 1988 by Scott O'Dell; cover illustration copyright © 1990 by Ted Lewin.

Hyperion Books for Children: From *Sees Behind Trees* by Michael Dorris, cover illustration by Linda Benson. Text copyright © 1996 by The Estate of Michael Dorris; cover illustration © 1996 by Linda Benson. From *Elena* by Diane Stanley. Text © 1996 by Diane Stanley; cover illustration © 1996 by Raul Colón.

Kalmbach Publishing Co.: From *Name This American* by Hannah Reinmuth in *Plays: The Drama Magazine for Young People*, May 1995. Text copyright © 1995 by Plays, Inc. This play is for reading purposes only; for permission to produce, write to Kalmbach Publishing Co., 21027 Crossroads Cir., P.O. Box 1612, Waukesha, WI 53187-1612.

Kids Discover: From "Ice Lands" in *Kids Discover: Water*, June 1999. Text © 1999 by Kids Discover.

Lee & Low Books, Inc., 95 Madison Ave., New York, NY 10016: From *Dear Mrs. Parks: A Dialogue with Today's Youth* by Rosa Parks with Gregory J. Reed, cover photograph by Mark T. Kerrin. Text copyright © 1996 by Rosa L. Parks; cover photograph copyright © 1996 by Mark T. Kerrin.

Libraries Unlimited, Inc. (800-237-6124): "Who is Best?" from *Thai Tales: Folktales of Thailand*, retold by Supaporn Vathanaprida. Text © 1994 by Libraries Unlimited.

Little, Brown and Company (Inc.): Limerick from "Write Me a Verse" in *Take Sky* by David McCord. Text copyright © 1961, 1962 by David McCord. From *Yang the Third and Her Impossible Family* by Lensey Namioka, illustrated by Kees de Kiefte. Text copyright © 1995 by Lensey Namioka; illustrations copyright © 1995 by Kees de Kiefte.

National Geographic Society: "Smoke Jumpers" by Janice Koch from *National Geographic WORLD* Magazine, August 1994. Text copyright © 1994 by National Geographic Society.

Harold Ober Associates Incorporated: From "Children and Poetry" in *The Langston Hughes Reader* by Langston Hughes. Text copyright © 1958 by Langston Hughes; text copyright renewed 1986 by George Houston Bass.

Oxford University Press: From "Musical Instruments" (Retitled: "Brass Instruments") in *Oxford Children's Encyclopedia*, Volume 4. Text and illustrations © 1991 by Oxford University Press.

Penguin Books Canada Limited: From *Little By Little* by Jean Little. Text copyright © 1987 by Jean Little.

G. P. Putnam's Sons, a division of Penguin Putnam Inc.: Illustrations from *Tomie dePaola's Book of Poems* by Tomie dePaola. Illustrations copyright © 1988 by Tomie dePaola.

Random House Children's Books, a division of Random House, Inc.: From *Satchmo's Blues* by Alan Schroeder, illustrated by Floyd Cooper. Text copyright © 1996 by Alan Schroeder; illustrations copyright © 1996 by Floyd Cooper. From *Off and Running* by Gary Soto, cover illustration by Eric Velasquez. Text copyright © 1996 by Gary Soto; cover illustration copyright © 1996 by Eric Velasquez.

Marian Reiner: Earth Songs by Myra Cohn Livingston. Text copyright © 1986 by Myra Cohn Livingston. Published by Holiday House, Inc. "Souvenir" from *The Singing Green* by Eve Merriam. Text copyright © 1992 by Estate of Eve Merriam. Published by William Morrow & Company, Inc.

Boonsong Rohitasuke: Cover illustration by Boonsong Rohitasuke from *Thai Tales: Folktales of Thailand*, retold by Supaporn Vathanaprida.

Scholastic Inc.: From *We'll Never Forget You, Roberto Clemente* by Trudie Engel. Text copyright © 1996 by Trudie Engel. From *Seeing Earth from Space* by Patricia Lauber. Text copyright © 1990 by Patricia Lauber. Published by Orchard Books, an imprint of Scholastic Inc. From *Summer of Fire: Yellowstone 1988* by Patricia Lauber. Text copyright © 1991 by Patricia Lauber. Published by Orchard Books, an imprint of Scholastic Inc. From *Aesop's Fables*, retold by Ann McGovern. Text and cover illustration copyright © 1963 by Scholastic Inc. Published by Apple Classics, an imprint of Scholastic Inc.

Simon & Schuster Books for Young Readers, an imprint of Simon & Schuster Children's Publishing Division: From *Frindle* by Andrew Clements, cover illustration by Brian Selznick. Text copyright © 1996 by Andrew Clements; cover illustration copyright © 1996 by Brian Selznick. From *Woodsong* by Gary Paulsen, cover photograph by Ruth Wright Paulsen. Text copyright © 1990 by Gary Paulsen; cover photograph copyright © 1990 by Ruth Wright Paulsen. From *Black Frontiers* by Lillian Schlissel. Text copyright © 1995 by Lillian Schlissel.

Sports Illustrated for Kids: From "Slammin' Sammy" by Alan Schwarz in *Sports Illustrated for Kids*, July 1999. Text copyright © 1999 by Time Inc.

Walker and Company: From *Iditarod Dream* by Ted Wood. Copyright © 1996 by Ted Wood.

Photo Credits

Key: (t)=top; (b)=bottom; (c)=center; (l)=left; (r)=right

Page 41, Rick Friedman / Black Star; 63, Parallel Productions; 70, Tom Raymond / Stone; 87, Image Club Graphics; 133, Bill Ross / Corbis; 162, J. Nettis / H. Armstrong Roberts; 162, Photodisc.com; 186-196, Ted Wood; 197, David Swift; 199(t), Charles Mauzy / Corbis; 199(b), Harcourt School Publishers; 221(t), Joseph Sohm / Corbis; 221(b), Jose Azel / Woodfin Camp & Associates; 246, World Sat International / Photo Researchers; 247(t), NOAA / Mark Marten / Photo Researchers; 247(b), Earth Imaging / Stone; 275, Peter Skinner / Photo Researchers; 276-277, Erwin & Peggy Bauer; 278-279, Yellowstone National Park; 280-281, Jeff Henry / National Park Service; 281, Yellowstone National Park; 282, 283, 284, Jim Peaco / National Park Service; 285, Jeff Henry / National Park Service; 286(l), Jim Peaco / National Park Service; 286(r), Ted Wood; 287(background), Jeff Henry / National Park Service; 287, Rick Falco / Black Star; 296(t), Kunio Owaki / Corbis Stock Market; 296(b), Keith Gunnar / Bruce Coleman, Inc.; 297, Ken Kinzie / Harcourt School Publishers; 298-299, Chuck Place; 300, NASA; 302, Tourism Nova Scotia; 303, NOAA; 304-305, Terraphotographics / BPS; 305, John Broda / Woods Hole Oceanographic Institute; 306-307, US Coast Guard; 308-309, Chuck Place; 309, Chuck Place; 310, BPS; 311, Black Star; 311(background), Chuck Place; 322-339, NASA; 339, Rick Falco / Black Star; 368, Library of Congress; 389, Steve Gravano; 422, Corbis; 423(t), Leslie Harris / Index Stock Photography; 423(b), Edward F. Wolff / Earth Scenes; 419, George Rinhart / Corbis; 424, Phillip Gould; 427(all), William Joyce; 434, 435, Phillip Gould; 457(r), Tom Sobolik / Black Star; 464, Alan Schein / Corbis Stock Market; 466-467, 468, Marty Sohl; 469, 470-471, Lloyd Englert / San Francisco Ballet; 471, courtesy, Evelyn Cisneros; 472, Marty Sohl / San Francisco Ballet; 473, 474, Marty Sohl; 474-475, Lloyd Englert / San Francisco Ballet; 475, 476, Marty Sohl; 477, Bonnie Kamin / San Francisco Ballet; 478, courtesy, Evelyn Cisneros; 478(b), Lloyd Englert / San Francisco Ballet; 479, 480(t), Marty Sohl; 480(b), courtesy, Evelyn Cisneros; 480(background), Lloyd Englert / San Francisco Ballet; 481(t), Black Star; 481(b), Lloyd Englert / San Francisco Ballet; 512, Culver Pictures, Inc.; 513(t), The Granger Collection, New York; 513(b), Culver Pictures, Inc.; 527, John Harquail / Black Star; 555, Margaret Miller; 582-583(all), Ken Kinzie / Harcourt School Publishers; 600, Werner Bertsch / Bruce Coleman, Inc.; 601, Bryan Hemphill / Photo Researchers; 618, Black Star; 619, Ron Kunzman; 668, Tom Sobolik / Black Star; 692-693, Corbis; 698, John Mitchell / Photo Researchers; 700-701, Library of Congress; 703, 704, Solomon D. Butcher Collection, Nebraska State Historical Society; 705(both), Nebraska State Historical Society; 706(both), 707, 708, Kansas State Historical Society; 709(both), Solomon D. Butcher Collection, Nebraska State Historical Society; 710(l), (c), National Baseball Hall of Fame; 710(r), Nevada Historical Society; 711, Black Star.

Illustration Credits

Kristen Funkhouser, Cover Art; Anne Smith, 4-5, 18-19; David Groff, 6-7, 136-137; Dave LaFleur, 8-9, 244-245; Marc Mongeau, 10-11, 366-367; Will Terry, 12-13, 350-361, 488-489; Kris Wiltse, 14-15, 598-599; Ethan Long, 16-17, 43; Jesse Reisch, 20-21; Russ Wilson, 22-41; Lyne Biding, 46-47; Rocco Baviera, 48-63; Kees de Kiefte, 72-85; Cheryl Phelps, 90-91; Lori McElrath, 92-105; David Scott Meir, 106-109; Beata Szpura, 111; Ande Cook, 114-115; Michael Steirnagle, 116-131; John Mantha, 138-139; Gil Adams, 140-153; Suling Wang, 164-179; Steve Björkman, 184-185; Steven Noble, 202-203; Lee Christiansen, 204-219; Miles Hyman, 224-225; Rich Nelson, 226-237; Kurt Nagahori, 238-239; Wendell Minor, 248-269; Rob Wood, 320-321; Chris Lensch, 348-349; Tim Ladwig, 370-381; Rafael Lopez, 382-385; Sarajo Frieden, 390-391; Carleen M. Powell, 440-441; Floyd Cooper, 442-457; Tomie de Paola, 482-485; Melinda Levine, 490-491; Jerry Tiritilli, 492-507; Allen Garnes, 514-527; Jennie Oppenheimer, 528-529; Donna Ingemanson, 534-535; David Golden, 536-555; Eldon Doty, 564-565; Sheila Bailey, 566-575; Eric Westbrook, 576-577; A.J. Garces, 584-593; Thomas B. Allen, 602-619; Cathy Bennett, 624-625; Russ Wilson, 626-639; Steven Kellogg, 640-643; Tom Payne, 648-649; Margot Tomes, 650-669; Janet Hamlin, 670-671; Lyse-Anne Roy, 676-677.